FROM BLUEBERRIES
TO BLUE SEAS

PRESS

A Superior Publishing Company

P.O. Box 115 • Superior, WI 54880
(218) 391-3070 • www.savpress.com

From **Blueberries** to **Blue Seas**

Sailing Adventures of a Midwest Farmer

or

Real Sailors Don't Need a Dodger

Carol & Pete,

Curtis C. Bush

So good to see you!

Enjoy the adventures.

Curt Bush

First Edition

ISBN-13: 978-1-937706-15-9

Library of Congress PCN Card Number: 2016938937

Published by:

Savage Press
P.O. Box 115
Superior, WI 54880

Phone: 218-391-3070
Email: mail@savpress.com
Website: www.savpress.com

Printed in the United States of America

Foreword

This tale is told as a compilation of several things. Mostly it is a memoir, and as I wrote this book at a makeshift writing table in my warm log cabin during the long, bitter, cold, winter following the "big sail" the clarity of my memory of the adventures herein sometimes amazed me. It must have to do with the detail oriented and open-eyed (yet unconscious) visual recorder that my brain has running most all of my waking moments. When I brought back those mind pictures of circumstances and events from that visual recorder in my mind, it made putting those parts of this tale to words much easier for me. For the sake of honesty and accuracy, I have tried to tell it like it was, as close to a telling of the real thoughts, emotions and circumstances that actually were.

I kept a daily journal of events, thoughts, and feelings. Sometimes I only put down single words...what I thought were key words that would later trigger a more detailed recoup of the particular thought or feeling. Sometimes, in the journal, I wrote out more complete descriptions or phrases, to try to capture a moment that I thought was, from a sailor's view, worth mentioning. I thought it may have passed as a required ship's log too, had the Coast Guard inquired.

Journal entries that I replicated herein are italicized to give the reader a sense of chronology as time and daily events transpired.

When I was connected to cyberspace I would write and send emails to friends back home and new friends met and made along the way. This was a third way that helped me record some parts of the journey and relay and entertain the folks who were following me in their hearts and minds. As I write now, the emails help to jog my memory and in the book they are italicized also.

Some basic sailor lingo that I have used throughout this book are common words that may need some defining for the non-sailor readers and that, I hope, makes this tale a bit more poignant, personal and interesting for all readers.

Here goes: I always try to sail the shore from which the wind originates, thus the term "windward". Off the windward shore the waves are smaller. Sometimes a sailor will call the side of the boat toward the wind the "weather" side. The side of the boat from which the wind is leaving is the "lee" side. If I sail downwind, "run" to an island, I have approached the island on its lee shore, where the waves are big. If I sail around to the backside of the island and duck behind it to get out of the waves, then I am in the "lee" of the island, yet on its "windward" shore or the "weather" side of the island. I hope you can follow these few terms and my brief explanations; they have confused me at times but I think I have finally got it straight.

Over time sailors have evolved (devolved?) a language that gives specific terms to the "points of sail" or the direction that a sailboat travels with regard to the wind. If a boat is traveling directly down wind it is on a "run". If the wind is from the side of the boat but still taking the boat downwind, the boat is on a "broad reach". When a boat sails 90 degrees off the wind, with the wind coming directly over the side of the boat, it is called a "beam reach". When a sailboat is going against the wind (upwind) or "close" to the wind, it is on a "close reach" and when a boat sails as close to the wind as it can and still make "headway" it is "close-hauled". Most sailboats can sail upwind to about 45 degrees off the wind direction.

I took a few photos along the way, not many, and I hope to include some for those readers who are visual like me. They too, helped me to recall and draw the best word pictures that I am able.

A word of caution about single-hand sailing. There is always danger lurking. The single-hander must first and foremost, stay in the boat. There is no one on board to come around and pick you up should you get tossed overboard. Broken bones or deep cuts can be life threatening if sailing offshore and alone. Storms offshore or near-shore, can be white-knuckle scary alone and disastrous if caught unprepared.

Sailing is a relatively recent skill set for me. Lifetime sailors who grew up sailing may recognize some terminology shortfalls or a set of circumstances they would have handled differently. That's as it should be. My goals were only to enjoy each moment of each day and to live to sail another day.

Lastly, this tale was told as a labor of love...a tale of a life changing adventure that I wanted to take you along with, to share, to entertain, and perhaps bring a smile, or a chuckle even, to those with too busy lives, and only armchair dreams.

— *Curt*

Introduction: The Dreamer

Okay, the truth is, this book is really a tale about some of my dreams, but really, who would be interested? Who out there would want to read about a bunch of unrealized fantasies? "Dreams of a Midwest Farmer??" I don't think it would work. My kind of book needs some adventure!

The redeeming part of the dreams that make them an interesting story (I think) is that they really came true. With some effort and determination, the dreams of adventure and accomplishment really happened. Honest!

The dreams that came true, the ones you will read about (if you don't quit now) aren't about inventions or discoveries or earth shaking events that I made happen just because I'm so special. They are circumstances and events similar to some that have happened before, to other ordinary folks; but I think they can make for good storytelling. You be the judge.

From my earliest recollections, as a kid of rural northern Minnesota, dreams of adventure, or daydreams of any type, were an undeniable part of my makeup. Daydreams came naturally to me, as naturally as lying in the grass on a warm summer day and watching the clouds sail by…did I say sail by?

Any old daydream seemed to suffice…all I needed was some leisure time and the dreams would happen. Maybe they were an escape from less pleasant circumstances, regardless, they were easy to slip into.

It seemed that the daydreams caused me to have a short attention span, or vice-versa, and I suppose that modern psychologists would have labeled me with some professional jargon, an acronym no doubt, representing a certain challenging mental handicap that would have given just cause for my short attention to classroom lessons. They may have unintentionally given me a medical excuse so that I could dream onward without prejudice, but back then I didn't need any excuses. If I didn't have the leisure time to dream I would simply make the time; at church or at school I became a well-practiced dreamer and consequently I was never a very good student, either of faith or knowledge. But the key here is leisure time. I think that I was, early on, planning for a life with plenty of time to dream, and to explore those paths down which those dreams would lead.

Canoe outings, fishing trips to the Boundary Waters Canoe Area Wilderness (though when I was very young it wasn't declared a wilderness yet) or building a new shack or tree house in the woods near home; all were the fodder of new dreams for me. Dreaming taught me to reminisce, to recollect, and to reflect. Dreams of better fishing next time perhaps or of "discovering" the lake at the end of the next portage. Dreams of having more free time for a longer fishing trip (they were always too short) or a longer summer to build shacks of logs, old lumber, and rusty nails.

There just didn't seem to be enough free time with summers so short, school taking so much time; then Sunday school and church stuff on the weekend, and if that weren't enough, Saturday night was bath night.

Somewhere around the age of 8 or 9 I really began to enjoy reading. The first book that I remember really getting into was an adventure novel by Farley Mowat called *Lost in the Barrens*...easy to read and a book a that a boy dreamer like me could step right into. In it was the stuff of daydreams come true; exploration and discovery in the far north. Farley became my favorite all time author...still is.

Best of all, books of adventure drew me in during a part of my boyhood when a childhood illness had kept me bedridden for months. I still couldn't play with the other kids at school recess; I had to rest instead. I had to take penicillin everyday and I wasn't supposed to play sports. But when no one was looking I would run as fast as I could, climb trees...or lay in the grass and dream. The illness is distant history now, but I always had a youthful zest for life, daydreams to follow, and a lot of time to make up for.

Another of my favorite authors, Sigurd Olson, wrote of the far north and of the near north, of fishing and wilderness canoeing expeditions. Sigurd understood me. He could sit on the shore of a remote lake and dream just like me. He could feel the spirits of the past in remote and lonely places. He could sense the tiniest details of the forest and had learned of the interconnectedness of all the parts. He came to understand how all things in nature worked together. He could see the big picture. Sigurd became a real boyhood hero for me. He was a staunch defender of wilderness places and was one of the key people who saved the boundary waters of Minnesota from developers and profiteers. He was real. He had courage. He knew the value of wild places. He went his own way.

And what does all this personal boyhood history have to do with the blueberry farmer turned sailor, you might wonder? Like any good farmer will tell you, it was about planting seeds. Seeds of adventure, seeds of wonder about faraway places. Seeds sown far from the cities and the crowds and the noise. Seeds that grew up with the boy.

The Winds of Gaspé

Yesterday's sail around the point of the Gaspé Peninsula was as trying as any rugged sailing day of my brief maritime career. The waves were scary big and I like to think that I don't scare easily. The scrambles to keep Sweet Breeze upright bruised my old body in ways and places that I had no time to notice. The near knockdown by a breaking wave really got my attention. The big waves were lashing us from behind. I felt we needed more speed, more sail, to gain the steerage needed to steer around the breaking tops of the biggest waves. But how to hold steerage now, right now, just for a few seconds, while I lengthen the head-sail in this maelstrom of wind and confused seas?

I managed to time it while in the trough between waves, lashing the tiller for an instant while I tried to uncleat the furling line for the headsail and thereby let out a bit more canvas. It worked for now. Steerage was better now but also a wind gust could more likely push us over or force the bow down into a wall of water as we surfed down a cresting wave.

I lashed the tiller again and dashed below to grab the sturdy companionway hatch cover that I had specially reinforced, dashed topside with it and slid the hatch into place blocking the opening. If we were to get knocked down flat I had to keep the seas from filling the cabin. A cabin full of icy North Atlantic seawater would likely end this adventure, and all future adventures, for me, and for my sweet old sailboat.

I checked that my knife was handy to cut the painter, that thin umbilical between the towed dinghy and Sweet Breeze. The dink was filling with water and crashing into the transom behind me when the bigger waves picked it up and tossed it forward. If it sunk it would act as a sea anchor slowing us and leaving us vulnerable to getting pooped. After dragging it for 2000 miles I would cut it free in an instant if it endangered Sweet Breeze.

Here I was, a few miles offshore in some of the most challenging wind and seas anywhere on the globe...off the Canadian coast of Quebec's Gaspé Peninsula... known through sailing history for the fierce and sudden winds swooping down from the mountains and rock cliffs.

That brilliant morning of fast sailing had quickly turned into survival sailing. I have had a few days of survival sailing in the last two months on the Great Lakes and in the last few years learning to sail on Lake Superior. Lake Superior teaches one quickly, surely, it yields no quarter, and gives no second chances. Older salts had told me that if I could sail Superior I could sail anywhere there was water. That day off Gaspé I was hoping they were right.

Once more I had gone and left an early morning's safe harbor. At the first hint of dawn's light, I had started the motor and quietly shoved off the dock at Port Madeleine, Quebec, into wispy gray coastal fog and out to sea. With some serious second thoughts I left the camaraderie and comfort and hopeful wonder of the company of Susanne. I thought about that warm smile of hers, how it welcomed me into port yesterday as I motored past the end of the dock where she was fishing.

She was a teacher on summer leave and a boater from Montreal. She spoke better English than me. With her smooth Quebecois' accent she had invited me aboard her boat yesterday. I studied her paper charts of the water ahead as she made us tea. We learned what little that an hour and a half's conversation could reveal about our current lives and our history. That evening we walked the rocky beach at low tide and shared a little more of ourselves. She asked if I would stop at the Port of Gaspé forty miles down the coast, where we could meet up again. I told her I didn't know...that it depended on the winds and the seas...how driven I was feeling to put on miles.

Those were my thoughts as I left another safe harbor...thoughts of Susanne. Would I ever see her again? Two ships passing in the night? How many times on this journey to the sea had I left behind acquaintances, potential friends, before friendship had been given a decent chance?

Here I was, not knowing what the day would bring yet once again with perhaps that overdose; bitten by that affliction of false confidence in both myself and my little ship...the anticipation, and that sense of adventure drawing me away from a safe harbor...the feeling that I could *probably* handle whatever the winds and seas had in store for me that day. It was the 'probably' part that should have given me pause that morning...that, and lingering thoughts of Susanne.

And now I was amidst another survival sail. To the left was the open Atlantic. To the right the towering cliffs of Gaspé. Behind me the biggest waves I had yet encountered...15 feet? Perhaps the occasional 20-footer? Hard to tell. They were steep sided walls of icy water, close together and confused. Only one option for the single-hander on that day. Survive.

The winds of Gaspé live on with me today. I still feel their power, their force... unforgiving and uncaring to the unwary or unprepared sailor. The winds of Gaspé live on with me today...today as I digress...and still I have thoughts of Susanne.

The Blueberry Farm and other Dreams

The tall, lanky shed on posts has a family of old tractors living in it now. They cohabitate in a crowded space, pressed up against one another, with no noticeable anxiety even though it is a mixed and colored family crammed into close quarters— Ford blue, Allis Chalmers orange, John Deere green, and Farmall red. But it wasn't always this way.

Sweet Breeze in her home at camp.

The tractors used to be scattered about the woods near this camp, resting, waiting for the next project in need of their powerful engines, pulling power and lifting arms. This three-year-old shed was not built to house *them*, however. The roof was twice as high as it would need to be for a tractor shed. They came in after the boat left. You see, the tall shed was built to protect an old sailboat while it was being restored, by me, back to a sail-able condition and a sort of basic live-aboard health.

This shed was a part of the dream. It cost more to build than the sailboat it was intended to shelter. Even the trailer I bought, to haul the boat and its cradle back to camp, cost more than the boat. Yup, I got her at a bargain price.

But she wasn't just any old sailboat. She was a 1962 Pearson Brothers Triton; a classic plastic. She had a heavy hull and a deep, full keel with some 3000 pounds of lead in her butt. The hull was hand laid fiberglass throughout and thicker than most modern sailboats. Deep in her belly was an "Atomic Four" inboard engine; a power plant famous for dependability or infamous for troubles, either one, depending on its service record and care. This old boat was indeed a large part of the dream.

But for now I must digress again, for some 25 years ago I had another dream. This dream began to take shape during that "midlife" period of raising two kids and working full time to try to "get ahead", whatever that means. It was sometimes a segment of a lifetime that was just too busy for a proper dreamer like me, but I had thoughts and hopes of "someday" having the time to adventure forth and follow some dreams.

Blueberry Farm Beginnings

Back then I had bought a long neglected pastureland of 40 acres from an old second generation Finnish farmer. It was probably cleared by his father who had immigrated to northeastern Minnesota around 1900 looking for a better life doing what he knew best, farming. The cows had been absent from the meager forage of the pasture for a few years and trees and brush were creeping in to reclaim it.

The land purchase was financed by my oldest brother who always seemed to have some extra money for speculating. He lived far away, in a completely different world, in southern California. In retrospect, I suspect that speculating with investments was his form of adventuring forth.

I had previously bought another part of the old dairy and rutabaga farm from Jalmer and had put up a homestead of our own for my young family of two kids and a very tolerant wife. We then lived adjacent to the forty-acre parcel of spruce swamp and brush land that we had just purchased.

Myself, being composed of farm and soil roots (my father and grandfather were farmers of sorts), and being a tree farmer in my own right, I was curious about the land and the soils and the potential for a sale-able crop. Maybe a peat harvesting operation as well; some sort of a living off the land that would eventually lead to my dream of self-employment. I had no preconceived notions, I just wanted to evaluate the resource and think creatively.

I had learned, from my informal lessons, taught to me by Mother Nature herself, that the plants growing on the surface are a good indicator of the types of soil beneath them. If undisturbed, plants will grow where they are best suited for the soil, the sun, and the water they need. Plants on this old pasture had 10,000 years or so, since the last great North American glaciation, to migrate to their favorite places to grow.

The health of the plants tells a lot about the health of the soil too. (Come to think of it, the health of humans and most other animals is about the health of their environment or of how they adapt.).

On further investigation and with a visual analysis of the soil removed and examined from the several test holes that I dug in various places around the property, there appeared to be a diverse and interesting soil profile left by the last glacier. Over the seasons and life cycles of the last 10,000 years, the plants on the high ground had left about a six-inch deep organic topsoil but in the bog land of the black spruce and tamarack, the organic peat was as deep as four feet!

Another encouraging discovery of the cropland potential was the total lack of rocks, stones or boulders; those hard and forever gifts of the glacier that inhabit most of the thin soils of northeastern Minnesota.

The plant cover on the surface was a mix of lowland spruce/tamarack bog and upland mixed brush and hardwoods. Soil tests showed acidic soils everywhere but very acidic peat in the lowland areas. The most obvious indicator of the soil's ability to support a potential domestic crop seemed to be the obvious one, i.e., the prolific growth of *wild* blueberries thriving on the margins between the highland and the lowland. Aha!

About this time the University of Minnesota Experiment Station at Grand Rapids, MN had developed and was promoting their new and unique half-high blueberry plants that were a "cultivar", or a variety of blueberries that combined the hardiness of wild plants and the productivity of the "domesticated" plants. I visited with the plant experts and listened and learned. I learned that these new plants had a lot of potential given the right soil preparation and water and sunlight.

That new, old pastureland seemed to have just the right soils for blueberries. Deep sandy loam on the high ground and organic, acidic peat on the lowland, but they were on different parts of the property. No problem there, as I had some old, heavy, dirt moving machines (I'd had an excavating business in the past). There was my backhoe to dig with, my dump truck to move with, and my tractors to mix the peat and loam on the high ground.

I dug trenches in the loam and mixed in the peat. There was over a mile of trenches, if they were laid in one straight line, but they weren't. They were in three small fields of about an acre each with rows about eight feet apart. In the largest field the rows were laid out in parallel curves that gave it an artsy, aesthetic appeal that I liked.

The sites for the three fields were chosen because they were on the highest ground and were slightly sloped and best of all, the deep loam was totally rock free.

When I started to really believe in the potential for making an income from the farm I hired Jim, the man with the big tracked excavators who lived nearby, to dig three fairly large ponds in a low area near each of the blueberry fields and I installed pumps and underground water lines and a drip irrigation system for each field. Each of the three thousand plants would have their own water source.

These were the beginning steps toward reaching my dreams of building a blueberry farm and of working for myself. This was not a dream that was widely shared or supported by friends or family. I was stepping way "outside the box" here. I sensed some quiet skepticism and maybe a raised eyebrow. No one had a blueberry farm in northern Minnesota on so large a scale. Why was I not satisfied with the status quo; a good job, a good family, a big car, several TVs and a pension?

The primary support network for the blueberry project was my own innermost dreams. They didn't box me in at all. They weren't slaves to conventional thought or lifestyle. I think the dreamer in me came up with some creative ways of dealing with the challenges as they arose. I think the skeptics only made me more determined.

This project was not to be just an ordinary blueberry farm, whatever that might be, but it had to be a farm that was aligned with my values; one that would be self-sustaining without a lot of off farm inputs. I wanted to farm as though the earth really mattered. I didn't want to be spraying chemicals around the farm. I wanted it to be a low impact farm that conserved the soil and had large areas of natural flora, some woods and ponds to provide habitat for local wild creatures.

I wanted a crop that would be valued in dollars per pound and not in dollars per ton like the big farms. Blueberries could be the high value crop that this farm needed, and finally, I wanted the harvesting to provide a fun picking experience for the human creatures and a sustainable income for me.

As a business venture, the farm struggled for the first few years but it did eventually develop into a profitable and most pleasant way to make some money on the side (I had a full-time job also), but the blueberry plants thrived immediately in that special soil and I cared for them like babies.

My biggest challenge was in marketing the crop, which, in this case meant getting enough customers to come and pick them when they were ripe and ready. Eventually word got around and after some years of creative marketing and struggles, the farm's three thousand blueberry plants produced berries by the ton and the customers arrived in droves and picked every ripe berry.

There were lots of rewards for me; the best reward of all being all the friends I made through the farm's pick-your-own customers. My dream of self-employment and living off the land had become a reality. I felt I had arrived, by my simple standards, as an entrepreneur.

I had proven to myself that anything was possible given some hard work, creative thinking, and determination. I felt that, as a whole person, I had grown with the farm and through the whole experience of risk taking into the unknown (the world of self-employment) my self-confidence had grown with the farm and the clincher was, now I had more free time to adventure out.

Sailboats and other Distractions from Work

Life on the blueberry farm was a good one but the call of the wild was always with me. The farm had very busy times and also times when I was not needed. Free time, leisure time, always important to me, was sometimes filled by just lying in the grass and dreaming, and sometimes it would allow me to pursue adventure near and far. My canoe trips on several North American rivers could be the subjects of books in themselves (good reads, I would hope). Canoeing the Missouri, the Yellowstone, the Green River of the Canyon-lands area, and the Moose River to James Bay of northern Ontario, Canada, were some of the far adventures.

The nearer adventures were mostly to the beloved Boundary Waters Canoe Area Wilderness. Usually solo trips with super lightweight gear. Usually in the spring or fall, when I was most likely to have the lakes and campsites to myself, and when the bugs were not yet so numerous and hungry.

They were usually rigorous trips with sore shoulders and neck muscles from long days of paddling and were rewarded by the view of the moose at the end of the weedy bay and the loon's lonely call at twilight. There was the radiant warmth of the friendly campfire, perhaps on an island camp, warding away the chill of a frosty evening. There was the snug chrysalis of the flannel lined sleeping bag, and the aroma of boiling coffee in the morning and as always, the silent, near, and watchful companionship of my dog.

There were a few days, when the wind was right, that canoeing was not so rigorous, but instead rather relaxing. I had conducted lots of early and spontaneous experiments with simple ways to catch some wind in a canoe, the simplest being to hold a broad bladed paddle up into the wind. On one small canoe I had devised a mast and sail that was barely usable for anything but downwind sailing, but then I knew little about the curious effects of a deep keel.

Once on the Moose River of northern Ontario, we lashed together two canoes with poles into a very stable double hull craft. Then we arranged a large square sail (tent fly) mounted forward between the hulls and supported by two more poles (masts). A very brisk wind on that one afternoon propelled me and some canoeing buddies for miles at some amazing speeds, north toward the salt water and whales and seals of James Bay. That exhilarating experience and the respite it afforded after days of paddling were enough to capture my interest into the possibilities of wind propelled watercraft.

My farm dog was always with on canoe trips. She was a most relaxed and quiet canoe passenger and a snuggler to sleep with. She is watching me as I write this. We have been partners now for fourteen years and she is as healthy and spry as I pretend to be. Ah, the unconditional love of a dog…the subject of many a good book.

At other chore-free times I would escape to the places of my boyhood fishing trips with my dad. The Sawbill Trail of northeastern Minnesota was a favorite haunt of mine for exploring the backcountry for brook trout streams and lakes. The streams we called "cricks" and the lakes we called lakes. Berries were prolific in the Sawbill country and when I was a kid we picked hundreds of quarts as a part of family camping and food gathering outings. Mother canned and froze the berries and winter deserts often left your tongue and teeth blue, and your stomach wanting more. Mom was an amazing cook and she seemed a tireless provider for Dad and six kids.

Another boating experience had a lasting effect on me. Some time within the blueberry farm years a friend had asked me to sail with her on her Lake Superior sailboat. Sue Wilmes and I sailed together three or four times on outings on the big lake or on the St. Louis bay and harbor. Once we had a brisk northeaster blowing off the lake and we streaked along the bay on a beam reach at seven knots. Faster than her boat had ever gone before said she. I was hooked on the quiet sense of speed; the wind's awesome power. Sue let me steer and tweak the sails and she taught me the basics of how stuff on a sailboat worked. This seemed to me to be the ideal way to travel on water. Sleek and quiet and secure with no sore shoulders and neck muscles. No motor either, except to get in and out of the tight places.

The boat's cabin below had all the comforts of a home, a quite modest home like mine anyhow, and it offered complete protection from the elements, provided someone was minding the helm above. It was like a camper on the water in which you could travel anywhere in the world.

You could bring some friends along if you wished, and the boat even gave me a hint of security from the horrors of what Lake Superior could do to small boats (and huge freighters as well). Lake Superior has a history of being unkind to boats at times, and her bottom is littered with wreckage, large and small. There are hundreds of wrecks in Whitefish Bay alone, on the eastern end of the lake.

Sailing still felt right to me. The kinetics, the geometry, the vectors and forces began to make sense to me as I gained some little experience during the short northern summers, sailing with friends, on their boats, on the big lake and in the harbor; and I started to read lots of books about sailing adventures.

Sailboat Number One

On a drive through some local countryside I spotted a tiny sailboat on the side of the road with a For Sale sign taped to it, so I stopped, of course, to check it out. It appeared to be a home built project of plywood and paint, some ropes and a crude wooden pole, and in a mostly completed stage of construction. It was resting on the ground, listing heavily and looking forlorn, like it needed some water to rest upon and get its life back into balance, you know the feeling if you have ever listed too far to one side.

I bought the boat and hauled it home to the blueberry farm where I could assess its needs. Her needs were many and typical of most sailboats, but she was a well-built hull and had great potential. Need number one was a trailer to rest it upon and transport it to water. It would have to be a custom made job with just the right cradle to fit her unique hull and it must be a strong and lightweight trailer so that my little truck could pull it; so off to my junk pile I went to shop for parts. Here was an old rear axle from a Rambler car of the sixties and there I found some lightweight steel beams salvaged from an earlier project.

Trailer building was not new to me. One of my many, many work careers was as an industrial education teacher and in learning the processes of welding and metal fabrication (in order to teach them) I had gained these skills for a lifetime. Welding and fabricating with steel is fun, a great creative outlet, artful, and almost forever. Still today, I would feel lost without a welder close at hand for tractor repairs or making parts for other machines.

Sometimes when a fun project is in the works, workdays voluntarily begin very early and end late. The trailer quickly took shape after some long days and evenings and "Sea Mouse" soon was resting on her cradle with wheels. She was a real trailer sailor now and my first real sailboat. She had the crisp and certain lines of a boat with a purpose. Her job was to teach me more about rigging and single-handing. All twelve feet of her spoke of fun and learning.

Sea Mouse and I did some trailer sailing together. We sailed near my workshop with her hull still on the new trailer. I would step the mast, hoist her sails, and test her lines and her rig for ease of handling and strength. She had white tarp sails, a jib and a main, and I may have needed a steering wheel on the trailer if the wind got stiff and she took off across the yard on her three trailer wheels. She stayed put of course and I experimented time and again with ideas for making her rig easier to handle.

The tamarack mast had a slight bend in it but I was not concerned. That just gave the boat some added character. However, the rings around the mast that secured the main sail (mains'l) to the mast and were supposed to slide easily up the mast as the sail was hoisted, often didn't slip well. They would bind and get stuck when hoisting the sail or when dousing it. It would mean standing on the deck, while hoisting, to help feed the rings up with the sail—not a good place for a sailor to be on a small, heaving boat in cold northern waters. This would not do.

And so I replaced the rings with larger ones that I cut from a three inch PVC pipe. Before sliding them onto the mast I carefully rounded over the sharp inside corners of each ring with a small drum sander mounted in an electric drill. They slipped better both when hoisting and dousing the main. I ran the main halyard (the line that goes to the top of the mast and raises the sail) through a pulley block at the base of the mast and back to the cockpit, a typical and simple way of rigging in order to hoist a sail without having to go up on the foredeck to do it.

More trial and error and retrial got me to the point of having some confidence that her sail handling lines and rigging could work out adequately, but there were some definite issues with the outboard rudder that needed to be addressed. I felt that the rudder itself was okay, a substantial plywood affair with plenty of surface for good steerage, but the hinge arrangement fastening the rudder to the transom seemed marginal at best and way too weak to bet your life on.

This was fortunate because it gave me the opportunity to fabricate (I love to fabricate stuff from steel scraps) a pintle and gudgeon (hinge) from some scrap steel objects that could be cut and welded back into a heavy duty hinged rudder attachment.

That accomplished, a new tiller seemed to be in order to replace the ax handle now serving as the helm. Ax handles are really fine handles but generally look better on axes than on sailboats, or so my personal aesthetics had determined. After looking over my assortment of wood scraps and digging tools I discovered and envisioned the perfect tiller for the Mouse. It was a handle from a post-hole digger, the kind with two handles. Now, thought I, a post-hole digger handle would be a fine and proper looking tiller mostly because so few people would recognize it for its original purpose. Off to town to the hardware (and etc.) store shopping for a "new tiller" I went; a tiller without any "marine" connections, (marine connections that would automatically inflate the price by a hundred dollars or so).

Just a word of praise for that local, hardware and everything else, store. They have so far survived beyond the opening of the new "Mall*Wart" super store. Sure they sell their share of low quality goods from abroad, but if they only carried American manufactured goods their shelves would be nearly bare. I tell my friends my motto for that favorite little store that I patronize: "If L&M Doesn't Have It you Don't Need It." The store owners would probably want to pay me lots of money to use my motto.

A new coat of purple paint on her hull and white on her deck with purple accents put the Sea Mouse in fine form. She was an eye catcher and a miniature version of an old fishing vessel that was sailed on the big bay out east and called a Chesapeake Bay Skipjack. She looked in ship shape and ready to sail.

Dear friend Marna and I took the Sea Mouse to a small local lake for her maiden voyage on a warm summer day with warm lake water as a comfort, should any unexpected anxieties arise. The trailer trailed behind the truck, as it should, straight and easy. I backed her into the lake and Sea Mouse floated off the trailer with no serious leaks, just the minor seepage that wooden boats tend to have until they swell up (with pride) and seal themselves.

I should mention at some point that Marna can be a rather strong-minded woman and is used to having things of comfort near at hand. Sea Mouse was not exactly built for comfort but Marna's flexible spirit of adventure exacted reasonable compromise in the form of some simple boat cushions to sit on.

As on all sailing occasions with her, it wasn't long before she reminded me that she was once a sailing instructor at her summer camp in northern Wisconsin. Though that was quite a few decades ago she still felt the need to let me know that her expertise was, as yet, active in her memory, near at hand, available and within my earshot, and was certainly necessary to hear again if we were to have a pleasant sail together. She told me some of the fine points of sailing and if I suggested something new she was quick to remind me that, "I know that!" After she tired of being skipper, helmsman, and sailing instructor she retired to the galley, presently a picnic basket on the Mouse.

Marna and I sailed the little boat to the far end of the lake tacking and reaching into a light wind and making progress. This was as it should be! I had clamped on a small outboard engine but it was not needed. We were making headway tacking back and forth and having a picnic lunch with only the sound of the sails catching wind— no motor noise. The wings were all working...sails, rudder, and dagger-board keel. Sea Mouse sailed like Mother Kerry's chickens (a small bird that is light on the water and that I would meet a few sailing years later on the North Atlantic).

The little (first) sailboat and I headed for bigger water on our next outing— the Duluth harbor and the estuary of the St. Louis River. The harbor is protected from the forces of Lake Superior by a miles long spit of white sand called Minnesota Point. Harbor entries from the lake are channels through the sand wide enough for the largest of ships to enter but not for the wrath of a northeaster. The harbor area is a complex of giant iron ore docks and grain elevators, coal shipping docks, one remaining shipyard and huge freighters and small boats, most all of which were larger than the Sea Mouse and some were over one thousand feet long. When sailing alongside a thousand-footer one feels a sense of awe and respect and a strong desire to keep at a safe distance. The diameter of the propellers on those big freighters were about the same as Sea Mouse's entire length or at least of her beam (width).

Waves in the harbor and bay can reach two to three feet in really strong winds so I kept an eye to the weather, as sailors always should (and as I would, some years later, be reminded of, again on the North Atlantic). No hard lessons with the Sea Mouse however, just a lot of fun and a lot of learning about wind and waves and the wings of a sailboat.

As my proficiency and confidence grew there came a time to test either or both. I had this thought of sailing the Sea Mouse around the entire shore of Lake Superior.

I would have to watch the weather closely of course, stay near shore, keep her off the rocks, and camp on shore where ever I found a friendly bit of sand shore to drag her onto for the night.

It certainly would be doable. Kayaks and canoes have done it and native canoes perused her waters long before the Europeans arrived. The trip would take a few months, and summer months were of course the only option as the near-shore waters of the big lake freeze solid for months at a time in winter.

It was late September, blueberry picking season was past already and I thought perhaps I could get a good start yet that fall and finish the circumnavigation next summer. Plans proceeded and I got my gear together and practiced loading her little cuddy under the deck with all the essentials. Packing her small quarters and leaving room for me, the skipper, navigator, etc., was indeed a challenge. Too much stuff would make my comfort a compromise. Too much weight would make safety a compromise with only about a foot of freeboard (the distance between the lake surface and that point where water could enter over the deck) on the Mouse.

With the compromises somewhat balanced we set sail one morning in early October for the south shore of the big lake. The near shore weather forecasts looked good for the next few days, with light winds and small waves predicted.

Leaving the Superior entry and sailing into the lake created a tightness in my belly. There was such a liquid immensity before me .The lake was pretty calm, but the vastness of water to my left and right and straight ahead made me feel pretty small in a pretty small boat. If Lake Superior was thinking about me at all she must have thought what an insignificant particle on her surface we were, the Mouse and me. We hardly made a ripple between us.

With both sails hoisted and sheeted down tight we still weren't making much of a ripple. The three horsepower Johnson outboard on the transom would need to come to life or we might just sit there until the next storm. The motor gave us the thrust we needed for headway on down the south shore of the big lake. Swells left from the last blow on the lake reminded me of what the other extreme of lake conditions can be. Today the lake was kind to us.

Together we motored and sailed and motor-sailed down the lake moving ever closer to the south shore as we headed east with a little southing. All the details of that day and the next two are mostly forgotten, which means they likely weren't all that exciting. I do recall timing a swell so as to ride it to the shore and make a dry landing on a sand beach in the late afternoon and then dragging the Mouse a few feet farther ashore for safe keeping overnight. Loaded with gear, she was a heavy drag. It was an isolated beach of sand and boulders and I felt welcome there. Looking west, back down the lake, I thought I had made good perhaps twenty miles. I erected a tiny tent in the sand and spent my first night, as a sailor on passage, (though I didn't know then how short this passage was soon to become).

The next day was much like the previous one with the views of the south shore ever fascinating and intriguing, mile after mile. I remember the greens, the yellows, the rust colored sand and the high clay banks sliding toward the lake with whole trees and boulders in their slippery grasp.

I don't think I had a nautical chart of the lakeshore then and I remember watching for the mouth of the Bois Brule River, the Iron River, and the square cut hills above Port Wing, Wisconsin. That was all the further I had been before, by boat, along the south shore and I have always had a good memory for topographic landmarks.

The ancient valley of the Bois Brule was a grand landmark of the shoreline when out on the lake a few miles and I would use it years later for position and location but at that point I was too close to shore on this venture to view this grand valley where Lake Superior once drained south and west to the St. Croix, the Mississippi, and eventually the Gulf of Mexico. That was back in geologic time when the glacier had melted and the lake was hundreds of feet above the current 602 feet above sea level. Now the big lake drains east out the St. Lawrence River, east to the Atlantic because the land surface rose, sprung back after the glacier retreated (imagine the weight of ice a mile or more thick) and the Brule River then reversed itself and ran north into the lake instead of south, draining the lake. Wow! Earth history is fascinating.

Light wind and waves were the order for this, the second day of my grand passage around the lake. With late afternoon bringing me close to the hills above Port Wing, and the outboard not running so good anymore, we entered the breakwaters to the safe harbor. As I recall there were lots of people about and no quiet place to pitch the tent and call home for the night, so I headed back out to the lake under sputtering engine power and the idyllic sand beach that I had passed just to the west of the harbor. I tried to time the swells again and get the Mouse hard ashore for the night.

Sometime during the night the light wind shifted and blew with a purpose from the northeast. I checked on the Mouse at first light and discovered her afloat and a few boat lengths down the sand. I think her hawse line was barely holding to a rounded boulder and I felt lucky she was still in the neighborhood. She was lurching around in the cold surf as I loaded her in knee-deep water, shoved off and fell aboard over the transom. We were back on the beach before I could bend a sail or start the outboard. How many times I tried this maneuver I don't recall but I remember that I was soaked and bruised and cold before we got in deep enough water to start the engine. Around the break walls and back into the safe harbor we limped with a sick motor and water in the bilge, which was also the floor of the boat and where I, the skipper, helmsman, pilot, etc. also sat.

This was not a heartening start to my third day on the lake. We docked in the harbor and I hiked over the road and the sand dunes, back to the lake's shore to assess my possibilities of having a third day of sailing. For quite a while I contemplated the building surf, dark gray and cold. The waves were probably born some two hundred miles to the northeast off the Canadian shore. The sky was dark and so were my thoughts of returning to the lake, to ride on the Sea Mouse and into the wind and the waves, on that cold autumn day.

Back at the boat I listened to the marine forecast and it sounded like the next few days would be much like today with northeast winds and waves too big for me and the Mouse.

I gave in to my better judgment and called Marna and Sue, my prearranged boat haulers, to come and get me if they were available. Port Wing is about 60 miles by road from Duluth. They could and they would and I waited for their arrival.

As it turned out, the weather on the lake never did leave me with an opportunity to trailer the boat back to Port Wing and continue with this sailing challenge that fall. And I think I was glad. And the challenge went away. And a new and larger sailboat snuck into my sailing dreams.

Sailboat Number Two

Looking at used sailboats on Internet web sites can eat up an afternoon, or a few; sail boaters know what I'm talking about. Most of my Internet surfing was done at the local public library in a big soft cushy chair. I kind of knew what I was looking for… another trailer sailor, about 20 feet long, easy to sail, fiberglass, swing keel, and within my always limited farm budget (no federal farm subsidies for me, thanks).

I found one and negotiated a deal with Jake, her owner, in Traverse City, Michigan. It was on its own trailer so that part would be easy. She was a San Juan 21. Though far from its birth home in Washington State near the San Juan Islands she was known as a well-built and popular boat for day sailors and weekenders and my little truck and I were headed for Michigan.

Two things on that adventure remain active in my memory. One was the kindness and hospitality of Jake and his wife offering me supper and a place to stay until morning and the 600-mile drive home. Was this a Midwest friendly thing or was it a boating thing, I wondered. This was one of the first of many acts of kindness that I was to experience in my days of sailing.

The second thing I recall vividly was the drive home and the nearly white out snowstorm across the U.P., wipers going at top speed, both hands on the wheel, keeping the speed up for the hills, careful on the gas so no spin-outs. I knew the Upper Peninsula of Michigan was known for lots of snow but not in October, thought I.

Oh, and a third part of that journey comes easily back to memory. Strong east winds at the Mackinac Bridge where I was warned by highway patrol, upon approaching the bridge, that my small truck and big boat were a questionable safe passage over that very high and long structural wonder. They let me go with the warning to go very slowly. I did and needless to say, my new boat didn't float away that day, neither off the bridge nor the snowy roads. We made it back to the blueberry farm some twenty hours later.

She was the typical bleach bottle boat, all white fiberglass. The next spring I began modifications on the San Juan, mostly rigging changes and some wood trim on the cabin top and sides to give the boat some character and contrasting color. Of course I thought she was the prettiest San Juan around with the wood trim and she did turn heads with some eyebrows (above the windows) and unique side dressings of dark mahogany.

The San Juan 21.

It was a fine sailing and forgiving boat. She barely forgave me once when I took Marna out onto Lake Superior one fine summer evening, our first sail together on the San Juan. I really wanted to show Marna how sweetly she sailed.

Some dark clouds drifted from the west out over the lake as we left the harbor under the Aerial Bridge and sailed on a straight run (downwind) working up the north shore a few miles. The dark clouds started to bunch up and created some strong gusts on the lake that suggested, perhaps, that it would be prudent to head back toward the Duluth Ariel Lift Bridge and the safety of the harbor. This being our first outing together in the new boat I wanted Marna to experience the upwind capabilities of the new twenty-one, her stability, and my skills with sail handling. We did a 180-degree turn about and bad things began to happen.

The gusts increased. We were on a starboard tack near the windward shore yet, but we were fast losing headway and gaining leeway out into the open lake. This was not right. This boat should cut up into the wind at least to a 45-degree angle off the wind. Questions flashed through my mind as the boat heeled far over in the gusts and we were sliding farther out into the lake and further away from the protection of the windward shore. We must come about and tack back toward the north shoreline where the waves were being born, not to the lee where the waves were piling up. But she would not cross over the wind and come about. I tried several times, building speed and quickly heaving the tiller across to port and still she would not cross the wind to the port tack.

The force of one gust of wind ripped the tail of the main halyard from the cam cleat that I had installed on the cabin top and down came the mains'l about halfway flapping madly in the wind while turning the boom into a dangerous club.

Marna captured much of the loose main and hung on to it for dear life as I worked to get the outboard engine started, for at this particular point the sails were a mess, Marna was scared, and I was totally confused as to why the boat would not sail to the weather nor come about towards shore.

The outboard came sputtering to life with me reaching out over the transom and down to the throttle and the tiller, the boat heaving about, and with the full power of all three horses pushing, she came across the wind and headed toward shore with the jib back winded momentarily and Marna struggling mightily to flatten the half main and get it powered somewhat to help. The engine's tiller didn't feel right and as I looked back at it I could see the engine mounting clamps loosening and the motor trying to jump off the transom and into the lake. If only I had three hands at this point. I held the engine down with my elbow so it couldn't jump into the lake and somehow managed to tighten the mounting clamp back onto the transom bracket with the other hand all the while hanging half my body out over the rear of the boat and my leg over the helm to hold our course steady. We began to make progress toward the windward shore. Whew!

Marna was a trooper during that sailing fiasco. I remember the set of her chin as she had one arm wrapped around the boom and the other hand tugging as hard as she could on the leach of the main to get us some power to sail to weather. She needed to summon up all of her inner courage and camp instructor experience to hang on to the boom, the boat, and the sail. She seemed to have no desire to debate any of my shouted instructions, which was unusual for her. Things began to settle down with the engine and sail each steadily pushing and pulling us closer to shore where the wind and waves were losing their fetch.

I think it was about then that it dawned on me what our problem was and I began to laugh (a bit of a sheepish laugh it was)…as we had sailed out of the harbor downwind out onto the lake I had *forgotten to lower the swing keel*. Of course the boat could not sail to weather or tack across the wind without a keel. I dove below, lowered the keel and the whole personality of the boat changed. and Marna's face regained some color.

We got the main back up, the engine secured to the transom and shut it down, the jib crossed over to the right side and back to the harbor we sailed. I felt later that we were lucky we didn't get knocked down flat in a gust with the keel up high in its housing. Maybe we were lucky that the mains'l halyard broke free when it did and de-powered the main. That may have been what kept us upright.

But that is the story of a forgiving sailboat and of Marna, a forgiving first mate, who sailed with me another day after some quiet time to recover on solid ground. That was one of the hard lessons I was to learn as I kept going out onto the lake on my various sailboats over the next few years. Maybe a swing keel is not the best option for a forgetful sailor.

On a single-handed sail back down the south shore of the big lake there once happened another valuable lesson that has stuck with me for years. It started with the twenty-one and me leaving Port Wing, Wisconsin's safe harbor one early morn. There was a northwest wind with manageable waves of one to two feet greeting me as I motored out onto the lake past the breakwaters. There was a fishing tug leaving at the same time, heading out to check their nets and we waved, as boaters usually do. I was on my way back to Duluth so I knew I would have to tack back and forth to gain the westerly headway needed.

Of course, real sailors don't need a dodger, but after a couple of hours of tacking out and back along the south shore, and making some headway, the wind and waves gradually built until spray over the bow became annoying and chilling and the waves slowed progress considerably. Waves may have occasionally reached about a three-foot height by now and as noon approached, I was thinking about lunch and taking a break from the pounding and the tedium of the helm.

Examining the shoreline through binoculars and peering with wet, cold and naked eyeballs I thought I could make out a small creek estuary protected by a sand bar that was bending around the mouth of the creek. This was a common feature on the south shore, along this portion, where the sandstone, boulders, and clay banks are constantly being weathered into sand beaches.

I figured that with the swing keel up in the housing and the hull then needing only about a foot of draught to float, that I could possibly motor up into the creek's mouth and there find some protection from the waves, if not the wind; a break from sailing and an opportunity for some lunch. This was, of course, the leeward shore, where the waves were about the steady, tireless business of making new sand from rocks and boulders, but I thought that if I headed her in toward the creek mouth and caught a wave just right I could zoom in behind the sand bars' protection from the waves.

Sails were doused and the new to me, (but ancient) five horsepower Firestone engine that I had recently refurbished, caught quickly and purred to life for the run to shore.

As shore approached, the confidence that I had in my plan seemed to sink with the boat as it slid into the valley between waves. Closer yet to shore, it began to look like I had underestimated the power of the waves and the extent to which the now breaking waves pushed the boat around, beyond what my steering and the motor could counteract. If I continued nosing toward shore on this course I could see bad things happening as boulders were showing up in the shallows just under the surface. They were not turned to sand yet. They would do severe damage to the boat. Then wham, we banged down hard on a rock. Quickly enough, I reacted by cramping the engine's tiller and the boat's tiller hard to port and coaxing the full unthrottled five horses to push us back out into deep water. A miscalculation based upon inexperience on an unknown shore and a narrow escape from another wrecked boat on a Lake Superior shore. Whew!

"When in doubt go out!" This lesson I had almost learned the hard way, as with my many other sailing lessons, but I could not afford to learn all about sailing the hard way. Thankfully, most of the learning I did about sailing, came from books written by others, both novices and accomplished seamen, and reading of sailing adventures was to be the focus of many a long winter evening.

Reading books of outdoor adventures has always been one of my favorite leisure time activities and I always seemed to find leisure time in my lifestyle. When I was a boy, the canoeing and wilderness trekking stories, written by real life adventurers that so fascinated me, were drawing me into a longing for a real life, one of a kind adventure for myself. Single hand sailing at sea seemed to be the ultimate challenge to one's mental toughness, skill with boat handling, inner spirit and grit. Sometimes I wondered how *I* might handle such a rigorous test, alone at sea.

I had read all of the sailing books of the local small town public libraries and was building a collection of my own as well. I was becoming a voracious reader of sailing adventures and from them and my own experiences I seemed to be settling into my own idea of what a personal sailing adventure might be.

Sailboat Number Three

I think I first saw my next sailboat while browsing on Craigslist. Sailboat number three cost me my two current sailboats, my old Chevy dump truck, and some cash. The owner of the Commodore (the new boat) and I negotiated the deal which we felt was to both of our advantage. I didn't use the dump truck anymore and he had a young family and a farm that he was developing. His teenage son loved the potential of the Sea Mouse and her sweet lines and hard chine. I think his dad knew of the history and potential of the San Juan twenty-one.

The Commodore sure was a pretty boat. A twenty-six foot black hull, a spacious cabin with six feet of headroom, an outboard rudder and a four-stroke, six horsepower outboard motor mounted on a high quality transom bracket that would allow the motor to be raised or lowered as needed, and a matching tandem axle trailer to boot. She was in uncommonly good condition for a 1980s sailboat.

The Commodore had a fixed, shoal draught keel and needed only three feet of water under her. The shallow draught would allow me to enter harbors and backwaters where deep keel boats would run aground, yet it was a keel that was permanent and one that I couldn't forget to lower into position!

She didn't need much for exterior or interior dressing to make her a pretty boat and an eye catcher. I added some anyway, mostly because I learned to love working on sailboats as much as sailing them. I was gaining skills and knowledge with each boat and the modifications that I accomplished. I was acquiring a good store of high quality rigging gear and the skills for the best and strongest procedures for running lines to the cockpit for single-handed sailing. I was buying some special power and hand tools for working in tight quarters and I thought I had a good eye for making a boat good to look at and safe to sail.

The Commodore was a bit too heavy for my small pickup truck to safely tow. (Come to think of it, so was the San Juan. When I went to pull the San Juan from a sandy ramp to trade her for the Commodore, the truck, trailer and boat were all stuck in the Superior bay and I needed a tow from a big pickup truck to get things back on dry ground). I enlisted the help of a full sized pickup and her skipper, Ken Peter my friend, neighbor, and sawmill operator. The transport went well and together we got the boat down to the Superior, Wisconsin harbor and backed her down a steep launching ramp and afloat. I tied her off on the launching dock and sent Ken home with some money and lots of thanks.

Randy and I motored around the nearby marina for a while to warm up the engine and get the feel for how she steered. Tomorrow I would want to head out to the bay and hoist sails and see how she felt under wind power, but for now we tied up at the guest dock of the local marina. I slept on the boat. She was a very plush and comfy camper on the water. Still just a floating camper, not a floating motor-home like some of the newer boats.

The first sailing adventure down the lake on the Commodore wasn't an uneventful sail, but I guess I can say that about most all of my many sailing adventures on the lake. The first day we made it to Cornucopia where a small fee at Dave Tillmans' Siskiwit Bay Marina gave us access to our own slip and dock for the night. My son Randy came along on this, her maiden voyage down the lake, where the Commodore took us beyond the sight of the Duluth hills and the familiar narrowing of the western end of the lake. The view was of water all around when this far down the lake. Randy and I spent a peaceful night on the boat, me in the V-berth forward and Randy on the starboard settee in the saloon (main cabin of a sailboat, not the saloon in the nearby town).

Morning found us thinking about breakfast at the restaurant, a short hike into town away. Before we left we met some fellow yachties who had sailed into the marina during the night. (I had no way to know at the time that these folks would become friends and we would meet again in faraway places). They had a large and lovely top quality sailboat. Sue was skipper and Thom Burns the mate, and we all hiked up the road to town for breakfast.

On our return to the marina, Thom liked some of the modifications I had done to the Commodore and he suggested some others that I hadn't thought of. Both he and Sue lived in the Twin Cities where they had spouses and businesses. (Thom's business, _Northern Breezes Sailing School_, would play prominently in my sailing future.) We parted ways but gave each other contact information to keep in touch down the road (lake?).

Randy and I sailed out toward Eagle Island, the first one when approaching the Apostle Islands from the West, then kept to an easterly course between Sand Island and the mainland. The Sand Island strait is well known by sail boaters and especially remembered by those who have grounded out on the shifting sands. Though maybe a mile wide, the strait may only be three feet deep for long stretches. I was aware that only shoal draught boats should attempt the strait, all others should take the long way around, northeast out to the lake-ward shore of Sand Island, then east past the Sand Island lighthouse where one could then choose most any passage between the rest of the islands.

The shoal draught of the Commodore was the ticket for keeping some water between the rippled sand bottom and her shallow keel. I think there was usually a foot or so of water that kept the two solid items from contact (maybe an inch or so but what does it matter). We passed near the island where once there was a fishing village and year-round residents. Summer cottages were all that remained now. With an east wind and late afternoon approaching, we headed back west to a protected bay in the lee of the big island. There we set an anchor and took the dinghy to shore to explore the beach and see who could find the coolest looking rocks. All was well with the Commodore and the crew, the big lake, the protection of the island to our windward, and the quiet onset of evening.

Long before daylight the boat was pitching enough to wake me up with a queasy stomach. It's always hard to tell by looking toward shore if a boat has dragged anchor or is still in the same position as when you were falling asleep with the gentle rocking of the swells. The shore looked imminently closer now in the beam of a four-cell flashlight. The wind had shifted during the night from east to west. I was sure our position was approaching a critical distance both from shore and from the bottom as the boat rode on anchor over the building waves.

I started the outboard and woke the crew (Randy) to haul in the anchor rode as I motored toward deep water. At a guess of a ten-foot water depth we tried to hold steady and dropped two anchors hoping to finish the night with some sleep. That was not to be. Building waves made sleep impossible. The crew hoisted anchors and we set sail to the west; when in doubt, go out!

Daylight found us rounding the outside of Eagle Island and close reaching into a sou'wester back to Duluth and a workday for Randy on the morrow. Some good and easy lessons about anchorage and wind shifts behind us. The winds were steady and brisk and we made landfall at Superior, Wisconsin before dark.

That summer the Commodore and I sailed three more times, farther down Lake Superior than I had been on any previous boats, to Cornucopia and beyond, to Bayfield, Wisconsin, and the Apostle Islands. That was a big leap for me, to sail down the lake for ninety miles, single-handing a 26-foot sloop rigged puff bucket, gaining some confidence and lessons from the lake each time.

One particular day among the Apostles provided me with both a small measure of confidence and a large helping of humble pie. It began with a brisk and early morning sail from Cornucopia east to the Sand Island strait and right up into the shallow harbor at Little Sand Bay on the mainland coast. I tied her up there at the public dock among the power boats and went for a walk with a twinge of smugness knowing I was one of the few sailors who could enter this harbor due to my choice of the shoal keel.

I walked over to a reconstructed fishing camp where authentic fishing gear and boat hauling winches and the net drying racks, their wood frames graying and cracking in the northern sun, all brought me back to an earlier time of hardy folks who made a living from the lake. They often went out on the lake to check their nets before daylight, without a professional forecast of what this day on the lake would bring in terms of wind or waves or storms. Some didn't return. But by the 1940s the catch was diminishing. Over-fishing, pollution, and invasive species were changing lake ecology in all of the great lakes and here in the coldest and deepest of lakes the slow growing fishery was also over-fished and damaged.

The sea lamprey had worked its way up to Lake Superior through the ship canals that man built around the falls and rapids of the huge rivers between the lakes. This eel-like fish was not a handsome looking creature and as a boy I have seen many large trout and salmon with the open scars on their sides where the rasping, sucking mouth of the lamprey had sucked out the fish's life juices.

The rainbow smelt swam up with the lamprey and reproduced in such vast numbers as to change the lake in unknown ways. When I was a kid we could easily dip net a few hundred pounds of the small fish from rivers and cricks. Smelting was great fun and the small fish were great eating. Smelting was one of the first rites of spring when the snow-melt swelled the north shore rivers and at the time we had little knowledge or concern about invasive species. Smelting was a party.

Salmon also were not native to Lake Superior in modern times but were introduced as another experiment toward "improving" the sport fishery potential of the lake. Generally they were not a success, I believe, and potentially harmful to the recovery of naturally reproducing native lake trout and brook trout.

Most folks don't realize that arctic grayling, a gorgeous fish with an overly large dorsal fin, was also native to Superior. They reproduced in the rivers of the south shore before the robber barons sent in legions of loggers to strip the white pine (the native peoples' spirit tree) from the land and drive the logs down the rivers. The log drives disturbed and changed the spawning beds and the sawdust and bark from the sawmills clogged the gravel beds where the fish laid eggs and where the fry were well oxygenated and learned when to forage and when to flee.

With the white pine mostly gone and small trees and brush replacing them there were subsequent large changes to the water cycle or hydrology of surface and sub-surface waters. The pines and their enormous root systems stored and released water in ways that kept the rivers flowing at steady rates. With the big trees gone there was more flooding with quick runoff after spring thaw and silting increased as soil was exposed to heavy rains. The arctic grayling could not adapt to this rapid change and went the way of the passenger pigeon.

As I developed a plan or outline for this book I did not envision a chapter on local ecology or an exposé of the major blunders exacted upon our so very precious water, mineral, and soil resources by our lifestyles and those before us. But how can one write of farming or sailing or just living without taking notice of the beauty and bounty around us? How can one live in that beauty without wanting to learn of its intricacies, secrets, or protect it? Anyhow, back to sailing.

The Commodore and I left the sheltered and shallow little bay heading northeast for Raspberry Point. The offshore winds from the hills seemed pretty gusty so I decided to hoist only the main so as to lessen the spooky effect of the gusts. I seemed to have struck a good compromise between speed and safety. I was trucking along at a good pace without excessive heeling in the gusts.

When sailors sail among other sailboats I suspect that they, like me, notice the set of the others' sails, how it compares with my use of the wind and what I may learn from or wonder about with their particular attitude toward the wind. Two boats were about a half-mile off my port beam plying the wind westerly, opposite my easterly heading. The first thing I noticed was that they had both main and jib flying and were meeting the gusts in what looked, from my perspective, like a dangerous heel.

As I watched, the second boat, the one nearest me, was knocked down flat in a gust. I knew what to do and wasted no time. I started the outboard and motor-sailed as fast as I could to the flattened sloop trying to spot sailors in the cold and lumpy seas. It took me forever, it seemed to get near this possible tragedy in the making, but I got over close and circled. I could see two people on board and the boat had righted herself but the mast was broken off and was somewhere down in the lake, below the surface, trailing in the tangled rigging.

When I hollered to offer assistance they waved me off as they were trying to start the outboard. They got the engine running while I circled the boat once, myself concentrating on keeping my boat upright in the lumps and bumps and gusts. They asked where the nearest safe harbor was and I pointed to Little Sand Bay, where I had come from. I wanted to get close enough to their boat to hear their needs but not so close as to get hung up in their mast and rigging hanging over the side of their boat and adrift in the water. I offered assistance again and again they waved me off. Were they too embarrassed to ask for help or a tow? Did they understand the seriousness of their situation and the cold water?

Whatever their plight became is unknown to me as I had my own hands full with the developing situation because I was getting further from the windward shore than I wanted to be and the waves were getting too big for my comfort. I took a heading to the southeast, back near shore, where only the wind was an immediate contention and not both the wind and waves.

As I rounded Raspberry Point and crossed Raspberry Bay, the shelter of the windward shore made for an interesting but not uncomfortable sail. Entering the strait between the mainland and Basswood Island brought the wind to my nose as my heading curled toward the southwest. I had to motor-sail with the main pulling and all six horses pushing to keep steerage and maintain a course to Bayfield, the safe harbor ahead.

Wow! These gusts were tremendous. I was making little headway and I couldn't release the tiller long enough to douse the main and if I couldn't get it contained on the deck I thought it would get blown to rags or over the side. This single-handing in a blow was sure showing its shortcomings.

Without a down-haul on the main, or lazy jacks to contain the sail, I felt my best choice was to leave the main up and keep trying to claw my way to Bayfield, get behind the break wall and get that main down. The mains'l would only luff now and was not helping with forward pull. The motor was not strong enough to keep pointed straight into the wind if the mains'l caught any side wind for power. I tried several times to fall off the wind slightly but it felt like that would take me to a broach and a knockdown. The wind was too strong, the boat too light, and the sail too tall.

Lashing the tiller would only give me seconds to leave the helm and get the main down and under control on the deck before the boat broached to the wind and waves. That looked like a bad choice and a poor risk considering I was surviving okay in the present state of confusion.

Instead I let the main-sheet fly, kept my head low under the boom and somehow got the thrashing loose end of the main-sheet swirled around my neck but got it loose before the flailing boom yanked the sheet and stretched my neck. Whew again! The outboard had just enough power to keep some steerage and keep her pointed with the sheet swirling and the boom flailing and the mains'l luffing and me without enough hands to get control of anything but the tiller. There were times however when the bow would get blown off the wind and I would stretch out and back over the transom and cramp the tiller of the outboard hard to the side to bring the bow back to the wind, all the while waves and spray washing me down and chilling me.

When it took cramping both tillers just to maintain steerage it should have dawned on me that this was too much weather for me and the boat that day. We inched our way to the break wall after what seemed like hours of enduring this crazy summer afternoon trying to manage two tillers in a small hurricane on the big lake. I got the mains'l down and met my new friend Kay Bakke on the city dock as she helped me tie up against the strong off-dock gusts. She was the skipper of a charter sailboat docked nearby and had wisely chosen not to take out any customers this "brisk and breezy" day.

That afternoon I watched some other sailboats come into safe harbor. I talked to the owners of a trailer sailor that they were strapping down to its trailer, asked them about their day and where was the mast for the boat. They too had been de-masted and had cut loose the mast and limped to shore under motor power. And you thought I was exaggerating about this blow on the big lake.

There were some lasting and humbling lessons learned that day. One was to rig a sail so that it could be lowered in a blow, single-handing it, without risking a broach. Another was to have enough engine power to maintain a course and steerage in a blow. Third, was to have a heavy enough boat and deep enough keel to withstand the side forces that wind and waves can exert on a craft, and fourth, if all of the above still didn't feel right then do a 180 and run with the wind back to the lee of an island and wait out the blow. These lessons changed my direction toward a more seaworthy boat and ideas for sure-fire rigs that a single-hander could safely single hand.

The Cabin-on-a-River Dream

There came a point in my life where the chores of the blueberry farm began to interfere with my dreams of summer adventure. The responsibilities of keeping things looking good and producing well were weighing heavily on some warm days and cutting seriously into my playtime. I began to wonder what life would be like without the cares or worry that ownership of a farm and a home and all the associated stuff brought to bear on one's life. Where could one go or sail then? Where *couldn't* one go or sail then?

The sailing adventure books that I loved to read were seriously corrupting my engendered sense of capitalistic enterprise and dedication to work. I would ask myself, "If not now when; when I get old?" "Hey," I would answer, "You're sixty already, how old do you have to be?"

Across the oceans of the earth adventurous folks were sailing. Around the world some had sailed and some very few had done single-handed crossings of the great seas and had even circumnavigated the globe, alone! Alone! Alone for weeks and months at a time. Completely at the mercies of the winds and the seas. They must have been strong-minded sorts. Alone in the unknown. Strangely, this had an appeal to me.

I had mentioned to some friends about my thoughts of selling the blueberry farm and most seemed incredulous that I could be serious about selling out. I guess the farm was becoming a local institution and they thought of me as institutional. But as my mind moved closer to the change that I seemed to need, a life without daily chores became more and more appealing. I imagined myself footloose, able to wander and explore at will—explore both myself and the world of nature and culture.

Not having lawn to mow or equipment to maintain, nor having to pull weeds forever with no end in sight, nor having to plan and organize and prepare for the mad rush of picking season—not having these responsibilities seemed essential if adventure was to be my future. It was at about this period of the farm's growth and maturing that crowd control at picking times was a hectic and wearing part of the business. Cars were the biggest hassle. Parking and traffic management became a huge challenge in the tight quarters of a small woodland farm. But that was my fault, for I had tried for many years and with many creative incentives to attract pickers and a burgeoning market for my berries.

The capitalist part of me wanted to profit as well as possible while at the same time providing my customers with the best blueberries that the soil and the sun and the rains could provide. Making enough money to make this idyllic farmstead life to be also a viable living, was always a challenge and farm income was my only income at this stage of my work life.

Okay then, if the farm must go what would be my source of income and where would I hang my hat? On a tree limb? I did have a small, very small, pension and some small dividends from some investments but the sum total there would barely pay the utility bills for a modest house. But wait, I wouldn't have any utility bills or a house to support if I didn't have a house.

My newly proposed budget did not seem that complicated...very low income with very few small bills. But where would I live, on a sailboat? In a camper perhaps? I did have a small pickup truck, old but paid for, and I knew that I loved to travel and camp out (in relative comfort) and so it seemed prudent at this time to buy a small (tiny) pull behind camper. Marna and I drove out to the factory in west-central Minnesota and we pulled home a little camper called a "Scamp". Thereafter, if the farm sold quickly I could always go "Scamping" wherever I decided to park it.

It looked like I had a plan for a balanced personal budget with an affordable economy of scale, that is, minimal costs to fit within a minimal income and it was beginning to look like an unencumbered lifestyle was in the making with more adventure in the future.

During the process of selling the farm two other possible opportunities for adventure presented themselves, or perhaps more accurately, I deliberately worked to make them happen. One involved a lifelong dream of having a cabin on a remote river or lake where a peaceful, low cost and simple lifestyle was still possible in far rural Minnesota.

My son, Randy had bought a home and some rural property thirty or so miles north of Duluth. While visiting him and my grand daughters I took a walk behind his house and back to the river that bordered his rear property line. I was taken by the old growth pines along the river and the bend of the river where the rapids gurgled over boulders and gravel beds. It seemed so remote and untouched, so like a perfect place for a cabin on a river.

This was a typical mixed woodland/farmland area that is like much of northeastern Minnesota. A hundred years ago, or a bit more, the land thereabouts was partially subdued by ambitious immigrants, mostly from Scandinavia, who managed to eek out a meager income and pursue the American dream of a better life. They followed after the lumberjacks had cut most of the pines and had only to dynamite and grub out the stumps in order to have the beginnings of a pasture or cropland.

Now, a hundred years later, the cleared land was slowly returning to forest and brush. The cows had mostly gone as had most of the farm families.

Behind Randy's house and along the high banks of the river, those few old growth red and white pines had somehow survived the onslaught of the timber barons (robber barons) and the homesteaders. I envisioned, that if the thick cover of balsam fir trees were opened up a bit (they were almost impenetrable) and a small road put in, there could be a cabin on a river here and a camp of boyhood dreams.

One of life's lessons that I learned early on was that few things are gained unless one is to venture forth, and so I formulated a plan to approach the landowner with a reasonable proposal to purchase some of the fifty or so acres that she owned along the river. Long story shorter, she agreed to my proposal and I bought from her about twelve acres of woodland along the river.

Very soon after the deal was consummated and made legal I hauled my old tractors up to Randy's yard and began laying out the route through the woods for a driveway back to camp. This was an exciting time for me and I think the tractors sensed it too. I loved my old tractors and I think they loved me. Together we had history. We were about the same age. We had each done some hard work in the past and we still had the strength for more. This driveway was to be put through some challenging terrain but I believed we were all up to it. We couldn't wait to begin.

There was a small, nagging hitch in the back of my mind. Remembering my personal philosophy about the ownership of property (real estate) equating with the loss of personal freedom, and having eternal chores to do, worry, and costs, I reconciled all these things by planning for a small, simple, and maintenance free camp establishment. I found that I could rationalize away my fears of ownership by utilizing alternative plans for all of the camp's services and my own meager wants. Hey, if it works for me....

The blueberry farm sold quickly and easily, without advertising and for even more money than I was asking. Some great folks who were former pickers (customers) of mine bought the farm and we became friends through the process. I parked the Scamp just down the road from the farm at another old farm that my brother owned in absentia (he lived in southern California). It worked out well for a temporary camp and the first summer of no chores.

Days were spent driveway clearing for the camp, thirty miles to the north. Running my old tractors was not a chore at all but instead was one of my all time favorite activities. It turned out to be about a quarter mile long driveway winding through the woods and across a steep ravine with a small creek in the bottom. Some new, local friends donated a large diameter used culvert for the bottom of the ravine and I pushed dirt with the old tractors for several days to make an access across that was not too steep to be navigated in winter. When the road was roughed in all the way back to the cabin site I drove my truck in for the first time and set up a tent and spent my first night at "Camp Cotton".

The tent was the first structure to meet my camp's immediate amenity requirements. I have always liked tents. As a boy, tents meant adventure, whether in the real wilderness of the Boundary Waters or in the neighbor's back yard. Spending a night with friends meant stories and jokes and goofy boy stuff late into the night. The Camp Cotton tent felt like home and worked out well for sleeping quarters...for a while. Rainy periods made the tent floor damp and food and clothing eventually soaked up some dampness and musty odors that didn't seem healthy. Also, mice had found their way into the tent and were taking up residence and setting up a camp of their own.

The pursuit of comfort was never high on my list of things to pursue, but with the rain and the mice I knew a better home was fast moving up on my list of things to pursue. With the new driveway's surface graveled and smoothed and roots and stumps removed, I headed thirty miles to the south and hooked the truck up to the Scamp and headed north. Dry, warm, and without uninvited guests, the Scamp became the first real lodge at Camp Cotton and nights and rainy days were spent in indulgent comforts. If I could figure out a safe and dependable heat source, the scamp could even work out to be my winter home…perhaps.

A pole between two trees with a blue tarp slung over it and the four corners tied down to stakes driven into the ground, made the camp's first tool shed. That shed was soon filled to bursting with hand tools and stuff that I started to haul north. Stuff that mice had little interest in. Lots of stuff, handy stuff, kept nearby where I could lay my hands on it without a search, preferably everything within sight for this was my modus-operandi for efficiency and productivity. I could never find things if they weren't immediately visible.

There were certain methods and tools that I had become accustomed to in order to feel productive. Grease guns, gas cans, pry bars, socket sets and end wrenches, shovels, axes, chainsaws…these were just a few of the tools that I needed to put in a day good day of woods work.

More dry storage space seemed to be in order to get stuff out of the weather. I dug and hauled a few cubic yards of sand with the Allis and dumped it and smoothed it and packed it in a place that seemed to be the right location for another shed.

With the sand for a foundation and some money for compensation, I hired a fine crew of young guys to build a ten by twelve foot wooden shed with a shingle roof. It turned out really nice, sturdy, good quality. I stood back and admired its cute shape and decided that this was all of the real estate that the camp and I would ever need for our new life together. I had a dry home and a tool shed/workshop. A real camp on a river. Life was good. Who could ask for anything more?

It is finally time now to take you, the reader, back again to that tall lanky boat shed currently full of old tractors. Remember that shed? As it happens, that shed is located back in the woods about a quarter mile from the main road, back on a driveway that winds through the woods and across a steep ravine and leads to a camp on a river. Remember that it was built to house a sailboat?

Sweet Breeze, my Last Sailboat…?

At the time I didn't know what I was looking for. There were lots of sailboats looking for a new owner at various marinas in Duluth and Superior. It was fun for me to poke around marinas, looking at boats large and small, some with signs attached that caused me to look twice. The signs suggested that they were available to buy.

I had asked Joe, Radke, the manager of Barker's Island Marina, to show me some of the boats on the lot that were advertised on the Internet and elsewhere, but when we went into the huge shed to get a ladder for boarding the boats out in the yard, we passed by an old boat in the corner that caught my eye. In the rearmost, dusty corner of that huge boat shed, I was drawn to an old, abandoned looking sailboat with the overall appearance of what I thought a traditional sailboat should look like. Was it for sale I inquired? Joe thought perhaps it was, he could check later, but for now he suggested, we should haul the ladder out in the yard to climb aboard a couple of boats that I might find interesting.

We did check out a couple of boats and they were okay, but as I explored them I think I was slightly distracted with some persistent thoughts and wonder about the old girl in the corner of the big shed with the attractive and seaworthy lines. She had caught my eye. Back in the dusty corner of the shed. with the ladder up against her, I climbed aboard that old boat for the first time, the first time in what would eventually be thousands of boardings and thousands of miles of sailing. The original bronze tag mounted on the transom said she was a "Pearson Triton", hull number 239.

Later that day, finding a wi-fi service connection for my laptop, I did a little Internet research to learn something about the history and specifications of a "Pearson Triton". I quickly found out that it was an old, classic plastic, North Sea design with a dedicated following of owner sailors. There were "Triton" racing clubs on the east and west coast and a national "Triton Association". Whoodathunk...that old thing?

There were hundreds of Tritons sold in the 1960s. They were hand-laid fiberglass and were one of the first commercially available boats of that relatively new production method. She was built in Bristol, Rhode Island in the early sixties, designed by Carl

Alberg after the seaworthy Scandinavian boats plying the dangerously unpredictable waters of the North Sea.

All the notoriety aside, I liked her looks and struck a deal. I next had to figure out a way to haul that heavy old boat away from the city and up north to my new home in the woods.

From all the available information I could find, I determined the weight of a Triton to be somewhere between seven and nine thousand pounds; that would mean a trailer with a capacity of 10,000 lbs. or so would be needed for its transport. I thought about borrowing or renting a trailer so that I wouldn't be buying more stuff, however, I couldn't figure out how I could get the boat off the trailer to return it once it had arrived north of Duluth about 35 miles at Camp Cotton? The boat was 28 and one half feet long with a deep keel hanging below the hull another 4 and one half feet. As you might imagine, that made for a very top heavy and ungainly object for me to try to handle with tractor loaders at camp.

I soon arrived at the conclusion that a heavy-duty trailer dedicated to hauling the boat and also cradling her at camp, needed to be purchased.

With a borrowed full size pickup and with the new trailer behind, I headed for the marina where Joe and the crew would put the boat and its steel support cradle on the trailer with a boatlift. All went well early one Sunday morning before the church traffic as the truck labored with its heavy burden up the Duluth hills and northward to the Camp Cotton "boatworks". And she did need some work.

Things were moving pretty fast. It sure looked like the boat and me would need some protection from the elements, especially during the long cold winter months if I wanted to reconstruct her cabin and get the boat cleaned up and ready to sail for next summer. Those were not chores that I wanted to do out in a snowstorm. This is when it looked like some more camp real estate was necessary in the form of a tall, lanky, boat shed.

Another sand foundation, some more money, and another hard working crew put the tall, lanky shed together in about four days, and Sweet Breeze was under cover again. Boat number four was home.

Remodeling an Old Boat

The interior of Sweet Breeze's tiny cabin was all disassembled. It looked like the former owner had begun the process of reconstituting and reclaiming her inner beauty in order to bring it back to original condition or better but he had evidently lost interest in the project. So far, the best part about the cabin was the six feet of headroom.

Assessing what I thought should be changed seemed to be impossible without first reassembling all of the original woodwork and furniture as it was designed to fit together. But wait! Simply climbing up onto the boat was a project in itself. This would never do. How was I to carry my tools and materials on board? Everything up and down a ladder? No, thought I, that is too dangerous, too risky, too much exposure to a sailor's dreams ending in a fall. A better and safer access method was needed.

One of the most convenient advantages of having a well-stocked home junk pile is the efficiency with which suitable building materials can be acquired. With hardware and lumber stores mostly thirty miles away in any direction, having a ready source of project supplies was imperative if I were to build anything efficiently, and the limits of my immediate enthusiasm to get started would be severely tested by the delays of securing materials from far away places. There are parts of my personality that allow infinite patience, sometimes toward intricate projects, and even some women friends of mine with their mysterious and intricate personalities, but when a fun project is the focus of my attentions, I really want to get started... now!

There was enough old lumber stored at camp to begin most small projects and the immediate search turned up two heavy planks about fourteen feet long to begin a sturdy stairway to the deck of Sweet Breeze. I decided that the stair treads should also need to be of a sturdy and strong nature so I cut a trial one from a big black ash log right near the shed that I had salvaged from my own woodland. The log was already up at a nice work height as one of the top logs on a log pile that I had deemed too good to cut up for firewood.

"One must have the proper tools to do a proper job." That was pretty much my motto throughout my career of building and repairing things around home and for others. My chain saw collection included a heavy old one given to me by my brother-in-law who probably just bought it because it was cheap, five dollars if I remember right. For cutting stair treads it was perfect with the twenty-inch bar cutting through most of the length of the tread and the heavy weight of the saw helping on the downward cut.

I thought the stair treads turned out perfectly. A full two inches thick by twelve inches wide and as long as I would like. Plus they had the rough cut marks of the big course saw chain and would give good foot traction if wet.

The completed stairway was hoisted into position running parallel to the length of the boat and a sturdy black spruce handrail was harvested from my woodland lumber store. By now, you, the reader probably would think "sturdy" is one of my favorite words…it is and it is also one of my favorite building concepts, which brings me back to the interior of Sweet Breeze.

The bulkheads (support enhancing dividers within a boat's hull) and the interior wood trim were all made from real wood back when Sweet Breeze was built. Bulkheads were made from three-quarter inch marine plywood, quality lay-ups of Douglas fir without the voids of most modern types of plywood. All of the interior trim work was of a dark mahogany, again, solid as the tree it was cut from. High quality woods were readily available back in the 60s. Sweet Breeze has little or no chipboard, pressboard, fiberboard or other types of board where poor quality trees are disassembled by mechanical or chemical means and then the pieces or fibers are pressed back together to form a board of any dimension required.

(I can't resist the opportunity to sermonize a bit: If the North American forests had been utilized in a wise and sustainable manner with an eye toward future use and multiple use there would be high quality woods available virtually forever...instead they were exploited for the sole purpose of making money, fast and easy, still are. Ninety-nine percent of the original white pine in Minnesota was cut within about a 30-year span 100 years ago. Now the process of recreating building materials and lumber from chips or dissolved fibers brings to mind what happened to the wheat kernel. Once a tiny miracle storehouse of protein and energy and fat, modern plant geneticists have restructured it into a highly productive but far less nutritive source of bulk. Ground into flour (the wheat germ and bran somehow removed) and then bleached (everything white is pure) it then needs to be reconstituted with nutrients to approach the real food value its original forbears had a hundred years ago and it still doesn't come close. The farmer in me cringes as I think about our industrialized food system).

Sweet Breeze looked easy to put back together again. All of the wood trim pieces were piled into the V-berth but before screwing them back into place a fresh coat of a light colored paint on all of the surfaces seemed proper. I cleaned and painted floor to ceiling, cabin sole to coach roof, bilge to anchor locker. A high quality oil based paint with a gloss finish seemed proper because it would wipe down and be easy to keep clean. Ah, what a fresh coat of paint can do to fifty-year-old surfaces and odors.

She was looking spiffy with the glossy light walls and the dark wood trim. She was also looking very dated and quite basic with a cabin layout of two setees in the saloon for sitting or sleeping, a galley consisting of a stainless steel sink and a drawer, an ice box for a fridge, and nothing for a head. This is where layout and planning and great joy within me comes into being. The challenge of visualizing and figuring out how to make things fit and be practical in this small space was a huge creative outlet for me.

The reconstruction began with the main table in the saloon. It was designed to fit across the walkway into the forward parts of the cabin and folks could sit on either side and eat or play canasta with the table between them. However, with the table in place there would be no access to the bathroom (head) or closet or V-berths forward of the mid-ship bulkhead. It didn't seem like a well thought out floor plan.

The best options for the table situation seemed to be to move it to another location or to reduce the size of the table. In a practical sense, there aren't too many options within the tiny confines of a small boat cabin like this. There are some definite limits as to how and to where things can be mounted to the boat's structure. For one thing, there is no headliner in a boat of this age (an interior wall up next to the hull). The hand laid-up fiberglass hull is both the outside and inside of the boat. On the inside it is painted and on the outside it has a gel coat of smoothly finished fiberglass so anything mounted on the hull must either be glued onto it or drilled through for fasteners to attach.

Personal philosophy of boat integrity comes into play here, i.e. how many holes through the hull, especially below the water line, would you like your boat to have? Best answer: none! Second best answer: as few as possible! So mounting interior furniture on this old boat is pretty much limited to fastening to the bulkheads, the three-quarter inch thick "ribs" that divide up the space below. Any glued attachments to the surface of the hull are at best temporary and could not have much weight or forces upon them.

It was decided. The table would be both reduced in size and moved to the port side and supported against the bulkhead at the forward end of the settee. This location made it possible to squeeze by the table to go forward without taking the table down. I liked how it turned out and a crew of two could still eat upon it or play cribbage upon it, probably not monopoly, and it would suffice as a rather reduced size chart table.

At the aft end of the port settee was the door that swings open to gain access to the icebox. Not wanting to mess with ice, this nice and fairly large cupboard was assigned to be the tool chest. When the door was swung to the open position, up against the back rest of the settee, I used it as a support for a small table that I designed to swing up to function for a table and down to get out of the way. Around the edge of both tables I fastened fiddles about one and a half inches high to keep things from flying off to the floor. Fiddles also make attractive borders for tables or shelves. These I made from some oak flooring scraps acquired from a friend and darkened them with some mahogany wood stain to match up closely with the real mahogany elsewhere. My work always turned out a little crude but it was "sturdy".

The galley really needed some help. There was the sink, the drawer, and the missing countertop above the drawer alongside of the sink. The counter top was nowhere to be found but the opening it covered looked like it could possibly be the location for a small fridge if the drawer was removed. Internet research turned up a tiny, high quality 12-volt fridge (with a compressor type cooling system like the one in most kitchens) that could be set at any temperature and had a fairly low current draw on the ship's batteries. That seemed like the ticket and was ordered online.

A few days later, when the fridge arrived, I slipped it into its planned opening and built a secure wood frame to hold it snuggly in place and finally installed a 12-volt outlet under the sink for the power source. I plugged it in and set the temp. It started right up and began cooling in minutes. This little fridge was expensive but worth every penny as time and future voyages would tell.

Every ship's galley needs a stove but the designated galley corner of this ship was already stuffed full with the sink and fridge. There was only one corner left to mount anything in the saloon and that was the starboard forward end against the bulkhead there. It looked like that if the stove could be mounted high enough above the cushion of the couch that one's feet would fit under it and the couch could still be used as a bed. Off to the Internet to find the right stove (wi-fi service meant a one mile drive to town to the parking lot behind the community center where I could get a weak signal).

The right stove turned out to be a used stove from a boat in Florida that I found on eBay (one can find anything on eBay). I made the installation with foot room under it and judiciously planned the route for the propane line to feed the stove. Propane, or any heavier than air gas, must not ever, ever, leak any where on a boat. I checked and rechecked the whole installation from the tank to the stove, for leaks at all the connections, with soapy water and a soft brush and routed the line where it could not get damaged or wore through. It was a fine stove after a little cleanup and some hot tea was in order for to sip while working on a very cold boat.

Most sailboats have a head (bathroom) that consists of a toilet appliance, a holding tank, and a flush system with water that works much like the common household one. After a long voyage the holding tank is pumped out at a marina into another tank and then the marina's tank is pumped. "Pump out" is not always a pleasant procedure. Also, the boat needs to have a water source on board or a seawater supply to use as flush water. There was not much about the whole idea that appealed to me.

I did a little Internet research about an alternative option for boats. At my camp in the woods I had installed a composting toilet and the process of letting natural bacteria dispose of human waste seemed like the best one. There were some small models of composting toilets available that were made for boats and a friend had one on his boat that he swore by as the no smell, no mess way to go. Another on-line order later I was trying to figure out the best fit for the new head in the tiny closet space where the old one must have been. I found it would fit, just barely, if I mounted the whole unit on slides so that it could be moved in order to turn the agitator that aerated the waste for "enhanced aerobic composting". It was tight quarters but it worked, and I didn't plan on spending a lot of time in there.

The composting head was just a simple, common sense approach to dealing with something no one wants to deal with. The principle of keeping the liquid and solid waste in separate chambers is the key to not making a smelly mess. It worked well and I only wound up emptying the solid waste chamber once a year, long after the sailing season ended and the longer that it composts the more like soil it becomes. It's always emptied on dry land on your flowerbeds or scattered in the woods. I made a toilet on the same simple principle for the main cabin at my camp in northern Minnesota. In the wintertime I slide the waste from a tray, newspapers and all into a hot wood fire in my heating stove and it is soon reduced to ashes, no pathogens or hazard to ground water. I scatter the ashes in the woods.

There was a large drawer on the lower sides of each of the settees but they only made fractional use of the big empty space under port or starboard settees down next to the side hulls. I removed the drawers and took them apart and salvaged the solid mahogany front panels. I fastened hinges on the lower edge of these and changed them to doors over the drawer openings for access to all that unused space. Then I cut two more access openings under the cushions in strategic locations to give access to the rest of the unused space under both couches/ berths/ settees. Things were shaping up and starting to look like a place one could live aboard, or at least overnight now and then.

As modifications progressed, I needed to step back and look upon them and see an improvement over the original design. It was important to me not to just change the layout but also to make it a better use of space, a safer space, and a more convenient space.

One of the improvements toward safer sailing was to remove knobs, protrusions, and round off sharp corners. Those sailors among us that have been in rough seas know how easy it is to lose your balance on a rocking and rolling boat and bounce your body off things. Serious injury can result if those things are sharp or stick out far into an open space. Round corners don't hurt so much when bodies are thrown against them.

The electrical systems on the boat were mostly original and in good shape. The engine compartment was not the nightmarish tangle of spaghetti, wires hanging about inviting a short circuit and a fire as I have seen on some old boats. Wires were neatly arranged and fastened down like they should be. Some were even labeled with their function. About all I did, in order to consume less current and prolong battery life, was to change the lamp bulbs throughout the cabin. I replaced the 25-watt original bulbs with ONE-watt LED bulbs and had about the same amount of lumens (useable light). Amazing.

The VHF marine radio was old but looked in good shape on the outside but with no boats nearby I would have to wait until I could test it at the marina and see if it would transmit and receive.

Then, of course, being a music lover I wanted a good stereo system. To the Internet I went and ordered a car stereo; AM-FM, CD player. I could have ordered a marine type, one for another hundred dollars but I didn't! Once installed, home was shaping up, I had tunes.

The engine compartment was in good shape. The Atomic Four had been modernized with an electronic ignition, a modern alternator instead of the original DC generator, a completely new fuel system from the tank to the carburetor, and a new carburetor and cooling system. I hooked up a garden hose to the cooling system and started it up. It purred like a kitten. All engine systems were a "go".

After cleaning up the bilge a bit I installed an electric bilge pump with an automatic float switch that would turn the pump on if the water reached a certain level. At this point I thought the cabin was adequate, safe, and livable and went topside to assess what was most needed.

Midwinter Break

It was about this time that I got a phone call from Thom…the Thom that I had met the previous summer down the lake at Cornucopia. He asked me if I might like to sail in the Caribbean for two weeks, or so, in February, a month away. He was chartering some sailboats in the British Virgin Islands and needed a cook on one of the boats for the second of the two weeks. The first week I could be his guest on another boat and I could bring a guest as well.

It didn't take Marna or me long to come to a decision to take Thom up on his offer. In exchange for Thom's costs for the vacation we agreed that I would work on his training boats stored on the hard in Duluth. (On the hard is sailor-speak for land.)

The sailing vacation was a great experience for me and Marna. She said it was her best midwinter vacation ever. We were part of a flotilla and sailed on newer fifty-foot long boats and we had our own cabin in the starboard quarter. This was way more comfort than I needed but Marna soaked it up with ease, no complaints about the need for more rigor and hardship in her life. And who was part of the crew on our boat but Sue. The same Sue from the morning chat and breakfast at Cornucopia on the south shore of Lake Superior the previous summer. She brought along her friend Jeff, (her husband) who I learned in the next few days was an all around good guy.

I think we stopped at all of the islands in the British group throughout the week. We had great food on board and at restaurants and gentle trade winds for warm and mild sails. Warm water sailing had some very attractive qualities when Lake Superior was your only standard.

The second week I took over as cook (and first mate!) on another boat as Marna flew over to Puerto Rico and then back to the snow. Another Tom was the captain of this boat and a fine one he was. This was a teaching boat that the students needed the experience on in order to qualify for a certificate that would allow them to charter boats on their own. This captain Tom took the students (five big hungry guys) and me around the islands with everyone taking the helm, handling the sails, setting an anchor, retrieving a man overboard, and learning some basic navigation techniques. The students were tested on their sailing skills and I was tested on my ability to find fresh fruit and veggie provisions on the various islands and do some creative cooking in large quantity. It was a great week with some great guys. Nobody jumped ship because of my cooking.

The labor exchange worked out well and it gave me the opportunity to learn about the systems on Thom's different boats, marine diesel engines, and some of the more modern rigging that the newer boats employed. I made mental notes of ideas that I might adopt for Sweet Breeze.

Completing the Old Girl

It was back to Minnesota for me and back onto the topsides of my old boat for more improvements. Ground tackle (anchors) was next on my mental list of *critical* needs for the boat.

In the past, with the Commodore, I had a bad experience with anchoring, a really bad experience. Once upon a time, on Lake Superior in the Apostle Islands, after making a bit of a rough passage on the Commodore, I dropped the hook in a quiet bay of Stockton Island. Chickie and I took the dinghy ashore to hike back to some old abandoned sandstone quarries that I wanted to explore. Chickie loved going ashore for obvious reasons but also to run off some energy.

There were some swells coming around the point and into the bay but I was not too concerned about the security of the anchorage. The previous night was spent at Big Bay off Madeline Island and the anchor held just fine in the sand and we had a good night's sleep.

One last glance out at the boat before heading off toward the woods trail stopped me short. The Commodore looked farther out than before. It was, I was sure of it, and was drifting out toward the wind and waves of the channel beyond the protection of the point. If I didn't catch it quickly I would not catch it and it would wind up on the rocks of Presque Isle Point.

I threw on my life jacket and pushed off the dinghy and began to row with all of the energy and skill that I could muster. Speed was of the essence here. She was about three hundred yards out and would soon enter the channel. Once it made it to the channel I would have to let it go. I would not risk my life with the dinghy in the waves (or maybe I would).

After perhaps fifteen minutes of extreme effort I reached the boat and dragged my fatigued body over the transom, tied on the dinghy and took a deep breath (a breath that would tell later about the effort of rowing expended). But no time for rest now. We were starting to get tossed about by the waves but I got the outboard started, shifted it into gear and headed back for Chickie who I could see as speck on the beach and was running down the shore in my direction thinking I had abandoned her. The engine promptly quit. What now? Could I get the mains'l up in time to sail back into the bay before we met up with the rocks of the next point?

Why engine? Why now? I gave it a final restart try and it started right up in neutral; shifted into forward and it killed. That told the error of my ways immediately. The prop was not free to turn. I hoisted the motor up on its swinging bracket but still could not reach down far enough to unwrap the anchor rode from around the prop. Back into the dinghy I climbed, got the rope unwrapped, threw it on deck and climbed back aboard. This time we were headed back into the bay, toward calm water and my now frantic four-legged companion on the shore.

It's now getting way too late to make a long story short but the essence of this fiasco involves my trust in a stainless steel attachment clip with a spring loaded latch that, in my inexperience and ignorance, I had used as a final hardware item to clip the rode to the anchor. It had somehow unclipped itself from the eye on the anchor. What a hard lesson to learn about the proper way to attach ground tackle—a lesson that I was reminded of for the next few days as each deep breath would cause me to cough up a small amount of blood with a little chest pain involved. With the exertion of the rowing there must have been some minor hemorrhaging in my lungs. I had read about horses blowing blood after being ridden way too hard but I never thought I would ride myself that hard. I recovered quickly though and took shallower breaths for a couple of days until my lungs healed.

I had a spare anchor aboard, dropped it over the side and went to get my now elated little dog back on board with me. The rest of that day was spent in an effort to gain headway into the wind and waves toward the safe harbor at Bayfield, Wisconsin. It was not to be. There was not enough engine power aboard to make headway and when I tried to sail and tack, the boat felt like it was going to get knocked down flat in the wind and waves. We hid behind Hermit Island until evening when the wind subsided and the water settled down.

Besides the anchoring lesson, the heavy seas and wind later that day proved to me that I didn't have the right boat for extreme conditions on the big lake. The shoal draft keel did not make the vessel stiff enough to take on a good blow. I felt that the boat was just too light for the conditions that could create sailing drama quickly on Lake Superior. Also, a boat should have enough engine power to get us out of trouble under most circumstances. Two critical lessons learned that day.

Back to the outfitting of Sweet Breeze and the ground tackle lessons. I decided she needed a substantial anchor platform off her bow with two oversized anchors for differing bottom conditions. They would have 20 feet of five-sixteenths plated chain behind the anchor, the weight of the chain to help hold the anchor down and pull it into the bottom. The chain would be secured to about 200 feet of five-eighths nylon rope and the rope and chain and anchor would be ready to drop at a moment's notice. I constructed a heavy oak anchor platform where the anchors would be secured but always ready to drop in a hurry.

To make this mass of chain and rope ready to use and not tangle it would need to be stored in a dedicated locker in the bow forward of the V-berth. The space was available and I divided the locker area in half with a plywood wall so that the rodes from the two anchors could never tangle (foul) together. For the rodes to enter their assigned lockers and exit freely, I cut holes in the deck directly above where the rodes would lay as they were pulled in or winched in. To finish off the holes I installed some heavy PVC fittings (for household plumbing) to serve as hawse pipes, so that the chain and rodes would enter and exit the lockers smoothly. I could have bought some expensive bronze or stainless steel hawse fittings to do the same job as the PVC...I could have.

I imagined that the heaviest anchor, the plow, on the starboard bow would be a slow and hard retrieve, by hand, to get it back aboard and the rode properly stowed. An electric windlass, and a below deck mounted one at that, seemed to be the ticket, especially for a single-hander like me. If it were arranged and wired right I could raise and lower the anchor from the cockpit, my personal rule as the safest place for a single-hander to be when topside. If I had to work on the forward bow while sailing, having the windlass mounted below deck would make for one less tripping hazard. Important for the single-hander not to trip and fall overboard...real important.

The electric windlass cost about a third as much as I had paid for the whole boat. I was okay with that. It seemed to be a critical part of making the anchoring aspect of single-handing that much easier.

On eBay I found two used sailboat winches and mounted them on either side of the coach roof just forward of the companionway. These I thought would be useful for hauling on lines run back to the cockpit for various sail handling chores like reefing and hoisting. I mounted the winches on oak platforms with plenty of backing support by means of aluminum plates on the inside cabin roof.

Topsides looked good enough for now. Rigging all looked okay and I would give it a better going over when stepping the mast at the marina.

Back down below I thought of a couple of other improvements to get started on. One major convenience would be a foot pump to pull lake water to the sink for washing dishes, hands, or other body parts. The on-board storage tank had limits but the lake surely didn't. Done.

The side windows and the forward hatch were crazed and glazed and were probably the originals. They let some light in but looking out through them was something like trying to see with fogged glasses. They had to go. I cut replacement glass from quarter-inch thick polycarbonate using the perimeter of the old ones for a template. I installed the side windows within their bronze frames and made a completely new oak side-frame for the new "glass" in the forward hatch cover. What a difference; to be able to see out!

Another nice convenience would be a 110-volt inverter to supply household current for those devices that one occasionally thought necessary on board, like chargers for all the electronic gadgets we have now. It could power the charger for the backup VHF-GPS hand-held radio that I thought might be useful, chargers for electric drills, cell phones, laptops. Easily done.

The cockpit sole (floor) had a small access hatch to get at the stuffing box, transmission, and the rear of the engine. With the hatch open, one could get one arm within and not much else. I couldn't see what I was touching with that one hand and certainly couldn't accomplish any complicated tasks with that sort of minimal access. This would never do.

I found (on the Internet) a large aluminum hatch cover that would provide reasonable access to those critical parts below, ordered it and got my saber saw out for the big cut. This turned out to be one of the best improvements I ever did to that boat. Now I could easily check the engine oil level and replace the flax in the stuffing box and disconnect and pull the propeller shaft that allowed me to replace the cutlass bearing just forward of the prop. I can't imagine doing these tasks through the original access hatch. One would need mirrors and arms like an orangutan. What were they thinking?

The Single-Hander

With all of my sailboats, safely single-handing them was the top priority when on the water. There was a credo that I had adopted (whether I had read it somewhere or made it up myself, I don't remember) but it was simple and stuck with me: "stay in the cockpit and live to sail another day". To stay in the cockpit meant running all the lines that controlled the sails back to the cockpit, then there would be no need to go up onto the cabin top or to the forward deck, especially in a blow where one can get tossed overboard as the boat merrily sails away.

My boats were all sloop-rigged, fractional rigs with two sails, the forward sail (jib) not being as tall as the main sail. A sloop has only the two sails. It is pretty easy and straightforward to redirect sail control lines at strategic places through pulley blocks and fairleads back to the cockpit. It's also a lot of fun for me to figure the routing for the lines and attach the necessary hardware. There is something simple and satisfying about the simple physics of redirecting forces on lines and watching how it works.

From the cockpit of a properly single-hand-rigged sailboat I should be able to hoist the main and unfurl the jib. I should be able to reduce the size of either sail from the cockpit (called reefing) as winds pick up and thus keep the boat from being overpowered by the wind. I should be able to furl the headsail (jib) completely and secure it and I should be able to douse or drop the mains'l onto the boom and secure it. All of these basic sailing procedures the single-hander must do one way or the other and my choice is from the cockpit when possible.

It sounds simple enough and in calm weather things will sometimes go as planned. In heavy winds and waves, things almost never go as planned. Those are the times when I wished I had three hands and arms. When the foredeck is awash with waves and spray and things aren't working as planned I have had to crawl forward going from handhold to handhold and keeping my body low for balance in order to untangle some line fouled on something and crawl back to the cockpit. Not fun, but exciting and sometimes a part of sailing.

To complete the modifications of the rigging, for single-handing from the cockpit, I needed for the mast to be put up (stepped) and the mast support cables (shrouds and stays) to be fastened and snugged up and it was about this time that I thought Sweet Breeze was ready for the water.

To the Water She Goes

I had to borrow a heavy full sized pick-up truck again for the transport to Duluth. Before leaving camp I measured the distance from the ground to the highest part of the boat, which was the mast laying on top of the boat. It was about 12 feet, low enough to clear bridges and power lines as I had driven the planned route previously and checked approximate clearances. The lowest things I encountered were about 14 feet or higher from the roadbed.

There is something scary about transporting that top-heavy load. It must be the thoughts about all of the things that can go wrong. I had a kind of tightness in my chest for the first few miles. I loosened up as the highway miles sailed by plus I had left very early in the morning to have lighter vehicle traffic so I could drive slower without holding up those in a hurry.

Charley and Tom at the marina thought they could pick the boat up off the trailer and put her in the water yet that morning. Such good service. They had a special kind of hoist called a "Travellift", just the right piece of equipment for handling boats of all sizes.

Sweet Breeze floated and my sailing buddy (another Randy) helped me to step the mast with an ancient hand-cranked crane that the marina provided. Things went well. Sweet Breeze and I motored over to her assigned slip, her home base for the summer.

Marina Life

Thinking back, after all of the Marinas that the recent "big sail" has introduced me to, I feel that I need to do justice to this particular little backwater marina, where my new, old boat and me were to call our home port for the next two summers.

Maybe its because it is located away from the beaten boating paths or because of its long and colored boating history, but this little marina in the Riverside neighborhood of Duluth, is an interesting micro-neighborhood in itself. It is west, up the river about five miles from the busy harbor where most of the local sailors sail and keep their boats. It's on the side of a wide spot in the river that has recently been given its own name, Spirit Lake.

The most recent Native American tribe that called this part of the St. Louis River home are the Ojibway or Anishinaabe or Chippewa...three names for the same people. I suspect that the whole estuary of this river, where it widens before entering Lake Superior, was a summer home place for the natives with excellent fishing, waterfowl hunting and the late summer harvesting of the wild rice that thrived in the shallows. That was before the logging of the old growth pines and before the paper mill way upstream and the huge steel plant just a mile upstream changed the quality of the water, essentially ruining the river for fishing and recreation for many, many years.

Anyhow, the paper mill no longer uses the river for its private sewer and the steel plant is defunct and mostly gone and the river is flushing itself and recovering from the chemicals and we call this part of the river Spirit Lake now, probably out of a belated sense of respect for the original people who settled here and maybe because there was some new local pride in the cleaning up of the river.

The fish have returned to the river but the natives can't. The local native folks now live west of Duluth about twenty miles where the white folks' government said they could live. There were lots of plans for building up and "civilizing" the banks of the St. Louis and I suppose the Indians would have gotten in the way of the "progress" and the "civilizing" so they were assigned to an area now called the Fond du Lac Reservation.

My guess would be that the natives were the first to use the marina. The boat lift was probably of a different model then as were their boats, but I can picture in my mind the summer fishing activity, the canoes and canoe building and the summer shelters of bark on the shore, the waters teeming with fish and ducks and beaver and moose in the shallows. That was before the area was "civilized" of course.

Some time later World War II began over in Europe. The need for American ships was great and the Native's marina was converted to a shipbuilding factory. Iron ore, from the Grand Canyon like mine-pits dug into the Mesabi iron ore range of northern Minnesota, came by the trainload, down the western Duluth hills to the steel plant just upstream. The finished steel came downriver a short way where "Rosie the Riveter" and others converted the steel plates into ships as long as 500 feet at the bustling Riverside Shipyard.

Eventually the war ended and the shipbuilding center was closed and the facilities became a marina again. From that point in time to present I confess to knowing little about the conversion of the property to a marina for pleasure boats. However it happened, it sure became a great place to call home for boaters and campers.

Seriously, this marina has it all. A great view of the river, the islands, the Duluth hills; you can park near your slip, so not much of a problem provisioning your boat or keeping tools handy. Waterfowl, deer, bear, muskrat and beaver and good fishing right from your dock.

Charley and Tom have improvement projects in the works all the time. Many of the rental slips have trees and grass and maybe even a campfire ring. Many a pleasant summer evening has been spent at a gathering around a campfire, where neighbors get together in this unique setting on the western waterfront for conversation and a beer or a sunset on the water.

Marinas seem to develop their own particular personality over time. This one I would call a blue collar marina where you can work on your boat, paint the hull even, and in the spring you can hear the occasional whine of a power tool getting a boat ready for the water. And the coolest part of the marina is the sense of family that boaters and campers develop after returning each summer, from all around the countryside, to enjoy this unique marina and the good fishing in the river where sturgeon and walleyes have returned. Or to discover those hidden campsites on the islands that await your discovery by boat or canoe or kayak.

Boaters seem to be a friendly bunch. I'm not sure why, but perhaps it's because boaters rescue one another sometimes, like car travelers used to do. Whatever the reason, Sweet Breeze and I seemed to be a good fit for this small community at the water's edge. Neighbors Dennis and Randy were usually available when a boat project required another hand or the lending of a tool forgotten at home.

Neighbor Dennis was a walking encyclopedia. Whatever the subject, but particularly boating, Dennis was always eager to delve into his memory bank and tell you, no, pontificate on, the purpose and origins of a boating term or a rigging method. He may even bless you with the Latin derivations of a term or of an object and some of its historical background for good measure. He and his wife spent the winters in Florida and the summers in their camper at the marina. Tied to their dock was the Julia Mae, a unique little trailer sailor that Dennis built from scratch (and plywood).

Randy, my neighbor a few slips down, had a totally special boat too. He built it from the ground up, mostly from oak cut on his own land about 150 miles southwest of Duluth. The boat was a wooden schooner of about 50 feet, built in his barn over a period of about six years. He made the whole thing, even the pulley blocks for the rigging and she was a beauty.

Randy and I were hatching out similar dreams. Both involved spending some time on Lake Superior learning our boats and gaining more experience at sailing. Then, at some future time heading east, out the great lakes to the ocean and who knows where from there. We seemed to have similar sailing personalities being mostly lazy sailors. We weren't out to see how much cold water or abuse our bodies could withstand but instead thought sailing should be fun, exhilarating, warm even. Sometimes we would plan a trip off to the far reaches of the big lake together each single-handing our own boat but most often Randy would have guest crewmen aboard for whom there was plenty of space on "Rover", his big schooner with the two pine masts.

Back from a sailing sojourn on the lake, the time was spent changing or improving or fixing our boats, trying to make things work as good as they could within the bounds of our expertise and our checkbooks. Each sailing outing would reveal some aspect of sail handling that can be refined a bit or some system on the boat that should be modified and improved.

More Sailing Lessons

On one of our first occasions to sail together we headed up the north shore of the lake toward the Canadian coast and the hundreds of islands beyond Thunder Bay, Ontario. With little wind we motored into a fog bank after leaving Duluth. We quickly lost visual contact and we would try radio contact occasionally, but my VHF didn't always seem to work right.

I didn't have a chart plotter or GPS gadget on the boat yet but I was confident that I was on an accurate compass heading that would keep me about a mile out from the rocky north shoreline and on a course roughly parallel to the shore. Freighters would be farther out in the lake but I would keep a close eye out for fishing boats and nets. After about three or four hours, still in fog with no shoreline in sight I decided to angle in left, toward the shore where the fog was usually less dense and I could recognize some structure on the shore to see where I was.

The northern shore of Lake Superior is mostly a rugged coast of rock ledges and cliffs and boulders but gets very deep very fast offshore a short ways. Sometimes the lake is fifty feet deep just fifty feet offshore. This I knew was the case from a lifetime of exploring the coast and checking maps of the coast and charts of the waters, so I had little concern about running aground unless I got within a stone's throw of land.

At about a quarter mile out or a little less I could start to make out the shoreline and changed course to the right in order to run parallel to the shore until I could recognize some feature that would tell me where I was. There on shore I could see some homes or structures that I recognized at an area called Castle Danger.

I knew where I was then and headed back out to sea and then clunk and wham and jolt, the three worst sounds a sailor can know, put me in a near panic to stop the boat before I ran further onto the rocks. I immediately tried full reverse of the engine to slow the boat and get us out of this rock pile and the engine revved high and quit and wouldn't start. When I looked over the side all around me were boulders down about four to five feet in the crystal clear cold water.

The lake was calm with gentle swells and we were stuck in a boulder field with an engine that would crank over but not fire. It was an awful feeling, the swells would lift the boat up and not so gently set it back down with another jolt onto another rock.

I called Randy on the VHF radio thinking that the only way I would get out of this boulder field was with a tow. The radio worked so I knew he wasn't too far away. I told him that I had found the only boulder field off the north shore and I had run up into it and was stuck and asked if he could turn around and come and tow me off. He said he was already at the Split Rock lighthouse but would return.

With each grinding jolt I tried to think fast and come up with a way to get this boat out of here before there was serious damage to the keel or rudder. With the ten foot spinnaker pole I discovered that I could reach bottom and push the boat around slightly, but which way to go? Everywhere in all directions all I could see were more boulders. My first inclination was to keep working the boat outward, toward offshore, where it had to get deeper eventually.

As the boat rose off one rock with a swell I would try to time my push with the spinnaker pole to move the boat slightly toward another opening between boulders and out to the depths beyond. This technique was working, it was exhausting and we were moving, but the boulder field was not getting any deeper and seemed to be getting shallower. After a half hour of this intense struggle I had moved her maybe twenty feet and wedged the keel fast between some boulders. The only way out was back the way that we had entered this unique offshore rock pile.

With the same technique, and all of the strength that I could muster, I managed to move the eight thousand pound boat back a foot at a time as she rose from a swell and settled back down with a jolt. Finding purchase for the spinnaker pole amongst the boulders was tricky. Sometimes it would slip off a rock when I was pushing as hard as I could and I would nearly go overboard with the pole.

Without the clear water allowing me to see the bottom I don't think I would have had a chance of freeing the boat from the grip of the rocks but behind the boat I thought I could see a small area where I could turn the boat 180 degrees or less and get her facing the path where I had entered the rocks. I got her backed up into the slightly deeper area and ran from bow to stern with the long heavy pole swinging the boat slightly with each push as she rose on a swell and clunked back down on a rock.

It looked to be slightly deeper in this new direction and maybe I could pick out a channel between the boulders. I had to try.

The slightest hint of an onshore breeze was beginning so I tried to push the boat in the direction that would put some wind power on the main sail and give us a slight reach into the wind, and hopefully some power forward, as my body at this point was about out of power. It was working. We were clunking and inching and clunking our way back toward where I thought was our entrance point of the boulder field. I looked for blue paint on the rocks that started to point the direction out. The water was definitely, if slightly, deepening and there were fewer clunks as we bounced along. One last clunk and the water dropped off as suddenly as an hour or so before I had ran my sweet little boat onto the rocks of Castle Danger.

The fog had lifted and I had undone an error that could have wrecked the boat if there had been waves to grind away her hull on the rocks. Rover was coming around the point to the northeast and I sailed with enormous relief to meet my rescue ship and her crew.

Randy and Val (his first mate and wife) seemed a bit incredulous like "what had been my problem?" I dropped the main as the boats came together against fenders and we rafted together for a while as I caught my breath. As I was telling them the process of getting the boat unstuck I went to lean against the bulkhead, maybe to steady my shaky legs, only I missed the bulkhead and fell headfirst down the companionway. Good that I had rounded off the sharp corners below.

I came up only a little bruised but I think the stupid move of leaning against nothing and the fall told of the exhausted state that I was in. The adrenaline had run its course with the efforts to free the boat and Val and Randy could see that I needed a recharge so we made our rafting more secure and we headed up the shore under the diesel power of Rover. I went below for a while and fell into an exhausted sleep.

Some days later, upon close examination of the charts of the north shore it looked like I had run up on the only offshore reef on about one hundred miles of shoreline that was shallow enough to ground my boat. How's that for bad luck…but then I think of the good luck, that the lake was calm and we had escaped the hold of the rocks with little or no damage beyond some scrapes and scratches. And what a sailing lesson…yes, it was the hard way to learn but as unforgettable as was the intensity of the scramble to get free. It was to be the last time that I ran a boat onto the rocks but not the last time I was to run my trusting old boat hard aground, however.

Another Lesson

Farther up the north shore of the big lake I asked Rover's captain to turn me loose. We had motor rafted through the night taking turns at the helm of Rover but with the new day came some breezes that suggested a try at some sailing.

Sweet Breeze didn't need much of a wind to get up and go and we still had no motor power as I hadn't taken a look at the engine yet to diagnose the problem. It was a sailboat after all and if I needed some assistance there was always Randy and Val and Rover's trusty diesel.

Rover motored away and I hoisted sails to try to catch up, but there was no catching up in the light air. After an hour or so Rover was but a speck on the horizon and I thought to hail him on the VHF and ask him to slow down. I think this was one of the times that my radio decided to take a rest because Randy wasn't answering. Oh well, Sweet Breeze was a sailboat after all and in this light air I would get somewhere eventually.

The afternoon wind picked up as it often does on the lake and with it our speed and of course the waves picked up as well. It was a west wind too, great to run with, a bit gusty as I recall.

In order to avoid the building waves on the main body of the lake I ducked into the chain of about a hundred Canadian islands that would keep me in their lee and the waves at bay, plus it was one the most intimate and interesting and intricate parts of the whole huge lake. I had a paper chart of this section of the lake and spent some intense study trying to determine which island was which and what was my position with regard to the islands, the channels between them and the many hidden rock shoals.

It looked like I had gotten myself between a rock and a wet place here. My options were to continue through this maze of fascinating islands, unsure of my exact position, unsure of the exact position of the rock shoals, and not sure that I wasn't heading down into a blind bay that was not a channel with an exit. The wet option looked to be to duck back out into the big lake and try sailing downwind in waves that were building to an unknown future height. With the memory of submerged rocks so fresh (yesterday) in my mind I chose the latter of the two options.

The seas and wind did continue to build out on the lake. They weren't scary big yet but they kept me busier than a lazy sailor likes to be. An accidental jibe, with the mainsail way out against the spreaders, could be a small disaster and I was getting wore down with steering and sail handling and staring at the shoreline, then glancing quickly at the chart trying to pick out where the entrance to the Nipigon Strait was. I knew that whatever option I chose, the only way to make it happen was to sail the boat, no motor to get me out of a jamb. There was a point where I began to wonder, how do I get off this lake quickly 'cause it's really wearing me down. About then I could see the white speck of the Lamb Island lighthouse and from past adventures I remembered it as on the right at the entrance to the strait.

This was my first experience with big seas and single handling my new boat and I was unsure of what to do next. Could I jibe her around to the side opposite of the boom and get the main down that way? Then what? Unfurl a bit of jib for a more controlled sail? How would the boat handle the waves when she came about to take them on her beam? How would I keep her pointed into the wind while I tried to capture the main? How could I maintain steerage with no one at the helm? I had no answers. I only knew that we were surviving on our current course and with vigilance we could make it a few more miles to the strait.

I hate to admit it but I think about now I was starting to get scared. My nature is to start cussing about then…loudly to the wind and to myself for getting into this scary fix. I can utter lots of bad words and oaths sometimes, as sailors are sometimes prone to do…words that I would not want my granddaughters to hear. This was a time to spew some choice words and phrases forth and just maybe it bolstered my courage a bit hearing this tough and nasty talk into the wind and waves.

We held to the same course and I spotted a sailboat over to the left in the islands just in time to see it disappear behind an island. He must know the islands, the channels and shoals and shallows. I envied the boat as I worked my boat cautiously to the left hoping to follow him through the remaining few island channels. He was going too fast for me to follow and I would lose view of him for long periods behind the huge hills of the islands. Forget that, we were on our own again.

As if there weren't enough immediate challenges, in the sky to the northwest the clouds were darkening and beginning to bunch up, and having grown up as a cloud watcher I knew a thunderstorm was imminent, but we made it to the lighthouse and past the shoals, although here I must make another sheepish admission.

There was a large dock that I spotted where the lighthouse tender could keep his boat and if it was deep enough to tie up to I thought perhaps I could weather the thunderstorm there. I called the lighthouse on my not so trusty VHF radio to ask if I could tie up for awhile and how deep it would be on the northeast side of the dock. There was, of course, no answer (I found out later that the lighthouse has not been tended for many years) so on up the Nipigon Strait I sailed. For better or worse, to call for assistance on the radio two days in a row, is not something a sailor like me cares to admit. In retrospect, I can't imagine how I could have sailed up to that dock in those winds and waves without ending up on the rocks. On past the lighthouse we sailed and as we got behind Brodeur Island the waves and wind dropped way down and sailing became fun again (with one eye to the sky).

We were in the lee of the west shore of the strait now and the wind and waves had dwindled to the point where I was wondering if I could sail another two miles or so to a bay on the left of the strait that would be sheltered from the thunderstorm by the high hills to the west, back of the bay.

The little boat caught enough air to come about to the wind and sail up to near where a moose was having supper at the head of that most welcoming bay. We had made it together. Here I dropped the two heavy bow anchors while the bow faced west, drifted back and dropped a third off the stern not knowing what to expect from the soon to arrive storm. I secured the sails and anything loose topside and went below with the first big raindrops splatting on the deck.

The storm was way more bluster than blow, but one never knows. Sometimes their violence can be scary severe. It became a delightful evening as the storm sailed off to the east, the rain sailed away too and the dark sky went orange and yellow and the bluffs across the river were set aglow in that certain light that sneaks between the clouds of a late evening. A day of sailing on this big old lake can show a sailor many moods.

Lessons of the day were many and left me such questions as: how can I steer the boat, watch and manage the sails, read the paper chart closely and accurately determine my position in hazardous waters all at the same time? The answer that kept coming back, as I tried to do all this stuff in my mind, was that I can't do them all at once and yet there are times when I know that I must. No answers for the single-hander there! Only more questions.

More questions: How can I drop the mainsail in a blow when the waves are big and the boat is feeling overpowered and we are running downwind with no engine and no one at the helm but me? Some answers (for the single-hander) that I came up with had mostly to do with a positive reefing system that could pull the main down a little at a time. Still, I had to do it from the cockpit while somehow maintaining steerage. Something must be done for this situation could be a common one with fair winds and full sails. I knew I must find answers to all these questions if I was to have fun sailing alone on the big lake, and live to tell about it.

Up at first light and hot tea courtesy of the brand new (used) galley stove. My attitude was in a positive place. How could it be anything else in such a gorgeous place on such a morning promising a great day of bright weather to follow.

The way that the inboard engine quit yesterday, so suddenly without any hint that it wanted to fire on any cylinder or even cough, told me that the problem was likely to be with the ignition system. With hot tea, a fresh attitude and daylight it was time to check out the power plant below.

The first easy inspection area was within the distributor. The distributor cap comes off by releasing two simple spring clips. There was the problem! The rotor had broken into pieces. Ha! Not a big problem if only one has a spare rotor. I knew that I didn't so on to plan "B" (but I was not yet sure what that was).

I had a bottle of that good quality polyurethane glue that has that hairy fella on the label, however most of the rotor's black plastic body parts were laying in the bottom of the distributor but at least one had fallen below the base plate and I couldn't retrieve it. (That would fall within the parameters of Murphy's Law). I think that I had all of the necessary stuff to glue the rotor back together if I could get all of the pieces together. The only way to get all of the pieces was to remove the distributor from the engine and disassemble the mechanical advancing mechanism that was hiding the lost rotor parts. Thank goodness I had cut that big hatch into the floor of the cockpit as the distributor was almost directly below and accessible.

All of the above was done and with the distributor in my lap I was able to clean the rotor parts in alcohol and fit them up and glue them together on the shaft in their former position. Then I wrapped the gluey mass with rubber bands to act as a clamp to hold it together for a few hours until the glue dried. Time to go sail. Who needs an engine on such a day as this? It's a sailboat, right? Up the Nipigon Strait we sail, one of the most scenic passages on this adventure...or anywhere on the big lake for that matter.

It's way too late to make this long story short but the results will sum it up. After reinstalling the distributor some hours later, the engine started right up and has run fine since. That glued up rotor is still working fine three years later, but now I carry a spare.

There was another day of big winds and sailing stress about a week later on the return trip to Duluth. It began with a brisk northwest summer wind the morning we left Grand Marais, Minnesota, my favorite safe harbor to stop over for a night or two when heading up or down the north shore.

The morning wind was manageable as it swooped down the Sawtooth Mountains and out onto the lake. Val and Randy and Rover, with me and Chickie (my dog) and Sweet Breeze alongside thought we would sail across the lake on a close reach to the south-southwest toward Bark Bay, an open water passage of some forty miles. As with many of the best laid plans of mice and men....

A few miles offshore I was having second thoughts as the waves and wind picked up. We were on a close reach banging along against the sharp seas and getting wet and cold. Rover was pulling ahead with the diesel and the wind pulling. I kept looking back at the windward shore. These waves were still building.

I hailed Rover on the VHF to let him know that I was going to turn right, tack and try to sail back to the northwest with Carlton Peak as my land heading. No answer. Probably no transmission from my shaky radio. I found out later that the fun was mostly absent from their crossing and that Val was terrified (this on a 46 foot, 22 ton boat).

We came about. We bashed and struggled toward the shore where the waves were being born. With so little progress I started the trusty Atomic Four and gained some speed and bashed harder. Wave tops were washing over the bow and cold spray in the face kept my focus on making progress toward some easier sailing, smaller waves, lower anxiety, fun perhaps.

With the genoa furled up, the main pretty much unmanageable and the engine working hard we were making slow progress. That round domed landmark called Carlton Peak became more sharply defined on the horizon. Waves seemed smaller even as the wind increased as we drew near the windward shore at Tofte, Minnesota. Once in smaller seas near shore (I checked carefully on the chart for shoals) I had planned on reefing the mains'l down to its only reef point in order to get a better sense of control in the wind gusts.

The conditions were such that I could not see leaving the helm for the seconds, or the minute even, that it would take to get the main down to the reef tack grommet and secure it along the boom. I would need to bring the halyard forward in one hand while holding securely to the pitching boat with the other hand while hooking up the reefing tack with my third hand while steering into the wind with my fourth hand. It just didn't seem doable.

Down the coast about six miles was an industrial harbor with a power plant and taconite loading facility. There, I thought, I could get out of the wind long enough to reef the main, get the boat under better control and continue progressing down the shore.

The waves were not an issue now as I sailed offshore about a half mile out. But the wind gusts were still tough, and there were no safe harbors nearby. Of course this, I knew, was always a concern on this part of the lake where harbors are mostly about thirty miles apart. In between were only cliffs and rocky points and a very few gravel beaches of mostly course gravel that would not give an anchor purchase. So Taconite Harbor it was, the stacks of the power plant now in sight.

We made it into the harbor and tied up to and old concrete seawall. It was about then that I noticed that my beautiful mahogany spinnaker pole was gone. Had I forgotten to secure it? Yup, that would be me. In a hurry to get back to the helm from the foredeck and I forgot to secure it. Double darn and some much stronger words too were needed here...directed mostly at myself. I loved that fine old pole with the bronze clips on its ends and fine feel. Damn! I was pissed; at myself.

We climbed out and went for a short "walk" and had some lunch, etc. Off the water the weather seemed like a perfect summer day and it delivered a brisk wind to keep the bugs at bay as well.

I reefed the main as well as I knew how. This reduced the area of the sail to about three-quarters of whatever the full main had. I knew that it was about 15 miles down the coast to the marina at Silver Bay but at the time I didn't know just how quickly those miles would pass, being lulled a bit by the swells in the protection of the harbor.

The afternoon gusts would come sweeping down the hills and hit the water with gusto. I could see them approaching me (I was about a quarter mile out now, hugging the shore) as the surface water would dance and shiver (cat's paws) and the tops of waves would become airborne and swirl off into mist with the wind.

It was fun. It was spooky. It was new to me, feeling the strength of the gusts and the strength of this old boat. That day I learned she could take just about anything and lots more than I could. Remember, I am a butt lazy sailor after all.

We clipped along with the reefed main pulling and all of the weather helm that I could handle without breaking the tiller. Experienced sailors would ask why I didn't let out some headsail to balance the main. In retrospect I don't know the answer except to say that I was surviving and clipping along at seven plus knots and I didn't know what the boat nor I could handle beyond a thirty-degree heel and more speed. I think I was also concerned about lashing the helm long enough to unfurl a small part of the jib and secure it. The reefed main was still more sail than I thought prudent and I would let her round up to take some of the pressure off the rig, though I tried to hold course between gusts and loved the speed.

The strongest gust of all came down off a big rock headland and cliff called Palisade Head. Again, I could see the wind coming and got one hand on the mainsheet and one on the tiller and braced my feet across the cockpit. I think we both shuddered a bit but handled it like old salts after two hours of watching and timing the gusts.

Two yachties helped me dock at the marina and asked me what it was like out there. I probably answered something like, "Ya, it was a bit gusty all right." They told me that somewhere nearby wind gusts were clocked at 50 mph, but I thought that might be a conservative estimate, from my perspective on an offshore course in a sturdy old boat.

I was still mad at myself for losing the spinnaker pole, however there were a couple of critical issues with the mains'l that I noticed when I doused it and captured it on entry to the marina. The uppermost two sliding things (forgot what they are called) had been torn from the grommets at the luff and head of the sail but they still came down the track with the sail and it would be easy to re-lash them with some strong ceasing line that I had. Also, one or two reefing grommets had been torn from the foot of the sail where I probably had them tied too tightly to the boom.

More lessons, but all's well that ends well, I guess. That old boat saved my butt again.

Every Sail is an Adventure

The next summer's sailing expeditions on Lake Superior were mostly enjoyable ones and the two new high tech additions to the boat made single-handing almost too easy. One was an autopilot and the other was a chart plotter.

The autopilot would steer the boat to whatever magnetic course that I would set it to. It consisted of a linear actuator, controlled by the signal from a small computer that received a signal from a flux-gate compass. Suffice it to say, it was an electronic gadget that I had my doubts about, but I installed the various parts carefully with lots of fore-thought toward the best location where parts would not get wet or be disturbed by stray magnetic waves. I came to call it "Otto".

It took awhile for Otto and I to become friends. He had his limitations, but then so did I. He could steer the boat wonderfully while motoring or motor sailing and on most points of sail as long as the seas weren't too big. We came to accept each other as captain and crew with few disputes as to our rightful roles.

The chart plotter is an amazing device. It receives signals from satellites hovering up in the sky somewhere, then it interprets these signals to a screen upon which you can tell exactly where you are on the planet. Within this device are stored all of the maps of the coastal waters of North America plus the great lakes and the Bahamas, no, really, right down to the detail of each red nun (A red nun, besides being a Catholic sister from the Communist era, is the red buoy marker on the right when entering a harbor that resembles a nun's habit.) and green can (Buoy always on the left when entering harbor.) and yellow buoy, each island, water depths and shoals, tidal currents are shown, and a whole lot more. It wasn't perfect either but again, neither was I.

Now I could tell where I was (where the boat was) relative to shorelines, reefs, islands, marked channels, deep or shallow water, you name it. I never did name this device but I often praised it with kind words, out loud so that it would hear.

With the addition of these two devices I had acquired that third hand I often needed as well as that extra pair of eyes that can see landmarks, even in the fog. I gradually became better at handling the boat alone and gained confidence in the stiffness and seaworthiness of that tough old boat.

Although one expedition stands alone as a real boneheaded one on my part.

Randy on Rover and I had sailed up the shore again and spent the night riding at anchor in a big shallow bay called Grand Portage Bay, about 100 miles up the shore from Duluth. For hundreds of years, perhaps thousands, this bay had led the Indians and their bark canoes and then the French voyageurs to the start of the Grand Portage Trail, a nine mile overland path up through the hills to a point on the Pigeon River where canoe travel was again possible. From that point canoes could access all of North America to the west and northwest. The trail was enormously important for commerce during the fur trade era, when beaver hats were the rage in Europe, and Europe had no beaver left. Trade in beaver "plews" to Europe had kept the Indians busy trapping and the voyageurs busy transporting trade goods west and furs east.

That morning the lake was a bit riled up but we decided to sail out to Isle Royale, some twenty-five miles out in the lake, riled or not. It's the largest island in Lake Superior and about fifty miles long and a national park to boot.

I had only the furled genoa to sail with because of a broken gooseneck at the bitter end of the boom, where it connects to the mast. That put the mains'l out of service until I could find someone who could weld stainless steel. It had broken the day before when a keeper nut unscrewed itself and the swivel self-destructed. No matter, in the morning's stiff wind I thought the big gennie would be enough power... and it was!

This sail didn't start out well. While we were rafted up discussing sailing strategy and what part of the island was to be our destination a big swell must have swung into the bay and snuck up on us because our boats were heaving such that they tossed the fenders aside and clashed hard. Rail to rail they banged and grated and Sweet Breeze took a hard beating against the heavy steel outboard chain plates on Rover's beam. We quickly untied our rafting lines and pushed the boats apart but the damage was done. Sweet Breeze would need some fiberglass repair and a stanchion base re-bedded. It was not a good start to the day but after a few bad words (quite a few as I remember) and those telling, slow head shakes that men sometimes do when a string of oaths seems inadequate, we set sail. Most of the oaths were mine, being that Randy is a more civilized sort than I.

Chickie, the world's sweetest dog, was my sailing partner up the shore as usual but she hopped over to Rover some time while the boats were rafted up. Have I introduced you to my dog yet? I forget as I write this (have I told you that I am getting forgetful? (I forgot if I may have mentioned *that* before too.) Regardless of any possible previous omissions, my sweet dog deserves a complete introduction, and who knows, the reader may need a reminder too.

She has been an important part of my life for fourteen years. I rescued her in the nick of time from an animal shelter that was over-full with dogs, which meant they would have to begin a process of euthanizing the dogs that had been there the longest. I went to the shelter on a good will mission to retrieve a dog that some friends had lost on a camping trip up the shore and it turned up there. Chickie was in a cage and was quietly conspicuous, with all the other dogs yapping and wagging, saying, "pet me" or "take me out of here!" Chickie was silent and smiling shyly and oh so pretty. Her eyes reminded me of a special girlfriend I...well, we were once very close.

I returned home with the friend's dog but fell asleep that night with the vision and memory of Chickie's bright eyes, mournful yet hopeful, following me around the room as I visited with the other dogs. Next morning I was up about six and soon on my journey the fifty miles back to the animal shelter.

At the shelter, I took her outside on a leash to learn more about her personality and her responsiveness toward commands and rewards and affection. She must have passed my tests because we were soon heading home together. They knew little about her history at the shelter and I didn't much care. Chickie's eyes have been following me around the room for 14 years now.

She was a trying girl at times, but in between she made up for it; always quiet, never demanding, always happy, and thankful for the rescue I suppose. Chickie has never had a bad day, at least from her perspective, and we have been through a lot together; canoe trips, camping trips, cross-country ski trips and sailing. She became a favorite of both pickers and volunteers at the blueberry farm and folks often remembered me, through her.

Well, that morning sail turned out to be an adventurous one over to Isle Royale. The lake was lumpy to begin with and the lumps got bigger. The headsail (genoa) had plenty of power to pull us along on a broad reach with a west wind and us on an east-southeast heading. I liked the physical movement of the boat as she slid up and down on the waves, that were maybe three to four footers, and they helped to push us along at about six knots. The big island and the smaller ones on its western end were getting closer and bigger and more clearly defined on the horizon as the miles melted quickly away.

The wind and the waves built as the miles flew by and I was beginning to adjust my course just to the east of the Rock of Ages lighthouse which was by now standing clearly on the horizon. It's hard for me to estimate wind and waves, their height and intensity, while sailing, but perhaps wind strength was 25 to 30 knots and wave height building to six feet. I was now on a course to take me on the absolute shortest distance that would get me behind the nearest island and shelter from the building waves. There may have been an occasional eight or ten foot wave that I was ever vigilant to watch for and I would try to veer slightly to the right and let the highest breaking part of the wave pass just ahead of the bow, then quickly steer back to the left slightly so that the next wave would lift us and scoot us along on a surf. You could feel the acceleration as Sweet Breeze slid down in the trough.

I tried to adjust my one sail to keep a seven-knot speed yet not feel overpowered by the gusts. It was an exhilarating sail and let's just say I couldn't get to the lee of the first island fast enough.

We sailed lickety-split on a run down the length of the bay leading to Washington Harbor and down to the huge dock at Windigo where Rover was already tied up. It felt so good to be on gentle seas and have solid ground but a few feet away. I soon learned that my stay here was to be surprisingly short and no solid ground would I feel under my feet until back on the mainland.

The national park ranger approaching my boat on the dock did not look like the welcome wagon host. I think his first words were "I understand that the dog on board that other boat belongs to you, correct?" "Yes," I replied.

"Are you aware that dogs are not allowed on Isle Royale?" was his next question. Of course I said that I wasn't aware of that rule or I wouldn't have brought her over.

He then said that I must then take possession of the dog and immediately leave the island. He explained that the wolf population on the island was deeply endangered because of a virus that dogs had carried to the island some years ago and there were only a few wolves left.

I did know that the moose/wolf prey-predator symbiosis had long been studied and observed on Isle Royale. There were books written about the studies and wolf researchers from all over the world had used this natural laboratory to observe at close-hand the social structure of the wolf packs, their interactions with other wolf packs, and their part in the island ecology. I had read some of those books but recalled nothing about dogs being a threat to the wolves.

I felt embarrassed and a little foolish for not having informed myself of the issue with the wolves and the rules applying to visiting the island. Ranger Steve caught on to my sincerity and relaxed his demeanor a bit. I tried to explain to him that the lake was in an anxious mood right now (much like his own) and with only one sail I didn't know if I could safely sail back to the mainland until the lake settled down.

That was about where in the exchange that Ranger Steve asked me more about the broken gooseneck; how was it broken and how could it be fixed. He even brought the part up to the workshop at the Windigo ranger station to see if they could weld it. Chickie and I were quarantined and could not leave the boat.

On the other side of the dock from us was the biggest motor yacht I have ever seen on Lake Superior, perhaps 100 feet long. The skipper-owner of the boat had taken an interest in my dilemma and, contrary to the stereotype one might automatically assign to such a vessel's owner (sipping martinis in the sun on an upper deck with some perfectly appointed women and some perfectly manicured poodles, perhaps?) he was going back and forth to his workshop on board and searching for the right part to make the broken gooseneck perform in a pinch. (Boaters of all shapes and sizes are always looking out for one another.)

We cobbled together a jury rig of stainless steel clevises (heavy duty sailboat fasteners that can connect most anything to anything) that would serve as a temporary gooseneck until I could get to Grand Marais and a welding shop for a proper repair job. Ranger Steve pointed to a protected bay about a half mile away and said that if I were to anchor in that bay with Chickie and promise not to leave the boat nor to take Chickie ashore that I could stay there for the night and leave first thing in the morning. That seemed like a most welcome and reasonable request, preferable to the fines and possible jail term that he could have assigned me for my ignorant transgression.

Randy carried Chickie over to my boat and we shoved off for the protected bay.

That afternoon at anchor was most trying. I knew Chickie had to pee but that she would not pee on the boat, ever. She whined and put her head in my lap. I knew what she wanted, into the dinghy and to shore—fast. But I couldn't. No way. I had given my word.

I think it was harder on me than on her, watching and hearing her discomfort but unable to help her. I tried to read but I couldn't stay with it. I tried to enjoy that gorgeous summer day in a sheltered bay on a wilderness island, but I couldn't. All I could do was talk to her and try to comfort her.

Almost at bedtime I brought her below and put her on the port settee which was her bed on board. I knew I wouldn't sleep with her whining and the compassion I felt for her. As a last ditch effort to get her to pee, I did! Right below her bed on the floor of the cabin, where she would smell it and where it drained into the bilge. Then I went to bed.

I heard her jump down onto the painted wood sole (floor) of the cabin when she thought I was asleep. I could hear her peeing, for the longest time, and I think that I was more relieved than she. The floor could be flushed with a bucket of water in the morning. I was so relieved.

We both slept well that night and were off at the crack of dawn for Grand Marais, Minnesota, a dog friendly little town with a welding shop, about forty miles down the lake.

It was a good lesson to learn, that is, check with the rules and regulations before sailing into national parks, or nation states even. I meant to learn it well but sometimes I forgot stuff (as Canada customs officers would remind me while on the "big sail").

The lake had settled down, too much so, to make good time, with very little wind. Once we got over close to the North Shore I began to glass the bays for a likely place to anchor or dock where we could get ashore and walk in the woods and do a proper pee. I felt guilty for getting us into that fix that made her suffer so, and I apologized profusely. She, of course, loved me unconditionally.

We did find a small bay with a shallow "T" dock where I found enough water to tie up at the end. We went for a long walk down a rustic little road and then a trail through the woods and she peed several times, just for the fun of it.

Each summer I had tried to be a good student of the moods of Lake Superior. The big lake was a good teacher if you were paying attention. Neither my boats nor myself suffered any lasting damage in the six years or so that we plied her waters. She had taught me respect for how quickly her moods can change and how I must sail accordingly.

It was the steadiness of Sweet Breeze that really gave me confidence at sea. Sometimes I even felt almost competent, but both were often shaken when seas were building and I couldn't know how big things would get. That was probably as it should be. I think humble sailors have the best chance of longevity, perhaps timid sailors the best chance of all but I knew that the latter was not me.

I felt that the persistent dream of sailing east, to the salt water and beyond, was completely within the realm of my capabilities now. Honestly, Lake Superior was loosing some of its charm. Not that I had explored the whole lake, but, I think, like the blueberry farm, it was time to move on. I hauled Sweet Breeze home that fall for the last time. Next spring she was heading east.

Commitment to the "Big Sail"

The tall, lanky boat shed was full of tractors already so I parked her close to the cabin at camp and ordered a huge white tarp to cover her for the winter. I felt confident now that I had the right boat for sailing afar but, as always, with a sailboat, there were improvements that needed to be done to make one's life aboard more comfortable and sailing the boat more pleasant and safe.

If I made the right sort of tent with the tarp, I thought that I could work on Sweet Breeze under the tarp and out of most of the severe weather. I secured the tarp over the boat with weights and ropes and poles knowing how winter blizzards can take tarps into the next county or at least wrap it around the nearest tree. Being white, the tarp let in lots of diffused daylight for working.

There was no hurry to get started on the boat...next spring as the weather warmed would be soon enough. I could do some planning and dreaming and order the parts 'till then. I could lose some weight and get in better shape for the journey. I could order navigation charts of the Great Lakes and the St. Lawrence River. June first was months away and that's the day I chose for departure and the beginning of the *big sail*....

Springtime

June first is not that far away. I've gotta put the books down and get out of those vicarious adventures and get Sweet Breeze ready for the big sail. The real adventure. With the snow finally gone and an extremely long and cold winter behind me there is a feeling of rebirth and energy within. Maybe it's the brightness as the sun climbs higher in the sky with each day. Maybe it's the radiant warmth of that bright and shining mystery from which all the energy on the whole planet springs forth. With springtime a not so young man's fancy turns to what...boats?

Email Wednesday, May 22, 8:42 a.m.... Hey folks, will try to begin this summer's adventure sailing to salt water on or about June first. Will keep a daily journal and communication lines open by phone and email. Will need a crew of three to lock thru the Welland Canal around Niagara Falls... anyone for an easy adventure? Anyone for some other leg of the journey as well?

I am expecting to sail most of the way single-handing. There are lots of challenges that I want to experience alone. The weather here is not encouraging for a timely start for Sweet Breeze and me but we will make an early start if we can. Sweet Breeze is in the water now but I have yet to step the mast, rig and provision my little ship and get Camp Cotton ready for Terry Millikan, my summer guest and caretaker. I will keep you posted if you like, as progress toward departure and the daily trials and joys of the crossing of half a continent (about 2000 miles) becomes real. Halifax, Nova Scotia is my goal for this, the first leg of a landlubber's sailing dream.

     For now,

     Curt

What to do with my camp in the woods while I am sailing away toward the ocean? What about my little dog? There were lots of options but the best one of all just fell into place while having breakfast with some friends in Duluth.

Terry Millikan, an artist friend who was along that morning, lived in an apartment in the city on a busy, noisy street but was a country girl at heart. When the conversation about camp and Chickie came up she mentioned that she would love to get out of the city for the summer! Could she live alone in the woods? Could she drive to Duluth to work at her job? Could she put up with the mosquitoes at camp? Yes, yes, and her eyes lit up with the thought.

It worked out that she really did want to stay through the summer *and* take care of Chickie at camp as well. It couldn't be better for me. She was a responsible sort and could easily handle some of the more rustic accommodations. There would be no worries about my dog or my real estate. Lucky me, and she felt lucky too.

There were a few things that I wanted to get ready and finished for my camp's summer caretaker, guest and dog sitter. She was a gardener and definitely wanted to put in a vegetable patch. I tilled up my garden site and got it looking ready to plant. She came out and went over every inch of the soil removing the roots and live plants from under the soil. I could tell this was going to work out, she was a trooper.

I knew how bad the mosquitoes could get in June and biting flies in July can be an aggravation. Sometimes the bugs will drive a person right into the cabin, even on a warm summer day. The front of the cabin was designed to have a screen porch along most of its length but it was not complete. More screening and doors need to be installed to keep the bugs and small critters out. This I did. I got it bug tight so Terry would have a sanctuary.

My solar electric system was up and working fine but not yet complete. There were feed wires on top of the ground that needed trenches in which to lie and be buried. This I did. Things were looking up.

Window screens put on for the summer, some slate rocks laid for a sidewalk, and the place looked nearly perfect to someone like me who was not bent on perfect anything.

I'm starting to get some boxes, large and small, from the UPS man. Sailboat stuff. Expensive stuff.

A new VHF radio that works all of the time, and not just when you are broadcasting for a radio check, is the first installation project and an easy one. I ordered a good one. Same brand as the chart plotter that I have learned to depend on, remember, the device that tells me where I am and where I have been and how deep the water is and so much more?

My sailing friend, Kay, called once to tell me she had been talking to some friends who had sailed the St. Lawrence and some other foggy areas out east and they used a device described by the acronym AIS and that it was helpful in locating boats in the fog. AIS stands for Automatic Identification System. I found a new VHF radio that had the AIS circuitry included.

Now is probably a good time to tell you that I never wanted a boat loaded with a bunch of electronic gadgetry. Being a bare bones canoeist most of my life and a simple liver at that, I was prepared to learn to sail with paper charts and eyes and ears…possibly a depth meter too but that was about all that I wanted on a boat.

I had sailed with some friends once who had all of the latest gadgetry on their top quality sailboat and we spent too much time looking at screens telling us our virtual position without regard to the real world around us. It took the fun and the excitement away for me. The only senses needed to sail such a boat were sight and the touch of an index finger. You could observe your position on a screen and steer accordingly with the push of a button on an autopilot.

Years of canoeing had taught me that all of our senses can become active and acute after being in the woods for a few days and make one feel a part of the natural world on the water. I could hear the rapids ahead on the river long before I could see or feel their currents. I could tell a lot about the lake bottom by the lay of the land on shore. Drops of water on my head meant rain was imminent. But seriously, with experience, observation of the skies and clouds can tell a lot about weather to come without a radio and a forecast.

The various sailboats and sailing experiences I had acquired the last few years have changed my perspective a bit, not a lot. I had learned to survive with very few electronic gadgets on board but it wasn't always easy and it wasn't always fun. There were times when knowing precisely where I was in the dark or the fog and the distance from shore and water depth would have taken a lot of the stress off me as a single-hand sailor.

I did get the new VHF with the AIS feature. Installation was easy in approximately the same location on the boat as the old radio. The new one had a tiny screen that could tell you where ships were located around your little ship. It could tell you their heading and speed and bearing and could monitor their positions up to about ten miles distant and it had a loud alarm to warn you that ships were near. It seemed like a good idea at the time and could prevent me from running over a ship and damaging or sinking it.

The bigger project, that was also a completely necessary one, I thought, was to modify the cooling system for the inboard Atomic Four engine. The standard freshwater cooling system on the boat was a simple one. A pump would draw lake water in from a thru-hull fitting and push the water through the engine to cool it then push the water out the exhaust to keep that cool and then back to the lake the warm water would go.

That simple system worked great in fresh water but in salt water the engine would eventually corrode internally or possibly plug up cooling passages with saltwater critters. That knowledge came from reading, not from personal experience, and I didn't want to take any chances with that sweet running little engine.

The system that I ordered and installed had a heat exchanger that kept the salt water out of the engine. I installed another pump on the engine to draw in seawater and push it through the heat exchanger and out the exhaust. The original pump was re-plumbed so that it circulated an anti-freeze mixture through the engine and the heat exchanger continually and was a mostly closed loop system like on a car.

The tight quarters around the sides of the engine compartment didn't allow enough space to locate the heat exchanger there. The next best option was just aft of the engine with access through the big hatch in the cockpit floor. That was about the only other practical option and would have been impossible to install or maintain if I hadn't put in that big access hatch.

It worked out great. I filled the engine system with anti-freeze and connected the garden hose to the seawater intake and ran the engine until it warmed up, then adjusted the drive belts for the pumps. That fine little engine was ready for the sea.

Auxiliary engines can be a wonderful addition to a sailboat but they must be dependable and they must start when needed. Electric cranking motors for starting them are wonderful inventions but if they fail you have no other options to start the engine.

This little engine was originally designed to start with a hand crank too if the electric starter failed. Low compression gasoline engines have the potential to be hand cranked to start. Most of the old farm tractors that I have owned had the hand crank option so I was familiar with how it worked and the hazards of hand cranking. My oldest tractor, a 1928 model had no electrical system nor electric starter motor so hand cranking it was the only option.

I modified the end of the crankshaft beyond the new drive pulley for the water pump so that I could engage a hand crank. That was a bit tricky, but I fell back upon some of my metal working skills and came up with a simple system. Then I lengthened the shaft of the hand crank to get the business end of the crank beyond the obstacles of the companionway engine cover. Some day this simple system could save the day I reckoned.

The shaft that transfers the power of the engine to the propeller, the drive shaft, has a seal around it where it exits the hull and a bearing just in front of the prop to support the shaft. The device that seals the shaft to the opening through the hull is called a stuffing box. It works like an old-fashioned faucet valve that has a packing nut to compress a seal against the shaft of the valve so that water doesn't leak by the shaft when you turn on the water. The packing material in the stuffing box is a kind of a flax rope with wax impregnated into it. I took the unit apart and dug out the old packing and replaced it with new.

The bearing just forward of the prop is called a cutlass bearing. I thought it wise to replace that as well as long as I had the drive shaft out of the boat. It's a bronze housing holding a hard rubber insert with flutes or slots for water to enter and lubricate the clearance between the two surfaces.

The last thing that I wanted to accomplish toward readying the boat was painting the bottom of the hull. I bought a gallon of that heavy paint with the fine copper filings in it and rolled on a heavy coat. The copper in the paint is supposed to keep the sea critters from attaching themselves to the hull. Easy and messy.

Then I repainted the red water-line stripe all around the boat, mostly for looks. Sweet Breeze was ready to leave camp aboard her trailer for the last time. Another early morning voyage down the highways, boat in tow, heading for that little out of the way marina, some thirty miles to the south.

The Last of Last Minute Improvements

Email Sunday, May 26…greetings from Camp Cotton. Curt here wanting to share some of my thoughts on my summer adventure of sailing to the Atlantic.

There are so many things to prepare, and sometimes I wonder why I don't just stay around this summer and soak up the north woods. So far, this summer is so late in arriving and there is very rarely any warmth to soak up after a two-year long winter and a spring that just won't awaken from hibernation.

Sweet Breeze, an 8000-pound, 28-foot sloop-rigged, 50-year-old sailboat, is at the dock and starting to look like a sailboat. Mast up, sails rigged, but so many seemingly small issues of things that can be improved. I am, one at a time, fixing them as best I can. Getting things convenient; as safe as sail handling can be on worried seas; lines led to the cockpit where I won't likely get swept overboard in heavy weather. Checking pins, lines, screws and attachments. And checking them again.

There are lots of better sailors than I; more experienced, more confident. But sometimes I think I am right up there with some of the most determined.

When I think about some of the travels of past adventurers on the seas I can place better perspective on my somewhat lazy goals. When I think of the Native American forced treks overland on the trails of tears, or the Mormon hand carts pushed 1000 miles, or the pioneers in a sod hut during a prairie blizzard burning twisted hay and buffalo chips for warmth, then my sailing adventure to salt water is brought into perspective.

I am about a week from departure. I will miss my dog Chickie. She has been with me for fourteen years on many sailing and canoeing adventures but her age is starting to show. For me, at age 63, if not now, when? For Chickie, only the memories of adventures past are probably best.

More emails coming soon, Curt.

Remember the white-knuckle times I told you about when sailing downwind in the Canadian islands or into the wind through the Wisconsin islands? The real issue that made those sails unpleasant and downright scary was my inability to get the mainsail reduced in size or doused completely. I just couldn't do it all; steer the boat and get the main under control in conditions that felt like we could get knocked down if we broached or fell-off enough to get cross-wise to the wind. Those experiences didn't deteriorate into really dangerous situations only because the weather had mercy on me and the wind didn't continue to build beyond the scary velocities and into the, "Oh shit," velocities.

After lots of thought, the best I could come up with was a positive reefing arrangement of lines and pulleys that would haul the main down to two predetermined levels. I stripped the mains'l down off the mast and brought it to the sail shop where I had them install webbing and cringles for two reinforced reefing points. A single reef would pull the sail down to about three-quarters of the area of a full sail and the double reef would reduce sail size to about half of full.

I got together all of my old and new pulley blocks; the extras and spares that a rigging junkie like me has squirreled away for repairs and improvements. I tried each in different positions and arrangements until on a lightly windy day at the dock I could make the sail behave. With either of the two reefing lines back at the cockpit I could force the sail down, even when filled with light air, to the first or second reef and it would still keep a pretty tight sail shape for good power.

I know that it wasn't rocket science and any old salt could have rigged it in his/her sleep, but I was still pleased with how simple it was and how positively it worked to get that sail reduced without having to turn the boat and de-power the sail. Once the sail was reefed (reduced) the reefing tail lines should be secured around the boom to capture the loose foot of the sail, but it wasn't absolutely necessary because the lazy jacks mostly contained the loose fabric. Under harsh conditions, that could be done later when climbing onto the coach roof was not so dangerous.

Sailing and non-sailing friends alike were always encouraging me or reminding me to acquire and install certain safety apparatus. I appreciated their concern but I felt secure in what I had and in my ability to adjust to situations.

I did install jack-lines though. They were heavy one-inch wide nylon straps that ran all along the side decks, secured fore and aft, to which I could clip on a tether if I had to go forward in heavy seas. I modified a heavy, strong harness to wear and to which the other end of the tether would clip to me so that as I moved around on deck the tether would slide on the jack-line keeping me attached to the boat. Seemed like a good idea.

It was the end of May and June first was around the corner. Final preparations were going well. Chickie was staying with me on the boat, sleeping on her berth by night and napping under the trees by day. It felt good to be sleeping on the boat again and have Chickie nearby.

She was about fifteen now and getting a little stiff in the joints. Her sense of hearing was all but a memory. It was getting hard for her to get up and down the companionway ladder even though I had covered the steps with carpet to give her a grip. I had decided long ago that she would not be my mate on this sailing adventure, though I knew I would dearly miss her. She had been my partner through thick and thin for most hours of each and every day since she came home with me to the blueberry farm from the shelter. I made the difficult choice to leave her home; home for both of our benefit. It would be hard for me to get her to shore everyday, lifting her in and out of the dinghy, and find friendly landings where we could tie up. It was decided.

Email Thursday, May 30. I had a productive day of boat preparation Wed. I got the solar panel installed and wired. My hope is that it will run the autopilot so that I can sleep and rest at times, while sailing, without running the motor on occasion to recharge the batteries. I hope to use wind power and solar power as much as possible for this passage to salt water.

I have rigged two mainsail reefs to the cockpit so that I can shorten the sail in strong winds without having to leave the safety of the cockpit. Then I hoisted myself halfway up the mast in order to attach some small wheels to the shrouds so that the jib would slide across more easily on tacks, (some sailor lingo for you). Then up to the masthead in a boat swain's chair (boson's chair) to affix a wind direction indicator (masthead fly), with the help of special friends Randy, Dennis, and Kay and the generous folks at Spirit Lake Marina.

Later, Curt.

One of the last of the last projects to ready the boat for the big sail was to capture some sunlight and convert it to electricity to keep the batteries charged. This could be accomplished with a photovoltaic panel or by its more common name, a solar panel.

One of those boxes arriving at camp by delivery truck contained a 50-watt solar panel. I mounted it on the port side stern pulpit with a simple swivel affair that would allow me to adjust the angle so that it faced more directly towards the sun. Inside the cabin, near the electrical panel, I mounted the charge controller, an electronic device that keeps the batteries at optimum voltage without over-charging them. The wiring is simple and ultimately the sun's energy becomes directed into the batteries; the batteries store that energy and it can be drawn off to power the autopilot, the fridge, and the chart plotter; start the engine and supply juice to the other gadgets or systems on the boat. Done, tested, and functioning.

The primary source of electrical energy for the boat's systems would be the alternator on the inboard engine. It would put out as much as 50-amps of current when needed, but of course the engine would need to be running. Avoiding running the engine just to charge the batteries was the motivation for the solar charging system.

The fuel tank on the boat held only about ten gallons of gas and of course I wanted to burn as little as possible. I thought that an auxiliary tank would add some piece of mind.

There was enough space within the rear of the port cockpit locker for an additional three-gallon gas tank. Those three gallons could get me a few extra miles in a pinch or recharge the batteries a few times. The installation absolutely must be a secure and safe one. I would not have a gasoline container moving around and rubbing against things that could wear a hole into it. I made a simple wooden cradle that the tank would rest within and affixed it with a nylon strap and buckle to go around the tank and snug it down.

Satisfied with the installation, I began to route the fuel line, from the new tank, forward and downward toward the fuel filter trying to make sure that there was no possibility for abrading or pinching the rubber line. *Gasoline leaks on a sailboat are forbidden. It must not be.* Fire will surely be the result of a leaking fuel system and that kind of adventure will not be a part of my sailing…ever. I would check and double check all the fittings and line placement. Every part of the fuel system would be scrutinized.

Day of the Hero

A couple of years ago while at Marna's home high on the hill above Lake Superior, I would often scan the lake and the harbor from her deck. I liked to watch sailboats, see how they set their sails and look for boats that I could recognize.

This particular day there was a northeaster blowing and the waves were building on this, the western end of the lake. There were only two boats on the lake that I could see. Through binoculars, I could see that one was a Coast Guard powerboat. The other one looked like a sailboat with no mast. The coast guard boat was heading back into the harbor through the Duluth ship canal but the sailboat had become sideways to the waves and was taking them on her beam. Watching that boat toss made me very glad that I was where I was, high and dry.

I mentioned to Marna that the sailboat didn't look right and that if it continued on its present course it would be washed up on the beach of Park Point, and with the waves looking pretty big even from my high perch, a grounding on that lee shore would likely tumble the boat to wreckage in short order.

She encouraged me to call the Coast Guard station in Duluth to report what I thought to be an abandoned or boat in trouble. The Coast Guard officer who answered the phone thanked me for the call and called me back shortly to say they had been out looking for a disabled sailboat but couldn't locate it in the building seas. He asked if I would stay on the line and they would send a crew back out onto the lake.

I saw the rescue boat leaving the Coast Guard station and soon got a call from one of the crew on board asking me to direct them through the waves to the boat in distress. With phone in one hand and binoculars in the other I got them to change and adjust their heading until they were pointed at the sailboat. When they looked to be a hundred yards or so from the boat they spotted it finally and thanked me for my assistance. They put a towline onto the sailboat and headed toward the ship canal and off the lake.

About an hour later I got another call from the Coast Guard thanking me again. They informed me that there was one person on board, he had been involved in a fire on board and was burned and was taken to the hospital. Well, needless to say, I felt gratified and pleased that my own sailing experience caused me to recognize a boat in distress and following up on my hunch may have saved a life.

That story about the fire on board and the rescue was not my way of telling you what a hero I was that day (well maybe a tiny bit), but rather only to tell you one of the reasons that any fuel installation on my boat had to be done with the greatest of care. There were to be no fires or explosions for me to write about, OR NOT.

If ever anyone were to consider this book to be a reference on sailing or a learning tool, neither of which it is intended to be, but just in case it is, then I feel the responsibility to mention another likely source of an on-board fire. That would be a fault in the boat's electrical system that would cause a short circuit to occur. There is enough current in a charged lead-acid storage battery to heat copper wires until they are red hot and melt, and a shorted circuit will do just that. Poorly done or maintained wiring, plus a fuel system with a leak, equals all the potential needed for a fire or an explosion and fire.

All circuits on a boat should be fused near the source battery. Fuses, properly sized and located, will interrupt the circuit and protect the wiring and the appliance, should an overload or short occur. All wiring should be routed neatly and fastened so that contact with the vibrating engine or any other source of a short circuit cannot occur. Loose or loosened electrical connections can create resistance to the current and develop heat when under load. Poorly done wire splices can develop heat and/ or sparks. In short, don't take any chances with the wiring on a boat and if you don't feel confident in your abilities, have a professional do the new installations or replace the old. Enough said, but I felt that it must be said.

One of the last things that I did to help ensure that the systems on the boat could be kept in good order was to accumulate an assortment of spare parts. For the engine I had spare V-belts for the water pumps and alternator; a spare electric fuel pump and a complete alternator tested and ready to bolt on. I brought along a whole spare ignition distributor with breaker points should the new electronic ignition fail; spark plug wires and spark plugs, and an ignition rotor (the glued up one was still holding together).

For the rigging I had an assortment of good quality rope should replacement be necessary and a sewing kit for sail repair; then there were my boxes of nuts and bolts and electrical connectors and lots of sailboat hardware. I had made wooden boxes with dividers to organize and keep contained all of the zillion stainless steel fasteners and other small parts.

Remember that I have told you that I'm basically a lazy sailor? Very true. Sailing need not be, indeed should not be, a struggle against nature. Nature would win. Every time. Which leads to a lazy sailor's need for some good books for those days of holding tight at anchor in a safe harbor waiting out the weather or for those long evenings when this lazy sailor took to harbor in the afternoon, even though another ten miles would have been doable if he wanted to push it.

The basic books in the library of any sailboat should include the books of seamanship, sailing technique, knot tying, etc. I had all those. That was my reference library. I knew three knots (most of the time) and that was enough. I was in the need of an entertainment library...western novels, history, tall tales of sailing adventures.

My dear friend Michele was the perfect reference person. Not only is she a retired librarian but she helps out at a friend's used book store. She agreed to meet me at the bookstore and I left the store with ten adventure novels to round out my ship's library. My favorite historical novels are mostly about the hardship of pioneers settling the plains and traveling further west yet. I found a few of those. It almost made me hope for some nasty weather that would keep me bound at safe harbor.

Food and drinking water are almost as essential as books for a long sailing adventure. The beauty of provisioning a sailboat is that weight doesn't much matter. There will be no portages. I won't need dehydrated anything. Canned goods are a go. Lots of canned goods. Canned everything. I even had some canned bread, German rye from Germany, and lots of sardines.

I got some fresh veggies too. I had been on a salad diet most of the new year and I felt great. They may not keep well but I thought I would try to eat them up quickly and get more along the way. This wasn't a wilderness adventure where I had to bring everything I needed and carry it on my back between lakes or around the falls (Niagara?). There would be lots of places to stop and re-provision.

The weather at the western end of Lake Superior has been crappy. Northeasters, fog, and more east winds. June first was here but I could not see leaving until the west winds of summer started. No matter. There was still some improvements needed on the boat and I loved each day at the marina with my dog. I hugged her a lot. She tolerated me and gave my nose a moist lick (a dogs' way of kissing).

June second. In the gray early light a big ketch slipped silently out the channel toward the river. It always made me a little sad to watch. There was a deep feeling, a haunting feeling inside, something about wanting to join them on their journey. I could never identify the source of that feeling but it was to haunt me many times in the coming months. Maybe it was about single-handing…the aloneness. Maybe it was about the folks on board sailing out of my life and I would never see them again.

June third. Made my last trip to Camp Cotton. Got all the warm clothing that I thought I would need. Long underwear, a big bulky wool sweater from my friends in Ireland (I think they called it a "jumper"). I packed gloves and mittens and caps and a jacket with a hood. I gathered some warm weather clothing too, light nylon pants, several short sleeved shirts, long sleeved shirts of light cotton, even some swim trunks.

A sailing buddy had loaned me a survival suit. It was one of those big, bulky orange colored ones with flotation. It fit okay but it seemed pretty restrictive if one had to move quickly. I felt like the Pillsbury doughboy or an astronaut when I zipped up the front. I packed it into its own duffel and stowed it up on the starboard V-berth with my duffels of everyday clothing.

Special, special friend Marna would ask me all the right questions as I readied the boat. Did I remember this or that? Do I have enough of this or that? Sunscreen? Ibuprofen?

Marna on Sweet Breeze in the Duluth-Superior harbor.

There was one last rigging project that I wanted to have ready. It was simple yet something about it was baffling at times. It was an automatic steering system of ropes and pulleys called "sheet to tiller steering".

With the right arrangement of lines and pulley blocks the forces transferred from the sails to the sheets can also be transferred to the tiller in order to steer the boat. It is amazingly complex and fascinatingly simple all at once. It could be described as an instant feedback system that senses any change in wind force or direction and adjusts the course of the boat relative to the wind.

I found an Internet website that described in detail how to rig the system and I had accumulated all of the necessary light rope and high quality, low friction pulley blocks, plus some surgical rubber tubing from which I could make an elastic arrangement to oppose the action of the steering control lines on the tiller. In essence, tension from the mainsheet is transferred to the tiller when sailing to weather and when sailing with the wind, forces from the jib sheet are transferred to the tiller.

It fascinated me. I got it all rigged at the dock. Now to get some steady winds on my journey so I could try it out.

Marna, bless her heart, organized a farewell party at her house. The sun showed itself briefly that evening. Friends came from far and wide and we gathered on her deck overlooking that big cold gray sea. I had brought along the chart of the great lakes and the St. Lawrence and we set them up for folks to get an idea of the route and the winding watercourse to the sea. It was a fine send-off.

The last social sendoff was a gathering at the marina at Dennis and Linda's. We had a big campfire and grilled meats and a smorgasbord of foods and other wharf rats like myself came to enjoy it. Folks would ask about my destination. "Salt water," was my usual answer and beyond that I had no destination. I had thought of sailing down the east coast far enough to reach water that never freezes, maybe as far as the Carolinas or Florida even, but the trip was really about the journey, not a particular destination.

Marna took Chickie home with her to transfer her to Terry up at camp. Big hugs and squeezes for both Chickie and Marns, then early to bed in the boat for tomorrow morning I was heading east no matter the winds.

The Big Sail Begins. Friday, June 7, 8:00 a.m.

The chart plotter has a trip log feature that records the distance traveled on the water much like the trip odometer on modern cars. It showed that we (Sweet Breeze and me) had traveled 22 miles since leaving the marina at first daylight. I was below heating water for my second or third cup of tea while the autopilot steered us eastward.

The early morning was windless as we left the marina but at least there was no headwind. So many times I had sailed or motored down the river heading east toward the lake; past a great blue heron wading in the shallows, past the coal docks, past the huge old railroad bridge at Grassy Point that would swing open with some clanks and growls on ancient gears and bearings. So many times had I sailed past the iron ore docks, the sand and mud island that is white with so many thousands of shorebirds and gulls, then under the High Bridge connecting Wisconsin and Minnesota for the thousands of cars and trucks that passed each day. Then there was the bend to the south toward the Superior entry with Minnesota Point to port and grain elevators to starboard; and then finally to the east, through the channel and out into the big lake.

I wondered if I would ever sail this route again. Sure, I knew I would be returning to this north country to live, at least part of the year, but would I ever ply this familiar old watercourse again? Such were my thoughts as we motored out onto a glassy lake heading east.

The tea was always a comfort in the morning and I thought it was a good way to re-hydrate for the day. I would pop my head up every five minutes or so to look ahead and to the sides for boats. Charter fishing boats and other small boats were out on the lake trolling for lake trout. I would try to adjust my course so as to pass far enough behind their boat to clear the trolling boards and lines that they trailed. I thought that if they made a course change quickly the trolling lines may tangle, so it was easier for me to adjust my heading. There was no reason to hurry even if the shortest distance between two points was a straight line. I had all summer.

The engine was running perfectly but the temp gauge showed that it was not heating up to 180 degrees, what I thought would be a good running temperature for an old engine. According to the gauge, the engine temp would only reach about 140 degrees but that wouldn't hurt the engine though it wouldn't run as efficiently. I thought the engine thermostat must not be closing up to restrict the cooling water flow through the engine and I had purposely checked it in hot water on the stove to see that it was working properly before I had installed it. Another of those best laid plans gone awry.

With Otto at the helm there were lots of on-board projects that I could attend to when feeling ambitious. When I was down below, with the engine pushing us along, there were oily smelling engine fumes that seemed to accumulate in the cabin. I experimented with opening hatches and using the bilge blower to chase out the fumes and they helped but the air was pretty cold and going below for a while was my way to warm up my chilled self. There was nothing wrong with the engine to cause the fumes, it was just the fumes common to a warm engine and a closed space. I could live with it.

At about 2 p.m. the trip log said I was 71 miles out of Duluth. That didn't seem right. Cornucopia, Wisconsin was just a few miles ahead around Bark Point. I didn't think it was that far to Corny, but how could a GPS controlled instrument be wrong? Dennis called on the cell phone about this time. I told him where I was at about 70 miles out.

"No way," he expressed strongly, "something is amiss because it is barely 50 miles to Corny."

But it's a chart plotter that gets its signals from satellites high above. How can it be wrong?

"It is," he insisted.

Dennis convinced me that I should double check on the accuracy of the trip log. I agreed, but secretly wanted to believe that the gadget wouldn't lie. We were going fast and far and that was a good feeling.

With the paper chart of Lake Superior and my dividers I checked the distance from Duluth to Cornucopia using the scale of miles on the chart. I came up with about 45 miles. That seemed reasonable, besides how could I have motor sailed seventy some miles at only a four to five knot speed? The math said that four and a half knots times ten hours makes for a 45-mile day.

I double-checked the units that the trip log said. It was in NM or nautical miles. The other units that it could record in were statute miles and kilometers. That gave me an idea. Maybe the gadget was really recording distance in kilometers.

Multiplying the trip log's figure by the conversion factor for kilometers to miles of .62, I got 45 statute miles. Aha! It was a relief to learn that I still could use it to calculate distances traveled each day. That would make for an easy and accurate way to keep track of how far and fast this journey to salt water was progressing but the different units of measure for distance on paper navigation charts would continue to be a source of confusion at times.

While Otto steered I got some other small projects accomplished that first day. That sturdy and strong white oak anchor platform was showing its age already. It was only three years old but the glue joint, where I had laminated two boards together to get the right width, was opening up. That made it look cracked and weak. It wasn't weak but it didn't look good.

The only material that I had on board that would be easy to tie those pieces together with would be the aluminum flat bar that I had stowed under the port settee cushion. There were lots of other possible repair materials stored there too, but the flat bar looked like the best and easiest fix.

With the vice and hacksaw the pieces were cut, rough ends smoothed with a file, and with the battery powered drill they were screwed down securely. It looked better. If I were to sell the boat at the end of this sail it would make the platform look more substantial, though I was confident that the integrity of the whole anchor system was never compromised by the crack. Now the flat bar crossties would prevent the crack from opening up further, too.

I took the time to explore the chart plotter's many different features. Up 'till now I had really only used the navigation screen to keep my position known and my course plotted toward the next landfall. There were lots of other screens of which I knew little, tide charts for instance. I knew that they would come in handy eventually so I tried to figure out what they meant and how to read the screen. They didn't make much sense to me yet and the tide chart that kept coming up was somewhere on the coast of Maine. I wasn't sure what good that would do me at other locations. That tide stuff baffled me.

There was another screen that showed the nearest ports and the services they provided for boaters. I didn't need it yet because I was still in familiar territory. It just amazed me that so much information was packed into the memory of the gadget. I didn't know yet how many times I would depend on the chart plotter to see me through unknown places.

Speaking of gadgets, my cell phone charger won't charge and I cannot find where I hid the charger for my yellow rechargeable drill. I'm sure I brought it along. What good is the drill without the charger?

I only say I hid it because I must have packed it away in some obscure cranny of the boat and one of my greatest handicaps is that I can't find anything that is not plainly visible. Sometimes I think I should make inventory cards and tape them on or near the entrances to all of the many storage places on the boat. There are only so many places available to put things that leave them plainly visible. Maybe it's just an excuse that I have adopted for all the clutter that seems to surround me, that's what some of my women friends might think, but no, they just don't understand my makeup. Really, if something is out of sight it is, to a degree, lost! If, after searching behind a few things or within some compartment of the boat, I still can't find the item, I usually give up the search with some foul language and the hope that it will turn up or show itself later. Searching for things tends to make me anxious, the foul language tends to vent the anxiety.

Another thing that makes me a little anxious is entering tight little marinas. When you are single handing you must do things right. You don't have crewmen to fend off other boats or docks. For such circumstances though, I had made up a black spruce boat hook (pole) about ten feet long with a hook and a rubber tip at the end. It was about two feet longer than the aluminum extendable ones boaters commonly carry. That extra two feet made a world of difference when hooking a cleat or a cap blown overboard and it was stiff and couldn't collapse inward in a really hard push.

To get it off the deck and secure it so I wouldn't lose it (remembering the still hurtful loss of my beautiful spinnaker pole) I stored it against and up the mast, hooked over a spreader on the top and tightly wedged into a conduit clamp on the bottom end. With this long and sturdy hook I could push off other boats or grab a cleat and pull into a dock in windy and tight spaces.

Usually, however, I am completely at the mercy of the power and steerage that the engine provides. I have sailed into docks in light air but only into places where I knew there was some room to make a mistake. The Tillmans' marina at Cornucopia was not one of those.

It is one of my favorite marinas though because it was a family-run operation and they kept a well-stocked ship's store with real maple syrup for sale. Maple syrup was my sweetener of choice for all my sweetness needs. It is locally produced, healthy, delicious, and sustainable, unlike sugar cane or sugar beet products with their history of environmental degradation and slavery.

The engine on Sweet Breeze was so dependable. It always started immediately with a touch of the starter button. Under power in the forward direction the boat was very responsive to the helm. Under power in reverse it was another story. I could never discover any consistent way to steer her in reverse and was always baffled why. The steering was simply unpredictable in reverse but reverse was an excellent braking technique and I could sometimes get her aft end to shift sideways just a bit with the "prop walk" under power.

I used to practice and practice again docking her on windless days in Duluth. Sometimes I would do it just right, rarely, but I could seldom do it twice in a row. I had to settle for "docking without damage" as my goal and be satisfied with that.

After topping off my gas tank at the fuel dock and my sweet tooth at the ship's store I headed out to anchor for the evening. Around to the right at the end of the breakwater was a big sand bottom bay where I had stayed at anchor before. I knew that if the wind shifted during the night it would become an extremely uncomfortable anchorage because it had happened before and sleep was impossible that night. Back then I had weighed anchor in the middle of the night and cautiously slipped back into the protection of the fuel dock and tied up 'till morning.

The forecast this night promised no such disturbances to my sleep.

I rowed my dinghy into the beach for a picnic. Marna and Chickie had driven down from Duluth. What a friend! What a pair of friends! What a sweet final parting from my two best friends.

Through the Islands and Beyond

Saturday, June 8…up at 5:00 a.m. for the morning ritual of sweetened tea, two cups.

Inside the cabin it was a chilly 50-degrees. Outside the temp was probably 40 with a light north wind. I had put on a lot of warm clothing hoping to sail today. I get tired of the drone of the engine and shut it down whenever I can if I can still maintain some progress. It is a sailboat after all.

I was underway at 6:00 a.m. with a very light north wind and a very bright sun creeping above the vastness of the water to the east. I could see Chickie everywhere, underfoot and on her berth below. This was my first sailing adventure without her. Second day out and I missed her already.

Sure she was a pain sometimes, getting in the way at critical scramble times, hair all over the boat from her constant shedding, but, oh, that unconditional love, with never a grudge if I accidentally hurt her in my hurry to handle the boat. When she wasn't napping she would watch me and every move that I made.

After Otto took the helm I went below several times to fill and heat the teakettle on the stove. I made more cups of tea than I could drink but needed the warmth of the cup in my hands. As the teakettle cooled a bit I brought it up to the cockpit to use as a hand warmer. Gloves or mittens could not keep the damp cold from stiffening my fingers.

The cold dampness was chilling me thoroughly. It was beginning to affect my assessment of the day's progress. If I stayed the night at anchor in the Apostle Islands I knew I could expect a cold night on the lake. If I made it back to the south shore at Black River Harbor, a good piece up the lake beyond the islands, then I knew it would be much warmer in a shoreline harbor.

Could I make it to Ontonagon, Michigan, or was that too ambitious a goal? I wanted to have ambitious goals. It had been a very long winter in the woods and the sooner I got off Lake Superior the sooner I might find some summer-like weather. From the weather report on the radio I discerned that the water temp of the lake in my vicinity was 36-degrees and any moving air across the lake picked up the chill and brought it aboard.

We passed to the south of Eagle Island, making sure that I was south of the shoal that Randy and Rover had hit on a previous encounter. This, the smallest of the islands, has provided nesting habitat for the local birds and is off limits to human visitors who would be a disturbance to the nesting inhabitants.

Rounding to the outside of Sand Island and nearing the landmark of the Sand Island Lighthouse, the sun was getting high enough to heat up my dark colored outer clothing and the warmth was penetrating through the layers toward my skin. I took back all of the cold nasty thoughts I was having about the lake.

There were no cities anywhere near. The air was crystal clear and the sunshine was brilliant on the water. Some forty miles across the lake to the north I could clearly see my old friend Carlton Peak. It poked its bald and ancient head above Tofte, Minnesota on the north shore. For me it was a landmark of memories; of the camping trips and the blueberries and the brook trout of the Temperence River as it splashed through the hills and around the old peak only to roar through a canyon and disappear into the waters of the rocky shore. The chills were leaving my body and I was making peace with the lake.

I was feeling thankful to the spirit of the greatest of lakes. As Gordon Lightfoot, the songwriter so aptly sang, "The legend lives on, from the Chippewa on down, of the big lake they call Gitchi Gummi. The lake it is said, never gives up her dead, as the skies of November turn gloomy."

But this was June and it was a glorious day. I was even feeling a sense of confidence, in my boat, in myself, in my journey ahead. I knew this would be a short lived euphoria if the lake kicked up but my nature was to soak up all the warmth of the sun available and the late spring beauty of the islands. The opportunist in me took in what was freely given at any time and I was just thankful to be alive.

The lake was like that. Sometimes it brought out a gracious and soulful side of me. Sometimes it brought out my ego side; challenged me unmercifully and tested my tenacity for survival. My moods must adjust with hers.

One nice advantage of the icy waters of the lake was the cold that transferred through the hull to the storage areas under the settees in the saloon. My fresh veggies for salads were nicely refrigerated down there.

Remember, this was early June, it was supposed to be summertime, but I knew that in a few days the weather could change drastically and besides, in a few days I would be heading south down the St. Marys River to another of the great lakes. It must be warmer down south, right?

I had to motor sail most of the rest of the day through the islands. I snuck below in shifts, while Otto steered, and I cooked some oatmeal with lots of raisins planning on some warmth from the inside through the eating and chase out the last of the chills.

Fishing nets and rocky shoals were the main hazards through the islands. I was the only sailboat out. Some fishing boats were tending their nets for whitefish and lake trout.

The islands themselves were of a yellow-green hue that told me the trees were not fully leafed out yet. There were a few majestic white pines here and there sporting their spring green colors over the thick blue-black of their winter dress.

I wondered what it was about white pines that drew me so. Then I could see it in their profile. Their long branches held out to the side with a gradual upturn along their length; then the branch tips turned more sharply upward. They reminded me of open arms saying, "Come to me. Shelter under me if you wish," or, "we are in this world together, you and I."

Usually I recognize anthropocentrism when I feel it and avoid attaching it to natural things but in this case I think it's all right. If the white pine takes on some of the best of human qualities, or at least I see it that way, then it can only boost the lowly human to white pine status. Sometimes I think trees are smarter than people anyway.

The trip log at York Island said that I have sailed 120 miles since leaving Duluth. When I multiplied 120 times .62 I got 74 miles. That seems about right. Problem solved. Kilometers...converted to statute miles from now on.

The tyranny of the tiller is history on Sweet Breeze. Otto has broken those chains binding me fast to the helm and tossed them overboard. When Otto steers I can seek food or warmth or work on boat projects. I can read a book or take a catnap. Sometimes it seems too easy, but I love it.

Otto can steer a straighter course than I can, but of course he can't see wind gusts approaching and he doesn't know how to steer into the occasional big wave, but on a fine day like today he steers flawlessly. We are becoming fast friends.

There are lots of fish nets to watch for as I pick a route through the twenty or so islands. I keep Raspberry Island on the right and Bear on the left as I head down the most direct strait past the old fish camp on Manitou isle. Continuing southeast between Hermit and Stockton then bending back to the east brings me back toward the open lake with Michigan Island on the right. I begin thinking about lunch when I get past Gull Island and back into the open waters. Smoked whitefish and cheese, left over from the picnic last evening on the beach, and canned pumpernickel bread from Germany rounds out a tasty lunch.

4:00 p.m. leaving the Apostles behind me.

This is the farthest east that I have sailed on the south shore of the lake. Light air sailing along a rhumb line that will bring me to Black River Harbor, Michigan, 20-miles to the southeast makes for a relaxing afternoon. Looks like Black River Harbor is do-able. It's the only safe harbor nearby. Dark clouds are bunching up over the mainland some 20 miles to the south. If they keep sliding east they will miss me.

Sunny, but the wind is still very chilling.

Wearing long johns and insulated pants, two jackets and a cap pulled down over my ears. Summer on Lake Superior.

Easy sail, winds abeam, four-knot speed.

With Otto at the helm and the destination 20-miles away I began reading a book about a teacher on Isle Royale, Lake Superior, put together by her son from a diary she wrote in 1933. It was a tough and lonely winter for her, teaching in a cabin around a wood stove with eight students of all ages. Her contact with the outside world was mostly through a battery-powered radio that didn't always work. She could sometimes hear music and news from a broadcast station in Houghton, Michigan and it so brightened her day. It was a tough and lonely winter for her.

Can see the Porcupine Mountains of the U.P.

I remember a cross-country ski trip to the "Porkys" a few years ago. The great glides down the hills. Cabins in the woods. Saunas after dark. The snoring of tired skiers.

7:00 p.m. Tied up to the dock at Black River Harbor.

This has got to be the prettiest place to tie up for a night on the whole lake! Tall hemlocks and pines on the bluffs above the river. A natural harbor at the estuary just upstream from the river's mouth. An old C.C.C. era walk bridge across the river to the trail leading upstream to the falls; camping and picnic grounds in the park nearby. It looked like there was boat fuel available but no one around to pump it.

Sweet Breeze on the quay at Black River Harbor, Michigan.

After I tied up I moseyed down the dock and met a couple of charter fishing boat captains. They were tidying their boats up for the night. Jim has been fishing out of Black River Harbor for 50 years. Both he and Dan had big cabin cruiser powerboats with twin inboard V-8s. Lots of power, lots of gas. Jim said there are times when the power is reassuring. He said, "Most days she blows northeast for awhile just to remind you who is in charge."

Jim, 50 years on Lake Superior.

I took an evening hike up the river and it was quite a climb; no more chills inside and worked up quite a sweat on the outside. It was the primordial forest of my dreams. Giant old growth pines and hemlocks holding the clay bluffs secure from eroding into the river. The mist from the falls added to the ancient atmosphere of the dark forest. It was a quiet hike, alone again, a spiritual endeavor for me.

Fixed a big salad for supper but the mosquitoes were so thick that I had to keep the cabin closed up tight. Had a warm water wash-up bath and was soon fast asleep.

Sunday, June 9. Up at 2 a.m.—checked winds and forecast; back to bed; up at first light at 4:30.

It was a much warmer night in the harbor than it would have been anchored in the Apostles. Good choice, plus I'd gained another 20-miles of easting.

Underway this morning at 5 a.m. with a breath of a southeast breeze. Motor Sailing with a half tank of gas left on a heading of 50-degrees toward Ontonagon, Michigan.

We're making good time this morning; about a five-knot average speed with Otto holding the helm to the rhumb line.

It's warmer this morning, perhaps fifty degrees. East winds predicted to 30 knots today. Hope to make Ontonagon before seas kick up.

With the cold winds off the cold waters of the lake, I have been ducking into the cabin as often as I could think of an excuse to do so; cleaning and organizing even! Cleaning the inside of the windows and ports, and especially the two forward facing ports, would make a good excuse to get out of the wind for a while this morning. With crystal clear port windows facing forward I could stand below, out of that chilling wind, and still feel comfortable that I had a clear, safe, forward field of vision.

Perhaps now would be a good time to mention that I had decided not to have a custom made dodger installed on the boat; they were kind of a sissy thing after all. A dodger is a kind of tent that extends aft from the coach roof. It has clear vinyl windows that give good forward vision all the while giving protection for the helmsman from wind and spray. Real sailors, like me, often found them to get in the way of that touchy, feely intimacy with the elements that we sail for. They stick up high and catch wind and slow a sailor down. Like I said, kind of a sissy thing.

Boy, I wished I had a dodger that day. Damn, that wind chills a sailor to the bone. The dampness from spray carries that chill right to your skin—brrr—but like I said, they're kind of a sissy thing.

As a Minnesotan would say, "Okay then, put on more clothes," and I did.

The east wind became steady which gave me the incentive to try out my new "sheet-to-tiller" steering system. We were on a starboard tack, heading 30 degrees, plying the wind. I hooked up the control line to the mainsheet and back to the tiller with the proper bends through the proper pulleys and got it working well by tweaking the tension of the surgical tubing tensioner device on the leeward side of the tiller. This was great. Even Otto got a rest.

Jib-Sheet-to-tiller steering on a beam reach for hours at five-knots.

We crossed over the wind to a 112 degree heading and I re-hooked the control line to the other side and with a little tweaking again she steered beautifully on a port tack, close reach. Below I went to do some writing and reading and warming up my stiff old body. Who needs a dodger anyhow?

Dennis was my hero that day. He sent me a text that morning asking if I had a chance yet to try out the sheet-to-tiller steering. That was the reminder I needed to stop shivering and get busy giving it a try.

It worked beautifully; amazing even. Not only was the self-steering holding course but as the wind began to slowly veer to the north of east she followed the wind; that kept me sailing parallel to the coast.

The steady east wind was great, though I thought I'd never say that. It was 10 a.m. and we were about 20-miles out from Ontonagon.

3:00 p.m. at the mouth of the Ontonagon River.

Glad to have made it early. The waves were building steadily and slowing headway. I was starting to get soaked with spray as I tried one tack and then the other searching for the driest point of sail but, of course, I didn't really need a dodger.

Motored up the red-brown water of the river looking for the marina entrance. On the left bank is a huge modern looking warehouse building with a couple of folks fishing from the wharf. There are a few homes further upriver on the left bank with docks and fishing boats and even a sailboat at a mooring.

Off to the right over the bank I could see some sailboat masts, that friendly looking forest of aluminum, and around the bend was the narrowest of channels leading into the marina proper. The red and green channel markers looked to be only about 12-feet apart so some careful navigating was in order. My depth meter said

4.5-feet, which is what Sweet Breeze draws as I slowly motored in; guessing where the deepest channel was that would lead me to the fuel dock.

A big charter fishing boat followed me into the marina. After I had tied up I walked up the main dock to see if I could buy fuel.

My timing was perfect. One of the fishermen on the boat just arrived turned out to be Bob, the harbormaster carrying a huge cooler of ice surrounding a beautiful mess of fresh caught lake trout. I told him I was in no hurry for fuel; to go ahead and clean the fish and could I buy a small one, perhaps?

I went off to one of my favorite marina pastimes: checking out the old boats on the hard in storage and the few in the water. There were some cool looking old boats of all shapes and sizes that gave me pause and caused me to wonder on their history and their owners' stories.

This was a really nice marina but there was no one around but Bob and I. I moseyed on back toward the fish cleaning station and Bob had about a three pound lake trout cleaned up, set aside, and asked if I wanted it. He wouldn't let me buy it though, try as I did to convince him that the gas for that big fishing boat of his didn't come cheap and I really wanted to pay for it. Nope! He wouldn't take any money, period!

After topping off the gas tank with 7.6 gallons of gas—that's all I burned all the way from Cornucopia, Wisconsin with lots of motoring for two days—I got that trout cut into pieces that would fit into my fry pan. With lots of butter in the pan, and the lid on, I slow cooked that fish with an onion for flavor. It turned out exquisité...not exquisitely...but exquisité. Practicing my French for the waters off Quebec.

An unexpected guest showed up and I invited him down below to share a piece of fish. His name was Tom. He had a boat a few slips down and had noticed the jumper stays at the top of Sweet Breeze's mast and came over to check it out.

The old Triton does that. Folks notice something about her rig or her shape that draws them over. Some know right away that she is a Pearson Triton; others are drawn to the classic lines of her profile.

We. had some fish together and talked. Tom had sailed down to Fort Pierce, Florida last summer. Down the Erie Canal and then the inland waterway down the east coast. That's the route most sailors choose. Not out the St. Lawrence as was my plan. He was 75-years young, and fit.

I hadn't been to Ontonagon, Michigan since I was just a little fry. We had taken a family vacation to see the brand new, just completed Mackinac Bridge. It was considered an engineering wonder and it is. Our route back home somehow took us to Ontonagon. The only thing that I remembered about the town, as a boy of about eight, was a tavern that my dad brought me into. It was like a museum of stuffed animals; all sorts of North American fur-bearers and hair bearers and feather bearers.

We took Tom's car across the bridge and had a beer at a tavern on the main street. It had to be the same bar I was so fascinated with some 55-years ago. It was loaded with stuffed animals of all sorts; "mounts" I guess would be a more proper term. The thoughtful bartendress turned on the lights so I could better see all of the mounts and the artifacts and tools of the bygone age of logging.

It is a bit sad to me now to see all of the animals killed and put on display for us humans. I didn't know back then about endangered species or those we humans have extirpated. I think there was even a stuffed pair of passenger pigeons, once the most numerous bird in North America with flocks of millions that darkened the skies when passing over, or so I have read. The bird was a major food source for Native Americans over the ages. The invasion of that non-native species of which I am descended found ways to kill them by the wagonload and use them for pig feed. The last one died at the Cincinnati zoo in 1914.

Ontonagon now reminded me of the old saying, "Will the last one to leave please turn out the lights?" Main Street had lots of empty storefronts. The extractive industries that had kept the town alive and lively had extracted themselves into closure. The white pine had been cut. The copper mine had closed. The paper mill had closed. The ship building enterprise at the huge building on the riverfront had failed; but at the tavern the stuffed animals were standing still, their steady gaze staring down the few human visitors with their dusty, dimming, glass eyes.

Even the marina was nearly empty of boats. I was the only visitor. There were a few abandoned looking boats nearby but that is true at most marinas. Boaters lose their enthusiasm or the money dries up like the old peeling wooden hulls in the storage yard.

Once famous for mineral riches, this region of Michigan's Upper Peninsula was where the local Native Americans mined copper; before the Euro-Americans arrived, bought the land for some trade goods and some promises and went at it on an industrial scale. Ontonagon was once the home of the famed and sacred "Ontonagon boulder", a nearly four thousand pound chunk of pure copper that Henry Schoolcraft was guided to by some local natives. It now resides in the Smithsonian Institution in Washington, D.C.

To the west and a little south, above the town, rise the Porcupine Mountains. It is said that from the lake, the spine of the mountains resembles the profile of a porcupine, their namesake given by the natives. In a valley high in the hills lies the Lake of the Clouds and there is a wilderness state park established now as the hills are ever recovering from a century of logging and slowly reverting back to the habitat and beauty that draws naturalists, hikers, skiers, car travelers and forest dwellers, both fur-bearing and hairless.

I think the local residents of Ontonagon are coming to terms with the booming past and the quiet future of their isolated area...long sandy lakeshore beaches where one can stroll without seeing another soul...offshore sport fishing for trout in the lake; simple, small town summer homes at bargain prices. As nature returns, so are the people. Are the lessons of avarice ever learned?

Tom and his wife resided in one of the old lumber baron's homes (robber baron's) near the lakefront. It was a historic looking home with a small beach house and a caretaker's home nearby. Tom was a professional librarian, sailor, and this day he was a tour guide.

T'was a restful night I had in an almost too quiet marina.

Onward to the Waterway

Monday, June 10. On the water by 5 a.m.; warmer than past mornings; wind about 10 knots; no long johns needed.

A warm, lovely, and light southeast breeze—and me headed up a northeast coast—that puts me on a beam reach up a windward shore toward the entrance of the Keweenaw Waterway. Does sailing get any better than this?

Ten-Mile-Point is off to my right. Did its name derive from being ten miles from Ontonagon...I wonder? There is an abandoned lighthouse barely visible in the trees on the point.

An interesting shoreline, this Michigan coast. The names of the bays cause me wonder; Union Bay, Sleeping Bay, then Misery Bay. White sand beaches stretch for miles around the crescents of the bays. Two tall smokestacks stand smokeless and abandoned. One at Freda and one at Redridge. The relics of industry past? Copper smelters? Paper mills? If so, good that they are closed. If those traditional polluters belong anywhere it is surely not on the Lake Superior shore. A close study through the binoculars revealed no signs of life.

Wind shifting to the west then back to the northeast.

I put on more layers of clothing; four layers on top now with two on the bottom and a wool cap pulled down over my ears. I guessed I had my warm up weather first thing in the morning. If the wind would be steady I could go below for a while and get out of the cold penetrating air; Otto could steer, but not in these variable winds.

Dense fog bank near shore

I thought I could avoid getting into the thick of it if I headed further out; I turned to head out and it was a good thing as a fishing boat appeared through the fog. We wouldn't have clashed but better to keep plenty of water between us.

The wind quit again. We were eight and a half miles from the waterway entrance and it looked like the motor would be the ticket to get us there. Just to keep busy I estimated our speed and distance and came up with an E.T.A. to the entrance at 1:30 p.m.

Otto was at the helm again and holding course and I was hungry. I filled the fry pan with the leftover lake trout, two eggs, another onion and some canned pumpernickel. 'Twas a midday feast.

I had crossed over the Keweenaw waterway on the lift bridge at Houghton-Hancock about 20 years earlier. We were taking a mini-vacation, my wife and I, up the Keweenaw Peninsula. We thought we would spend some quality time together, camping, to sort things out or patch things up. That part didn't work out but we did enjoy the rugged beauty of the Keweenaw.

The waterway is part lake, part river and part dredged channel. It was made to be a shortcut across the peninsula for shipping traffic and also a harbor of refuge for ships to get off the lake in storms. Since the peninsula itself juts up into Lake Superior about 60 miles there is a significant distance and safety factor won if one can cut across the peninsula near its base.

We entered the Keweenaw Waterway around the lighthouse at about 1:00 p.m. Entering the breakwater channel brought me into the intimacy and challenge of close quarter sailing. After three days on the open water of the lake it was a welcome change. It was warm, sunny and I took off the layers down to a t-shirt. The long johns were history. After three days of cold winds or no winds the warm welcome of the weather seemed to uplift my spirits. There were people to wave at walking the shores. A dog running on the beach; not that I had suffered loneliness or the feeling of isolation but it just felt kind of warm and fuzzy, seeing these family outings on shore. Maybe it brought back hints of memories of times past when my kids were young.

Where were the sailboats anyhow? None on the waterway. None in the Apostles. Not one have I seen on the lake since leaving Duluth. Didn't they know it was summertime on Lake Superior? They didn't know what they were missing? Or did they?!

I gave up on the sailing, but not until the wind was dead on her nose. It was like a wide, slow river. We motored along green, tree-lined banks with foot trails and ATV trails visible. The woods looked buggy and thick. The shore-view changed to homes and cabins, and lawns became more the common shoreline habitat.

There were tiny, friendly looking cabins, where I mused that weekenders needed good relationships in close quarters. There were amazing log and stone crafted getaway abodes tastefully tucked into niches in the woods. There were the "starter castles", abrupt, white, and starkly conspicuous on lawns mowed down to the water's edge.

On the left bank stood a great old farmstead home, but there were no animals or tractors in sight, instead a hefty shoreline dock and a fishing tug tied up. More of my self-entertaining musings take me to an educated guess that it had gone from a farmstead to a fish-stead, instead.

There were lots of boathouses dotting the shoreline that made me wonder how busy the waterway might become on weekends; today it was just me and Sweet Breeze and a welcome climate change from an hour ago. There were apple blossoms and a woman digging dandelion roots from her front lawn. I happen to like dandelions. At least she wasn't spraying them with poisons but really, life is brief, wouldn't she rather be adventuring?

I knew that I needed at least 40 feet of clearance for the masthead of this old girl to pass safely under obstructions. The bridge ahead looked too low!

It always makes me feel sort of important, powerful even, when I call a bridge operator on the VHF radio and request passage. My simple and brief call brings all car and truck traffic to a halt and *I* have started the clanking of gears and the whirring of motors and the movement of tons of steel and concrete out of *my* way.

Some bridges swing out to open a passageway and some lift their span high above. This one at Houghton-Hancock was the lift bridge of all lift bridges. It was huge and very complicated looking from the water, and yet I was momentarily in charge. This was a different feeling from sailing on the lake where I was *never* in charge.

Houghton-Hancock Aerial Lift Bridge.

Below the bridge the scenery changed as the city of Houghton on the right bank dominated all views. I was motoring slowly because there were some fascinating structures. Michigan Tech University at Houghton had a building that looked like it should have been part of the NASA compound in Florida. Of course! It was an engineering school. I wondered if they had designed the bridge.

On the left bank stood another landmark structure—the head frame of the old Quincy Mine. From deep down in the bedrock copper ore was raised to the surface for 80-years until the mine closed in 1945. The gears and cables in the head-frame lowered the miners and raised the ore.

Another mile east and the river bends to the south and opens up into Portage Lake, a large lake in its own right; shoreline homes and summer scenes of greenery far to the left and near to the right. Life is good. I am warm and lucky.

If I weren't so focused on making headway I would make a sharp left turn now and head up the Torch Lake Canal. On the chart it looks like a fascinatingly intimate channel leading about five miles north up to Torch Lake. The lake has great depth and would make a good overnight hideaway. My thoughts at this point in the journey are about headway so I opt for another five miles-made-good; south across Portage Lake.

There was lots of seaway on the lake now but no wind. It is late afternoon and I was beginning to look for the marker buoys leading us back into the river and out to the lake on the eastern shore of the Keweenaw. Off the starboard bow were some vast marshlands with veins of shallow waterways stretching and winding back a mile toward the tree line. Herons and marsh birds would abound here but it is the nesting time and they are being shy.

There was a long seawall on the right side as the river began to open at the lake. I tied up to the wall for the night; my dock lines cleated onto big cast iron bollards strong enough to hold a thousand foot freighter in a storm. There were picnic tables and a park of sorts. There was a fisherman trying his luck. And there were a million mosquitoes.

I would have loved to heat up some supper and have a picnic at the tables but the bugs were too bad. They were worse than that. This must be the "Mosquito Coast" of Michigan. I stayed below in the stuffy cabin with my two new wood framed sliding bug screen hatch covers for the companionway. Quite a few skeeters got in before I got organized, but life was still good.

A few more fishermen arrived for the evening. They all seemed to know each other and that typical good-natured banter between them, loud enough for me to hear, drew me out into the bugs. One guy was trying out his brand new bug zapper/ tennis racket from Mal*Wart. It kind of worked I guess but you would have no time for fishing and might get a case of tennis elbow while swatting the thing through the swarms about your head.

He told me to take it and try it on the bugs so that he could fish a bit. I told him I would probably hit something with it and break it. He said he didn't care, it only cost a few bucks anyhow; all the way from China and it only cost a few bucks…with electronics on board and a battery? Somehow it doesn't sound sustainable to me but it was an interesting gadget and a big seller, I guess.

The first fisherman hooked into a good fish. He asked me to get a net out of his trunk and I netted it for him; a largemouth bass of about four pounds. That was enough excitement—and bugs—I dove back into the cabin of the boat for the rest of the evening.

It was a quiet night once I had killed off most of the skeeters in the cabin. If I didn't get them first, they would get me later. This was war.

I'm a real light sleeper and I remember that sometime during the middle of the night a car pulled up near my boat and sat there idling. I hoped it was someone looking for privacy, but then why park alongside me and the boat? I turned on a light in the cabin just to let them know that the boat was occupied and not available to charter or rent at 2 a.m. He (they) soon left.

Once, upon a time a few years ago, while sleeping in the back of my small pickup under the topper on the riverbank at a public park in Fargo, North Dakota, a similar thing happened. That time I could hear their muffled voices wondering if anyone was sleeping in the back and what I thought were some back and forth discussions of some bad sounding intentions. They came over and looked into the side windows of the topper. I was getting concerned but feigned sleep and my girlfriend was shaking.

The night was black as ink. Maybe I had read too many western novels, but what could they have wanted with us?

I remember lacing on my boots, tight as I could, getting my mind and adrenaline in high gear. The circumstances made it clear to me that their intentions were not honorable. I whispered to her to get her shoes on and to run as fast as she could if the fighting started, anywhere, just get away.

As they approached the back of the truck again, their vague silhouettes were outlined against the dim glow of the city. I thought that I could make out three of them, and I could foresee only two choices; try to scare them off or fight. I wouldn't run with Elizabeth counting on me, but I always kept myself in pretty good physical shape and was hoping that I could keep them occupied 'till she got away in the dark. Whatever happened, they weren't gonna harm my girl while I had any fight left in me. I couldn't see or hear if they had guns, one never knows in Fargo.

When they got within a few feet of the rear of the truck I slammed open the back door of the topper and shouted in my loudest, deepest and gruffest voice, "What in hell are you boys doin' botherin' us in the middle of the night?"

It caught them short; spooked them. They mumbled some half-assed excuse and couldn't get back to their car fast enough. They sped away.

Cars in the middle of the night stopping nearby still spook me, they always will.

Halfway Across Gitchi Gami

Tuesday, June 10. Day five and just about half way across the big lake.

Between the paper chart and the chart plotter there was close agreement on distance traveled so far. By multiplying the trip log by .62 and using dividers on the paper chart they agreed on 230 miles since Duluth.

Old Sol was peeking over the northeast horizon as I motored beyond the long breakwater at the east entrance to the waterway. It was a glorious morning with a forecast of light winds.

After a few miles I noticed that the fenders were still hanging from the lifelines and dragging in the water. So typical of me to forget to untie and secure them. Shit, shit, shit! I had two big blue ones and now only one tied on.

I had done this before! Me and my knots! I glassed behind me the five miles or so to the breakwater and nothing. Well, something floating a couple miles back but can't tell what…wood, loon? I hate going backwards. The silly things cost about 60 bucks. Oh well, I have spares.

Mad at myself for about an hour. I hate making the same mistake twice; or in this case several times over the years. My failings piss me off. I should be better than this; some mental self-flagellation this morning and damn-it I deserve it.

Everywhere I look on the boat I see Chickie this morning. I hear myself talking to her out loud. Sweet nothings. She couldn't hear me even if she was here. She has lost almost all sense of hearing. I miss her out here but things are easier without caring for her needs.

Her deafness creates special challenges now. She doesn't come when called. I have to get myself into her line of sight and give her hand signals to come to me, then she trots right over. Getting her to shore everyday, or twice a day, would cut into my forward progress and headway is my goal right now.

I have been trying to make 40 miles a day. Usually I get underway at the first hint of light and stop over for the night at late afternoon. The days are very long now. I feel that I should take advantage of it. I'm in the Eastern Time zone now but I pay little attention to the clock. The sun's position is a close enough clock.

It's about 12 miles across Keweenaw Bay on my 90-degree heading toward Point Abbaye. Sounds French—Abbaye. I know I'll see a lot of that language before this journey is over and I hope that I will learn some too.

Aha! Some light winds rippling the surface. Sails up. Motor off. Now I can hear the public radio station at Marquette, Michigan. I love public radio; the programs and the news are like old friends to listen to in the background. How can people listen to commercial radio with all of the anxious voices screaming at you to buy more crap? Different strokes I guess.

If I can make it to Big Bay harbor, that will give me my 40-mile day. Winds are light and come and go.

Still mad at myself for losing the fender with my poor knot so I go below and take my frustration out on the remaining mosquitoes; they're hiding out, waiting patiently for me to fall asleep again tonight. I don't mind a fly in the cabin, I even try to make pets of them, but mosquitoes must go. This is war.

Point Abbaye near to the right now and I can see the Huron Mountains through the haze. Geology books claim they are the oldest mountains east of the Mississippi. I have read stories about the Huron Mountain Club. It's a private organization of really rich folks (Marna would call them wealthy investors.) who have bought up large tracts of the Huron Mountains above Lake Superior for their very own hunting and fishing retreats. They allow no one entrance into their sanctuary except club members. I hear they have hired security guards to patrol the perimeters and keep the riff-raff (like me) out.

The Huron Mountains viewed from the island with the lighthouse.

It seems a mixed blessing that such a gorgeous natural area is in private hands, but I'm sure the owners are good caretakers and smart enough to keep the forests healthy and the trout streams flowing clear. I'll never be able to explore the area but I'm glad it is protected. If it were public land, a national forest for instance, it would not be held safe from exploitation, I fear.

The club has been around for a long time. Henry Ford was a member and would bring his pals Thomas Edison and Harvey Firestone up there on vacation.

This sailboat is a grand little vessel. The gas sipping inboard propels us along smartly at only a fast idle. Without the engine we would make little headway today, with no wind strong enough to boost us along. I hate to run the engine so often. I wanted this adventure to be wind powered but with no wind my adventure would only amount to sitting out on the lake for days at a time. That would be okay too, for a lazy sailor like me with a good library on board, but I wanted to see the country. Yup, it's all about me.

All the boat's systems work well. She sails well. She motors well, hour after hour. She handles easily and anchors securely. Still, I catch myself thinking of a bit larger boat that I explored. It was for sale in Duluth; a 33-foot Glander. The cabin on the Triton becomes cramped at times even for the single-hander. The Glander's extra space would make for a big change from the normal bumping around in tight quarters that I was used to. Maybe if I had a larger boat I could find a sailing partner. Maybe if....

Searching for wind, we headed out into the lake on an east-northeast heading. When we got there it was not what it looked like from a distance. That breeze petered out too.

As long as we have to motor along I decided we might as well have some scenery to look at so we took a hard right turn on a near-shore course toward some interesting views. Through the morning's foggy haze loomed some high, rocky archipelagos. Was it Fatu Hiva? The Azores? Tierra del Fuego? No, I believe it must be the Huron Islands of Lake Superior, but my imagination worked well to entertain me.

The Amazing Archipelago

Rocky and rugged, they have stood up high against all that the lake has thrown at them. Isolated from the mainland by three miles of water there weren't many visitors here any more now that the lighthouse was abandoned.

In Bonnie Dahl's book, *The Superior Way*, she tells about the old dock and trail to the lighthouse. My curiosity is piqued. It looks tricky to get to the dock, but, today, with the calm seas, maybe I could do it.

The white pines on the islands draw me. The big lighthouse on the highest hill intrigues me. Charts show very narrow channels approaching the dock. A rock shelf bottom with huge scattered boulders means no mistakes by me!

Here we go with the main down and the depth meter on. The water is so clear here that I can see the pink granite boulders 20 feet down. The dock looks like a new one but it's short. The approach has rocks on all sides two to three feet down but with the motor and the long spruce boat hook and the calm seas I got the boat pushed and turned and wiggled into dockside, touching nary a rock.

The island was a fascination. First, there was an old boathouse with a rusty rail car and rails askew but leading out under the clear water along the dock, to haul boats out with.

The trail to the lighthouse was itself remarkable with a concrete bridge across a ravine and old concrete steps with a handrail. Honeysuckle and other wild flowers lined the path where thin soil on otherwise bald rock gave them a foothold.

The lighthouse itself was constructed in 1868 of pink granite blocks fitted with mortar between. As an integral part of the light tower, the light keeper's house was of squared granite blocks and brick as well. It looked like it would stand for a thousand more years. I thought that the granite might have been quarried right underneath where the structure now stood giving it a solid granite base.

I think that I recall a bunkhouse for the occasional work crew. The bathroom was an actual "brick shithouse" and it might last another thousand years too. The coal storage building was still intact and hauling the coal up the steep path must have been quite a chore. The mindless destruction of vandalism to the vacant buildings was nearly absent here.

The whole of the community of buildings gave me pause to wonder about the bustle of activity that the warning of ships once entailed. Before the sophisticated electronic navigation gadgets were invented this light was considered essential to keep the ships off the rocks at night. Now a navigator has an array of screens that sweep the vicinity and show the location of his ship relative to rocks, shoals and other ships. On the darkest of nights or in the densest of fogs, location, bearing, and heading can be precisely determined with a glance at a lighted screen; but the lonely romance of the keeper of the light is rekindled here, in my mind, with this visit to the highest part of the Huron Islands.

Once back on the boat and motoring east past the last island I still felt in awe of the quiet, lonely, magic of the islands. I was so glad that I had taken the risk to stop and explore such a remote and pristine archipelago. The diversion from the lake refreshed my enthusiasm. The builders should be proud of their everlasting light tower of granite.

Big Bay

I had to do something with my smelly t-shirts besides stuff them in a duffel. I put out a laundry line trailing far behind the boat with t-shirts attached at intervals with strong spring clamps. After dragging for a few miles they were retrieved and looked pretty clean and smelled pretty good.

I need to say this. As a culture we use way too much soap. I only use soap for dishes if they are greasy. I seldom use soap on my hands. Warm water is an amazing solvent and leaves my hands clean and soft. Clothing? So far so good! No soap. Lots of agitation in the clear, fresh, water of the lake.

Got on a boat cleaning binge while Otto steered us toward Big Bay. Cleaning binges strike me so seldom that I know I should take advantage of them when I am stricken. I scrubbed the sink 'till it shined. I polished the rest of the cabin windows and took the galley stove to task. That was enough for one day.

Big Bay is indeed a big bowl along the Michigan shore. At almost two miles across, I had to keep glassing the shoreline to try to spot the channel leading to the protected harbor that the chart plotter showed. On close approach it looked like some sand shoals had narrowed the entrance but I made it okay.

There was no one home at the park building or the fuel dock but there was a phone number for fueling assistance. They soon arrived from a town nearby and I topped off my tank with gas.

To spend the night they required payment of thirty dollars to tie up further down the dock, which I ordinarily wouldn't mind but there were no services available as I recall. Fifteen dollars to drop anchor out in the harbor sounded better because I had that water buffer between me and any late night visitors.

A family came down to the harbor to pull their boat which needed some expensive sounding repairs to the out-drive. I supervised as Tim, Bob, and Zack did the work, besides, my hands were wrapped around an ice cold beer they had given me.

I learned that the town of Big Bay was only about a half mile walk up the hill and I was about out of half & half for my tea; a very important addition to my comfort beverage of the early morn. I tried to get some physical exercise each day as well. Walks were my exercise of choice.

I met a friendly sort of fellow on the main street in town. Wayne told me to stop back at the hotel later and talk sailing; he was the owner of a nicely refurbished grand old hotel from the logging era called the Thunder Bay Inn. Henry Ford once owned the building and converted it to an inn in the 1940s. In 1959 the Inn was used in the filming of the classic movie, *Anatomy of a Murder*. Wayne and his wife have their own little piece of Americana that they oversee.

We talked sailing over a big taco salad. The conversation almost turned toward politics once but we felt the wind beginning to shift, fell off just in time and jibed back into sailing. Wayne had dreams of sailing my adventure, and I wrote down his email address so that he could follow my progress. I knew I was lucky to have the freedom from stuff and responsibility so that I could adventure forth, but it was always my intention to be free, and a part of a loosely formed lifelong plan...after all.

Wayne offered to take me back to the boat in his car and I accepted but of course I was so bold as to ask for a brief tour and history of his tiny town. He drove us down to the big closed factory on the shore of the big inland reservoir lake just below the town. It was a former Brunswick sawmilling factory where they had made the flooring for bowling alleys. Before that it was owed by Henry Ford. He used it to prepare the wood side panels for cars with real wooden sides called Woodies.

It didn't take but a couple of minutes to tour the town. The closed down factory buildings are what draw me anyhow. This was just about the right sized town for me *and* it had a hardware store.

Back at the boat I remembered at the last minute to pay the 15 dollars for mooring but I didn't have the right change. Wayne's last words as he drove away were to not worry, he would take care of it...typical of the folks I was meeting along my journey.

Who's in charge...?

Wednesday, June, 12. Another early start; no wind yet but no fog either.

Motored ten miles already this morning and have Granite Island Lighthouse on the horizon. Through the haze I can see some huge harbor structures at Marquette, Michigan on shore to the right. I still can't make out what they are through the binoculars but they must be huge.

Passed Granite Island on the offshore side with a heading pointing us at Grand Marais, Michigan. It's 80 miles away yet but it's a straight shot across Marquette Bay. That would be too far for one day, most likely, unless brisk winds abeam gave me about a six-knot average speed and the forecast mentions nothing of the sort.

I must be dreaming. This far offshore the waves would be really uncomfortable if in my current daydreams such a wind were to stir up the lake. We were about eight miles offshore passing the island; way too far out to be caught in those kind of winds for long. The only time I would ply winds that produce that kind of speed would be down a windward coast about half a mile out. Just dreaming about fast sailing, I guess, after so many days of putting along.

Speaking of fast sailing, once upon a time, (here we go again) about a year ago I had spent the night at Silver Bay Marina, one of the few safe harbors on the rocky north shore of the big lake. Chickie and I were up at the crack of dawn and tuned into a marine forecast telling of brisk northwest winds and I could hear the jiggling lines and hardware topside, already, as my tea water was heating.

I left the marina about six a.m. with the first gray light of dawn. It became a perfect beam reach heading southwest down the coast. Sweet Breeze wanted to show her stuff; I could sense it. We made the 1:30 afternoon lift at the aerial lift bridge and into the Duluth harbor. Honest. I forget the math but it was close to a 60 mile run in 7 and a half hours. It was the fastest that I have ever sailed over any considerable distance and it wasn't uncomfortable. If she heels to 20 to 25 degrees and if I've done my job well with the sails she moves right along. She carried a big bone in her teeth that day.

This day, a year later, was for motoring, yet there were some promising ripples to the southeast off the starboard bow.

Never mind wind. I was getting into reading a pocket novel western of the Indian wars of the Llano Estacado, otherwise known as the Staked Plain of the Southwest. Being the lazy sailor I mostly am, those slight breezes just confuse me and take me back off the plains of the southwest, thinking, should I hoist sails or shouldn't I?

I got into boat cleaning again, without soap I might add, just to pass the time. It would not set well with my conscience to rinse or dump soapy water into the lake. We were riding over the surface of ten percent of the worlds freshwater; all in one lake. In some parts of the lake, away from the cities, you can see down 50 feet to a rocky bottom.

There should be no soap or other polluting household "necessities" in this lake. Not by me anyhow. I know, the TV ads have taught us for many, many years that without lots of soap products we will smell bad, our homes will be taken over by bacteria and fungus and we will die a premature death of infection and no one will attend our funeral unless we are cremated. But guess what? They want to sell you stuff.

Thinking of the Glander 33 back in Duluth, while listening to public radio. Every time I bump around in the close quarters of the cabin I think of that spacious living area in the larger boat. Cleaning has played itself out for awhile.

Lots of time for thinking out here. A large part of my focus on distance is directly related to sailing as far as I can get, yet getting back to Minnesota sometime in September for my daughter's arrival from Germany for a visit. Not just her, but the new grandbaby and the father, Mr. M. J. Bach, a German fella my daughter became attached to in her yuppie days of world travel.

The breeze has not much strength for sailing but is just strong enough to chill me. I have on several layers of clothing still. The offshore wind is a bit warmer than usual but it cools down quickly after blowing over the water for a few miles.

I calculated the average distance traveled per day since leaving Duluth. I came up with 52 miles. Not bad for such light winds.

Have decided to spend the night around Grand Island, near Munising, Michigan.

As a freighter passed to my left heading east I tried my new AIS locating device on the VHF radio. The AIS screen showed its position relative to Sweet Breeze; also the speed, heading, bearing, and the name of the vessel. Pretty amazing.

I took a southing course down the channel between Grand Island and Wood Island with light air and the motor keeping up speed. Grand Island to the left has some beautiful homes and what appears to be a camp for kids. There is some great summer scenery here. Wood Island and Williams Island on the right look uninhabited by people.

The wind had warmed, the sun was brilliant, the scenes idyllic. Rounding the corner to the left around the green marker buoy at 5 knots and wham, hard aground I ran her up into the sand.

What have I done now! One should look down once in awhile into the clear water when sailing through an unknown channel. My whole relaxed mood went into adrenaline mode. I looked down now to see rippled sand to port and forward and aft as well. Looking aft, I could plainly see the furrow in the sand that the keel had plowed. This was an awful feeling. How abruptly my daydreaming world had changed. Now what?

I looked all around for boats. It would take a big boat to pull me off this bar. The shock of the situation was waning and the problem-solving mode was entering my brain.

What were my options? I could wait for the tide to rise and float me off the bar, but of course there was no noticeable tide on the big lake. I could flag down a passing boat and hope for a powerful tow, but of course there were no boats. I could….

I had to do it myself. Okay, try engine power combined with all the strength that I could muster pushing off the bottom with the big, long, sturdy boat hook .We pushed and we pushed, the engine and me. We couldn't even turn the bow of this little 8000 pound tub to point it toward the deep water.

Okay, Plan-B. I was not sure what that was going to be just yet.

I sat down on the cockpit seat, in the thinking position, with my chin in my palm rubbing my whiskers (well, perhaps I'm embellishing a bit here but you get the word picture, right?)

Looking back at the dinghy that I had been dragging for nearly 300 miles, an idea came to me that I had read about once. With the dinghy, I could row my heaviest anchor out to starboard, to deep water, drop the anchor overboard and row back to the sailboat and try to "kedge" the boat off the bar with the windlass.

Yes, that would be Plan-B! I would take the heavy plow type anchor. That one should dig into the sand and that was the one the electric windlass would retrieve.

I rowed the anchor out about 150 feet beyond where the water suddenly dropped off. It was tricky dropping it off the stern without upsetting the little boat, but I managed.

Back at the sailboat, with the motor at full speed forward I tried the windlass switch and I was amazed as the bow started to swing to follow the taught anchor line. It worked perfectly. We were unstuck in a jiffy, afloat, and winding in the anchor. Huh? I guess sometimes the best-laid plans do work.

The chart showed a little bay that I named Muskrat Bay that was protected by a hook shaped point called Muskrat Point. It was a part of the larger bay at the south end of Grand Island. The chart showed a sunken wreck in the bay but that could be avoided with a slow and cautious approach. After dropping the hook in that safe looking little niche, I took a deep breath and let out a big sigh and spent a lovely evening at anchor. Soon after, the jet skis were silenced by the twilight.

I tuned into the marine forecast because I had read a text message earlier that afternoon, from an old friend in Manitowoc, Wisconsin, that said to watch the weather; that there were big winds predicted. My marine forecast said light winds for the morrow from the north-northwest. I fell asleep looking forward to tomorrow's sail along the coast and my first ever viewing of the Pictured Rocks National Shoreline and the huge dunes of the Grande Sable, and slept like a babe.

Thursday, June 13. Early start at daybreak…motored wide of the sand shoals off the point.

Once I got through the strait between Sand Point and Grand Island I bent both sails to a close reach into a northerly coming from the Canadian shore 150 miles off the port bow. This put me on the lee shore. Definitely not where I felt I wanted to be with the lake kicking up a bit.

After days of motoring, the exhilaration of the wind in the sails again, became short lived. That morn the wind got stiffer and the waves got steeper. I remember looking back toward the protection of Grand Island and considered turning around. Nope. Too far along already. It was a fast and rugged sail but still, Grand Marais, the next harbor of refuge, was a full paper chart away, about 30 miles.

I remember nothing of Pictured Rocks or the Dunes of Grand Sable. The boat was heeling excessively and starting to pitch wildly in the seas. My attention was fully on staying in the boat and getting some feeling of control back. I reefed the main once, then reefed it again a short time later. The cockpit reefing system worked pretty well if I let the boom swing wide to spill some of the wind from the sail. I didn't dare leave the cockpit to tie down the foot of the main with the reefing ties. I couldn't tie the lines with one hand only and I surely wouldn't release both hands to tie. My rule was, *always*, when leaving the cockpit, keep one hand on a secure part of the boat.

While working with the sails and steering I got as seasick as I have ever been. I concentrated on my work and holding my breakfast down.

As soon as I got the boat under control the wind died, but the waves continued. Big confused waves from all directions. Without the full sails to buffer the motion of the hull the boat would pitch then yaw then roll and the sails would slat with a bang. It was hard to stay in the boat.

I shook out the reefs, then vanged the sail to flatten it. Then I cinched the boom down tight on center trying to stabilize the boat with the air pressure on that tall, waving sail. Nothing that I tried helped much. I took two motion sickness pills. I had never taken two before but it helped.

After I got the motor started and began making headway in the most confused waves ever, the wind started up again from the north harder than ever. With twenty miles to go to Grand Marais and safety, I think I pretty much switched into survival mode.

The wind was veering slightly behind the beam now. I felt that I had to get the main down and try a reduced headsail, together with the engine pushing, to regain some control on a broad reach. The propeller was out of the water half the time it seemed and I was concerned about the engine over revving. I tried to find the correct throttle setting so it wouldn't rev so high when the prop was out, yet still give me some steerage when it was in the water and pushing. Otto was useless in these seas so I lashed the tiller hoping to gain some time and control as I scrambled to douse the main.

The main got stuck half way down of course leaving me just two options now. Climb up on the coach roof and pull it down and secure it to the boom or just leave it and let the wind blow it to rags. Of course the latter was not a real option if I wanted to save the sail, so up I scrambled working with one hand getting it down and bunched and tied to the boom all the while hugging the boom with my arms and my elbows; all concentration on not getting pitched off the boat. This was not the day for a lazy sailor like me.

A wave must have hit the port beam as I was squat walking and crawling the few feet back to the relative safety of the cockpit. I remember being pitched down onto the cockpit sole onto my big plastic baling bucket which I crushed into pieces with my right kidney and hip. No time right now to worry about pain or internal damage.

Too much to do. Steer the boat. Manage the headsail; keep it full. Watch for the biggest waves and try to take them on a forequarter and still maintain headway. I could see Sable Point now. Grand Marais was about eight miles beyond.

Hooray! The wind was taking a break again, but there was no way I was going to haul the main up and balance the boat. I knew that would bring back the gusts with a vengeance. It's part of Murphy's Law of Sailing.

Hey, I'm writing the book now so I made it to Grand Marais. I remember motoring down the channel and waving to the fishermen on the west breakwater as if to tell them, hey, I made it, so whatcha think of that. I wonder if they weren't thinking about how foolish that sail boater was to be out in the lake with that norther blowing across from Canada. The sailboat did well. This boater survived.

Thinking back as I write this, back over the thunder storms that lay ahead and the northeaster in the North Atlantic, the fog and the tidal currents, and all of the weather that the next three months were to throw at me, Lake Superior was in a mean mood that blustery June day and in my memory it was by far the toughest day of sailing of the journey. Lake Superior was like that...kind to you one day and the next she would toss you off the boat and think nothing more of it. She is always in charge. I won't forget that.

If I was really trying to put some miles behind me, such an early afternoon stopover as I had at Grand Marais, Michigan would have grated on me. As it was there was a great sense of relief as I tied onto the fuel dock and stepped a bit tentatively, wearily even, ashore.

Grand Marais, Michigan reminded me of Grand Marais, Minnesota, 150-miles across the lake to the northwest. The breakwaters were similar, protecting the harbors from the open lake, and the towns were situated right along the curves of the inner harbors. They were both likely dredged into harbors from the original swampy, or "big marsh" flats that the voyageurs called "grand marais" in their native language and used them for canoe trade stopovers to and from Montreal.

Just like across the lake, a friendly fellow stopped by on his bicycle. He said that he recognized the look of my old boat. We talked sailing for a bit. He thought I was only the second sailboat to stopover from Duluth this year. I was curious.

The other boat, he said, was heading to Australia by sailboat. I was intrigued but he didn't know much more, only that they were a family and were here about a week ago. Wow! Duluth to Australia! And I thought that my adventure was being adventurous.

I asked Terry, my friendly docksider, about the possible safe harbors farther down the lake. He said not to bother with Little Lake Harbor, though it was a nice 30 mile jaunt down the shore, it was always too shallow for a sailboat to wiggle into. He strongly suggested that the harbor around the hook of Whitefish Point, would be my best choice and had a deep entry channel.

In retrospect, it always amazes me how quickly my mind and body can shift from the intensity of riding a bucking sailboat to the calm reassurance of a walk on the land. Two hours ago I was concentrating on the seas and always trying to think of a better way to handle the boat. I was cold and wet. My stomach was queasy. I was tired and a little angry at the lake and/or the marine forecasters, those computer generated voices that drone on and on are so tiresome to listen to but also reassuring at times.

Friday, June 14. Today I have been one week on the lake.

Yesterday was a hard day. I'm a little stiff this morning. My lower back is achy and my butt is sore. There are some bruises on my arms and a small cut across on my cheek. All in all though, I feel great.

Yesterday afternoon, with a topped off gas tank, I had motored off the dock a ways and anchored near another sailboat in the Grand Marais harbor. It was a cool night, probably in the 30s but great for sleeping. We anchored near another boat that was moored.

When I anchor near other boats I am never feeling confident about the mysterious possibilities of the boat's swing in changing winds. It seems simple enough, that arc that a boat at mooring or at anchor swings through, but the radius of the arc depends on how much rode is out and the strength of the wind and the other boat's arc and...? I usually try to reason through all of these factors and then anchor far enough away from a boat to give more leeway for the likely errors of my guesswork and also to help assure a good night's sleep.

This mid June dawn had the promise of allowing the sun to creep over the horizon soon. I lit both burners of the propane stove to chase the chills from the cabin and my achy old body. I hugged the hot tea mug with both hands.

In order to make the harbor at Whitefish Point we would need to leave this cozy harbor soon. Whitefish was about fifty miles, and a stiff day's sail or motor sail. As usual, an early start and an early stopover was my M.O.

I motored out the channel to the end of the breakwaters in the hazy gray of first light. Then I struck an eastward heading to get a feel for the lake and the wind. We sailed east about a mile when I decided that the lake was still too lumpy from yesterday's blow.

Down with the sails and back to life the engine came and back to Grand Marais Harbor we went. I guess I was being cautious for a change. My stomach was a bit queasy already and I didn't want it to progress to that miserable flu-like feeling that came next. There wasn't much wind out there to dampen the motion of the boat. The afternoon was supposed to bring a south wind, or so the forecast promised.

Email Friday, June 14, 2013 at 8:58 a.m. Taking a day off the water. At Grand Marais,

Michigan…the Sportsman's Café. About time I gave you all an update so that your pins and needles are dulled and restful sleep returns.

Not to worry about this salty old dog. The lake has been mostly kind to me. Yesterday she reminded me who is in charge. Confused seas and winds made for a trying sail as wind and seas built with the morning. Headed out from Munising, Michigan about five miles to get some sea room and some fetch for long tacks. Pitching and rolling made me feel queasy in five to six foot seas. I was below studying a chart and knew that I must get up in the wind and clear my head with the horizon in view.

I thought about turning back. The forecast was for light northwest winds, which became cold wind from the north at 20-30 knots with me on the lee shore and waves coming across from Canada. Kept my tea down. Reefed the mains'l once then twice then doused it altogether. Went forward to secure the main; when not looking some big waves hit, don't remember how exactly, but made it to the cockpit with a thud. Landed hard somehow. Sore hand and butt today and slight cut across my cheek; looking like a salty dog now.

Made it to Grand Marais safe harbor. Noticed that I lost my long spruce boat hook that was "secured" along the mast. Darn it, and worse. I loved and depended on that hook to grab docks and things. It was my long, single-hand arm.

Two more days to the Soo Locks; then to lower Sweet Breeze into the Saint Marys River flowing to Lake Huron. I'm sure I won't miss Lake Superior.

Have met some very interesting folks in ports along the way. Black River Harbor, Ontonagon, Chassel, Big Bay, Munising, and here in Grand Marais; all U.P. towns with hearty fishermen.

Sweet Breeze has been flawless in all systems. So far MY flaws have cost me little.
'Till the next layover with wi-fi; your vicarious sailor….
Curt.

Fishermen are a hearty breed. They were lined up on the break wall, sitting on plastic pails, waiting for a whitefish to bite, before the sun. Parkas and hoods and layers of camo clothing were in style today. I hoped their hearty determination produced some fish.

It was still too early for the restaurant to fix me the substantial breakfast that I thought I deserved after yesterday's struggles and exertions, so I sat in the early sun across the street warming my bones and watching the town come to life. Facing the morning sun felt too good to leave. I'm usually not hungry in the morning because of my late night snacking while I read but I wanted to get my little Netbook booted up and write the folks back home.

There were four folks at the next table all of whom were busy concentrating on a cell phone type gadget in there hands. They were tapping and pressing and sliding their finger across the face of their gadgets and were not speaking to one another. They looked up, one at a time to give Jane their breakfast order, then immediately returned to tapping and pressing and sliding.

Jane called me "Hon" and "Sweetie" as she took my breakfast order. I figured she liked me because I was a sailor and had survived Lake Superior and I was the only customer she used those terms to address. Wi-fi and an omelet and Jane, was a good start to a day.

The hardware store across the street had opened and I was thinking about looking for some way to replace my lost boat hook. He had some long two by twos in the lumberyard out back but I had no way to shave it down to a handy size.

The hardware man was a sailor too. He had a small boat in the harbor and said that I was sailing his dream. He was the second person in two days that told me that. Every time I hear that, I am reminded of how lucky I am.

It was early afternoon when I decided to motor back out past the break walls and check out the lake conditions though I was being entertained by the small seaplanes that were landing in the harbor. I had happened in to Grand Marais on seaplane weekend. They were fascinating to observe and their lines were sleek and attractive but they sure were noisy little airships. One of the several planes landed ever so sweetly, skimming the surface, then taxied over to the sand beach and gunned the motor, pulled right up on the beach on wheels and the skipper stepped out on solid ground.

Leaving the Grand Marais harbor in early afternoon the lake had settled down enough to tempt me to hoist sails and try for some headway. The wind was about on the nose now so motor sailing seemed the best option. I flattened the sails as tightly as I could to get them to pull a bit and to dampen the roll of the hull.

Why do swells have that name? They are not swell! They make the boat roll and the sails slat, then crack they go when they fill with air. Pulley blocks bang as sheets get taut then slack then taut again. They are definitely not swell. They get on my nerves fast.

Wind direction started to make a change for the better as it gradually shifted from the northeast to the north and eventually to the northwest. I was picking it up on a broad reach now (wind behind the boat about 45 degrees off course); the wind on the quarter and the late afternoon brought the kind of sail that Sweet Breeze and I liked best.

I think I could see Whitefish Point now and beyond to the east was a vague outline of the Canadian shore. Gargantua was somewhere over there in the distant haze. I was closing in on the easternmost waters of the big lake. Waters with an element of legend. It has been called the graveyard of Lake Superior. There were ships and their crews in the depths; ships battered by storms and broken open. Whitefish Bay gives me a chill when I think about what is on the bottom, as I sail along toward its mouth.

I used the heavy spruce whisker pole that I had made at camp, to push out the genoa and keep the clew way out and down to catch as much wind as she could. It was a very light wind off the port quarter but strong enough to keep the sails working and the boat gently rolling along at three to four knots. It had become a lazy day with me dozing off while Otto steered and the afternoon sun on my back soaked out some of the soreness.

This had become the kind of steady wind that would be perfect for my "sheet-to-tiller" steering system. I had yet to try it on a downwind point of sail. I should have known that getting out the gear and getting it all rigged up was a sure way to kill a nice, friendly wind. That sweet breeze on the port quarter knew what I was about, and she gradually died away to nothing.

Was that Gargantua far to the east on the Canadian shore? With a name like that it must be that high headland barely visible to port bow. I'll bet that it was a landmark to early mariners.

Made another pot of hot tea to warm my hands and my insides. Four miles yet to Little Lake Harbor. Twenty-two miles yet to Whitefish Point. Too far to make the safe harbor around the inside of the point by dark.

The paper chart says that Little Lake Harbor is often subject to shoaling at the harbor entrance. Have decided to check it out cautiously to see if I can get within the protection of the harbor.

No chance to gain entry into the protected waters of the break wall. We touched bottom in sand even before the entry channel. Anchored outside of the entry in eight feet of water and a sand bottom. Dropped the plow anchor forward and backed up with full power to set it deep in the sand. Set a stern anchor in order to try to limit the swing of the boat so that it doesn't start to roll with the swells.

Buttoned up topsides and went below to make supper and warm up. Opened up the lid to the engine compartment to get the engine's heat into the cabin. Chilly night forecasted around 35 degrees.

If the winds stay light all night we will ride at anchor just fine. If the wind kicks up on this remote part of the lake I'll hoist anchors and head out into the lake and ride it out until daylight but that would not be a pleasant way to spend the night; not for a lazy sailor like me who loves a restful sleep.

Saturday, June 15, 5 a.m. From my nest in the V-berth.

I can see the first orange glow of daylight. It was an easy and restful night at anchor. It could have been the opposite with no safe harbors within twenty miles.

The hot, sweetened tea warmed my innards and my hands on that crisp and penetratingly chilly morn. The hot chai is my simple method of starting a day just right. I thank the spirit of the lake for the restful night and the promise of good sailing with an offshore southeast wind pushing ripples across the lake to the northwest.

Thinking back to the tough and dangerous sailing of two days ago, and soaking up the sweet sailing of this day, one becomes thankful for the quick turnabouts that the lake throws at a mariner. Maybe it proves the old Midwestern adage that, "If you don't like the weather now just wait a few moments."

This is my eighth day on the water. Lake Superior is kind this morn. The only difficult day was the day of confused waves. The rest were easy but today is the best yet; offshore wind on a broad reach, holding a five knot average speed. We should make Whitefish Point at about 10 a.m. if the wind holds.

In my mind, at least, Whitefish Point is a kind of a milestone. The eastern end of the lake is in sight from the waters off the point; the mysterious Canadian headlands of Algoma, Gros Cap, and Gargantua are beckoning through the haze. The panoramic view from the water is not intimate; instead it makes me feel small…and I am small out on this huge body of water. Those invisibly small molecules of water under me and those of the air about me give me the imaginary ego of a giant, but a glance around me, afloat on this inland sea, brings me instantly back to the reality of my insignificance. Those were my thoughts that morning rounding Whitefish Point; the view in each direction leaving me small within yet vast without. Perhaps I was feeling in balance.

As an old lake freighter steams by I checked the AIS screen (automatic identification system) for her name. She was the Michipicoten. I called her on channel 16 just asking for a response to a radio check to verify my transmission and reception at perhaps a five-mile distance.

"Loud and clear." Then I asked if Sweet Breeze was clearly visible on the ship's radar screen and that was affirmative as well. Good to know and good practice for my radio communication skills.

The entrance to Whitefish Bay narrows down enough that it could be called a kind of shipping bottleneck. It's about ten miles across from the end of the point to the Canadian shore but the islands and shoals off the eastern shore crowd most of the ships to the lane near the point. Ships have collided in the fog around Whitefish Point and there are wooden ships and iron ships in the depths.

Lesson #3: When entering an unknown harbor of refuge, stand your boat off at the entry and climb onto the coach roof for a thorough visible check for shoaling. This only works, of course, when the water is clear and you can see down a few feet.

I made this lesson up after the fact. We ran into the harbor at Whitefish Point around noontime that day. We literally ran into the harbor at Whitefish Point. What we really did was run hard aground onto a sand shoal at the entry. I could have easily seen the shoaling in the clear water if I had taken the precaution of a visual assessment from the bow. Instead, I was relying on the advice (mistake number one) of the old mariner at Grand Marais, Michigan: that the Whitefish Point harbor was always an easy access. But to be sure, I had the depth meter on and was closely observing adequate depth (mistake number two) until I grounded her fast. If I had observed Rule # 3 the next hour of angst could have been avoided.

It was sand all around me now about three to four feet down. Sweet Breeze liked the sand to be down there at least 4 and a half feet or she became very stuck; and she was. Now what?

There was deep water all around but it was ten feet away, in all directions. Before I got too concerned about this latest predicament (and that wouldn't have taken long) two fishermen in an old steel skiff came in from checking their nets and asked if I would like to be towed off the bar. Guess what my answer was.

In my journal I wrote that it took about 40 minutes of pulling from several different directions to gain floatation. It took both of their engines plus Sweet Breeze's inboard at full to wiggle and turn and gain an inch, then two. That was a total of 230 horses of engine power. The 5/8-inch nylon towline was sawn halfway through but held together.

Must I learn all lessons of seamanship through negative experiences? Why can't I just read about the groundings of others and absorb that experience from the ground up, by capillary action, or osmosis? Somewhere it must be written that sand shoals are often very steep sided and can sneak up on you. Somewhere it must be written that depth meters don't look ahead but can only tell you what is under the boat right now…and somewhere it must be advised that the lone seaman should take all suggestions from others, even locals, with a precautionary note.

I know now that I could have seen the shoal at the mouth of the harbor if only I had stood high on the coach roof and examined the waters ahead. I think that the deep channel along the seawall to the right would have been obvious by the dark colored water. But no, I was keenly watching the depth meter which showed ten feet, then ten feet, then ten feet, then three feet as I ran really hard aground. The "really hard aground" part of the grounding didn't have to be either. If I was approaching the entry very slowly it could have been a bump and a quick reverse to back off.

I do think that my learning experiences could have been much avoided if I had another crewmember aboard. These are the lessons of the single-hander, and I needed to pay attention or my next grounding might not be so soft or so quickly resolved.

The fishermen were native fellas from the Bay Mills reservation down the coast. I paid them a pretty generous tip for their efforts to free us from our sand trap. It was a difficult towing and they deserved it to be generous; then I bought a whitefish to cook for supper from their tub holding the fresh catch. If they came back to fish tomorrow I thought I'd ask if I could go out fishing with them: I would love to learn about their fishing methods and just have the experience of a day on the water with them.

For the overnight, I tied up to an unused finger dock. There were several fishing tugs at most of the docks but there was an unused one opposite a big sailboat that suggested to me there was good depth at that dock. Barn swallows were nesting under my dock just a couple feet away but they wouldn't sit still for a good close-up photo.

After I filleted out the whitefish I placed the remains on a rock nearby to watch the gulls indulge. It was a tug of war by several in several different directions. Small pieces broke off but the head and side skins and backbone and tail were all of one unit yet and a big gull swallowed the whole works. He tried to fly away for a peaceful repose but was too heavy to lift off the water. Other gulls pestered him hoping for some regurgitated morsels. The fish remains must have been as heavy as he/she was and I think it would be some time before flight would again be possible. The heavy gull swam off looking most uncomfortable.

A mile-long gravel beach curved outward to the southeast from the harbor and beckoned me for the hike out to the tip of the gravel spit. Most of the shoreline, back a few feet from the water, was flagged with signposts that said not to enter because it was the nesting habitat of piping plovers, an endangered shorebird. The bird had been absent for many years from its nesting sites here but in recent years a few have returned and fledged offspring. I think I saw a plover as it was walking on spindly legs; when it stopped it became really hard to spot with its camo plumage, the colors of a stony beach.

Another sign was to notify the hiker that the beach was privately owned but that you could walk along it as long as you didn't *collect* any rocks. The rounded stones were gorgeous. I had already picked up a couple of small ones to be those smooth and lucky pocket stones I liked to carry. Not to be a picky old wordsmith, but to me, a "collection" of stones meant more than two very small ones.

After the whitefish supper, which was good but not to compare with the lake trout at Ontonagon, I started the hike out to the lighthouse point and the shipwreck museum. The access road led me about two miles to the east through what I would guess are overgrown dunes of former storms way back in geologic history. The dunes were barely discernable now for the veritable plethora of ground covering plants. Ground covers of blueberry and cranberry, blackberry and, above those... choke cherry. Many other blossoming plants were creeping along wherever sunlight penetrated through the Jack Pines. Juniper of at least two types was interspersed here and there, seeming to not like close neighbors of the same species.

The White and Jack Pines formed a sparse canopy, likely because of the harsh, unprotected landscape of the point. The pines were a scraggly lot, which may be why they were still there. They looked to have little commercial value as lumber or wood fiber sources. The arms of the pines pointed to the east, groomed by the persistent strength of the prevailing westerly's.

The point was a stopover and nesting site for lots of migrating birds; raptors, water birds, and songbirds. The Audubon society was recently involved in trying to limit development and preserve habitat for the feathered migrants that depended on the point for a rest stop or a home. So far the birds and the Coast Guard are cohabitating on the point without too much conflict.

The enormous complexity of nature seems only to be exceeded by the enormous ignorance driving man's quest to dominate nature. In a teaspoon of organic soil are thousands of tiny critters and perhaps a billion bacteria. Man is always trying to improve on nature and her processes. What I'm getting at here is that Whitefish Point was once a prime shooting place to kill hawks and other raptors for a government sponsored reward, called a bounty, as they passed over on their annual migratory journeys. Ignorance and the desire to kill things are usually the root causes of such stupid, mindless slaughters. Maybe we are a little further along in our understanding of the natural interconnectedness of all creatures, great and small, but not much further, I'm afraid.

I think it was a Saturday, and of a late afternoon because the lighthouse and museum of the great lakes shipwrecks were closed. Something about all of the shipwrecks on the bottom of the lake nearby gave me that queasy feeling, kind of a shivery thought.

I met the nicest family on the beach and offered to take their picture with their camera, a simple kindness that often leads to friendly introductions. They were Tom and Bette and two year old Promise from Lansing, Michigan. Something about their warmth was memorable to me, maybe it was just that...their warmth. Being alone for hours or days on the vast reaches of the lake may have made me into a human sponge ready to soak up some genuine human warmth.

Back at the boat, I recall having a glass of wine and contemplating my own fate. Should I take the time to go fishing tomorrow if invited by my fishermen/ boat towing native friends or should I get an early start across the huge expanse of Whitefish Bay and get through the Soo locks and down to the St. Marys River? The west winds forecasted for tomorrow would help me across the bay and I hate to miss out on a favorable wind.

The trip log says that I have traveled 715 nautical miles (kilometers) so I multiplied that figure by .62 and I got 430 miles…sounds about right.

The composting toilet aboard has got tiny black gnats taking up residence within. Darn!

Sunday, June 16. Late morning, up at 6 a.m. Fog and mosquitoes and light rain.

The native fishermen arrived and are fogged in just like me. It is an unsettling thought to be out in the shipping lanes in a dense fog. They have decided to weld up the leaks in their steel skiff to pass the time productively until the fog lifts. I have decided to "supervise" the welding since I had been trained to teach welding and they good-naturedly put up with my light-hearted banter and presence.

There was no question about taking me fishing with them that day or any day. They said that it would be against some DNR regulation and they could lose their license if caught with me on the boat. I didn't understand but it must have had something to do with their fishing rights as Native Americans and having a white boy aboard would violate some law. I didn't feel it was my place to question it further, but I was a little disappointed because it would have been fun and interesting to help and learn. Those young men were making a living from the lake, as their fathers and grandfathers had before them.

By my nature I guess I usually reach out just slightly, maybe with just a smile or a wave, and sometimes it turns into a memorable acquaintance. We're all in this together, right? Merlin and his grown daughter Jamie stopped by Sweet Breeze for a visit. Native folks, also waiting for the fog to lift so they could tend their nets. Merlin usually went out alone but Jamie had the day off and came along with her dad to help.

Both boats of fishermen headed out for their nets just before noon. It was still foggy but I guess they thought it would lift soon. I was right behind them but everything was feeling tentative with me, though I did get past the sand shoals at the harbor entrance with no problem.

Visibility was about a quarter mile now, plenty of time to avoid a freighter I felt. Still, it was a spooky feeling for me out on notorious Whitefish Bay, alone in the fog.

Heading south, I kept our course to the west of the shipping lanes and watched our position on the chart plotter. I could hear the growl of the deep horns on freighters as they blew warnings into the fog. I could almost feel the air vibrate when they were close and sounding warning. The VHF/AIS showed me their position relative to our position so I felt pretty secure.

There was a slight northwest wind fetching across our starboard quarter that I had caught on a broad reach in the fog. I figured the wind would blow away the fog and it did as the afternoon got brighter. At the time I didn't realize that fog would be an unwelcome morning guest all too often aboard Sweet Breeze, for weeks and months and many, many miles ahead.

Anvil clouds forming ahead as I tentatively crossed Whitefish Bay.

The lifting and thinning fog allowed some glimpses of Ile Parisienne about five miles to the east; a remote, curiously long and narrow north-south stretch of an island with some visible signs of habitation or commerce on its southwestern shore. Intriguing name too but I know nothing about its history. (Aha! A little research while writing this book is telling and gratifying to me in that I learned that the island is mostly a conservation reserve held by the province of Ontario, Canada. The island is completely undeveloped except for the lighthouse on the southwest corner).

I welcomed the warm rays of Old Sol as the fog thinned and finally disappeared. The broad expanse of the bay no longer felt spooky, now just vast. The tendrils and veils of fog lifted, as did my spirits. The legends of dangerous storms however, started to creep in and pollute my enjoyment of the swift sail because big, tall, enormous, cumulonimbus clouds were forming to the southwest. They were on shore yet and moving east, but I could hear the thunder and see some lightning bolts dancing in the blackest parts of the anvil shaped clouds, even though they were 20 miles away.

My charts didn't show any likely safe harbors nearby on the western shore. My hope was that the storms were going straight east. Not northeast, which would carry them out onto the bay and I might sail into them. Should I slow down my progress to the south, I thought? I watched and I watched as I sailed and I sailed. The darkest storm clouds were getting no closer. Full sails and a secure feeling followed. I was sure the storms would pass to the south of me and my little boat, so we sailed along as fast as we could for the narrowing of Whitefish Bay toward the Soo.

Again, the vastness of Whitefish Bay held me a bit spellbound and in cautious awe. The narrows were in sight now and I could feel both a little confidence and the joy of sailing returning. A few big raindrops splattered around the deck but they were from the very northern fringes of the thunderstorm clouds. Life was good but I was to remain alert and humble and observant, ever vigilant. No more did I want any of the anxiety of running aground. I tried to train myself to always think ahead; plan and prepare the boat for each new move or trial. These were some of the thoughts this old single-hander was having that afternoon, sailing into the next challenge of how to lock down the river.

Part of an early celebration of one great lake behind me was to try some of the "cherry flex" from the fridge. That was a concentrated paste made from tart cherries and given to me by yet another kind and friendly couple that I met briefly at Whitefish Point safe harbor. I guess the concoction was considered to be good for the body's joints, a kind of natural glucosamine-chondroiten. Something so concentrated from healthy fruit just had to be loaded with nutrition. It tasted good and I loved fruit, especially tart cherries, and if it lubricated my joints too, then why didn't medicine always taste this good.

Sault Ste Marie. Monday, June 17. Cleaning up the boat this morning for Kay.

Locking down yesterday late afternoon was too easy. I called the lockmaster on the VHF radio and asked for instructions. He said to proceed down the left channel and enter the lock and stay to the left when the light turned green. I could handle that.

I put fenders on the port rail and motored into the Poe Lock, an enormous structure that could accommodate Sweet Breeze plus a thousand foot ore carrier plus another 150-foot boat behind that. Thankfully, we, my boat and I, were the only ones using the Poe.

The attendant in the middle of the lock's north wall threw me a line and I asked for two, one forward and one aft. I had imagined the process and thought through what I guessed would be the best way to control the boat as we descended 21 feet in turbulent waters. With a fore and aft line loosely bypassing a cleat on the deck I thought that I could stand in the middle and control the boat with light tension on each line.

It worked great. Me and my little tub dropped down the 21-feet without a hitch. When the barrier gate rose and the green light went on we motored out of the largest lock system in the world just like we did it everyday.

There were lots of locks ahead before the salt water and I hoped they were equally as easy, but they had rules. Rules on the Welland canal system around Niagara Falls required a crew of at least three to line down the several locks. Beyond Lake Ontario, the Canadian locks down the St. Lawrence River required a crew of two. I had to make some plans for future crew....

Speaking of crew, Kay Bakke had arrived at Sault Ste Marie, Michigan at 9 a.m. and I must make way in the cabin for her gear and all the other stuff that a woman deems necessary. She was to take rest upon the starboard settee, captain's orders (that would be me). Her gear would be stowed wherever there was room. I wanted her to be as comfortable as the cramped space of our cabin on the sea could afford.

Kay and I first met at a boating safety class that was offered by the power and sail squadron at Duluth. She had gained the proper Coast Guard licensing in order to skipper commercial boats and worked summers sailing charter sailboats out of Bayfield, Wisconsin. Bayfield is at the doorstep to the Apostle Island's National Lakeshore and some of Lake Superior's finest sailing waters.

She had never sailed through the North Channel of Lake Huron nor the St. Marys River connecting the lakes of Superior and Huron. Of course, neither had I so we talked by cell phone and as I made my way down the lake we made our landfall meeting at the Sault (pronounced *Soo*: an obsolete French term meaning rapids or falls). Sault Ste Marie meaning falls of the St Mary River. (Where I was heading I needed to practice my French at every opportunity).

Email Monday, June 17. At a marina on the downtown waterfront of Sault Ste Marie. We're in the St. Marys River now. Lake Superior is conquered…well…we may have become tolerable friends. I walked downtown and had a beer and some Mexican food to celebrate.

Friend Kay Bakke is to join me for as long as she can stand being mate, steward, cook, Navigator…in short, "at my command." We both look forward to sailing through the 1000 islands of the North Channel of Lake Huron. Lots of interesting and intimate sailing among the islands while trying to keep our bearings.

Yesterday was a bit trying as I left the harbor at Whitefish Point around noon when the fog appeared to be lifting. After it thinned I could see big, dark anvil clouds forming in the skies to the south. Big thunderstorm clouds they were, but they moved east and were not a bother.

Whitefish Bay is huge and a bit intimidating. "The Graveyard of the Lake," it's called, with hundreds of ships and sailors on the bottom.

It all worked out with a fast sail to the locks and the 21-foot drop to the tranquil river below.
Adventures to all,
Curt.

Kay was a good packer of her stuff…not too much. She arrived by bus and was hungry. Still in good humor after an all night bus ride…now that's a real trooper. This sweet little marina, the George Kemp Downtown Marina, provided bicycles, so we biked downtown and had a brunch, all the while joking and catching up.

I spent the afternoon biking around town while giving Kay some time to catch up on her sleep in the cabin on her new bed where her feet slid nicely under the galley stove when she stretched out. It was easy for me to keep busy. Right next door to the marina was a museum ship named the "Valley Camp" and I had to take the ship's tour. I had never been aboard an ore carrier before in 60-years of living near the Duluth-Superior harbor where they are very common. About time.

Sometime that afternoon another small sailboat slipped quietly into that sweet little marina. I noticed it later while on a tour of the docks. Mostly big powerboats were the common vessel there, so the sailboat stood out and caught my eye.

A big friendly looking dog was moored at the intersection of the sailboat's finger dock and the main access walkway. She was big and she was friendly but the skipper either wasn't home or was napping so I quietly slunk away.

Doug was rummaging around in his Cape Dory 25 when I returned an hour later. I think I had seen the mast of his boat rolling a bit, waving at me, which indicated someone was likely vertical and moving within the cabin.

What a nice and gentle and tired looking fellow was Doug. He was on his way to Duluth from the New York City area and had been on the water for about a month. Doug and Birdie, his dog, were delivering his boat to the head of the Lakes in order to ultimately get the boat to Montana where he was moving back to. He'd had about enough of the big city and the big city ways. I hoped there was a big lake near his new home-site in Montana but I guessed he knew what he was doing.

Doug and Birdie at Sault Ste. Marie.

We were on similar journeys but in different directions. Adventurers both.

Doug and Birdie came over for a visit with Kay and I later, and there I learned more of his journey and of his trials. He still looked really tired and aged, 70-years I guessed.

He had taken the Hudson River north to the Erie Canal then west and north to Lake Ontario by way of Lake Oneida and Oswego, New York. From Oswego he sailed across Lake Ontario and once up on the north shore of the lake he took the old Trent-Severn waterway system across southern Ontario to Georgian Bay of Lake Huron; then through the islands of the North Channel and up the St. Marys River and here he was. Sounds easy?

The Trent-Severn system of canals and locks and rivers and lakes was an early and short way around Niagara Falls and connected Lake Ontario with Lake Huron bypassing Lake Erie entirely. Originally a canoe route, Canadians made it passable for small ships with lots of digging, marine railroads, and lock construction.

Doug had consumed enough of the quantities of healthy food that his wife had packed for him. I think he was ready for some French fries and a burger. He gave me lots of nuts and whole grains, which I much appreciated and he thought he just couldn't eat any more. Then he gave me paper charts of the North Channel and Georgian Bay and asked me to return them by mail, somewhere along the way, to his home in New York.

My only donation toward the success of his voyage across Lake Superior was to tell him of my experiences with grounding and shoaling. I still needed my Lake Superior chart book because it had the upper St. Mary's River system but I afforded him a word picture of how to safely move into the harbor at Whitefish Point and then just generally cautioned him about sand shoals at the entrances of the south shore boater's refuges. We wished him well and thought perhaps (hoped) we would meet again. I didn't think until later that I should have bestowed to Doug my copy of *The Superior Way*, Bonnie Dahl's invaluable treatise on sailing the big lake.

And Down the St. Marys....

Tuesday, June 18. Kay and I left the Marina to find Canada customs and check-in.

We searched up and down the Canadian shoreline of Sault Ste Marie, Ontario but could not find the customs office that we were told was there somewhere. We got an entry number over the phone eventually and lots of confusing directions from different customs officials on what should be the proper way to enter Canadian waters. We spent an hour or two trying to be legal and proper with our check-in but nothing was resolved so down the river we went.

The Edwin Gott, a thousand foot ore carrier, followed us down the river. We gave way and moved over to the right edge of the channel so the Gott could pass, then *we* followed the *Gott* down the river, which seemed to be a better plan.

Before looking at navigation charts of the St. Marys river, my mind was in the short river mode; thinking two huge lakes connected by a short river with rapids, just like in the Boundary Waters Canoe Area Wilderness. The scale here was so much larger. First, the river was a braided type with different channels. The northerly route around Sugar Island looked to be the most interesting and scenic but there was one bridge with only a 35-foot clearance. I figured Sweet Breeze was at least 40-feet to the top of her mast. That meant the southerly route, the one that the ships took, was to be our route to Lake Huron.

Not only was the river much longer than expected but more interesting as well. It wasn't twisty-turny of course because it was modified with straight cuts to accommodate the huge ships. One channel was blasted through bedrock. It looked like slate. There were also large lakes with channel markers to keep us from meandering out onto the broad shallow flats. Part of the route was divided around both sides of an island so that up-bound and down-bound ships weren't squeezing through the narrow cuts.

One night and half a day later, Kay and I were still getting along splendidly. Of course, I knew that I was one of the easiest people in the world to get along with but I didn't yet know about Kay.

We nearly hit a red nun buoy channel marker but that was the only navigation issue we had down the river. Seems the helmsman was soaking up the scenery all around at the time and got a little off course. I think Kay was below deck at the time resting.

Lime Island was an interesting afternoon stop. It was a historic shipping and commercially important stop for the early lake freighters. Coal was stored there for the steamships to replenish their power source and limestone was quarried on the island and "roasted" to make lime for cement. I wonder if the earliest locks at the Soo were constructed of cement from the Lime Island kilns.

There was a friendly couple that told me the history of the island regarding its role in early shipping. They were volunteers who stayed on the island for the summer and care-took. There were always questions left unanswered (and usually unasked) about the history of such places before the Euro-Americans. I wondered what the island's significance was to Native Americans. With its location along a water-travel route, I'll bet it was a stopover place or a summer camp.

I think that Kay would have liked to spend the night dockside at Lime Island. A good idea, such a pleasant place, but the wind was blowing nicely onto our starboard quarter...you know what that means by now, right? A broad reach with good speed and gentle boat motion. I just couldn't pass it up after all the breeze-less days I had spent motoring on Lake Superior or tacking into northeast winds. Afternoon winds, especially quartering winds, were hard for me to let pass. They meant speed, miles-made-good, and pleasant sailing. Toward what end? What goal? Let me try to explain...somewhere in this book, likely many places, this author feels the need to try to put into words what coastal traveling by sailboat is really about.

There are many advantages to this type of boat travel. A sense of complete *freedom* is probably the one that draws me most. The freedom of choice to go, or where to spend the night...it could be anywhere on the water. Freedom to decide how fast to go, or how slow. Nary a rest stop, nor a campground, nor a motel, need the sailor be watchful for. She/he need only watch the weather forecast for wind direction and velocity.

Winds and weather will determine your campsite for the night. If the sailor has equipped the boat with adequate ground tackle (anchors and their hawse lines or rodes) there may be no need to look for a dock or a marina or an established mooring. With good anchors and associated equipment, all you need for a good night's rest is a bottom that will hold fast your connection to terra firma. And if you prefer a steady boat while you sleep, and most sentient sailors would, you will look for a protected cove or an island that blocks the waves, or perhaps a small bay that cuts back into the hills and offers protection from three sides.

Checking the navigation chart for a protected anchorage on the near shore is fun for the map lover like me; with forecasted wind direction being your main criteria for finding that sweet little bay of your very own, your pirate cove. Planning your time in order to arrive at your safe anchorage before dark is always a wise goal. That afternoon, Kay and I were heading for our choice of a good night's rest toward Drummond Island and a cove down into Rabbit Bay of Sturgeon Bay. After Kay had her graham crackers and milk, her evening comfort food, she was a happy woman and we were at peace with the world. We put out two different types of anchors onto an unknown bottom to assure a good night's rest. Lastly, we selected an alternate harbor of refuge should the wind shift during the night and we would need to move.

Ah, the freedom of sailing. The greatest freedom of all is the lack of roads. That's right. Not a single road. Not a speed limit either. Well sometimes there are at marinas and marine mooring areas to help remind those who don't realize that boat wakes can bother others.

You can go anywhere in the world if you can make it to the coast; anywhere, anytime you would like. How free is that?

Nobody groping your crotch before boarding. No long lines or traffic backups. No waiting for help if you run out of gas, just wait for some wind. No ticket line waits and no flat tires. I have to wonder why everyone doesn't sail! I think it would be a more peaceful world.

The First Thousand Islands

Wednesday, June 19. Lovely and cool morning.

Windswept pines of the Thousand Islands.

Kay and I were up early (skipper's choice) and the sunrise found us picking our way, carefully I might add, along the northern shore of Drummond Island heading north to get around Chippewa Point before we could strike an easterly course. We were checking the paper chart against the chart plotter looking for hazards. Lots of shoals to be mindful of between small islands and narrow straits; motoring along and hoping for some wind as the sun rose and began to heat up the shore-land structure.

When the land warms and is alongside a cold body of water there should be some air currents stirring through convection; the less dense warm air rising off the land should draw cooler air off the water, or so dictates my basic knowledge of physics. A thermal siphoning of air currents...?

We did start to get some variable breezes. It was looking like a good forty-mile day with the early start and an early stopover somewhere ahead.

Kay and I were getting along nicely so far. She laughed at my jokes. She didn't try to take charge. She agreed with my choices mostly, and when she disagreed she did so in the most diplomatically cautious way so as to spare my fragile skipperly ego. Yes, we were getting along splendidly. She had all the makings of a first class mate on my ship. Oh, and she also helped to manage the sails and steer.

The trip log registered 893 kilometers this morning. That would be about 534 miles since leaving Duluth on June seventh. Let's see, today was the nineteenth so twelve days divided into 534 equals 44 and a half miles per day. Not a bad average for all the light winds and the stronger winds that were foul. There were still a few miles (about a thousand) to go before salt water and ocean tides and strange sea creatures, but we were in the second of the four great lakes that I would traverse and that was a kind of milestone for me.

We caught the afternoon breeze on the starboard beam. Sweet Breeze wanted to get up and go with the wind. So did I. Kay, not so much.

The breeze became a wind. It was offshore and that was what we needed for some speed and some *not* really big waves. Kay steered us along at some great speeds and sometimes the prolonged gusts heeled us more than we liked. We reefed both sails one time and held the same speed with less heel. That felt good. That we; not the wind, still had control of our little ship. We could always reef more if the wind continued to build and we were approaching a grand and deep bay to our right as we passed Cape Robert.

There was a miles long fetch down this bay to Bayfield Sound so we expected some big bumps on the water and big winds. It was bumpy and lumpy and another sail reef kept us feeling in better control across the mouth of this bay, and with double-reefed sails we still maintained about a six-knot average speed.

I was glad that Kay got to experience some fast sailing on a boat that gives a stiff presence to the wind and a reasonably secure presence to the passengers. We made Gore Bay with evening light. That stiff wind gave us not a 40-mile day but a 70-mile day. Kay thought it was her steering that made the difference.

My journal notes said: *Gas, beans, and Spam for a celebratory supper after a 70-mile day.* On closer examination of my scribbles I saw the gas part was crossed out and further down the journal it said that we got gas(oline) in the morning after the marina opened. I guess both versions could make some particular sense.

Kay was really impressed with my Beans and Spam Delight. We both slept like rocks.

Thursday, June 20. Got gas and paper towels and toilet paper and a smoked whitefish at Gore Bay…a great looking small town. Locals up early jogging. An island community.

We were traveling too fast through the North Channel of Lake Huron. It's the kind of sailing waters that should be savored and sipped, like a hot, spicy, chai tea. One should spend the whole summer.

There are many more than 1,000 islands. Some estimates say 30,000 islands. With that many to choose from the sailor-dreamer could find one to call his very own, or to imagine it at least for a day. Then, one should sail around it and ask, "Now, where should the cabin be located on my island for the day? Shall I orient the cabin in order to watch the sunrise, from my wicker chair on the porch, or the sun set?"

I already have my cabin in the woods on a winding canoe-able stream where the evening's setting sun slants through the branches of tall white pines along the river and paints the log walls of the porch with splashes of that warm, brilliant, orange-yellow. The long sitting bench allows room to sit between the streaks of evening sun and watch the lighting change and listen for the owl's evening conversations.

On the east side of the cabin, the rising beams of morning sunlight sneak between the tapered tops of the balsam fir and streak into the cabin's kitchen, where the tea water is always hot.

My cabin is on an island too…an even larger island than Lake Huron's Manitoulin, whose coast we had sailed along for forty miles yesterday. The island upon which my cabin sits is called North America and it sits somewhere near the middle of that very large island. I imagine North America as a huge island in the sea.

Manitoulin, with Gore Bay cutting into its north shore, is a vast island in one of the planet's largest lakes. It's the largest island in a freshwater lake on the whole of our planet Earth. It is located east a bit of the geographic center of the island of North America. Manitoulin has another "largest" to its credit. It has the largest freshwater lake, on the largest island in a freshwater lake. I'll sum it all up to say, Canada is a huge nation state on the huge island of North America and is so lucky to have the North Channel of Lake Huron within its borders.

Looking back within my daily journal—my written memory of the day's events and thoughts, and my guide for this, the larger journal—it is glaringly brief these days with Kay. Conversation and human interaction must have taken the place of the intimate connections with all that surrounds me that I was noting before her arrival. A whole day passes with only a couple of scribbles of my thoughts.

It seems to me that journeys into new and special places are best remembered when done alone. The light, the sounds, the delicate intricacies that the senses feel, see, and hear; are noticed more and more deeply without distraction. This may not be true for everyone, but for me the absolute presence of mind, the clearing away of past and future, is most nearly accomplished when alone. Maybe that's why I have canoed alone so much. Conversation and sharing have their places but my thoughts wander when in conversation with others. Past memories and future wonderings are awakened within my own thought processes when others are present and I am listening to and stimulated by their thoughts. My alertness is far less alert when I concentrate on listening to another's words.

We made our way through the islands and marked channels and I thoroughly enjoyed Kay's company. Honest! She is a trooper (my highest compliment to a partner in adventure).

Our next planned stopover was to be at the town of Little Current, Ontario. We got there early that afternoon.

Lost My Crew Already

Email Thursday, June 20, 5 p.m. Kay and I are at Little Current on the eastern end of the North Channel of Lake Huron. She is trying to arrange transport up to Hwy. 17 going west with ALL of her bags. I walked around town asking strangers and stopping at businesses, trying to be creative and find her a ride. The closest I came to finding her transport was at the auto parts store. They would take the van in the morning to Espanola but couldn't take passengers. What a dumb rule.

I found a really good guy from Oklahoma...Sooner...than later, who said he would take her there and he had a big ass SUV with lots of room for bags.

We spent the night last at Gore Bay on Manitoulin Island after a good day's sail of about 70-miles. I fixed her a wonderful dinner of Spam and beans. The bean can said it contained real onions. It made me wonder what the other kind of onions were like.

I will leave early in the morning for waters unknown, heading east, then south across Georgian Bay.

At the Soo I met a great guy from Long Island, New York sailing to Duluth with his dog. His name was Doug.

Out for now, back to channel 16.

Curt.

Kay and I compliment personalities well and I learned a lot from our sailing adventure together. I tease her a lot. She doesn't get mad. She laughs at my jokes and I like her.

It was only about a 25-mile sail and motor sail to Little Current. The city had a large and handy and clean and pleasant marina on the right bank as we entered the narrows leading to the city.

I had told Kay about how Sweet Breeze had a mind of her own when backing the boat under power. Unpredictable she was, Sweet Breeze, not Kay. How she answered the helm in reverse seemed to depend mostly upon her mood. Much like some women I knew.

"Hah," said Kay. "Let me try."

And try she did.

Kay backed Sweet Breeze into a finger dock that we had chosen. Into the dock. Not alongside it. Second try, too far from the dock to reach it with a boat hook and pull it in tight. Third try, etc. I encouraged her but reminded her (and her captain's license) that Sweet Breeze had to be in the right mood.

There were a couple of wharf rats (marina regulars) on their lawn chairs nearby and it pleased me that we were providing them with some entertainment to go with their beer and brats. Kay gave up eventually and agreed that she was indeed a fickle girl in reverse. I took the helm and praised Sweet Breeze so that she could hear me above the motor and after a few try's she decided to slide backwards alongside the dock pretty as she pleased, emphasis on "as she pleased."

Once again, the first person I met, sitting on a park bench along the jetty, was someone of the best of personal qualities and someone I would remember long after. He was Dave from Oklahoma...a sailor who pulled his trailer sailor north each spring to spend the summers exploring the waters and small town cultures of Lake Huron's North Channel. He and his wife came north together and this year he even brought their teenaged grandson who had some mental challenges that may have made vacation times challenging for all. That told me more about what kind of a person Dave was. Sometimes I feel pretty selfish wanting to enjoy beautiful natural places alone or with only a critically selected companion (that usually being my dog).

The city dock area had a clean, hot shower building, and plenty of hot water. We were "parked" right next to the downtown area of the small town where there were restaurants and a curious shop of cheap imported goods of which I have zero interest, but I had to check it out as a cultural window into what some of the local folks might buy. I learned that Americans had no monopoly on the desire for "consume and throwaway" goods.

I talked to Dave again on one of my wanderings to and from downtown and told him that I thought Kay had had enough of me and asked was there a bus route or train route that came nearby where she could catch a ride heading west back toward Sault Ste. Marie?

Dave thought if there was a bus it would stop at Espanola, a town about twenty miles north that resides on the main Trans Canada highway. Kay learned from the Internet that there was such a bus and an approximate stopping time at Espanola and Dave volunteered to run her up there in his SUV in the morning. See what I mean about folks?

Its Just You and Me Again, Old Girl

Sure I talk to my boat. I would talk to my dog too if she was along.

I know what you're thinking. He's been alone in the woods too long and he needs to get out more. Well you're probably part right, but what is normal anyhow, you might ask, and I might ask if "normal" is really something to strive for. I know it's not a goal of mine and I'm going to keep talking to my boat.

Friday, June 21. Summer Solstice: the longest day of the year. Up early to get Kay and her gear to Dave's car at 6 a.m. I will miss her suggestions and her perpetual good attitude. She was sharing and helpful. She was relaxed and quick to see humor in situations.

After Kay left, Sweet Breeze needed my mechanical attention. The engine's oil level was down a half quart...not bad after so many long hours of motoring and tanks of gas. I carried extra oil for such occasions. I added a few drops of oil to the cup that leads to the bearing on the distributor shaft also. I tried to remember to do that after each tank of gas burned.

The engine oil was taking on a dark color, normal after lots of hours of steady running, but not black in color, just a medium brown.

My conundrum: How to get some miles-made-good without favorable winds or the push of that dependable little motor. Shall we sit out on the lake's swells with slatting sails and me going nuts with the motion and the noise, waiting for a breeze? Motoring it would have to be, again and again. I had already burned way more gas than I thought I would need to make progress, but progress was my goal, no certain destination in mind, but progress to the east was essential, in my mind at least.

Motor-sailing east. Good that the channel is well buoyed with the red and green, nuns and cans, as their shapes are called. We went around Garden Island to the north trying to pick out the safest passages through shoal filled waters. Passing the big one called Strawberry Island, I wondered if there was once a strawberry farm there or was it loaded with wild strawberries? I was always wondering about place names and conjuring up historic reasons for them. It was part of my entertainment. Single-handers do that. What about Espanola nearby and the Spanish River? Was Ponce de Leon here looking for the fountain of youth? I didn't think so. Too much water to search in this neck of the woods. Was Magellan here looking for the Northwest Passage?

I remember that there were some other entertaining thoughts that I was entertaining, like: Should I stop at Killarney, that quaint town on the north shore that I had heard so much about, or should I make way to the south and shoot for the islands off the Bruce Peninsula? Could I make the safety of those islands before dark? What was the weather forecast for the western half of Georgian Bay, those big open waters of northern Lake Huron? My journal said the waves were one to two feet and the wind from the southeast. I opted for progress down the east side of Georgian Bay.

Winds weren't good, light and variable, but water depths were safe on the east side of Big Burnt Island. I was heading straight south toward Cape Smith, expecting southwest winds as per the forecast. Presently only light winds from the east-southeast.

Cape Smith. Was it like Cape Horn on the tip of South America? Could I round the Cape in a blow? Cape Smith that is. More single-hander mind entertainment.

Cape Horn has the most notoriously dangerous sailing waters in the world.

Storms were common off the Horn. Waves and winds reached seriously epic proportions. Old time sailors called the far southern seas the Roaring Forty's way down in the south 40-degree latitudes. Single-handers who have made it around the horn are few. Single-handers who have tried are many.

Well, I was in the roaring northern 40s rounding Cape Smith, and in my imagination it was really Cape Horn today, but I had gotten lucky. The waves were not 40-feet high yet. Perhaps the seas would build to those heights with the afternoon winds. They were two feet high now and I had successfully single-handed the Cape... Smith that was.

My playful imagination was seeing coastline here as likened to Tierra del Fuego at the tip of the Cape Horn. Remote, inhabited mostly by natives. There were no towns or dwellings visible. There was no smoke on the shores (Land of Fire in Spanish). I made a hard left, 90-degrees, toward Squaw Island, just to be safe. This would get me beyond the reach of their war canoes should they not be peaceable.

My journal again had recorded the thoughtful detail of aloneness. Playful imaginings. Deep thoughts, and serious thoughts about navigation in unknown waters. Always studying charts to be aware of the nearest places of refuge should the lake decide to kick up. No southwest wind yet, still southeast and light.

There were islands ahead with some possible safe anchorages. Rabbit Island, then Club Island and farther out I could see the shallow hump of Lonely Island, though with that name it didn't sound welcoming. Shoal grounds were frequent and scattered. On the Canadian paper chart some hazards were called "shingles," some "ledges," some "banks," and some were called "patches." They all kept my attention focused on my position. I knew the bottom here was mostly all rock.

The gas tank was getting low but the wind was freshening. The direct course south took me between Rabbit Island and Club Island where there were some shingles and some shoals down a few feet and some bare rocks surfacing. My journal recorded 5 p.m. as we slid between the islands with an east-southeast wind giving me some speed on a close reach.

Would like to make the Otter Islands off the tip of the Bruce Peninsula before dark.

On the chart there appeared to be some protected coves between the islands for a hopeful and restful overnight anchorage. I estimated the distance and my speed and believed that I could make it by dark...10 p.m. or so.

I got a text message from Kay saying that she caught a bus heading to Sault Ste Marie. She knew there was a bus to Duluth from there because that was the route she took before to meet me. I'll bet she is a happy girl making some connections toward home; and she is out from under the tyranny of orders from the master of the ship.

While sailing with her, Kay would make some hints to me that now might be a good time to wear a life jacket while sailing. Most times out far from shore, alone, in 40-degree water it makes little sense to me. Sweet Breeze would sail away from me faster than I could ever swim (I was never a strong swimmer.) If she was on autopilot steering and I got tossed overboard. Twenty minutes of consciousness while bobbing in the cold water would only be a hopeless and trying twenty minutes of eternal goodbyes to friends and family and dogs.

However, if I was steering the boat *and* I had remembered to drop the boarding ladder and I got tossed overboard in seas, I would have a chance, a slim chance, of reaching the boat but only if she rounded up into the wind and stalled. I may even be able to board the boat without the ladder, being in that critical moment of knowing that life and death were at hand and then calling upon the untested adrenaline of determined survival.

Last summer in Lake Superior, I practiced boarding both Sweet Breeze and Rover from the water. I wasn't strong and wiry like a 16-year-old but I did manage to board both boats from the water without assistance. I found that if I could hook the back of my foot around a stanchion and with my arms pulling mightily on another stanchion base that I could roll myself up onto the deck, just barely. Good to know that I could do it, but that was in calm seas.

The only way that I could board Rover, the two-masted schooner with her high decks, was to climb the anchor chain until I could hook my foot around a bob-stay chain and keep inching my way up to the bowsprit. That took every ounce of my strength too and could most likely not be done in seas.

My personal thoughts toward safe boating are much like safely driving a car. Don't crash your car and don't get tossed overboard. Concentrate on defensive driving and boating. So far so good. No car crashes or motorcycle crashes and no boating accidents. I really do concentrate on being present and fully aware of my surroundings and immediate hazards. The thousands of miles of motorcycling, and some near crashes, has sharpened my conscious presence to a fine edge, most of the time. Those other times...well, so far so good.

I have added 13 wooden handholds to Sweet Breeze both above and below decks. I can traverse topsides and below, stem to stern, from handhold to handhold always having at least one hand gripping a solid chunk of well-attached oak.

As with most of my sailing days during the last two weeks I was alone on the water. No sailboats or fishing boats. Where was everyone? It was summertime after-all, though colder than most. These were times on the vast open waters when a melancholy mood sometimes touched me.

Journal Entry: Thinking of Marna and Randy Bush and all of the other people I miss. So lucky am I to have dear friends and family. I do Miss Chickie. I pet and scratch and cuddle other peoples' dogs when I meet them. Dogs are great. Most dogs like me—those that don't must be troubled.

Sailing five to six knots now on a close reach. A perfect ride on Georgian Bay—she is kind to me today. If the wind keeps I'll make Otter Island by dark. Don't really want to stay at Lonely Island, just the name I guess. No boats anywhere—all alone on Georgian Bay.

Otto steering perfectly on a close reach heading south.

From the notes in my journal, I can tell now that I must have spent lots of time below after the wind became steady that late afternoon. I would sit or lie on the starboard settee and read, or write in my journal. I wrote three pages that day.

From the berth I could see the magnetic compass that I had installed above the galley stove and would check it occasionally to verify that Otto was holding course. If there were shoals or any bottom hazards within a mile, I would climb topsides every ten minutes or so for a visual check of my surroundings and a position check on the chart plotter.

This day the wind was steady and across the beam and I loved this little boat. She would hold a six knot speed If the waves didn't get too big on a beam reach like this.

Cape Smith was fading away on the north horizon. Otter Island was still not visible to the south at 6 p.m. but if the wind kept east and steady I still felt I could find an anchorage by dark.

My journal writing is legible this day. That means the seas are yet not too rough. Some days my journal scribbles are barely discernible—written in code—the code breaks down to: *Stop writing, go topsides before you get seasick.*

There are times when the cabin of Sweet Breeze seems just too cramped; even for one person there is hardly room to move without bumping into something. If the boat is pitching around there seems to be lots of nearby things to give your hip or your knee or your kidney a bruise. On the other hand, in tight quarters there is not enough room for your body parts to gain enough speed to hit anything too hard.

When I mentioned to Kay a few days ago, that sometimes the cabin seemed a bit tight, even for me, she said she was glad that I was coming to my senses. That 33-foot Glander in Duluth had a roomy cabin and lots of potential as a more comfy live-aboard. Perhaps next summer I could do the "sail to the sea" again in spacious comfort? I wondered if she sailed as well as Sweet Breeze and felt as stiff in a blow? I wondered if maybe I could have a sailing partner if the boat was more roomy and afforded a few more comforts. Ahh, I had a sailing partner right now, she was all I had, she was all I needed, and she was Sweet Breeze.

Fast sailing got faster. I could see the humps of islands ahead; too far away yet to tell which is which. Maybe twenty more miles. I could definitely see Fitzwilliam Island. It was by far the largest of the archipelago that stretched from the tip of the Bruce Peninsula to the southeast tip of Manitoulin Island and across northern Lake Huron. Fitzwilliam was coming up on the right but the whole of Georgian Bay was to my left and the easterlies were pushing up some lumps.

It was astonishing! A huge white ship appeared off the port bow. It looked like a small version of a cruise ship and was heading northwest at what looked like a fast clip. Sweet Breeze wasn't the only boat on Lake Huron!

That sighting gave me a boost, not that I would admit to needing one, but the tedium of twelve hours on the endless cold water with wind and waves and small islands my sole companions; I had a sense of companionship and warmth from that sighting. There must be people on board.

In the fading light, the flashes from the lighthouse on the north tip of Cove Island also gave me a sense of companionship. I could see on the chart plotter that the southeastern tip of Cove Island indeed had a cove that would shelter me from three sides. That became the target of my adjusted heading.

I switched the screen lighting on the chart plotter to the nighttime red so as to save my night vision from the brightness of the daylight screen. It helped but was still too bright.

These were my most anxious times. Entering a rocky, unknown cove in the dark is a time for slow going and cautious approaches. My four cell flashlight would reflect off the above-water rocks and the chart plotter would show me the depth gradient; then the depth meter should get me into ten feet of water, or so, where I could drop a hook. That was my best plan. Not many other options.

The best plan worked well enough and got me within a few feet of shore. The problem that arose was the bottom. It appeared to be much like the nearby shore, a bald rock face dropping to a 40-foot depth just 40-feet offshore. Where was the sand or mud bottom I was looking for? Something for my anchors to grab onto? There would be no sleeping with my anchor sitting on a bald dome of bedrock.

I edged along shore looking for some indication of a holding bottom, then I spotted it in the flashlight beam. There was something floating at the head of the bay. A mooring ball…? How lucky could I be? Voila, eureka, etc. I inched up alongside and could see that it had a heavy one-inch line going down into the crystal clear depths. I followed the heavy line down with the flashlight beam and I sensed (cautiously) that there must be something substantial on the other end.

With relief and a sense of security, I was in for a good night's sleep after all. To be sure, once tied on to the bridle around the mooring ball, I backed Sweet Breeze off hard to see if we could budge whatever was on the other end of that heavy line down in the depths.

I had made a good 63 miles that day. There were gusty winds in the cove but I had to trust that mooring. It was by far my best option. I fixed something special for supper...sardines.

Tobermory to the St. Clair

Saturday, June 22. Up late and refreshed. Two weeks on the water. Sailing off to Tobermory for gas and some walks.

There was a nice wind left over from yesterday so I bent sails for the few miles to a tiny town on the end of the Bruce Peninsula. How gorgeous was this cove in the morning light, where just a few hours ago I had lucked onto a mooring ball in the darkest unknowns and vastness of Lake Huron. The whole area, now in daylight, reminded me of the rugged beauty of the Canadian islands of Lake Superior.

Email Saturday, June 22, 5:44 p.m. At a sweet harbor on the end of the Bruce Peninsula. Tobermory, Ontario.

Sailed across Georgian Bay yesterday with some occasional good winds of 15 knots. We sailed on a close reach at 5-6 knots for hours. Made good about 65 miles. Pulled into an island cove at dark but found a mooring buoy to tie up to for the night. Lucky me, with a rock bottom and gusty winds all night.

Left Tobermory this morn to sail down the east coast of Lake Huron. Thick fog on the lake so I turned back to this lively hamlet for the day. Will try for an early departure tomorrow. Need to make three 50-mile days to reach the outlet river down to Detroit and Lake Erie.

Hope summer is arriving on Lake Superior soon. Warm here on land. Lots of tourists. Will talk again soon.

Curt

Tobermory was a surprise. The bay leading into the town narrowed into a fiord-like finger of water right up into the downtown area. My first stop was the fuel dock on the right where the message said to call Carla, the harbormaster for assistance. She was friendly and pretty and I had to flirt with her...tastefully, I like to think. I couldn't help it. Paid her for fuel and asked if I could stay awhile at a slip dock...if I decided to stay the night I would come back and pay for that too. Carla was helpful and agreeable. Carla...I liked that name, I once had a very special friend named Carla.

What a sweet little town. Tourists everywhere but still it was interesting. It's considered the diving capital of Canada with shipwrecks nearby in some of the clearest waters since Lake Superior. Glass bottomed boats too. All sorts of boats have found ways to separate the summer tourists from some of their dollars.

I had to do some tourist shopping myself. There was a "fair trade" African import store that had some really artful and crafty handmade goods. I bought a carved stone abstract of a circle of figures holding hands that I named "We're All In This Together," one of my favorite recent expressions of unity.

Remember the big white ship that crossed my course yesterday? Well there she was tied up at Tobe. A huge ferryboat that looked nothing like a ferryboat at first glance. The whole bow section opened into a giant maw. When loaded from the stern with many, many cars and trucks and semi-trucks she could pull up tight to an off-load dock and open her huge maw and they could all drive off at South Baymouth on Manitoulin Island...hundreds of cars and trucks. She was that huge. She was the "Chi-cheemaun," meaning "big canoe" in Ojibwe.

With a full tank of gas and my quota of social interaction satisfied for now, we left our temporary dock with some serious intentions of headway down the eastern shore of Huron. Out the harbor, then to the left we motored, out around the first point, then on to Cape Hurd where we ran into a wall of thick fog. Nope...did not want to purposely head out into fog and sail by chart plotter and depth meter onto unknown waters...and motoring, so we couldn't hear other boats. Back to our dock and tourism and Carla we scuttled.

Eureka! I found some fresh homemade fruit pies that the church ladies were selling and bought a blueberry one...my favorite. That should last me about two days, less if I could find Carla and share a piece of pie and some conversation. I asked if

I could join a sidewalk hand-drumming group and we pounded out rhythms to the enjoyment of passers by who stopped to listen and occasionally move some part of their body to the throbbing of our rhythms. An interest in drumming must have came from some past life of mine...it was easy and natural for me. With a hand drum between my knees and an appreciative, smiling sidewalk audience, I felt more like a Tobermorian than a tourist.

I was fascinated watching the tourists. Most spoke a language that I didn't know and had brown skin. Pakistani and Asian Canadians perhaps. Whole families and lots of little kids, heading out the dock for boat rides, packing shopping bags with their treasures...like tourists everywhere.

Sunday, June 23. Up early, foggy, back to sleep.

It was 8 a.m. before we headed out into Lake Huron. The fog was thinning but still present. Port Elgin, the next safe harbor down the east coast was a 60-mile sail so go we must if we were to make port by dark.

Light fog swirled around us through the rocky channels to Cape Hurd and out into the main body of Lake Huron. I watched the depth meter closely as we followed the marked channel through the shoal and rock shelves. When we entered the main body of the lake the depth meter went blank—I think it only reads down to 300 feet. Fog was lurking around the corner of the point.

The fog was dense all morning out on the lake, on placid water, so I broadcasted periodic position warnings on the VHF and practiced blowing the conch shell warning horn in the fog; visibility maybe 100 yards. The fog would thin and I would get my hopes up, then it would so subtly sneak back, wrap around us and shut us in. Fog makes the world seem small and immediate.

One sailboat responded on the radio with a position fix and a short chat. They were about five miles away and heading north, closer to shore than were we.

The wind finally picked up but was on the nose. Fog as thick as ever or thicker. Hoisted the mains'l to dampen boat motion as waves were building. Tried to keep vigilant, staring off into the fog where the water surface melded with the air. There was no horizon. Liquid air and liquid water just blended and blurred into an open gray oneness.

We had a visitor. My dock mate at Tobermory, a power boater, saw me on his radar screen and came over to check us out. We chatted on the radio and I thanked him for checking on me.

More fog. Navigating by the chart plotter and feeling confident in its accuracy and function. What other choices do I have? More slow going. The wind begins with earnest now and the fog thins. I could see glimpses of land some five miles to the east, off the port beam. First time I could see land since rounding Cape Hurd several hours ago.

With the afternoon, the wind and waves and the boat's speed steadily increased. Sailing fast on a close reach again. Some young fellas heading south from a Tobermory weekend drew close to make visual contact to see If I was okay in the heavy seas. They had a big powerboat and I waved them away as if to say, "All okay here." They were lurching and crashing into the waves and I felt that I was more secure under sail than they were under power. Sails were providing me with not only forward power, but they provided stability as well. I was glad I was on Sweet Breeze—speed be damned. We were getting tossed around too, but nothing like the pounding of that big power cruiser. Sweet Breeze would lean way over and ride the wave up and then down. She rode the waves more like a sea gull. The powerboat was trying to push the waves out of the way. They were good boys to come and check on me, and I hoped *they* would be okay if it got rougher yet.

I think I held my course at about five miles out from the shore. The charts showed the near shore waters to be full of bottom hazards. Today's waves and contact with any hazards would have been disaster for sure. The waves were fetching up from the southwest and there was a lot of lake down there, a hundred miles at least.

The speed was satisfying. The waves kept me busy. Some waves were breaking at their high centers and I tried to steer around the froth. Mostly I was keeping dry at the helm, sometimes I would get a cold face full, but real sailors don't need a dodger, I guess. Another hour or two of this and I could rest easy at Port Elgin.

We pulled into a quiet harbor full of big and expensive boats, Port Elgin, Ontario, at 6 p.m. Filled gas tank and paid up for dockage for the night. It was a hot evening and a warm shower was in order. There was a nice little restaurant at the marina but the menu was mostly burgers and dogs and french fries...couldn't do it.

Just down the dock were the young guys who veered off course to come and check on me out on the big seas that afternoon. They were having a beer or three or four and had some pretty young women in bikinis as guests. I wondered how they could afford a boat such as they had. I chatted with them a bit. They were talking about their rough ride in their big cruiser. I remember teasingly telling them, "Good that I was out there single-handing in case they got in trouble." They didn't know if I was kidding or not...neither did I.

I had sardines for supper.

Monday, June 24. Underway at 5:30 a.m. for Goderich harbor 60 miles down the coast. Good breeze but on the nose again.

Motor sailing again. Tacking off course to try to fill the main and gain some of that free and current energy from the sun. That's right, wind energy is really solar energy in a different form. All energy comes from the sun. Air currents, wind, weather of all kinds are an effect of the sun's rays heating air and water and land.

I would rather use current sunlight and heat than use stored sunlight; that's what I filled my gas tank with yesterday—stored sunlight, ancient sunlight once locked away underground as petroleum. No, I'm not perfect. I wish all of the energy that I used was current sunlight, but lo, I burn petroleum, therefore I am.

Not sure what the forecast is for wind conditions yet. Weather Canada broadcasts in French and I am sooo lame with French. Sooner or later I will catch a forecast in English. I thought I heard something about 30 kilometer winds; that would be just like yesterday's sail. Hmm.

Last evening dockside, I wrote a long and interesting (I thought) and maybe even clever email to all the friends back home about the fast and wet sail down Lake Huron yesterday. Just as I was about to hit send the wi-fi router at the marina went out and I lost the message before it was sent and the hellwithit! Damn technology shit. Sorry, I meant to keep this a family G-rated book but It happens all too often at marinas. "Sure, we have wi-fi...here's the username and password." I am hearing that all too often and all too often it just doesn't work worth a damn.

I hear that a lot of Scandinavian and European nations have broadband Internet service and it is accessible to everyone and just about everywhere. "Ya, but that sounds like socialism!" Ya, but capitalism doesn't work worth a damn for some services. Okay, I had to get it out. I'll try not to get so political. Like hell I will! Sweet Breeze has her moods and so do I. Bad moods can easily be triggered by G.A.S., my own acronym for "gadget anxiety syndrome". Don't let G.A.S. get you! It got me last evening.

Otto is not working well this morning. Otto is my crew. Perhaps he didn't sleep as well as I did. He is getting his directions confused and stalls out. I need him healthy and will give him a long rest today. I can't be tied to the tiller on these twelve-hour sailing days.

Otto is the whole self-steering system but mostly I think of him as the linear-actuator, a big word for the servo-electric gadget that hooks to the tiller and steers the boat for me so I can do other useful things like cook or take a cat nap.

I unplugged Otto and while he was resting I rigged up the sheet-to-tiller steering lines and pulleys. We got a heading on a close reach again with the mainsheet tension moving the tiller just a bit to keep that heading. It was set up for the port tack; 220 degrees was our heading; my steering line system steered from 6 a.m. until 11 a.m. without me touching the tiller, no kidding.

The self-steering was freeing me up and I fell into a rehash of what I had learned at the marina last night. The reason that the young guys at Port Elgin could afford $100,000+ power boats to play with on weekends seemed to be the high paying jobs at the big nuclear power plant just down the coast. My dockside boating neighbor seemed to think that if the power plant were to shut down there would be lots of 40-foot power cruisers for sale real cheap. I'm sure he was right.

On checking in the bilge, there seemed to be more water than the usual inch or so at the lowest point. I hadn't pumped it for a few days but there was definitely more water than the piddly amount I was used to seeing. Hmm? I knew there was a small leak at the thru-hull fitting for the sacrificial zinc...that chunk of metal bolted onto the outside of the hull that is supposed to be eaten away by electrolysis, instead of other critical hardware parts, when a boat is in saltwater and acting something like a floating wet cell battery. That leak entered through the floor of the closet and was mostly tiny and insignificant. It still was, when I rechecked. Something else must be leaking. Hmm?

The long tack that we were on was taking us far out onto the main body of Lake Huron. The steady wind created some not so steady waves but nothing like yesterday.

It was cold out on the lake and I was spending a lot of time down in the cabin to stay out of the chilling wind. I noticed my hands were a bit shaky today. I attributed that to the hard sail yesterday and extreme grip that I had to use on lines when sail handling. I promised myself that I would use the rubberized gripping gloves so that I didn't have to squeeze so hard to grip the sheets or halyards. Also, there was a bit of a run-down feeling plaguing me today. Probably expended more anxious energy yesterday than I cared to admit. Queasy stomach feelings too but that was probably just because I was below in the cabin in seas. Such was my physical inventory that day after 2 and one half weeks on the water. I was okay though. Probably even better than that.

No shipping lanes were nearby. Nothing but water as far as I could see. Won't be in sight of land until I make the long starboard tack toward Goderich. That easting should get me better speed with full sails and wind on the beam. I would need the speed to reach Goderich before dark.

I have put on my gray, rain and weather protection jacket. It blocks the wind but it simply has too much Velcro. Sometimes it sticks to wool or to fuzzy control lines. Sometimes the jacket sticks to itself. Sometimes I can't get at the front zipper until I get all of that secondary flap closure un-Velcroed and out of the way. The more Velcro, the more I feel like clothing is getting way too complicated. I think that clothing items with Velcro strips everywhere are becoming a fashion statement or a supposed indication of quality. Whatever happened to good quality brass snaps? I suppose if I were trekking to the South Pole the Velcro type closures would be a welcome way to keep the wind out, but this jacket has just way too much hook-and-loop and elastic strings and plastic zippers. I wonder how Eskimos ever survived without Velcro. Animal skins and furs sewn with sinew...come on, how could that have worked?

I love the little Velcro strap on the back of my cap though. It allows me an infinite number of adjustment sizes to fit my head, even when my head gets a little swollen on a minor rant, like now.

Sweet Breeze is taking the waves on her right shoulder now as we have made the 90-degree tack toward Goderich and the east shore. I am staying below as much as I feel I safely can. The wind is cold and I am getting very red in the face from the bright sun. Re-rigged the self-steering for the starboard tack toward shore. Looks like 18 miles to Goderich.

I have taken two motion sickness pills over two hours. I'm so drowsy I can almost fall asleep standing. If I sit. I am out in seconds. Maybe I sleep for a minute or two or 30 seconds, but it feels good. Damn drugs. Made some hot and strong black tea to try to regain consciousness.

Took Otto apart and cleaned and greased the long screw mechanism that is attached to the servo-motor. Everything looked to be in good condition. Maybe it is the fluxgate compass that is faulty. Must check that too. I think I have brought a spare. That's the compass that gives Otto the direction, by electrical impulses, in which to steer. One time Otto was having a really bad day and wanted to steer the boat in circles. I discovered that I had stowed a tool bag full of steel wrenches near the fluxgate compass. How quickly I apologized to Otto that time.

Thinking back to the young women at the fuel dock at Port Elgin yesterday. Wonderful service...they were waiting for me to help dock-up. Maybe I had called ahead on the radio...I forget. They were learning how to capture the working end of a tossed dock line and make a secure knot to the cleat on the dock. I am sometimes a knot challenged sailor so I am never too quick to correct or criticize. After they had tied me (Sweet Breeze) up and went back to the gas pump for the long hose on the big reel, I quickly re-tied their cleat knots so as not to embarrass them. It was one knot that I felt that I knew. It reminded me of a quip I had heard on a Caribbean sail some years ago, "If you don't know knots, tie lots."

One of the girls would not smile. I teased, I cajoled, I quipped. She was exceptionally pretty and way too intense. I gave up. She would have to smile in her own sweet time. Maybe she would mellow with age...like me.

Nine miles out of Goderich now. Sweet Breeze is self-steering again with balanced sails and a lashed helm. What a sweet and secure little boat. There is a south wind, straight up the lake.

The industrial side of the harbor at Goderich was interesting with freighters and tugs tied up, but there was no marina for transients like me. My chart showed a public marina called Snug Harbor but it looked like it was closed. The name Snug Harbor, had beckoned me with visions of a restful night. Teen age kids were jumping and diving off a high jetty and I remember hoping there was no big chunk of industrial junk down there sticking up from the bottom.

Back out into the lake and around the break-wall to the north, I spotted some marker buoys and a powerboat that was headed inland up the Maitland River. The marina channel (I could see the forest of masts) opened up and split off from the main river. It was late but there was still an attendant at the fuel dock. We topped off Sweet Breeze's tanks and I turned in early...didn't use the power (hydro they call it), or the shower, just wanted sleep.

Tuesday, June 2. Today is my son Randy's 45th birthday. Wow! How old that makes me seem in numbers, but not in age or health. I feel pretty young and able at 63.

I left the marina before tea even. Today I wanted to make some real miles if I could. If the wind was right and stiff enough I thought I might make Sarnia and the St. Claire River at the southernmost tip of Lake Huron. It would be about 60 miles on a straight course from Goderich but the forecast predicted south winds again. Darn. Maybe they would be wrong; it happens often enough.

The harbor and marina did not seem pleasant at Goderich. Maybe it was just my mood. Maybe it was the ugliness of the industrial harbor on one side. I probably shouldn't be so fussy about my campsites for the night. I'm not canoeing in the

Boundary Waters after all. Safe harbors are always good to find before dark. After dark too.

The city of Goderich is known as one of the prettiest towns in all of Canada. I probably should have walked up the hill and explored but my mission was becoming more about making headway. Somehow I did not feel like I was making good enough time to get to salt water and back to Minnesota by September to be with my daughter and granddaughter who were coming for a visit from Germany.

I learned later that there is a huge underground salt mine at Goderich, the largest such mine in the world. That must have been what the big freighters were carrying from the harbor. The mine was deep and reached out under Lake Huron. Sounds dangerous to me. It brings to mind the iron ore mine near Crosby, Minnesota that I had read about. They were also mining ore under a lake but the ceiling of the mine gave way and the miners were trapped and drowned as the lake rushed down into the mine and filled it.

Think about what a catastrophe it would be if Lake Huron slipped into the huge underground cavity of the salt mine. It would not only be the end of the miners but it might make a salt sea out of Lake Huron and the waters downstream. Too scary to imagine.

I'm afraid that I don't have much faith in mining companies. Historically, the records show short-term jobs at mining locations, exploitative short-term profit motives and long term environmental consequences at *all* mining locations.

I wonder if this is where the salt comes from that arrives in the Duluth harbor by the boatload. The salt that is loaded onto trucks and scattered upon winter roads to melt snow, rust away cars and the steel beams under highway bridges; run off the roadways with the spring rains and pollute fresh water...there I go, wondering again. I have to say, scattering salt about on roads is just about the dumbest thing that we humans have come up with yet. Earlier "civilizations", when warring with their neighbors, learned to salt the cropland, essentially killing the soil for a few years, thereby starving out those who were considered enemies.

I guess I must be a long-term thinker and lover of the planet. I know I'm not a lover of money. That's probably why I'm sailing and seeing and learning and not working in a salt mine.

Thinking of sailing straight across Lake Huron if the wind is reasonably stiff from the south, though I hate to go west when my goal is somewhere to the east. I just don't want to motor all day. So far I am making some headway south as the wind is veering to the west. We are holding a four-knot speed at a heading of 150 degrees. The water sounds and the near silence are a simple, soothing pleasure for me. The old Atomic Four engine runs flawlessly but I would love for it to have a long rest.

I am determined not to take any drugs today for motion no matter how rough it gets. Yesterday they made me so drowsy I could have fallen asleep and slid over the side without waking.

I'm looking at some of the things that I love the most on this boat. Chickie's wool blanket on the port settee. I can put things on it and they stay put, unlike the plastic fabric blankets, polyesters and such. It still has a coating of her soft, downy hair, but that just adds to the wool of the sheep. The laughing photo of my newest granddaughter makes me smile every time I look upon it. The whole boat is a dream to sail; so easy and forgiving. I love this boat. GOOD MORNING LAKE HURON!

Otto is steering well this morning. The sun is peeking through some clouds. I love to sit below and write my thoughts in the journal while Sweet Breeze carries on, as though she knows the plan without my interference.

I'm noticing lots of chores that could use some attention. Somehow a bunch of socks wound up on the floor of the head and are wet. They were clean socks too. Must have flown across the aisle from the closet yesterday. Not a problem. Need to wash clothes anyhow.

Washing clothing is easy. I tie or clip the articles of clothing onto a line and trail them behind the boat for an hour or so. Then I haul them in and wring them out and clip them to the lifelines until dry. How easy is that? No soap in the lake. A wind powered washing agitator.

The fridge is getting smelly. It's time to empty it out and wipe down the inside and load it up again. Humidity builds up or condenses inside and some bacteria must find it a cozy place to cohabitate and multiply.

There is a hook on the wall of the head for clothing that looks to be in a dangerous place. Given the most unlucky heave at the most unlucky time a sailor could be tossed into that hook and some most unlucky injury could result. That hook must go.

Wind quit. Motor-sailing again. We will never make Sarnia at this rate. Noonish... wind starting up again. Setting up sheet-to-tiller steering again. Tacking west toward the Michigan shore. West is the wrong direction but at least we are under wind power.

The sheet-to-tiller steering is working well again as the breeze becomes steady. I hope Otto cannot guess my thoughts because in a steady wind I like the sheet-to-tiller self-steering better than the autopilot. It needs no electric power and makes no noise and seems like such a natural and effortless, almost magical method of minding the helm.

On bright days like today the solar panel has provided enough electricity to power the autopilot, the fridge, the VHF radio and the chart plotter. It still doesn't make up for all of the gas that I have been burning over the last two weeks but it is a significant complement to our energy usage.

I'll never make it to the end of the lake by dark at these speeds. Three to five knots of speed while sailing; not much, but quieter and more synchronous with the mood of the lake than motoring.

Grand Bend, Ontario is only eight miles away. It looks like the chart plotter shows a marina there but I hate to stop so early. Sweet Breeze has been sailing the rhumb line today for 30 miles on sheet-to-tiller self-steering with a few infrequent adjustments. I got some housecleaning chores done and some thinking done and a few more miles so Grand Bend it is.

Email Tuesday, June 25, 2013 at 4:38 p.m. Today I really did sail...not far, 45 miles to

Grand bend on the southeast shore of Lake Huron. Wind was on the nose at first this morn but she bent to the southwest and we picked her up on a close reach for about 30 miles. It was steady and not so variable, as has been the norm.

Having a spinach salad, really. My fresh veggie supply is almost gone so I must either walk to town or get into the canned goods stored on board. I think the walk is the better choice.

I left Goderich early this morn, the harbor of which was an industrial site with the largest salt mine in Canada shipping salt out from there.

We, Sweet Breeze and I, are at a lovely harbor now at Grand Bend, Ontario. They don't get much nicer than this. Bob, the harbormaster, gave me a cold beer and a cut-rate price after I whined about how broke I will be by the time I reach salt water paying 50 bucks a night.

This is the first good wi-fi connection I have had in a few days. I have lots to tell you but you will have to read the book. Tomorrow the St. Clair River leading past Detroit and down to lake Erie, but first I want to meet up with Shane and Mary and two kids who also left from Duluth and are on their way sailing to Australia. And I thought I was on an adventure.

Best to all of you; fair winds have put me in fine spirits.
Curt.

This is one of the nicest marinas ever! Bob, the harbormaster, got me an ice cold beer from his cooler. It was shaped just like a bottle of beer only it wasn't glass, it was aluminum. What will the Canadians think of next? More friendly people dropping by on their afternoon walks checking out the boats and asking me where I might be from. Most are amazed when I tell them.

Grand Bend looks to be the consummate boating community. The river goes inland way beyond the marina and is lined on both banks with boats and boat-houses and waterfront homes and winds its way for blocks. Big shade trees also line the banks, and are in the backyards of the homes that have porches and decks overlooking the river. One could sit and watch boats pass by for hours on a lazy summer afternoon. I could almost live in this little city and that says a lot, coming from a country boy.

The grocery store was about a mile away. Just the right distance for some exercise and sightseeing. A small backpack and a couple of reusable cloth sacks with sturdy hand loops would contain all the food that I could comfortably carry back. My little sailing ship became reprovisioned with blueberries, some veggies and some necessary cookies.

Wednesday, June 26. Tea on the lake at about 7:00 a.m. Forty miles to Sarnia and the start of the St. Clair River. Motored out into the lake looking for wind. Long sandy beaches here near the bottom end of Lake Huron.

Remember the dockside gent back at Grand Marais, Michigan who told me about a family from Duluth who stopped at Grand Marais and were sailing their way to Australia? Well, I found a way to contact them through some friends in Duluth. They were, at this moment, at a marina in downtown Detroit.

Shane and I talked a bit on cell phones and I liked him immediately. They had left Duluth a week ahead of me but I was hoping that I could catch them at some point. Maybe that was why I was always trying to maximize my daily sailing progress. I wanted to meet them. I wanted to hear their story. They were at a marina on the waterfront in downtown Detroit.

Detroit was about two days sailing away but they were having a layover of a few days while some family connections were being made. I learned from Shane where they were moored and the name of the marina. I was looking forward to meeting them...folks from home, adventurers.

After a few hours of motor sailing to get out around the extensive shoaling at Kettle Point, the wind picked up enough to tempt me to get off my butt and get some sails pulling. Twenty-five miles of sailing to the start of the river would do my spirits good; no more of the droning sound of the motor and I could re-engage with the simple, quiet joy of sailing. This was a sailboat after all.

I could see the Michigan shoreline now after nine days of sailing in Canadian waters and overnights at Canadian ports of call. If it weren't for a line drawn on a map, how would I know? I wish there were no nation states.

Why do we humans find it necessary to draw boundaries between peoples? It must have to do with fear or possessiveness. What if we had only the United Peoples Republic of North America? I suppose it might be a bit cumbersome to govern, being so large and diverse. But think of all the different ideas that could meld together, "in order to form a more perfect union." We would need no border guards or customs officials and could come and go as we pleased, north to south, east to west. Folks in Mexico might be talking "Minnesotan." Manitobans would be speaking "Alabaman;" or maybe not.

Sailboats were capturing some early afternoon wind at the very bottom of this huge lake. I welcomed the sight of sailboats out on the water. We followed a lake freighter and the marker buoys toward the entrance of the St. Clair River. This was getting exciting for me. I loved the intimacy of the near shores after days of sailing beyond sight of land...those days when fog or distance allowed water and sky my only vistas.

Port Edward, Ontario on the left bank. Port Huron, Michigan on the right bank; and now I feel the pull of the current as the lake narrows suddenly into a river channel. Over ground, our speed quickly increased to 9.6 knots. That was the fastest I had ever gone in a sailboat (a few weeks ahead in another river I would exceed that speed by almost two knots).

Down the St. Clair:

Sarnia, Ontario looks so modern with those tall buildings, all dark glass fascias. Port Huron, on the right bank has some nicely done waterfront parks with folks in business dress having lunch or walking and talking on their cell phones.

Power boaters fly by with not a thought about what their wake does to Sweet

Breeze. Some of those long, narrow, fast ones with the big V-8 engines are so loud that I can hear their roar for miles even with my damaged hearing. Does our auditory space have no privilege? Times like this cause me to wish that gasoline was rare and cost about 40 dollars a gallon and motor sports of all kinds became but a memory, lost in history. True, without gas I might still be back in Lake Superior or in the Thousand Islands of Lake Huron, but why would I care if it took two summers instead of one to reach the sea, or wherever it would be that this particular adventure might end.

So much to look at. My head is turning like an owl. Oil refineries on the left. Power plants on the right. Interesting shoreline development of all kinds...not always pretty, but interesting.

Leaving the cities and most of the industrial sites behind, the shores have become the chosen personal development plots for folks who must have money by the ton. These are not just waterfront homes. These are personal expressions of great wealth. These are statements that shout of an arrival into the unsustainable world of conspicuous consumption. The boathouses at the shoreline are nothing I could afford to build or rent for the night even. I think the guys mowing the broad lawns are most likely not the homeowners. I wonder if the homeowners ever thought to raise goats instead? They would mow the grass and fertilize at the same time.

Perhaps there has been a silent, but not too subtle competition between the U.S. shore and the Canadian shore for which river bank shall display the grandest of homes, you know, like Christmas lighting displays on neighboring homes in a Midwestern town? It looks to me like a toss-up. I could judge no clear winner as I sailed by with the swift current of the St. Clair doubling our sail speed. I do wonder where all the money comes from...Detroit, before the fall? These are probably not the homes of the power plant or the oil refinery workers upstream, those men and women who do the productive work everyday that we all depend on? Just a wild guess on my part. It sure makes for great sightseeing though, for a backwoods sailor like me.

Jet skis zoom by. Mom, dad, and both kids behind. I shouldn't be so cynical. When I was a kid I would have loved to do that. I remember the thrill of a ride behind my brother on his old BSA Lighting, which today is a real classic motorcycle. I thought then, it was as fast as lightning and it had that throaty deep rumble of power that made a ten year old boy feel mighty proud, hoping my buddies would see me rumble by on the back roads clutching the back of my big brother.

Sometimes I just wish that we, as a society would grow up. I think I have in some ways. Loud and fast are no longer my preferred ways of travel. I don't fly in planes anymore. I drive my little truck at below the upper speed limit and above the lower one. Still, I hope that someday soon, cheap oil will be history. Forty dollars a gallon for gas would clean things up and quiet things down. Perhaps we would learn to ride with one another again, converse, plan ahead, slow down, enjoy the journey.

The huge power plant on the Canadian shore is belching out some yellow smoke. That's not a healthy looking color for smoke. It may mean sulfur emissions or unburned carbon? Whatever it means, it does not look healthy. I guess if the stack is high like that one, the bad stuff will dissipate downwind and fall somewhere "else".

The immense power plant on the U.S. shore looks dead, closed, no activity. Perhaps it had supplied power to the huge automobile manufacturing plants at Detroit, or Flint, or Saginaw, which are also dead, closed, no activity. Those are the towns where cars and their various parts were manufactured before they moved to "greener" pastures. Pastures in Mexico or the southern states where lower wages for the workers would not mean a better car or even a lower priced car, it would simply redirect the cash flow within the corporation; greater profit to fewer people... higher dividends for the stockholders. The American way, in a post-Reagan economy.

I wonder if it's just a coincidence that those three abandoned Michigan cities that built GM and Ford are now holding top honors as the most violent, crime ridden, dangerous cities in the U.S. Maybe I should just sail more and wonder about such things less. Don't misunderstand, these thoughts don't trouble me, but awareness is important. Looking at our culture with the critical eye of long-range thinking is our earthly responsibility.

An hour ago a big freighter snuck up on us from behind. It is quite a surprise to casually check the view behind and be looking up at the prow of a ship. I must have been doing too much "wondering" again.

We are not needing anything but rest tonight so at about 7 p.m. on this gorgeous evening we are dropping anchor. The strength of the current will keep us pointed upstream. There is a park on the Michigan shore where picnickers are gathered. I momentarily sensed a longing feeling to join them and lay in the grass.

I thought it prudent to double check to make sure that we were anchored well out of the shipping lanes. It was time for a big salad and some chart study. There were lots of possible channels downstream leading to Lake St. Claire. The backwater channels looked so inviting and narrow, remote and intimate. I only wanted to make sure that my choice of channels was deep enough. I studied Chenal Ecarte on the Canadian side closely, then chickened out and decided to stay in the main shipping channel called the South Channel on the charts.

Thursday, June 27. Drizzle and fog. Gotta wait out the fog. Gotta see the sights and look out for ships.

While topsides reading the trip log for distance traveled so far, (974 miles) a ship slid by in the fog less than 100 yards off the larboard beam (old term for left side). I hardly heard a thing; just the low rumbling thump of the engines as she slipped by in the fog. It appeared like a ghost.

Ship's horns are growling out a warning up and down the river. Dense fog. Think I'll stay put awhile.

The AIS screen says that the Michipicoten is two miles downstream. That's the same freighter that I called up on the VHF for a radio check and a radar check up by Whitefish Point on Lake Superior. She was heading west then. Next I saw it heading down the St Marys River below the Soo locks. Now it is powering up the St. Claire in the fog against a two-knot current. Soon I'll listen for the low thump of her engines as she draws alongside and past my anchorage. That old gray and rust colored laker puts on lots and lots of miles. I'll bet she has some stories to tell.

Sweet Breeze is having a birthday party today. She is 52 years old this year and I think today was the day she was launched. Well, perhaps I'm just looking for a special occasion to praise her for our successful crossing of the second great lake. I don't know how to treat her special this day. She doesn't ask for much and she gives so much. But she is special and such a low maintenance friend. A friend once told me not to love anything that can't love you back...but maybe she does love me back or maybe she is the exception.

I am determined that this digital camera does not give me G.A.S. (gadget anxiety syndrome). All I would like to do is take a simple fucking photo of a lake freighter slipping through the fog. It has so damn many buttons and screens and icons and symbols that mean nothing to me. What a complex piece of crap. Fuckin' gadgets. It will not break my sense of peace this fine, foggy morning. Capitalist, consumer shit, stay away from me.

I've been searching for an FM radio station to listen to. Perhaps I should catch up on the news I thought. I haven't really heard any news for three weeks. I guess the world is probably doing okay even when I am not paying attention.

Hoping to find a public radio station because I don't think I can listen to the mindless, anxious chatter of the commercial stations. I'm wondering again...does the fast-talking and excited tone of the announcers really create the desire to buy the crap they are promoting? The only thing it creates in me is the desire to change the station.

As best I can remember, I couldn't find anything worth listening to so I started to fiddle with the AIS on the VHF (don't you hate acronyms?). I set the AIS range to two miles to warn me of nearby ships but if I set forth in the fog I think that a collision would most likely be with a fast flying sport-fishing boat. I wonder why they are in such a hurry; especially in the fog, isn't fishing supposed to be relaxing...never-mind, there I go wondering...*again!*

My conch shell horn was going to be my main warning system if I weighed anchor now. But why hurry off now, with scenery on the banks so interesting, and philosophically stimulating, why miss it in the fog? Even if my view is through the eyes of a complete cynic lately, it is still a view that stimulates more interest than the recent hours and days of open water sailing out on Lake Huron. Out on the open lake I was always squinting out at the horizon looking for land, or a boat, or anything... here was a shoreline so close I could almost reach out and touch it in the narrowest of channels. The forests, the marshes, the homes of people just like me, well sorta like me...all were fascinating.

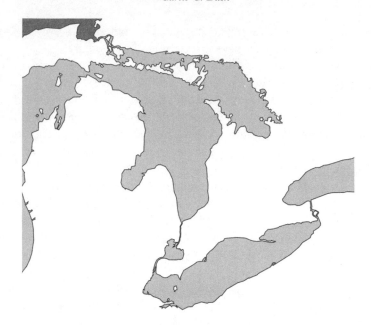

Lake Huron to Lake Erie via Lake St. Claire.

We weighed anchor at about 10 a.m. and slid out silently into the main channel. Yup, I chickened out. The Chenal Ecarte looked so intriguing. It was a waterway that left the main channel of the Flueve de Rue Claire just a few miles upstream from Lake St. Claire and wound around and through what may have been forest and marshland to the east...those intimate natural places where small boats and canoes can silently course among long legged birds, muskrats, and cattails.

That was how I imagined the Chenal Ecarte. Where it entered Lake St. Claire however, the paper chart showed vast mud or sand flats that could have meant a miles long backtrack if there were no marked channel through the flats and out onto the lake.

Sweet Breeze and I decided that the main channel was our most certain route to the sea though we did step off the main channel for a few miles at Southeast Bend, a big old curve of the big old river. This took us back to the U.S. shoreline where the sun was trying to show itself and the brightness penetrating the fog was most welcome. It was solid homes along the bank with lawns down to the water's edge.

My olfactory memory, being one of the body and brain's best recording devices, recognized the wafts of a chemical that drifted to me on the breeze. It's called 2-4-D and is a chemical poison that is sprayed all around the world to "control" broad-leaf plants. On lawns it will kill dandelions and plantains, probably earthworms and bugs and who knows what else. It has a peculiar sweet smell that I remember from my days of playing golf, where it was a staple in the arsenal of chemicals that most golf courses use. I remembered the smell from the roadside ditches that were sprayed with the herbicide to kill back brush.

You can't fool my nose. Here it was sprayed on lawns, for appearance sake, without the knowledge or concern for where it would end up during heavy rain events. A very close chemical cousin of 2-4-D called 2-4-5-T, was mixed with 2-4-D and was sprayed by airplane over the tropical rainforests of Vietnam to kill the forests. It was commonly called Agent Orange, was sprayed by the tons and some American soldiers and tens of thousands of horribly disfigured Vietnamese adults and children carry the chemical in their systems. How foolish must we humans be to devise chemicals that disrupt the most precious of life giving processes...*photosynthesis*. It's one of the most widely used plant killers in the world...still.

More thoughts entertain me (plague me?) as I motor-sail down the old South Channel of the St. Claire. Again it's the homes on the riverbanks. Why so big? What's this all about? Several families could fit comfortably into any one of those homes. Could the homeowner's even imagine the peace and comfort and secure feeling of my ten by twelve foot cabin? Would their ego fit into my cabin?

The houses are crying out to me, expressing the personality of those who dwell there. Are the homes, I wonder, a manifestation of one's ego or of one's spirit? Am I to admire their homes or am I to suspect that on moral grounds, they are living lives as though they believe there are no limits to what they deserve, or no end to this planet's resources? Is one's self-worth here expressed in square feet of living space?

Where are the homeowners? I see no one enjoying the decks, the lawns and gardens, the waterside docks and boats. I see only those who appear to be landscape workers with lawn mowers or wheelbarrows. For miles I have seen no people except workers. It's a gorgeous midsummer day. Are they behind closed doors in air-conditioned spaces? I wonder. Are they off at the office working to pay for all this? Where are the kids? Wouldn't they rather be on a sailing adventure to who knows where?

Interspersed, occasionally, are modest older homes, riverside cabins even, from bygone days of getting away from it all. I wonder if those older homeowners now think of themselves as small and inadequate?

I remember now: this book is supposed to be a memoir of adventure, not a treatise on ways to live, "as if the earth really mattered." Maybe we sailors have too much time to think.

We are entering the St. Claire flats now, where the river slows and deposits its billions and trillions of tiny carried particles which, in a few thousand years have built up into a broadly braided channel that we call a delta. This is the largest delta in the Great Lakes system and as the waters blend into Lake St. Claire the waters very gradually deepen and the sail-boater must be aware of his position with regard to the alignment of channel markers.

There behind some trees...perhaps a marina with gas. It would be my last chance for fuel before entering the lake for a 20-mile crossing. I should fill the tank in case Lake St. Claire has no wind. Alas, it was not a marina but a private boat storage area for the locals.

Some have said that Lake St. Claire should be considered as one of the Great Lakes. I guess it wasn't quite great enough but it is an interesting body of water. Too far to see across from the low decks of Sweet Breeze, too shallow in places to dare lose track of one's position or heading. Well, *I* think it is a great lake, though the water is not crystal clear like Lake Huron, but rather has that very light green opacity of midsummer small lakes, abloom with microscopic life.

It seems strange to see so large a body of water with marker buoys as far as I can see. They show the freighters the boundaries of the 27-foot-deep dug channel down the center of the lake leading to the Detroit River, leading down to Lake Erie. We need to stay within the channel as we enter this vast inland sea. She is a broad and shallow sea, with average depths outside of the shipping channel only around twelve feet.

We have less than half a tank of gas so we need some wind to get to Detroit. There is light wind from the southwest so we will be close hauled again with the sails as flat as I can stretch them; tacking way outside the shipping channel but paying close attention to position and bottom hazards. 'Twas a gorgeous day; bright, warm, light breeze—life is very good.

I must have been feeling good with the world as there was another sailboat crossing the lake and I wanted to try keep up with them...no, I wanted to beat them to the beginning of the Detroit River.

The skyline of Detroit is impressive, even from 20 miles away. If only I could find the marina where Shane and Mary are staying...the family sailing to Australia. One thing that helps to locate sailors are the boats and more specifically the masts. I'm always on the lookout for that friendly forest of masts and the usually friendly sailors aboard.

There were big black clouds boiling up in the western sky and I would have loved to have settled into a protected place before the storm blew in. It was just starting to blow. I remember watching the skyward developments with a feeling of haste. It looked like some real weather was imminent.

There was a yacht club on the right with a whole fleet of those little catboats that kids learned to sail on. It looked like the race was over or called off, probably at the discretion of the instructors in the powerboat. The fleet was being herded back into the marina. They were gathering their flock and heading for shore.

Just upstream from the downtown areas of Detroit on the right and Windsor, Ontario on the left, the river divides around Belle Isle. The right channel had some marinas, according to the chart, and I pulled into one that had fuel. We gassed up fast and got some instructions on how to find the marina downtown where Shane and family were staying for a few days. There was a bridge ahead downstream with low clearance and the helpful local gent said that Sweet Breeze was too tall to clear. We would need to go back upstream and around Belle Isle and back into the main channel, then, he said to look for the lighthouse on the harbor front. The marina was located right next to the lighthouse.

With one eye to the sky and one to the depth meter we got both motor and sails pulling back upstream. Around the sand bar at the head of the island we hurried, trying to make the best time we could down the Fleming Channel toward downtown

Motown. There was no place to hide out from the storm along the three-mile Belle Isle shoreline but the wind was brisk and we were making some fast tracks.

I have this aversion toward getting soaked in a downpour. I also have this aversion toward getting blown onto a lee shore in a thunderstorm. Always looking for alternatives, my best chance to survive a really big blow here in the river seemed to be to stay near the windward shore and motor about to keep pointed into the wind until it blew itself out, but until it arrived I was on a beeline for downtown.

Still no rain, just a few of those tell tale big heavy drops. Around the lower end of the island and across the river I could see a lighthouse. I had to get right up close to the harbor front to pick out just a very few masts against a backdrop of warehouses. Then I spotted the sign and the tiny slip giving access to the marina.

Shane's boat was a Pacific Seacraft, a model that I could easily recognize for its uniqueness. I saw this big guy near the boat and gave a shout, "Shane, give me a hand docking?" He was taken aback, that someone knew his name out of nowhere, but only for a second.

We were like old friends meeting up again for the very first time. I liked him immediately, but I knew that I would from our phone conversations. Rain was starting to get serious about getting us soaked so we buttoned up our boats and fell into our cabins and agreed to get together when the storm blew over.

While below fixing supper, I dutifully remembered to call U.S. customs. Two customs officers arrived in the rain, hearty souls out protecting American soil, I guess. They were pleasant and easy to talk with. But it was not always the case as I crossed back and forth over the international boundary many times on this journey down that confounded invisible line. The times that most bothered me were when I called in to report and I sensed an accusatory attitude coming across which seemed to be an attempt to put me on the defensive. Now really, think about it, would I call in to report if I *were* a smuggler or a terrorist? A couple of my interactions with customs officers on my journey left me feeling that I must be assumed guilty of something until I could prove myself innocent. I knew that every citizen's due process rights of both of our countries was not based upon such an assumption. What has changed?

Shane and Mary had a cabin full of kids and adults when the rain ended and I tapped a hello on their coach-roof. They had invited some folks, that they had met earlier that day at a nearby park, to join them for supper. It was a cabin full and it was noisy, but the generous spirit of our hosts was amazing. We divided up their last bottle of beer and Shane suggested that we take a hike to a liquor store he had discovered a few blocks away.

I agreed. I was not accustomed to the very noisy confines of a sailboat cabin packed with people...I was used to the very quiet confines of an even smaller cabin on Sweet Breeze.

On the walk to the liquor store the streets seemed deserted. Empty lots were common where factories and warehouses once stood. Massive and high buildings were falling apart or being torn down. Broken windows in otherwise perfectly serviceable looking buildings gave a sort of eerie feel to the neighborhood. A few cars passed by but we were the only ones out for a walk on sidewalks that were seldom walked anymore. The walks were heaving and cracking and grass roots were slowly pushing the broken pieces further apart.

I guessed we were winding our way through a long abandoned industrial neighborhood, just east of the downtown skyscrapers. It was indeed a different neighborhood than the anchorage in the St. Claire River of yesterday's eve, where those grand, yet ostentatious homes watched over their broad and manicured front lawns at the river's edge.

We seemed to be the only two white boys at the liquor store. I had the distinct feeling that store patrons were checking us out, something like, "what are you two boys doing down here, are you lost?" I guess we were the only two white boys in the hood that night.

Shane showed me where he had found a mulberry tree in a vacant lot. I had never tasted a mulberry before. The tree was loaded. They were a sweet-tart flavor and a wonderful taste delight.

It just seemed so incongruous—picking berries from a tree of an evening, with a guy I had just met, an Aussie yet, in the abandoned commercial neighborhood of a city steeped in the history of being a once prosperous manufacturing center, not only of the U.S. but of the world. However did I get here? Sailors are an adventurous lot I guess.

After their kids were put to bed in their boat, Mary and Shane brought over a few of those beers that we had lugged back. We talked into the wee hours...maybe until eleven. We learned so much about each other in such a short time.

Why, I asked were they returning to Australia after years of working and living and doing and being here in the U.S? Was it the sailing adventure? Only partly. They found it disheartening here in the U.S. They believed that little was left of the spirit of caring for one another. They felt life here was a harsh life overall...of making money and spending money and trying to accumulate stuff. What was different in Australia I wondered out loud? Shane responded, "Well taxes were certainly higher, but the social benefits were likewise greater; employers were required to pay a living wage and provide insurance to workers against medical calamities and everyday care. It seems to be less of a 'winner-take-all' society. More caring."

I wonder if I have ever learned to love a couple so much, so quickly. Our spirits connected. They will be with me the rest of my sail to the sea.

Friday, June 28. Today, three weeks on the water.

I remember that I was a late sleeper that Friday morn. There were some breezes blowing while I had my tea and there was no sign of any stirrings yet on Shane and Mary's boat so I shoved off, out the slip to the river and headed south, downstream, toward Lake Erie. My sailing motto was becoming, "With breezes blowing, Curt wants to get going." I never liked goodbyes that much anyhow.

The view down the river fascinated me. Detroit on one side, Windsor on the other. General Motors' monstrous office towers dominated the Detroit skyline. The blue lights that run up and down the sides of the towers were on. They must be making money again. I hope they are spending my bailout money wisely. No big parties, bonuses and pay packages for the execs anymore...I'm sure they have learned the lessons of their greedy behaviors.

Just downstream are some huge factories and warehouses but most look closed. Graffiti and broken windows are my first clue. Some small trees on rooftops and up against the sides of buildings are evidence that nature is slowly reclaiming the banks of the Detroit River. The largest shipping docks look dilapidated and closed.

A massive "CLYDE" crane sits idly pointing skyward, rusting and alone on a vast concrete flat where small trees grow up through the cracks. Clyde Iron Works of Duluth, Minnesota built huge cranes and small cranes and shipped them all around the world. The factory buildings in Duluth where the cranes were assembled are now the shelters for a hockey arena and restaurants. The crane brings back thoughts of home. The bleak scene before me brings back thoughts of Rome.

Occasionally I see someone fishing from an old pier. If they look out, I wave, as if to remind myself that we are all in this together.

The shore to the left, the Windsor, Ontario shore, is a contrast to Detroit. The city looks vibrant, alive, with trucks and commerce and things moving about. Windsor, just across the bridge from Detroit, is a relatively safe city where gun violence is rare, so I have learned.

I have been doing the owl thing again all morning. The riverbanks are fascinating to me. Monstrously large, blue painted warehouses on the Michigan shore are part of a U.S. Steel Company steel mill and it is showing signs of life. More oil refineries and power generating plants hovering near the water, and associated industrial looking structures stretching back from shore as far as one can see.

Downstream from the city shorelines, nature still has a firm foothold on the riverbanks. Great blue herons are wading in the backwaters. Tasteful waterfront homes show through the trees. I imagine what a Mecca for wildlife this river must have once been; the swift waters teeming with fish and shorebirds wading the near-shore waters. I imagine the sense of awe that the first white men must have felt when canoeing up this river; undeveloped except by nature; a kind of temperate rainforest, with trees leaning far out over the water. Even with the barge and ship traffic and the noise of the powerboats, there are still herons and all sorts of bird activity along the shores. There are big white swans tipping forward, feeding in the shallower water, trumpeters, I think.

Two up-bound container ships pass on the left as we hug the right side of the channel. From behind, a tug pushing a scow full of gravel very gradually overtakes us. A big power yacht plows upstream so hard and fast that its wake washes over our decks and I must hang on to stay in the cockpit and keep from getting tossed into the drink or onto some hard structure of the boat. The yacht's skipper was unaware, oblivious, or simply didn't care.

...All Small Craft Should Take Shelter Immediately...

As the Detroit river broadened at its mouth and the expanse of Lake Erie lay ahead, it was time to get the latest marine weather forecast and make a decision. Which shore was to be our course, the American or Canadian? There were dark clouds behind us up the river and I could hear thunder-rumbles in the distance. Environment Canada's forecast predicted northwest winds for the rest of the day. That was my cue. Our course was to be the Canadian shore of this, the third great lake, on our sail to the sea. That should give us the best chance for an offshore wind. It felt good to be heading east again, east toward the salt water.

There were two sailboats out on Lake Erie this morn. Both were yawl rigged. A yawl has a second, shorter mast way aft called a mizzenmast. She'll fly a small sail from her mizzen that I would call a jigger. Somewhere I'd read of the good control a yawl has when she bends a jigger and a jib. I think I'd like a yawl. That Glander back in Duluth was a yawl rig.

That afternoon brought some challenging weather upon Sweet Breeze and me. It began with my new VHF radio shrieking a blast of beeps followed by a weather bulletin for the western waters of Lake Erie. "All small craft on the western waters of Lake Erie should seek shelter immediately. Winds as high as 60 miles per hour are expected."

Yeah, yeah, yeah; I shut that damn thing off. Loud and unexpected sounds like that alarm startle the hell out me, gets my adrenaline flowing, which gets my dander up.

Actually, all one had to do to realize some real weather was imminent was to look skyward and I had been watching clouds darken and swirl upwards for an hour before the damn alarm on the radio almost spooked me overboard. Lightning was playing amongst the blackest of the clouds and the thunder—even I could hear it.

There was no getting off the lake anytime soon for us. We were ten miles from anywhere. Pelee Island or the Canadian shore was the nearest possible safe harbors and the Detroit River was at least ten miles behind us. We, Sweet breeze and me, decided to take our chances out in the lake, we really had no other choice. Remember, I thought, "When in doubt, go out."

My strategy was to batten and secure the boat (smart plan, duh) for 60 mph winds. The winds were blowing in the right direction at least. I knew that Lake Erie was shallow and infamous for fast-building big waves. I had all the faith in the world in Sweet breeze. My job was to get her prepared and handle her right.

With everything topsides as secure as I could make it, especially making sure the doused mains'l was made fast to the boom so that there was no possibility it could blow loose and make ragged in the wind. Then I set the headsail for following winds over the port quarter. I furled out only enough sail to keep us heading downwind without getting overpowered, maybe eight feet of sail along the foot. Sheets, halyards, and the furling line were double checked and made fast until I was certain that nothing could get loose and away under the worst of conditions.

We were a few miles away from the shipping lanes so that would not be a concern.

We were the only small vessel on the water as far as I could see in any direction. I hooked up Otto (my electronic-electric self steering device) and set him for a heading of 90 degrees and dove below as the rain and wind and lightning were upon us.

Otto did not steer well in big following seas but he didn't mind getting soaking wet in a downpour. I did. So far I was dry and warm and Otto was steering just fine. The compass on the bulkhead above the galley stove let me monitor Otto's performance. So far he was paying attention to his duties well enough and I don't think he knew that I was scrutinizing his work from below. I could see out through the side windows that the waves were building to whitecaps but nothing to worry about yet. Otto was still steering okay. I was a bit concerned about the lightning and the very tall aluminum mast. For a small boat she had quite a tall rig. So I stayed aft as far as I could, distancing myself from the base of the mast. We seemed to be putting on some nice speed with the waves pushing and that tiny headsail pulling. About the only sound I could hear, below in the protected belly of Sweet breeze, was the pounding dull roar of the torrential rain striking the coach roof.

Then it stopped, as suddenly as it began. The sky brightened behind us. It missed us. The main body of the storm was bowling and boiling along just to our south and passing ahead of our course already. The wind had never gotten stronger than 20 knots, maybe 25, as a sailor would be tempted to tell it later. Huh… that was nothing. Thunderstorms beware, Sweet breeze and me are gaining confidence.

My sense of safety and satisfaction was interrupted by the VHF radio crackling to life again. The Coast Guard had received a "mayday" call for assistance and was relaying the message to all boaters in the area that there was a man in the water hanging onto the side of a boat, but I could not make out the location of the boat in trouble with the scratchy broadcast transmission along with my poor hearing. Darn, I'd sure like to be somebody's hero today.

There looked to be another storm coming up behind the big one that mostly missed us. The wind and waves were subsiding a bit and there were the usual tasks at hand after a storm; mostly I wanted to get the sails set, pulling hard and maximize our speed in this following wind. Favorable winds were not the norm so far for this, the first three weeks of sailing, and I wanted to take best advantage of them.

We were sailing through an area of reefs and wrecks so I needed to do some position checks and plot a course toward Point Pelee. With Otto at the helm it freed me up to study charts and reckon our position and set a course.

Behind our course and to the south were the Hen and Chicks Islands, small and barely visible on the horizon. A ferryboat crossed our path ahead, heading south to Pelee Island, a large island amongst many smaller ones out in the middle of Lake Erie. Pelee has roads and farming and vineyards and a microclimate tempered by the waters of the lake. It's the Canadian tropics. The southernmost part of Canada. Once again, I am tempted to stop and visit but, once again, I also seem to be compelled by some unknown force to keep moving, to take advantage of the wind and seas and get some distance behind me. It is still a long way to the sea.

Have I told you that we have been towing an eight-foot dinghy and two oars for all these miles? Sweet breeze has been so patient dragging that little tub for nearly a thousand miles. Bailing the rainwater from the dinghy is a real challenge, but any water at all in the dinghy makes it incredibly hard to tow. Being all about sailing efficiency, I'm always trying to figure out a way of doing it while under sail. I could possibly board the dinghy over the transom and bail out the water while being towed... too scary...any misstep and the boat and dinghy would merrily sail away from me and into the sunset.

I have tried pulling the dinghy forward and reaching over the side, holding onto the sailboat with my toes, and bailing but it's too far down to reach. The little boat is too heavy to lift it manually by the gunwale while reaching over the side in an attempt to dump out the water. Once I used an 8-to-1 tackle hoist, that I'd brought along, and raised the dinghy by its prow up to the boom but couldn't get it high enough to completely drain it.

The intake hose on my manual bilge pump was not long enough to reach down to the waterlogged little craft. The best idea I could come up with was to tie my big sponge, my bailing sponge, onto the end of the aluminum boat hook and poke it into the water and wring it dry, over and over again. Not the most efficient method but I did have plenty of time. It was a safe method and there was a certain value in the exercise it provided.

There must be lots of fish in these local waters...the cormorants tell me so...and strange looking birds they are. After a dive they sometimes surface right close to us, I see panic in their beady little eyes as they grab a breath and dive back to safety in a flash.

They are not what I would call a handsome bird...a drab black coloration and a long thin beak with a hook on the end and an unbalanced looking body designed both for flight in air and flight under water. When wet, after coming up from a dive, they have the elongated look of a fat snake. I think that Native Americans once called them "snake bird". They "fly" underwater and catch fish. That hook on the end of their beak must be used to grasp a slippery fish. Back at Sault Ste Marie, on the St. Marys River I had stopped and talked to a fisherman who showed me a large whitefish he had just caught that was gashed open by what he figured was a cormorant's beak. He didn't have any nice words for cormorants.

How fast they must cruise underwater to catch a speedy fish. They are the birds you might see sitting on a piling, or any structure near the water, with their wings held broadly out toward the sun to dry their feathers. How do they know to do this? They don't really look all that smart. They're probably thinking the same of me as I sail by.

I heard the "mayday" marine emergency relay call on the radio again and this time I could hear the location—Sandusky Bay, way to the south, on the U.S. shore between Toledo and Cleveland. The boater was probably long since rescued...I hoped.

More storm clouds, thunderheads, I call them, building behind us to the west. We have been running wing-and-wing now for the last couple of hours with the big genoa thrust out into the wind by the heavier and longer of my two whisker poles. It catches lots of wind when poled out and it won't collapse with a slight wind shift.

Sweet Breeze runs pretty fast for an old boat with her deep keel and a lot of wetted surface dragging under the water. We could run downwind at five to six knots all day in a steady wind.

As the storm behind us drew near the wind piped up a bit and we were sailing too fast to feel secure. If only Otto could steer for a minute so I could go forward and get that whisker pole off the clew of the gennie and get it secured so I didn't lose it overboard. This was one of the most hazardous of my sailing chores...on the foredeck of a pitching boat with a heavy pole in my hands and a powerful sail thrashing the pole about. I risk using the pole because of the way it tames the genoa and then holds it far out past the blanketing effect of the main, where it fills with air so nicely on a run.

I looked very much forward to rounding Point Pelee and getting out of the wind and waves. It had been a long day since leaving Detroit and we had put some good distance behind us. We went way out around the point to be sure that we cleared any shoals that extended outward from the tip. Waves were breaking over the shallow areas. I hauled the gennie in to about half its area with the furler and made a slow jibe left, sailing winds-a-beam and waves-a-beam, just below the breaking waves and into the lee of the point. That relaxed feeling came over me again as it always does after several hours of fatiguing steering. The constant vigilance of sail watching on a fast, straight run is tiring, though it may not seem so.

We sailed a mile or so north up the point looking for an inlet into some marshes or small lakes that were shown on the chart. Just sand and gravel beaches, no inlets to sneak into for the night. We dropped anchor into sand and eight feet of water far enough around the point where the swells were not too big to sleep through. We drew up where there was a grove of tall and broad trees close to shore where they could help to break up any straight-line west winds should we get some blows during the night. There was barely enough breeze offshore to swing the boat at anchor even now, so the tall trees must be breaking up the wind nicely. That's all the planning I could think to do in order to get a good night's sleep, with no harbors of refuge anywhere within 30 miles.

There were some lights on the Canadian shore to the north...small towns or lakeside cabins and homes, looked like. Somehow the lights made me feel a little less alone riding anchor out on Lake Erie, on a stormy night, three weeks and 1000 miles from home.

Sometime during the night, as had happened to me a number of times since leaving Duluth, I awoke with a start and sat up in bed not knowing where I was or what I was doing. I could instantly see that I was on a sailboat...but why and where? Next I would look out the nearest window to try to get my bearings. Next, and it all happened very fast, TREES!! We're running aground. Quick, get up on the helm...I fly up to the cockpit naked as a fish to grab the tiller, get the sails under control!! By then I usually came to my senses.

The fresh air of the night. The shock of slamming open the companionway and bolting up the ladder as fast as I could would bring me back to reality. I was at anchor. I was on Lake Erie. Those trees were a hundred yards away. All was well. Get conscious sailor! Stop doing this to yourself!

It was the trees. I must have been dreaming I was sailing on the open seas and had dozed off. I was thrown directly into an "act now" mode from a sound sleep. It would take at least a half hour for the adrenaline rush to subside and sleep to return. How many times would this happen on my sail to the sea? Not every night I hoped... it was truly disturbing to me, usually a calm and peaceful sleeper.

Saturday, June 29. Up at 5 a.m., gray sky, very light rain, warm and humid.

At least I didn't have to huddle around a hot cup of tea anymore to warm my stiff fingers. We were as far south as our journey would take us...on this leg of our sail at least. From this point on we would be on a gradual east-northeast heading until the tip of the Gaspé Peninsula, far to the east and tucked far away into this old sailor's romantic sailing dreams.

The Gaspé...it conjures up big seas and high cliffs and gives me a shiver of anticipation, adventure...or dread. A sailor could get caught in a nor'easter out there (yes, he most certainly would).

I must be educable after all. I remembered to bail the dinghy of rainwater *before* getting underway...it is so much easier at anchor in calm seas.

Speaking of dreams, it was mostly a restful night at anchor, light rains on the cabin top, light swells to rock the boat. Just the one nightmarish start and the panicky dash to the cockpit in the darkness, and the warm light rain awakening a naked old sailor...then the smile and that slow, questioning head-shake again, when I finally came aware and awake. It made me wonder, those nightmarish starts in the night, somewhere, deep, deep down, just how affected my psyche really must have been about this sail to the sea. Perhaps I was becoming a real sailor, after all.

There have been some strange and intensely painful leg cramps at night. They wake me up at least once per night and I lay there wondering: should I move, will the pain get worse or will it subside? I usually try some very subtle movements of my leg as a test. Eventually, before a muscle tears itself, the cramp relaxes ever so slowly, and sleep returns. In the morning, as I recall the muscle cramp events, I wonder if something in my diet is missing or do I need to do stretching exercises? Bananas and their potassium may be the answer. Next port of call, bananas it will be.

Last evening, off the lee of Point Pelee, I practiced dropping and setting the big plow anchor a few times. If it entered the sand bottom right, and if Sweet breeze pulled it deep into the sand under motor power in reverse, I would be in for a restful night's sleep. If the anchor was not properly set so that it dug down deeply into the bottom but instead could slide across the surface, then the morning might find a sleepy sailor in a boat somewhere other than where he was when he drifted off to sleep. That night I felt the anchor was set well and fast.

The warm, humid sea air of Lake Erie felt good. It smelled fresh, rinsed clean by a rainy night. There were streaks of light that beamed down through the early dawn clouds onto the gray vastness of this, my third great lake.

We ran the motor to charge the batteries and to get out and under the influence of a light north wind. A warm wind, coming off the farms and forests of southern Ontario...warm tea, and warm wonderings of a new day and what it might bring; life was good. I was, after all, a lazy sailor...not out to test my stamina or abuse my body. When sailing, or anything else, I'll take comfort over stress any day but most days on the water provide me with at least a sampling of both.

We were on a heading of 60 degrees magnetic, east-northeast. Sweet Breeze was taking care of the driving and I was studying a paper chart, navigating, if you will. It finally dawned on me what all those lines on the chart were representing. Like a spider's web, the chart showed the Canadian side of Lake Erie to be crisscrossed with something. Aha! They showed approximately the location of natural gas wells on the seafloor and the pipelines laid to interconnect the wells and still more pipelines to bring the gas to a shore terminal. Good to know what all those squiggles mean should the need to drop an anchor arise.

It caused me to wonder why there were no gas wells or pipelines on the U.S. side of the international boundary. Was there only gas to be found under the Canadian waters of Lake Erie?

Were those old Brits at the Treaty of Paris of 1783 so smart that they knew just where to draw the international boundary line down the middle of the lake, so as to garner all of the gas for Canada? Just some of the entertainment that my mind conjures up, as a solo sailor shall do with idle time on his hands.

Speaking of gas, the gas gauge shows that we still have three-quarters of a tank of fuel after motoring some parts of the Detroit River and the quiet western end of Lake Erie before yesterday's thunderstorm scooted us along. Finally we are putting on some real miles under wind power alone. We always try to catch any breeze blowing by and put it to work for us, minimizing fuel consumption.

No need to motor for hours on this fine morning and wait for an afternoon breeze to start up...we had a nice north wind to start the day. With a light wind across the port beam and a four and a half knot speed, sailing parallel to the windward shore and Otto at the helm...what could be better? We were following a course about four miles offshore, but if the waves got uncomfortable we could move in closer.

The charts showed some safe harbors ahead, one way ahead. The near one was at Erieau, Ontario named Rondeau Bay and the far one (90 miles?) at Port Stanley. I wondered if the winds held steady if I could make it to Port Stanley. Ninety miles would be my best day yet.

Thinking of breakfast but not really hungry. Picturing Shane's big smile in my mind and it makes me grin, then laugh out loud, only to myself, alone out on Lake Erie at seven in the morning.

A Damsel Fly, much like a small iridescent dragonfly, landed on my journal. What a gorgeous and mysterious example of complex and mysterious life, and how lucky I feel that it chose my book, even as I write in it, for a restful perch. As we quietly slide along at 4 knots, I wonder to myself, what it could mean, or does it mean nothing at all, except perhaps that I have too much time on my hands to amuse myself. But still, the visit has left me wondering.

Marna called on the cell phone. The disturbance, a welcome awakening from the trance of my mysterious thoughts. She had been up to Camp Cotton to visit Terry, our mutual friend, and my summer guest, and caretaker of the camp. Terry had been busy. The place looked great...flowers and a veggie garden, and things were "cleaned up a bit" whatever that meant. I thought I had things perfectly cleaned up before I left for sailing. I remember her words, "Camp Cotton has never looked better!" Whatever.... She emphasized how happy Chickie and Terry were. That report gave me a warm feeling and another big grin to myself.

The dinghy is pulling easily again. I adjust the painter (tow rope) so that it has the lightest feel, the least tension, and it always surprises me what a big difference it makes if the dinghy is eight feet back or fifteen feet back. If I let it back until it is falling off a small swell that Sweet breeze leaves in her wake, the dinghy pulls with almost no effort. I can tell by the painter that sometimes falls slack.

I've been doing some simple math to see how far I might sail today. At four knots and a long day (16 hours) I could make Port Stanley, Ontario. At six knots and 14 hours we could also make it. A steady wind all day would be great but not to count on. Port Stanley looks to have a deep and protected harbor and is a bit over halfway down the entire length of the lake. That would be great progress...from Detroit to Port Stanley in two days. That shall be my goal.

The wind is veering east a bit from north. I pinched the sails up tighter and gained a little speed and a little more heel.

Lake Erie has been kind to me. Here I am again, a few miles off the windward shore, where the waves aren't big yet and I can glass the shore for scenery occasionally. I always try to sail the shore from which the wind originates (thus the term "windward"). Sometimes a sailor will call the side of the boat toward the wind the "weather" side. The side of the boat from which the wind is leaving is the "lee" side. If I sail downwind (run) to an island, I have approached the island on its "lee" shore. If I sail around to the backside of the island and duck behind it to get out of the waves, then I am in the "lee" of the island, yet on its "windward" shore or "weather" side of the island. These few simple terms have confused me at times but as I feel that the words of any well-written book should create pictures or visions in the reader's mind, and sailing terms are a handy shorthand, thus my definitions.

I love a good blow but I don't love big waves. Some of my Lake Superior experiences, especially on the north shore, have given me a life extending respect for the combination of big waves and strong wind. Either one alone is doable. The combination can be a frightening challenge for me alone on a small boat.

At least once daily, I listen to the marine forecast for wind speed and direction and choose what course gives me the best chance for a smooth ride. The forecasts are not perfect but they are often pretty close to the conditions and are the best option going for the boater, like me, without the fancy electronics that can show advancing weather on a screen. I'm just not good enough with watching clouds (though I have been a cloud watcher all of my life) and discerning their telltale patterns of weather to come, to depend on my own predictions. (There was to be a time ahead, on the North Atlantic, fast forward a thousand miles, where I should have listened to Environment Canada's warnings. It would have saved some high anxiety.)

Big waves are hard on me, hard on the rigging, and sometimes make a jumble of the cabin's contents if I don't have stuff well stowed, which is often enough. Big waves tire me out. They require constant vigilance. Otto can't handle them so I must steer, sometimes for hours and it is wearing and I am, after all, a lazy sailor. I have nothing to prove...except the adventure of this sail to the sea.

The wind is veering slightly east of north again so I pinch in the sails as tight as they will go now. Our point of sail is the highest toward the wind that she will go. We are close-hauled but still making pretty good time but if the wind veers more to the east we will have to leave our rhumb line and fall off to the southeast then tack back northeast later. If this old girl can hold a course 45-degrees off the wind then we are climbing about as high as one can expect.

Thinking about people. New friends and old friends. I wonder if I'll ever see Doug again. I liked his gentle spirit. He has probably made it to the far western end of Lake Superior by now. We met at the Sault, remember, two ships passing in the... at the marina.

Randy and Val were to leave the Knife River Marina, on Lake Superior's north shore, about ten days ago. I wonder how far they have sailed in Randy's hand crafted schooner? Will they catch me? Not likely unless I get wind or stormbound for several days. I wish they would catch me though.

Have Shane and Mary left Detroit yet? Will I ever see them again?

The freedom, the complete freedom of sailing has a sometimes sad, though gently sad, aspect. It's the parting of company with friends along the way. Real friends usually are slow in the making. Somehow, while sailing, friends happen more suddenly but are mostly folks that I'll probably never see again. Thus is the freedom and joy of sailing, flavored with a dash of sadness yet tempered with the anticipation of more friends on the journey ahead.

Something I seldom do while sailing...listening to music on the stereo. What prompted the desire to hear some music this late morning may have been thoughts of friends, the quiet solitude of sailing the length of Lake Erie, or maybe I just wanted to step outside of my sailing head for a while. Music is an old and trusted friend. Music, probably some Latin rhythms, my usual favorite, upbeat, syncopated rhythm, just like I'm feeling today.

I've been thinking about the history of Lake Erie, in my lifetime at least. I remember the scenes of masses of dead fish floating belly up in the 60s or 70s when the lake was considered nearly "dead" from pollution. When upstream a ways, at Pittsburgh, a river caught fire until it burned itself out.

I know that things are better for the old lake now, but then, how can they get much worse than "dead"? The fishermen and women are out in an armada around Pointe aux Pins (Pine Point). We sailed near one boat that was just landing a fish and shouted a query about what species they were after. "Rainbow trout and walleyes," it came back. That is some good news...both of those species need some pretty pure water to survive and thrive. We were, however, offshore on the Canadian side of the lake, and an undeveloped shore at that because the Pointe aux Pins is a Provincial Park. Now, if only we could sail across the lake and catch some walleyes or trout from the break wall leading into Cleveland harbor, now then, we would have a clean lake. But that doesn't take away from the good feeling about how far we have come. For all I know, maybe there are some clean and healthy fish in the waters off the U.S. shore too. I sure hope so.

One thing I am certain of, there are always corporate lobbyists (bribers) in D.C. offering their advice (and other things) to their corporate (owned) lawmakers, trying to get water quality regulations relaxed again...in order to maximize corporate profits, which will mean better wages trickled down to the workers and will of course translate into economic prosperity for all. Well, of course.

Around the point, the wind picks up from the northwest. This wind is nothing like what was forecasted: "Winds north backing to the northeast," but hey, I'll take this brisk breeze on a broad reach. We might make Port Stanley by nightfall. We're averaging about six knots over ground now and it sure feels good to be sailing once again...no motor.

This 22nd day of the "big sail" and second day on Lake Erie has had a little of everything. An easy morning sail at four knots until noon when the breeze quit and it got hot on the water; motoring for two hours in the heat of midday, then a brisk breeze over the port quarter and some real speedy headway. We could almost call this a 100-mile day if we make Port Stanley, which I'm sure we will now.

I miss my dog. I see her on her bunk. I feel her presence. Does she miss me? I doubt it. Sounds like her and Terry are having too good of a time to miss me much. They walk into town everyday. They walk my trail along the river and look for wildflowers and berries. She might miss me a bit. Wonder if Marna misses me--not likely either. Well that's...good. That means they are both being present-minded and enjoying the moments of their lives, just like me...mostly.

On the chart, the Port Stanley harbor looks deep enough and well protected but I may have to find the entrance after dark...always a stressful exercise for a single-hander, darkness and an unknown harbor. Without the chart plotter it would be really tough. I mounted the chart plotter on the port side of the companionway opening right where I usually sit while at the helm so I can monitor the boat's position relative to marker buoys, the entry channel, and any other navigation hazards that the chart plotter has on its map. It worked out to be the best location for me to try to keep from "running into stuff" (more sailor lingo).

My forward vision and my four-cell flashlight are my first choice for night nav but the chart plotter gives me the back-up confidence of having another crewmember double-checking our position.

We made Port Stanley at about 10 p.m. There were fireworks shooting out over the town. Did the town fathers know I was arriving after a 100-mile day sail? They must have...either that or Canada Day was being celebrated a bit early.

It was an easy entry in the dark. Wide and deep enough for some freighters of cargo, as it turned out. There was a kind of side bay to the right, inside the break walls and I could see some other small craft at moorings. I thought about tying up to the seawall, it seemed deep enough right up to the wall but decided against it. Anchors had served me well so far and if swells were to enter the harbor during the night there would be lots of motion against the wall.

There were more fireworks and I could hear live music and more celebrating. Probably, someone had noticed my safe harbor entry and anchorage, I figured. These folks sure know how to welcome a sailor to town but it was a long day, about fourteen hours, and though I supposed that they wanted me to come and join the welcoming celebration, I had a quick bite and turned in. The music didn't keep me awake for long and I had only one start in the middle of the night where I bolted up the companionway ladder, but came to my senses sooner than last night.

Sunday, June 30. Up at 6 a.m. with the sweetened and fattened chai tea that warms and comforts and makes a day start just right, but I was up a creek now, Kettle Creek, looking for a fuel dock.

There were masts showing the way up around the bend of the creek but first there was a low bridge, a drawbridge, a cool looking old fashioned looking drawbridge that would need to open to allow us passage. I got that sense of importance again as the early morning car traffic across the bridge was held up for Sweet breeze and her admiral at the helm. The two sides of the bridge went up about 45 degrees and we scooted 'up the creek', her mast slipping between the uplifted halves, rounded the bend, and passed some big fishing tugs on the right bank. I could see a fuel dock ahead and tied up...there was little current and no wind, so docking was easy.

It was called Stan's Marina...appropriate name at Port Stanley. It was owned and operated by a guy named Dave, however, who was really a good guy. He put on a pot of coffee and invited me to stick around and have a cup with him after he was done with the marina opening chores.

Some sport fishermen were putting in at the marina's back-down ramp where they could float their boats off the trailers. One group of three guys with not such good English and not much of a well-organized boat, had a dead battery, and couldn't start their outboard. Dave loaned them a battery pack to start the engine but then they asked to take the battery pack out with them fishing in case the on-board battery didn't take a charge. "Nope, might need that for other boaters today," said Dave. They went back and forth few times, quite a few times. Finally, Dave told them they could not take the starting pack but they could buy a new battery. Too expensive, they said...Dave gave up. They had no spare small motor nor oars but I think Dave was right to let them figure it out. He couldn't baby sit them anymore and wouldn't dicker on the battery price like they wanted and had other customers and chores. Stick to your guns, Dave.

The drawbridge opened on the half hour so I motored down the creek toward the beginning of the industrial part of the harbor and the bridge. The poorly prepared fishermen caught up to me and offered to buy my dinghy, the tub I've been towing forever…$100 cash. No thanks. Seems like there was a gap in cultures going on…here in Canada or the U.S. you might say good morning first, before trying to negotiate a giveaway price for a sailor's dinghy. Stick to your guns, Dave.

Northeast wind this morn. A light wind but the forecast is for increasing northeasterlies as the day wears on. Two possibilities are tossing about my head as the boat is being tossed about by some swells coming from somewhere. One is to sail across the lake, to the southeast, toward Dunkirk, New York, picking up the northeast wind on the port beam and making some real time albeit on a tack going away from the northeast corner of Lake Erie, where the Welland Canal begins around Niagara Falls.

The second thought I'm having right now is that I hate these fucking swells. Nothing swell about a swell. The boat is pitching in all directions without enough wind to fill the sails and dampen the motion. Can't get much speed with this wind swirling about either. I'm saying some of those words again that my granddaughters should never hear. Just a sailor talking to the wind and sea with sailor language, though sometimes we get along quite nicely, the sea and I, and I sing to her sweetly.

The third thought is to try to sail up the coast in these light and variable winds as far as I can and anchor in the lee of Long Point and sit out the northeasterly blow that is now forecasted for the next two days.

"Ick!" That's the word, in the journal, I used to describe the day's progress so far at 2 p.m. Perhaps twenty hard fought miles in five hours of sail handling on a boat being jostled perpetually by swells. Lake Erie had been so nice to me up till now. "Neptune…was it something I said?"

The north shore of Lake Erie between Port Stanley and Long Point has high sand and clay banks decorated with old tractor tires and various items of big, rusty farm junk. Occasionally a barn, or the roof of a barn is visible. Back inland a ways are the far-reaching, slow moving arms of the really huge three bladed wind generators. Many, many wind generators, hundreds since Lake Huron, reminding me of the power of the wind when harnessed to advantage, something I had been trying to do all day with little success.

By 6 p.m. we had made thirty-four miles. We were motor sailing close to shore and I was glassing the bank for some kind of inlet that we could snuggle up into for the night. There were some possibilities, but the water near shore was taking on that red-brown tint of the clay banks so I wouldn't be able to see into the depths to safely sneak up into a creek or river without the possibility of grounding out. We gave up on that idea, instead we dropped anchor in about six feet of water and backed it in, setting it into the sand, offshore about 200 yards. There were no bays or points to provide any protection on this shore.

Good to stop early. The bright sun was wearing me down. Fish were rolling and jumping around the boat but I didn't have any rod and reel. A fresh fish would have been a welcome main dish for supper. The swells seemed to be "sleepable" here and there weren't many other options besides sailing across the lake or staying put, here, near the beginning of Long Point.

Monday, July First. Canada Day. 1205 miles from home.

Twice during the night I awoke with a start, jumped up and checked the view out the windows, trying to think with a sleep-fogged brain why am I sailing so close to shore? Finally my brain clicks into a momentary wakeful reality of where I am and why and I snuggle back into Kay's sleeping bag. Up again at 1 a.m. checking the wind and the boat position relative to the shoreline, making sure we are not dragging anchor in the building swells.

Up again at 2 a.m. checking wind direction and speed and wondering if I should sail the twenty miles or so out to the end of Long Point and check the waves and options that could await me there. Weighed anchor and sailed away in the dark. Plenty of wind, but there is not a secure feeling in flying along in the blackness at six or seven knots. I was trusting the chart plotter too much. It doesn't show small boats or floating logs.

Too much wind now for full sails in the dark. Reefed the gennie with the furler, then brought the main down one reef. Twenty minutes later, brought the main down the second reef. This was not feeling good. Too dark. Too much wind. I doused both sails and began to head in to shore with the motor pushing us toward a cluster of electric lights that could be a village. Never should have left the anchorage. We made about ten fast and nervous miles in the dark. Not worth the risks, I felt.

Nor'easter on Lake Erie

We eased toward shore very slowly, watching the depth meter and the chart plotter to try to get as close to shore as possible where the swells seemed to dissipate in the shallows. Dropped anchor in five and a half feet of water which should have given us about three feet under the keel, but in the darkness the anchor chain twisted or fouled in some way that I just couldn't figure out in the dark. I didn't care, as long as it held us off shore in the building swells until daylight when I could reassess the situation.

Some of that comforting chai tea helped put me at ease after the, "shot in the dark" sail. I set the "man overboard" position on the chart plotter so that I could check periodically to see if we were dragging anchor. The M.O.B. button puts a mark on the screen at your exact location. The boat symbol should stay right on top of that mark...or the boat is moving from that point of reference. When anchored this shallow I must make sure we stay put. It looks like I got the Lake Ontario chart book out too soon...Erie is not quite done with me yet, nor I with her.

The wind is howling out of the northeast now. With the first gray light of dawn as a backdrop, I can watch the tops of the big white pines on the beach sway and bend to the gale. We are riding anchor in a semi-protected, slight indent to the shore about 15-miles from the tip of Long Point. Still, big swells must be rounding the point and curving into the lee. Why don't they just roll down the lake and leave me alone for a while. The lake must really be riled up now.

Checking the anchor rode by flashlight periodically for chafing. The rigging is humming now from the steady and strong nor'easter. It feels so cold in the cabin but the thermometer on the wall says 75 degrees. Still, I'm chilled. Settled down for some hot tea and a good book and a blanket. Can't hurry up the daylight.

With full daylight it looks like we're anchored about 200 yards offshore. There are lots of cabins and getaways amongst the pines up from the wide sand beach. Hearty Canadian weekenders are still here...joggers on the beach, swimmers even, young lovers smoochin' on a blanket. And here I am for who knows how long; hanging onto the boat to keep from getting tossed and bruised, and a bit queasy from all the motion.

At 10 a.m., lots of beach activity to watch and entertain me. Guess I'm easily entertained. Dogs, paddle-boards, and lots of folks wearing jackets and...shorts? I never quite understood the logic there. I'm a long pants guy myself. They keep my legs warm, protected from bruises and abrasions and cuts. I don't have to rub some (likely) carcinogenic chemicals on my legs to block the sun or to try to keep bugs from biting. I think it must be more about fashion than practicality. Some close friends who know how I dress might say that I am not always keenly aware of fashion. I wonder if someday the fashion will reverse itself, as fashions often do, where folks will wear heavy pants and little or nothing on top?

The weather forecast for today has been updated to twenty-kilometer winds, northeast with gusts to 40-K. Waves one to two meters (three to six feet). I think I'll stay put and hope for lighter conditions tomorrow, but it's sure no fun riding these swells at anchor for hours on end.

I tried to set another forward anchor plus an aft anchor in a half-assed attempt to position the boat and hold it so that the swells were hitting us forward of the beam (center side of the boat) and thus cut down on the rolling motion that gets one seasick. It's also hard to stay in a bunk when lying down on a rolling ship. I even tried lying down on the cabin sole (floor). That's where I was likely to wind up anyhow. Nothing that I tried seemed to feel right. Patience seemed like the best option.

Cleaned the fridge. Getting smelly again. Out of milk and need some half-and-half for my morning tea. I wondered if I dared to take the dinghy to shore and go walking, looking for a store with a few groceries. Would the anchors hold in these big lumpy swells with such short rodes payed out (called the scope, i.e. the ratio of the length of the line payed out to the water depth) or shall I stay aboard and risk my sanity?

The more that I watched the beach walkers and fun-havers, the more this tossing about on Sweet breeze grated on me. I readied the dinghy, tossed in a shoulder bag to carry some groceries, and very carefully timed the waves and stepped into the thrashing little tub, snubbed off on the port side, out of the direct waves but into the wind. It was a really tricky step-down into a really tossing dink.

Once on the shore, some local folks said there was a convenience store about a half mile to the west on the main road and I was off at a brisk walk, still thinking, worrying I guess, about the anchor situation of Sweet Breeze, one last glance over my shoulder to make sure she was still out there riding over the swells and not on her side, rocking on the beach.

This was near the narrowest breadth of Long Point and off to the right side of the road I found a trail out to the lake. I really wanted to see what the lake looked like on the weather side of the point. Were the waves as big as I suspected? I decided against it. I felt that I needed to find that store quickly and get back to the boat, though the walk on steady ground felt so steady and reassuring.

The roads were lined with vacation cottages, sometimes two deep, back from the streets. Lots of cars; three or four at each home or cottage. I guess Canadians are just like us, cars, cars, everywhere.

There were beautiful little gardens replacing lawns and so many plants that I didn't recognize. I was thinking there must be a uniquely warm microclimate here on the point with so many semi-tropical looking plants. That would seem a reasonable deduction with the water of Lake Erie on both sides, moderating the high and low temps.

Milkweed was in flower and that sweetest of smells...basswood trees in bloom, hard to capture in that wind, but I caught some whiffs and it brought back memories of the boy who loved to climb trees...me. Basswood often grows in clusters so that, high in the air, I could step or jump from tree to tree, branch to branch. Sometimes my buddies and I would play tag up in the basswood trees behind my house. It was a kind of test of courage and skill and no one was killed.

One other thing, a disturbing thing! There were a few lawn signs along the lanes, warning signs. Sprayed For Spiders...Keep Children and Pets Away...!" What in the fuck are these people thinking? "Yeah, hello, I'd like to hire you to come and spray some thoroughly untested poison chemical around my house....Yeah, I think I saw a spider yesterday." Lord, educate these folks, for they know not what they are doing! Aren't spiders predatory upon other insects? Aren't they part of a balanced and healthy garden? Indiscriminate spraying of poisons...will humans never learn? Did we not learn anything from the spraying of DDT? Trust the chemical corporations with your children's health if you so choose...I'll trust the spiders, thanks.

I found the convenience store and found it not to be so convenient. Lots of chips and junk food. Sold out of milk and half-and-half, sorry. I needed the walk anyhow. Just getting off the boat for a while was good for my spirit, my motion-suffering spirit. Six bags of Muesli and no milk.

From the Environment Canada forecast on the VHF I still keep trying to pick out some of the few French words that I recognize and fill in the rest with guesses. The waves were about three to five feet here on the lee side of Long Point so there was no reason to attempt any progress to anywhere. Sit tight. Patience. Hang on to something solid. I love my anchors, all three.

It's July already. Maybe we are halfway to salt water. I wonder how far the ocean tides reach up the St. Lawrence? I wonder if I can get back to Minnesota by September for my daughter's arrival from Germany? One thing I know, tomorrow I must try to get off this offshore anchorage. If this old boat and I must take a beating then we might as well take it trying to make some headway.

I tried sleeping on a makeshift pile of blankets on the cabin sole again. The motion was less but there was no room to roll over...the crowded, cramped feeling kept sleep at bay. Back up to my bunk on the settee, hanging on so as not to wind up back down on the sole.

Tuesday, July 2nd. Pitch and roll, pitch and roll...would rather pound through it than sit at anchor absorbing it for another day!

The early morning forecast is for decreasing northeast winds today on eastern Lake Erie. Good news. Anchors aweigh!

It wasn't that simple with three anchors out and being in such shallow water. First thing, start the engine and let it warm up. The waves, which were still really swells, were pushing us to shore with more force than the wind that was coming across the point and pushing us offshore. If I didn't do this right, we were shore-bound, probably wrecked.

The aft anchor was easy, just hoist and stow. The bow anchors were another story. Kneeling at the prow and hand-over-handing the Bruce anchor in I could see a problem. One anchor was tangled into the line of the other. With someone at the helm this would be easy, holding her steady under slow ahead engine, keeping us off the sand while I weighed and untangled the bow anchors. Alone, I had to have one anchor dug in at all times or we were headed for the beach.

It was not easy. Just when I needed the electric windlass most, the drive clutch released itself and let the big plow anchor back down into the very shallow depths. We were slamming down onto the sand now as the waves pushed us toward shore. Run back to the cockpit, bouncing from handhold to handhold, engine full throttle forward. Two anchors somewhere off the bow and anchor rodes trying to find the propeller. If we fouled the prop now, this sail to the sea would be over. This was Murphy's Law of Single-hand Sailing with no time even to cuss. Had to get sea room or beached we would be.

The engine was maxed and pushing. Each swell that raised and pushed us ashore was just slightly out-gunned by the engine pushing us out. The hard thumps on bottom became less hard. We were getting into deeper water. We were floating free again. Now to get out far enough to give me some time to scramble forward and untangle and hoist one anchor at least.

I scrambled forward, handhold-to-handhold, and got the windlass clutch snugged down with a winch handle that I kept tied alongside it for just such emergencies. Scrambled back to the cockpit, engine forward again, then up-anchor with the windlass switch, following the rode as best I could see over the pitching bow. This time the windlass did its job. Engine to neutral. Scramble forward and secure the plow and unwrap the other line fouled around it. Back to the cockpit, engine forward for more sea room and time to get the Bruce anchor aboard.

Fast-forward: we made it. Free of the sand, finally afloat and no damage done. Out into ten feet of water I shifted to neutral and bounced my body forward one more time. Dropped the Bruce anchor again, let out about 50 feet of chain and rode and cleated the rode off on a bow cleat, then took a deep breath. The Bruce had a good bite in the sand and we were out another hundred yards with some time and sea room. I really needed to reconnoiter. Did I fully comprehend how close my old boat and I were to the end of our sail together? It would have been entirely my fault. I should never have anchored that close to shore. We should have been 300 yards out and in 10 feet of water and suffered the heavier swells. What was I thinking? That little Atomic 4 saved my butt again. It never missed a beat. Always starts right up at my command and pushes when I say push. All of the latest updates and add-ons have made that engine what it should be...dependable.

We motored out along Long Point a ways and the wind and waves were sailable. With sails bent and reefed we were making some headway, not much, but it was so much better than riding anchor. Even if we had to pound our way across the lake to the U.S. shore, we were moving again. Close-hauled on an east-southeast heading we were approaching the tip of Long Point at three knots forward and probably one knot to the lee.

Dropped the Bruce (also called a claw anchor) while in the lee of the very tip of Long Point for a lunch break. The point was a fascinating view for me all morning, staying offshore about a half mile. Mostly sand dunes and pine and grassy areas between. No development that I remember. I would like to come back and hike it out to the tip, sleep overnight in a tent, then hike back. Maybe someday. It looks like a northern paradise, a Swiss Family Robinson place with pines for palms.

My sweet little 12-volt electric fridge hasn't worked for some time, the digital readout says its internal temp is at fifty-five degrees and getting warmer so I had better eat lunch from there before things spoil. I suspect that the refrigerant pump was not able to find the liquid to pump it around with all of the boat motion of late. I think that my stomach had some of the same symptoms as the fridge.

Sitting out here off Long Point in Lake Erie, having lunch and looking back I'm feeling kinda wimpy having lay around at anchor for twenty-four hours. I shouldn't second-guess myself I suppose. It was probably the smart choice. The winds are definitely lighter now and the waves are subsiding right behind the wind. I think that it's mostly because I don't want to be tied to the tiller in heavy seas for hours and hours, more than fear of the stormy weather; it seems like discretion is okay when the waves are too big for Otto to steer through. I think I'm doing a backbone self inventory. Should I have challenged Lake Erie through yesterday's nor'easter? The boat could take it if the rigging held together. Would it have made me a better sailor? I think, more than anything else, it would have made me a cold, wet, dog-tired sailor entering an unknown harbor in the dark of night on the New York shore and Lake Erie would not have cared one way or the other.

Marna called to my cell phone. Good to hear her voice. She is leaving Duluth today for Gloucester, Massachusetts to visit her mom. Wonder if I'll get that far?

Out around the tip of the point the waves are not so bad as I had suspected. On a close haul we're making some slow progress right down the center of Lake Erie and I can see the Pennsylvania or New York shore, not sure which. Falling off the wind to a close reach gives us another knot of speed, though our heading is now for Dunkirk, New York, on the other side of the lake and on an easting (90 degrees). The chart shows a safe harbor there. But wait...isn't that a sailboat ahead?

It looks to be a two-masted schooner, schooning down the lake with the wind. Through the glasses, my new Nikons, I can see four sails up...no five, is that a fisherman as tops'l? She's running fast down the lake. Better keep a close eye on her...could be a pirate vessel.

Close reaching to Dunkirk still but the afternoon sun is baking me. Went below to get out of the sun and read, letting Otto steer for a while. I started a new book, *Giants in the Earth* by Ole Rolvaag. A way good read about Norwegian Immigrants who settled the prairie lands of present day eastern South Dakota; their trials, their hardships and long days, their rare and simple joys.

Good thing I checked the big chart of the whole of Lake Erie because the Welland Canal, around Niagara Falls, does not begin at the far eastern end of the lake as I had guessed. The canal begins about twenty miles west of the lake's end on the Ontario shore at a town called Port Colborne, so that was where I really needed to head, not to the eastern end where the current of the Niagara might pull me in. She's a tough little boat, but not that tough.

Heaving To...or Not

With the afternoon wind having moved somewhere to the west and evening approaching our location it became clear that we wouldn't make Dunkirk by nightfall. That means a night spent out in the middle of Lake Erie. Shall I heave-to and try to stay out of the shipping lanes or could I stay awake all night and make some headway; gotta think about this.

Not having gotten a good night's rest at anchor last night was probably a deciding factor in my decision to attempt a heave-to and get some sleep, but not here! We were in a shipping lane and most of the middle of Lake Erie gets a lot of shipping traffic. The best option looked to be on the Canadian side of the shipping lanes. There was an area between the shore and the shipping lanes that was about six miles wide. If I could get the boat to stay still and quit sailing (that's what a heave-to should do) that should give enough room to get some serious sleep. Getting run over by a freighter would seriously delay the Big Sail to the sea.

Darkness is closing in now while we are crossing the lake toward the Canadian shore. The lights of a ship show to the east and lights are visible on the north shore. Motoring in the dark is worse than sailing in the dark. The drone of the motor clearly blocks all sense of hearing. No moon tonight, no stars...just the inky blackness. Checking the AIS shows the ship to the east is coming at us...can we cross in front... what direction, exactly, is he heading? This is definitely not fun. Being close to a ship steaming along at twenty knots in total darkness and guessing at a safe course is not my idea of sailing safe.

I guess you can figure that we crossed in front of the ship successfully, or I wouldn't be telling this tale. We avoided each other by 1.1 miles. That is way too close for such a vulnerable, helpless, out-of-my-control-feeling, skipper of a small boat. It may seem like plenty of distance, and in daylight it would seem so also, but the total darkness changes everything. No more nighttime sailing single-handed if I can help it, unless I'm out in the middle of the ocean, and even then there are hazards. Single-hand sailing at night in unfamiliar waters is a very humbling experience. Single-hand sailing anywhere is a very humbling experience.

I decided to heave to at a point somewhere in eastern Lake Erie three miles from the Canadian shore and about three miles outside of the shipping lane. Let's see now...backwind the jib, ease the main a bit, lash the tiller to leeward. Go below...sleep. The alarm on the AIS makes for a terrible awakening. It's two hours later and there is a ship somewhere near. Gotta get my brain to function and figure out where I am, where is that ship, what am I doing here? I can see nothing. Darkness. I have no idea what direction we are from anything. Lights in the distance...which ones are shore lights, which are the ship lights?

Started the engine and moved the boat some direction, any direction. Now the chart plotter comes to life and shows that we are back in the middle of the shipping lane that heads west from Port Colborne. I'm starting to get my bearings. We have drifted or sailed about four miles south while I slept for two hours. The magnetic compass...point this boat north and get outta here.

Still total darkness but we followed the chart plotter back to the man-overboard spot where we "hove-to" three hours ago. What we really had done was sail away in the dark while I slept. So much for my heaving to. We can practice that again another time, where we have more sea room and less ship traffic.

Sailing east-northeast toward Port Colborne in the dark. The first hint of dawn's gray light in the east will be most welcome. Hope this is my last night sail for a long while.

Locking Down With My New Crew

We motored up to the fuel dock at the Port Colborne marina for a gasoline fill and a slip rental. Here were the beginnings of a new chapter in my sail to the sea. Here was where my new crew was to meet up and see me through the locks of the canal around Niagara Falls.

Dave and Sue had volunteered to drive out from Duluth. They were both retired from the work world and, like me, were mostly in that late, play stage that we enter again if our health is good. We had been in touch on cell phones while they drove and I sailed and we tried to coordinate the meet-up for today. In order to traverse the canal downbound, pleasure boats needed a crew of at least two for line handling in the locks. Those are the rules.

Email, Wednesday, July 3rd. It's me again. Finally at a marina with wi-fi (that works) at Port Colborne, Ontario. There are eight locks ahead down the Welland Canal to Lake Ontario. Some locks will drop the boat 40 feet. Don't know much about the process but will learn as we go...we, meaning Dave and Sue from Duluth who are going to crew for me through the locks. Have sailed 1300 miles so far. 2000 to go to reach the Maine coast. Don't know how far I will go. Some days are pretty tiring and single-handing presents challenges that another crewmember would make easy. Still, health and attitude good, and wishing for following winds. Laid up on Lake Erie for twenty-four hours in nor'east gale and uncomfortable swells. Very tiring...hard to stay in the bunk or remain standing.

Detroit: one of my favorite stops so far, honest. Great marina on downtown waterfront. Met Shane and Mary from Duluth who are sailing to Australia with their young son Franklin. We talked late into the night and shared many parts of our kindred spirits.

Learning about seamanship everyday...about total self-reliance and taking good care of the ship so she can take care of me. Much more to learn...each day is different and single-handing a humbling adventure. One day at a time...Best, Curt

My crew arrived in the afternoon while I was doing laundry and having an iced tea at the marina facilities building. It was good to see old friends. Dave drove us around town with his pickup truck to get a few provisions and some motor oil for the Atomic 4. We found a jug of SAE 30 weight, the recommended viscosity oil for that precious old engine, at a Canadian Tire store. Enough for an oil change somewhere down the line.

One of my yachty neighbors at the marina offered me some helpful advice on making the Welland in one day...in the daylight that is, I didn't think that we could tie up or overnight within the canal and lock system. He said to get an early start, the earlier the better. Eric was a pilot boat captain. He brought the pilots out to the ships where they boarded the ship up a rope ladder tossed over the side, leading way up to the deck. Pilots were necessary to guide the ships through the canal just like pilots who were hired to steer ships into and out of harbors, like Duluth.

Dave spent the night in his pickup camper and Sue and I on the boat. I gave Sue the tour of Sweet breeze, which didn't take too long and showed her how to use the composting toilet and stowed her gear. She fit perfectly on the shortened starboard settee, being about a foot shorter than me; that was to be her berth for as long as she wanted to sail with me. After the canal, the plan was for Dave to hitch a ride back to Port Colborne where he wanted to explore upstate New York and eastern Ontario by pickup truck and camper. He and Sue were to meet up again somewhere down the lake after Sue had all she could take of my skipperly ways and philosophy.

I treated my motley crew to supper at the marina restaurant.

Sue reminded me of Shirley Temple in the morning. Her hair puffy and in a million tight curls. Her smile at the ready.

We were off as early as we could muster for the pay station, the canal wasn't free to use, but the machine where we were instructed to pay wouldn't take my credit card. It was one of those fail-proof automated voice machines that kept telling me to do the same thing over and over and over. There was, thankfully, a phone number to call if the machine was not working and the man said that I could pay cash at lock three. Whew! We were to wait for a call from the lockmaster, at lock eight, the first one, for instructions on how to proceed.

One of my favorite sights, another sailboat, pulled up alongside to pay their locking fees. They were heading downstream, just like us. They seemed a competent crew and an organized crew, Ian Bentley and Robin Ketchen their names as it turned out. Heading out to sea? Yes. Where from...Duluth, Minnesota, just like us. Wow, what a stroke of luck; my first opportunity to sail with another sailboat and they were really nice and they sailed out from the same little speck on the map on the far western tip of Lake Superior. I don't remember for certain, but I think that they left Duluth a week or two ahead of me. They were moseyin' along with Marley, their big black poodle, their bicycles, and their adventurous spirit.

Ian reminded me that my dinghy must be on deck and not trailed behind and some other locking info like fender placement on the boat for the various locks. I should know these things. I'm the skipper after all. I should have been reading the information book on the locks last night instead of that Louis L'Amour western. Such is my nature sometimes.

We were off following Robin and Ian toward the first obstacle, an aerial lift bridge. All is well and my crew is in good spirits. We will be dropping about 325 feet through the locks and the twenty-seven miles of connecting waterways between. Eight locks total. The first one has only a three foot drop, designed (I'm sure) to give newby's like me an easy and gentle introduction to locking procedure before the big forty foot drops on the locks ahead. I could feel some tightness and tension inside, not knowing quite what to expect.

With Dave and Sue, my line handlers, fore and aft, we pulled up behind our new friends in their boat. Ropes were dropped over the side from the wall above and I had my crew lightly loop their ropes around the far side of the nearest horn cleat on the deck, never to tie off the line on any part of the boat. They were to feed it around the cleat with just enough tension to keep the boat parallel to the lock wall and fend off the wall with a boat hook if necessary. That simple procedure worked well for me locking down single-handed in the Poe lock at the Soo where I had one line in each hand and dropped twenty-one feet. This three-foot drop wasn't much of a test of our teamwork. The next lock should have more turbulence with its forty-three foot drop and would need some attentive rope handling.

Thinking about Ian's bright smile and good nature as we pulled up behind them into the next lock. There was some waiting, in the canal, between locks. Ships were coming up the Welland as we were going down and the big guys had priority as we steered clear of their exit from our next lock downbound. A traffic light system of red and green and flashing lights in between, gave us the signals for when to wait and when to enter the lock.

Robin and Ian worked well together locking down and I suspect in most all of their boating endeavors, they were a good team. It brought back some old dreams of mine, okay fantasies, about having that special partner in adventure and a loving relationship at the same time and all the rest of that stuff that a romantic old sailor conjures up while alone for hours and days and weeks on the water.

The rest of the locks were fun, uneventful, but always interesting. We did have one lock rope tail-end that got tangled but we got it free in time.

It must have been an enormous earthmoving undertaking to dig and build this monstrous cut through the land. As we merrily navigate the canals between the locks my imagination takes me back to the times of steam powered shovels, and the masses of men and horses, for the machine and muscle power to move all of the earth and rocks. How was that volume of concrete mixed and poured for the lock walls and entries, I mused? I would like to see the massive gears and mechanical workings of the lock doors. And sadly, I remember the invasive species that swam up the canal; came up from the sea to wreak havoc with the fisheries of the lakes above Niagara Falls.

Since the last glaciation the whole biota of Lakes Erie and Michigan and Huron and Superior, and the rivers and lakes that connect them, have had 10,000 years to evolve, adapt, and specialize their species and their niches. The canal let a whole bunch of new creatures swim upstream and changed the biology of the lakes above the falls forever. Only time would tell the lasting consequences.

We motored out into Lake Ontario to an onboard wine and cheese celebration. I was feeling thankful to my crew, my boat, my ongoing string of good luck, good timing, good weather. The cheese was freshly purchased at Port Colborne and would prove adequate, though quite common. The wine however, had developed that special character that only time can impart. I had been saving the dregs of a fine old box of grape wine with other natural flavors for just such an occasion. It had been sloshing in that box for 1500 miles, tucked away in a locker where it was out of my immediate line of sight and memory and therefore safely reserved for this special time. Captain and crew were shipshape and in fine fettle aboard Sweet Breeze.

It was time to put away my Lake Erie chart book and dig out the spanking new "Lake Ontario and the Thousand Islands of the St. Lawrence Book" of nav charts. The Welland we had conquered. Ontario, the easternmost great lake and final passage to the river that leads us to the sea, lay ahead. I could almost feel the pull of the St. Lawrence.

Toronto, across the lake and to our left, was not quite visible in the warm afternoon haze. Hamilton, Ontario, was to our immediate left. Big cities had little attraction for me; it was the outflow of the Niagara River into Lake Ontario that was beckoning us down the lake about ten miles, on the right shore. Robin and Ian were pulling ahead in their long fast fin keel cruiser and we were fast (not too fast) in their wake, slipping along with winds abeam on a weather shore, Sweet Breeze's favorite point of sail, and no seas to slosh about the wine/cheese slurry within my crew.

The broad expanse of the mouth of the Niagara was a place of history and mystery. Fort Niagara, a remnant of the War of 1812 on the left looked like a fascinating discovery place for me, the sailor with a developing penchant for knowledge of the past. There were tents scattered around the grounds outside the fort's stone walls, not the bright colors of nylon tents but the warm tan of once white cotton canvas. Was there a rendezvous? I must stop there someday.

On the right, showing through the trees on the Canadian shore were some grand old homes and another old fort, not so big and everlasting as the stone and mortar one across the river, more wooden and white, and looking quite British.

Sailboat masts ahead on the right, as upstream against the river's substantial current we motored, with sails doused but at the ready, should the engine ever fail. The current of the Niagara was not a problem for the sturdy little Atomic 4, of course, but he was churning a lot of water and our speed over ground was reduced to a crawl. Wow, what a river. What scenery everywhere, both natural and cultural. I was doing that owl thing again, off to port and starboard swung my head. I didn't want to miss any of this fascinating part of this great river. My imagination was taking me back in time, only a few hundred years, to when there were Indian villages on the shores and to imagine what their towns and forts may have looked like; what the fishery provided then. Was I born too late?

Email, Friday, July 5th, 2013. At Niagara on the Lake, Ontario. Old forts and fascinating history to learn, green flora abounds. Must explore by bicycle. Will get back to you soon. Stay on edge of seat.

On our approach to the marina, the Niagara Yacht Club, Sue has spotted Ian standing high on his coach roof giving the old fashioned universal crossing arms wave signaling, "We are here!" We pulled up behind them, not too close of course with our heavy forward anchors preceding us, nearing their dinghy and other such delicate looking apparatus. Sweet Breeze could do some unfortunate and expensive battering and bludgeoning if the engineer/navigator/helmsman were indelicate with the speed and reversing controls. Often the most difficult part to a long day's seamanship trials is the final docking into tight spaces with million dollar boats but a few feet away.

Ian and Robin, our locking and cruising partners for the day, had already arranged that we could tie up at the fuel dock for an overnight, as long as we were first to fuel-up in the morning and move to a slip. What an easy tie up and warm welcome after a long day.

Ian and Robin locking down.

I suggested we take a short walk to town and find out about passenger buses that service the towns nearby and their routes to get Dave back to Port Colbourne. Possibly a restaurant and supper?

At the yacht club gate however was a locking contrivance typical at marinas. We could leave but we could not re-enter without knowing the combination for the gate. It was automatic with me...I knew that there was not yet a marina that could keep me either within or without, if I so intended passage. Asking another boater for the combination would have been almost cheating. As a kid, fences were put up as a natural challenge to my climbing ability, much like basswood trees. Baseball games and stock car races were a cheap ticket once you understood fences; and the fenced-in railroad yard at the nearby town was full of interesting treasures. Fences almost always had an end, or a gap to squeeze through. Sure, the gap would need to be a little gappier for me now, but still, I knew I'd be in my bunk tonight.

My first stop, just a block up the hill, was a small and elegantly homey sort of hotel with a portly and professional looking desk clerk. After I explained our need for transportation, he replied that a bus would leave the Fort at 8 a.m. with a first stop at St. Catherine's then a transfer, and on to Port Colborne. He even wrote the steps for the journey out on paper for me so that I could give Dave the absolute proper way to return to his truck...no worries.

Then it was off up the hill to find the bus stop at the Old Fort George. I was as intent on making Dave's voyage back to his truck as well plotted as my own voyage to the sea. Boldly, once again, I asked for directions. It happened that I had fallen in with a group of German tourists who had been to the fort and seemed pleased that someone was asking them for directions. They spoke English better than me, which I have found is the case with most Europeans.

There just wasn't much not to like about this pleasant town...Niagara on the Lake. I must return some day. Tomorrow I definitely wanted to see more.

Back at the marina gate to bring Dave the good news, and just as I begin to look for gaps and other entry possibilities, the gate slides open on its motor driven track, out drives a car, I wave, and in I go. Almost seemed like cheating. I must have looked more like a yachtie than a burglar.

The picnickers who I had chatted momentarily with on the way out earlier asked if I had any luck procuring transportation for Dave. I replied that it all was arranged and the next thing I knew I was seated at their family picnic table with a cold bottle of beer and some chicken in front of me. They were Canadians, brother and sister and their spouses. Teachers they were, in Cambodia of all places, and back in Ontario for vacation. It happens so quickly sometimes...they felt like old friends.

We made a nest for Dave on the port cockpit locker with some cushions and blankets and all was well, except for a little snoring, some loud snoring actually, back by the lazarette.

Sometime during the night the snoring ceased and was replaced with the sound of a chorus of raindrops striking the coach roof and Dave came below for shelter. I think I drifted off soon after with dreams of the simple and selfish challenges of single-handing.

July 6. Up early with the sun and the chai tea. Quiet time to catch up my journal.

Dave and Sue were off for the short walk up the hill to Fort George for Dave to catch the 8 a.m. bus back to Port Colborne, returning to his truck and camper at the marina. Sue would be back shortly, unless she was jumping ship on me. It was truly a fine morning; a light mist rising off the river, fresh smelling rain-washed air and an early morning stillness all around.

I got a text message from my son Randy, about my phone bill back home. My bill for June was over $500, and what was I doing to run it up so high? I was answering my phone. Time to shut it off before the phone company's standard international gouging practices bankrupted me. There arose in me a pressing need to go incommunicado for a long while here in Canadian territory. Maybe I should write my congress critter and tell him/her what the phone companies are doing. Maybe I won't bother since congress has been deregulating utility companies of all flavors for some time now, and since just possibly, the lobbyists on behalf of the phone companies could have more influence on the regulators than me and my tale of woes may exert. It's really too lovely a morning to think about congress or the sad state of our feudal plutocracy. Sue was back and we had a whole day on land to enjoy.

Sue and I learned of a bike rental place and Ian and Robin had their own bikes on board. I had heard that there was a falls on the river somewhere upstream so we made a plan to meet up with our new sailing and biking friends at the rental place after fueling our boats and moving to a finger dock. Robin and Ian had a motorized dinghy and so decided to tie up to a mooring offshore, a ways out in the current.

The mile and a half walk through town to the bike rental was good for a farmer/plant lover like me. Lots of the local residents/homeowners were really getting up to speed, my speed anyhow, about alternatives to standard lawns. Grass, i.e., lawns, were being converted into gardens up and down the tree lined residential streets. Some biological diversity was being introduced to the neighborhoods and the obnoxious sounds and smells of lawn mowers were rare.

This I recognized as not a small change, but a really significant change in community and personal values. It was evidenced by those gardens. People were using their property to re-create some healthy soil, some habitat for birds and insects. They were creating a natural way to slow and catch rainwater and let it percolate its way downward into the soil instead of running off to the streets. They were probably increasing their property value by the aesthetics of the added visual interest as well. As I walked the sidewalks of Niagara by the Lake It helped to erase the bitter taste (the congressionally approved larceny) of my phone bill, and besides, what book of sailing adventure would be complete without an opinion or two about some of the commonly stupid things we do and need to change?

The first requirement of a bike ride anywhere is to have hard tires that roll efficiently over the ground, so that's the first thing that I checked. Air pressure satisfied, the second requirement, for those bike riders not into pain and self-abuse, is to have a semi-comfortable seat from which to pedal effectively without damage to sensitive body parts. I had brought along a small pillow in case this second requirement could not be met. It could not. The pillow helped.

There were forested areas, along the bike path up the river, interspersed with vineyards and vegetable farms, views of the river, small towns, and generally an uphill climb as the path followed the approximate course of the Niagara. Mostly, I was able to keep up with the other three who were regular bike riders, but I didn't push myself too hard because the scenery, the greenery, the canyon of the river all held me somewhat spellbound. More of that owl-like head swiveling while trying to stay safe and not run into things. Trees that I didn't recognize were all too common to one who prided himself with identification of tree species and the unique characteristics of the more common northern trees of the forests where I had grown up in northern Minnesota.

As we approached the crowds and car and truck traffic of the nearby falls, sights of trees and natural things gave way to towering hotels and casinos and a zillion other creative ways and shops designed to separate the millions of tourists from their millions of dollars. There were shops with golden arches outside and food-like substances within. There were baubles and bangles and clothing and souvenirs to take home, and oh, the falls…spectacular in the enormous power and sheer immensity of natural forces at work. Here, however, was one of those journeys that exemplified for me the personal truth in, "Joy being found in the journey rather than the destination."

The bike ride back downstream was equally mesmerizing to my visual sense and easier and faster. I was pleased with my abilities where the gravitational pull enhanced my lack of stamina, i.e. coasting. It seemed that my body weight was no longer a disadvantage, as long as my bike had good brakes, that is.

It would be hard for me to overstate the scenery and simple joys of that bicycle journey 16 miles up the Niagara River. Perfect weather and amiable companions and a simple, efficient means of transportation, made it truly memorable. Along the way I even spotted some berries, mulberries, which I now recognized, and Saskatoons, also known as Juneberries, and I had to stop and eat my fill. There were lots of low-hanging fruit on the trees at some overlook places to pull over and view the river. Some great foraging opportunities for me. Crowds of people and no one picking these berries? They were instead, standing in lines to buy soft drinks and water in plastic bottles. Selfishly, it made me glad that their fears and/or apprehension, and likely ignorance, toward eating something not sold to them within the confines of a plastic container, was playing greatly to my advantage. I stuffed myself while some folks seemed to watch me and withdraw as though they thought I might be eating hemlock root and keel over in front of them. I guess it proves that, "You can take the boy out of the country but you can't take the country out of the boy."

On our walk back to the marina from the bike shop, we happened upon a woman walking; an older woman, in a white flowing gown, walking toward us on a sidewalk in residential Niagara by the Lake. Sue and I looked at each other as though we needed affirmation that we both had seen her. Was she some sort of apparition? No. She couldn't be. She spoke softly as she passed. Her skin was pasty white. Her hair was white. When she passed we turned to look at her expecting to see her disappear in a cloud of smoke or fog. I wonder still what her story was.

Thirty two miles of biking and three miles of walking later, found us back at Sweet Breeze and an invitation to join Ian and Robin for supper on their sailboat, *Passage*, moored out in the river about 100 yards. I swam out to their boat, just for good measure and to bathe and cool down. The swift current gave me pause however, so I wore a life jacket just in case I missed their boat and was swept out to sea by the great river Niagara. Good to have the assurance of the floatation. The current felt even swifter than it looked.

Our generous hosts treated us to sushi and wine and fruit and later to a ferry ride back to shore with their motor powered dinghy. Sue and I had lots to talk about before turning in to our bunks after a day packed with amazement, physical toil, and wonder. If everyday of our normal existence was so packed with adventure and "life" what fullness and good fortune we would have.

Email, Saturday, July 6th. I love the kind and thoughtful and supportive emails that folks have sent. They give me the little push that I sometimes need to keep going on this sometimes challenging adventure. As Dave and Sue and I were waiting to enter the Welland Canal up alongside comes a sailboat with a couple from Duluth. We followed them through the locks all day and out onto Lake Ontario to the mouth of the Niagara River. The canal and eight locks dropped us about 325 feet where we celebrated one more lake behind me. Sue will sail with me for a week or as long as she can tolerate me. Keep those emails coming. Hugs. Curt.

Sue was up early for her run. Sometimes I feel like a slug. Sitting around drinking my sweetened and fattened tea and writing while she is running all around town working off whatever...she doesn't have an ounce of fat on her.

The marine forecast predicts light southwest winds for the day, five to fifteen knots; perfect for that broad reach heading east down the windward shore of Lake Ontario. Summertime, and the livin' is easy aboard Sweet Breeze today.

Winds were lighter than light. So light that we had to do a lot of motoring and motor sailing. Having a lot of energy and perhaps being a bit bored Sue suggested that we could do some boat cleaning on this bright, warm July day. Huh? While I would never choose cleaning as a first choice with some free time to spend, I had noticed that there were some ants taking up residence in certain areas on board. Sue thought perhaps the ants were building an anthill up in the port V-berth where I had my sleeping quarters (nest). I did have a deck brush and pail; we had a lake full of fresh water to rinse with, and Sue's boundless energy. Swab the deck, matie. Those ants out foraging were going to have to swim for it, or scurry off to their onboard anthill, wherever that was.

While we were in the cleaning mood, we put out a drag line with some of our biking clothes attached to it and other sundry clothing that could use some freshening up. With a woman on board, those kind of ideas seem to take shape.

We motored up a small river to a marina at Olcott, New York, tied up and went to stretch our legs. The town didn't have any markets for us to get any provisions, but it did have a machine where we could check into U.S.Customs, which we did, and once again, it seemed so silly, the whole process of the back and forth checking in. The communications exercise caused me to wonder just how many smugglers or terrorists have called into customs before entering to do their business. I stood in front of a camera as he questioned me from cyberspace somewhere. Were there any passengers on the boat, he asked, and I told him about Sue and had her step in front of the camera. I wondered if those ants we washed overboard were technically considered passengers. American or Canadian ants, I had no way of knowing.

Sue prepared a great salad as we motored down the south shore of Lake Ontario and, as with Kay, Sue and I had a light-hearted banter or some philosophical discussion going most times when sailing was not a taxing operation and Otto was steering.

Toward late afternoon we motored up into another small river called Oak Orchard Creek and tied up with help from Bob, a local boater, at a dock on the east side of the river. The marina was a facility provided by the town and Bob was my first introduction to the friendly locals of Upstate New York.

At a nearby park I once again boldly asked a family of picnickers for directions to a local store or market. It was a birthday party and Sue and I were invited to join them...we did briefly and learned a bit about their family and of a market a mile down the road. Two young girls of the family had the prettiest eyes and of course I had to mention that to them and of course they giggled and looked at each other and thought who knows what about that old, crusty sailor from Minnesota.

Sue and I really just wanted a walk, more than we needed boat provisions. The market about a mile away seemed perfect; country roads with blackberries alongside and not much car traffic. There was a fishing tackle shop along the way where I bought a spinning rod and reel to use to try to supplement the protein stores on the boat.

On a hill down to the bridge across the river I had to stop and watch what I surely thought was the preliminary acceleration toward some young broken bones. There was a teenage boy who was riding down the blacktop hill while sitting on an office chair, the kind with the four small wheels. It looked like something I would have done at that age, with no brakes and no clue as to the outcome. He managed to come to a stop in the gravel before the river, the bridge, or any personal damage. He must have done it before. That was a good thing. I really didn't want to tend his broken body while waiting for an ambulance.

Brown's Farm Market was the best. Fresh fruits of all sorts. Blueberries in season. I bought a whole quart of fresh blueberries and sat down and ate them all. We bought a few other things that we didn't need and backpacked our treasures to the boat. What is not to like about this area.

We had it all. A scenic river and dock of our own. Some live music might be a nice touch, however. So honestly, this happened....floating down the river on a houseboat comes a lively bunch of musicians playing and singing some old rock-and-roll tunes. Whatever.

Then the local navy arrived next door (next dock, actually). A coast guard boat pulled up on one side and a sheriff's boat on the other and we were assured of a restful night's sleep free from the immediate threat of terrorists. I was amazed at the power plants on the back of one of the boats. Not one, not two, but three, 300 horsepower outboard motors on one fairly small boat. What were they thinking? Cheap fuel? Could that boat actually take flight? Do us taxpayers really have pockets that deep…? I had some other questions about their boat and recent activities that were best left unasked. I can be so cynical sometimes!

Sue and I went to sleep wondering about the ants. How could they get aboard and establish a colony? She thought they marched aboard like soldiers on the dock lines much like a wharf rat does. They clean up crumbs and haul away any dirt particles to obscure places and so keep the boat tidy, I thought. I guess the lightness and humor of our thoughts reflect the ease of our journey. We are friends so lucky in life.

Sunday, July 7th. Rain during the night, mostly slept through it. Heavy, humid, clean air smells of trees and plants. Sue up early and off for a run. Tea and writing for me.

The south shore of Lake Ontario looks green and lush from the water. I can see rows of what must be fruit orchards and simple old farm and waterfront homes. Nothing much pretentious about upstate New York. Not many homes shouting out the accumulated wealth of the homeowners here. Refreshing air, clean looking water that smells fishy, and a refreshingly simple looking pastoral lifestyle ashore. Upstate New York could call me back another day.

If we could find some wind and shut off the motor it would be idyllic. We could make it to Rochester and beyond with some quiet assistance of offshore breezes. We make good time with the motor too, but quiet time sailing is really what makes for quiet nerves and a feeling of oneness with the water and the world. It's hard for me to describe in words the peaceful feeling I get when the motor is shut down and the sails start working their magic. It must be something deeper than words.

An afternoon wind over the starboard quarter pushed and pulled us way beyond Rochester to a likely looking stopover called Sodus Bay and the Katlynn Marina. Bright sun on the water and the light winds made for long hot days and an early stopover was just fine with me; against my usual push for miles-made-good.

We were welcomed by neighbor sailors on the adjacent dock before our feet hit solid ground. John and Sandy were having a light supper of salad and wine and we could join if we so desired. John wore a t-shirt with the image of Geronimo and his small band of warriors and the message: "Fighting terrorism since 1492". The same one that I had on. Political allies we were. Fresh food allies too.

Monday, July 8th. Up not so early. Sue gone on a run. Hot shower and shave. Gas and go.

It was a short morning sail east to Little Sodus Bay where we sailed up alongside

Robin and Ian, who we had last seen in the Niagara River. They were out on the lake with Robin's sister, whom they had met in the harbor of Little Sodus Bay. Just a brief exchange of pleasantries later, saw us motoring on toward Oswego, New York where my recent phone and email contacts with Doug (of the Sault Ste. Marie stopover acquaintance) had arranged a meeting with Ann Gates. Ann was a new friend of Doug's that he had met on his upbound journey and she was the contact person who would get the charts of northern Lake Huron back to Doug for me. Ann was waiting at the dock.

The Oswego Yacht Club was another most welcoming safe harbor for yachties. Friendly locals and cold beer and a view of the lake and Oswego River. After fueling we moved to a transient dock for a free night's stay, alongside my new neighbors, Jean and Donald from Quebec City, way downstream on the St. Lawrence.

Old friend Dave also met us at the yacht club. He and Sue had prearranged to meet up and start their journey back to Duluth. Old friends and new friends all brought together by the common bond of boating. After a cold beer and some hugs, Dave and Sue and her gear were gone away quickly in Dave's truck, things were happening fast, and I had promised Ann that I would buy her supper at her favorite restaurant in Oswego.

She chose a good one. It was an Italian restaurant where a small salad was of a quantity to feed three lumberjacks. Then Ann took me to her favorite grocery store where I stocked up on everything that looked good and I didn't care about the weight because she would drive me back to the boat. I bought lots of real fruit juices in jugs... one of my many vices...milk chocolate, another one; the store had the good stuff, Swiss milk chocolate, so I stocked up.

Ann was a tall and strong woman. She was planning a late summer adventure down the Erie Canal to New York and beyond...a single-hander like me with a 30-foot sailboat. With some divorce unpleasantness behind her and two grown sons I thought the timing might not be right for a proposal of marriage and promise of a carefree life of sailing together. I saved it for the next port of call. My guess was that she would accomplish whatever goal she set out for herself.

I laid out some milk chocolate in an obvious place on my neighbor's boat from Quebec. Later that evening when I could hear that they had returned I went topside. They thought that I was the likely chocolate fairy and they invited me over for some wine. My $3000 boat alongside their $300,000 boat, their English a bit halting and searching but so much better than my French. No matter, sailors we were and once again a warmth bridged our language barrier. Jean (pronounced zshah) and Donald (pronounced like doe-nall') were old friends and retired professionals from Quebec City. They were on their annual sojourn upbound through the Great Lakes and like myself, thought that the yacht club here at Oswego was a fine and welcoming place to spend the night. Three sweetened sailors we were, with chocolate and port wine our bedtime snack. They were patient with my language curiosity and gave me my first lessons in French, knowing that soon I would be in French speaking Quebec for several weeks.

Thousand Islands of the St Lawrence

Tuesday, July 9. One month and two days on the water today. The Great Lakes are mostly behind me. Feeling slightly apprehensive about the next leg of the journey.

Dave and Sue are gone. Ann and Jean and Donald are left behind. Here I am again with that unsure feeling; that push-pull, an internal ambiguity that I'll call ambivalence. I once had a woman friend who said I was ambivalent about relationships. I had to look it up. She was right I guess. Women know these things.

Heading north out the Oswego harbor, but the river leading south behind me had a certain draw as well. It could take me to the Erie Canal and the short, easy, safe way to the east coast. The route ahead down the St. Lawrence River was a complete unknown to me. All that I knew is what I had heard from others; there would be fog, big winds and big seas out the Gulf of St. Lawrence and around the Gaspé Peninsula. That was the likely weather scenario, or so I was told, but I figured I could pick my way, sneak around the corner toward Nova Scotia in passable weather.

The short cut of the Erie Canal would shave about 2500 miles off the river route northeast to the sea...but deep down I knew which way really drew me. If I was in a hurry or had a destination in mind somewhere down the east coast, then it would be the canal. But this whole adventure was not about a destination other than getting to the sea. The only thoughts of clarity that were ever present with me were those of journeying, seeing, feeling, meeting the unknowns of all sorts. The Gulf of St. Lawrence and the North Atlantic around the Maritime Provinces of Canada would be my Cape Horn; my challenge to meet head-on, alone. I looked behind me a time or two but kept a northerly heading across Lake Ontario where the current of the big river would begin to draw us to the sea. The light southwest breeze over our shoulder confirmed that it was the right choice.

We would be heading northeast now, Sweet Breeze and me, for the next thousand miles or so until we rounded the cape at Canso, Nova Scotia. There we would make a hard right turn to the south-southwest for another unknown leg down another unfamiliar coast.

Intrigue might be a good word to describe my mindset as I crossed Lake Ontario. What must the flow and power of the St. Lawrence River be like? The St. Marys River was impressive. The St. Claire River scooted us along at nine knots at a 30-foot depth. Now the St. Lawrence had two more great lakes and all the rivers and streams that entered their waters to channel out to the sea. That is a lot of water. The whole of east-central North America is drained out to sea by the St. Lawrence. Once mixed into the North Atlantic waters the ocean currents would eventually take this water south to warmer seas where evaporation under hot sunshine would draw the water up into the atmosphere, there it would form clouds and fall to land again, water our crops and flow back to the sea. The life supporting water cycle, taken for granted mostly, not noticed or given much thought, the absolute sustainer of life as we know it.

The Thousand Islands of the St. Lawrence begins where the northeastern corner of the lake narrows and there begins a noticeable flowage. There were no visible signs of current but the speed of the boat over the bottom began to increase and the response to the rudder began to feel less predictable. There was lots of shipping traffic to keep track of and as usual in heavy traffic, I tried to stay to the far right side of the marked channels as the afternoon sun swung toward evening. The scenery fascinated me as always. A U.S. customs vessel with big outboards chased down an upbound foreign freighter, maneuvered up alongside it and the ship stopped in mid-channel. They worked out their apparent misunderstandings after a while and went about their business of shipping and the checking of ships.

Oh the sights you see in the Thousand Islands of the St. Lawrence.

One day without a woman on board and my boat is already looking messy, cluttered. Ants are still roaming the decks on their foraging duties. I think I read somewhere that ants were so essential to the natural balance of life on earth, their role was so critical, that most life would cease without them. I'm not sure if I believed it.

We were on the southern shipping channel, on the U.S. side of the river. The river is braided through lots of islands, more than a thousand. There were some homes on the islands to the left, and on the right were the pastoral scenes of rural New York. This was the beginning of that wonderful intimacy of river travel where around every bend were different sights to see...where the horizons were intimate. In my canoeing days I had always been drawn around the next bend; that ever-driving curiosity of the explorer I suppose. It was the same here.

It had been a long day of sailing and motor sailing...a perfect warm and sunny cruise from Oswego, a bit too sunny for my exposed skin. I could feel that sensitive warmth of near sunburn on my arms and face. A dodger or a bimini would have been nice, even for a real sailor on a real sailboat (not a motor home on water like Jean and Donald's Beneteau).

We were looking for a tie-up or anchorage for the night on the right bank. My navigation chart (a New York highway map) showed a state park with boating facilities called Cedar Point Campground and Marina. I could see some boats just past the swimming beach, but no sailboat masts, just powerboats. That had become an automatic caution sign for me, suggesting that the harbor depths might not be deep enough for sailboats so I tied up on the outermost jetty/dock and walked ashore to check out depths. The water around the docks was very clear with tall underwater plants, like looking down, suspended above a forest of trees, with some small fish lurking about. It looked to be deep enough for Sweet Breeze to coast into most slips. I hadn't been stuck on bottom since Lake Superior and surely didn't want that high anxiety helpless feeling again anytime soon.

Two cell phone calls from home: Marna with some newsy news of friends and family and Tom, my harbor chaplain back home, with news of the blessing he would ask upon Sweet Breeze on the coming weekend event at Barker's Island Marina in Superior, Wisconsin.

The state park was a good choice. Quiet...showers and fuel and an early bunk for me with thoughts and anticipation of the sights that tomorrow and this great North American river would bring.

Wednesday, July 10th...warm breezes greet me as I climb the companionway ladder.

Up and about at 5:30 a.m. and underway as soon as that first cup of tea is sampled. Chai tea sweetened with real maple syrup and fattened with half-and-half. I may have said that recipe before but I think it's worth repeating. Each and everyday needs some special self indulgence to start out right.

A westerly breeze blew Sweet Breeze off the dock and got her headed downstream on a broad reach. The white pines on the rocky isle midstream tell me that the westerly is the prevailing wind here. Most of the branches have been groomed by the wind and are reaching toward the east. Some of the trunks (boles to an old forester) have an ever so slight lean to the east. It could be a remote island in the Boundary Waters Wilderness, but for a home or a cabin perched amongst the rocks and trees.

Yesterday, on the very first large island upon entering the St. Lawrence, I sailed slowly by an old abandoned mansion. It was amazing in style and enormity and was in a thoroughly dilapidated condition. Windows were broken and holes were showing through the roof. I couldn't make sense of it and I couldn't sail by slowly enough to gauge or guess what it once was and what might have happened. Did someone build it and then ran out of the money to maintain it? Was it built for an Alfred Hitchcock movie and then abandoned? It didn't look like a Hollywood set...it was too substantial looking.

As I often do, while writing this book, I try to do some light research to find out just what it was that my daily journal took note of throughout my Big Sail. The fascination I had with the crumbling mansion of Carleton Island proved itself worthy. I learned that the Carleton Villa was built in 1894 by a New Yorker who made his fortune by selling a new invention of the times, the Remington Typewriter. History has it that he died in his sleep during his first night in his new summer retreat. It has been standing vacant for sixty years.

By far the most unusual home that I have seen from the water since leaving Duluth, is also on Carleton Island. Two adjacent farm silos have small cottages built on top with a walkway between them. It took me some views from different angles to figure that out. That is a really unique and good use of an existing solid foundation.

Ahead on the right, the Rock Island Lighthouse reminds me to keep checking my position. Reefs are numerous and rocky and this sailing tourist had better not get too engrossed in the scenery.

The Thousand Island Bridge is in view downriver. It looks high with lots of mast clearance...one of the reasons that I stay in the shipping lanes in unfamiliar waters.

I love the tiny islands. Some just large enough for a tiny cottage. Some tiny islands look like they might sink under the weight of the excessive homes that burden them.

The scenery on all sides creates lots of head movement on this sailor's part. Rocks, water, and pines...my favorite combination of natural features all juxtaposed in that contrasting blend of Canadian Shield topography, unique to the Great Lakes region. Two small islands have a connecting walk bridge which doubles the owner's real estate but still leaves me with the attractive sense of living on and in small spaces... and at the edge of a small island forest, with one tree.

My aesthetics draws me to the homes tucked back into the pines. Those with rock work and dark wood that don't proclaim their presence but give the impression that they grew up slowly, quietly, like the trees around them, from their natural surroundings.

My usual quest for maximizing my sailing speed is working against me now as I slip too quickly by some natural features on small islands that I would like to absorb more for the lasting effects on my visual memory. These are the intimate times when sailing only, provides the quiet view from the water that most car travelers never see. I take a few photos, but very few. My preference on this whole sailing adventure has been for memory photos. For me, being present, acutely present, and recording my surroundings with all my senses is the ultimate multi-dimensional photography. It's a selfish sort of sightseeing. The difficulty is in sharing with others later. Words are often sorely inadequate.

Though I would enjoy sharing this special part of this special journey the aloneness provides an awareness that I treasure. I may make a comment aloud occasionally or ask Sweet Breeze if she's paying attention but beyond that, it's all about soaking up the sights.

The river here simply amazes me. Heavy steel marker buoys are tipping slightly downstream and the surface shows the water wrapping around the body of the buoy. There are lots of osprey nests, I think, or some other birds building bulky nests on the tops of the buoys.

It looks like rain and feels like rain; humid and warm and thick feeling and smelling like heavy, tropical air. I love these kinds of days. The earth feels so alive and so do I. Weedy bays tucked up into the islands on both sides look fishy. The ospreys would know.

With only a very light wind over the starboard quarter we are still carrying a remarkable speed of five to six knots over the ground. Sometimes we are going faster than the wind as the sails slacken but our speed still holds at six knots. The depth meter shows it as deep as 200 feet with a swift current flow. This river's power is amazing.

More rocks and pines and water and scenery that only gets better. More homes on the islands that I could never afford (nor want...remember, I lived well in a ten by twelve foot cabin, and still had trouble finding my glasses). Then, almost hidden in the pines is an unobtrusive little place that I could love and call home. Some homes shout, "Hey, look at me," and some whisper, "Try to find me in the pines," resplendent in their shyness.

Back at Camp Cotton, on the river in northern Minnesota, I made a bench in the pines high above the river. When the mosquitoes are few it's a good place to sit and watch the river go by. Here, on the St. Lawrence, I have this feeling that the river is watching me go by.

Still swift, with eddies on the surface yet depths of 130 feet, this old river has carried me along at five to seven knots for nearly twelve hours. We pulled into the yacht club at Brockville for a brief respite and some chart studying. I was starting to think about a harbor for the night and about how to find a crewman to help me lock downbound on the locks ahead. The four Canadian and two American locks ahead required at least two aboard when locking down.

To this Midwesterner, unlikely sailor, the warm wind and the heavy air gave hint at some weather in the near future. Those big puffy cumulonimbus clouds were climbing higher and darker in the west. The charts showed a marina at Iroquois, Ontario ahead on the left, somewhere down an abandoned channel that looked like it had once led to a lock that was no longer used. I spotted a sign on the left side of the shipping lane ahead, on the sud-ouest (southwest) end of Iroquois Island. It said Marina and had an arrow pointing left. I had some serious reservations about the looks of these backwaters...were they deep enough for sailboats or was the marina just for shallow draught powerboats?

Email: Thursday, July 11th, 6 a.m.... Imagine every drop of water entering all of the great lakes flowing to the ocean in one great river...the St. Lawrence. One hundred fifty feet deep and swift with surface currents that toss Sweet Breeze about and not 1000 islands but 1800 have we passed on our run down from Lake Ontario. A stiff wind of 20-knots on the quarter, plus the current gave us an easy 60-mile day. Nearing the first of seven locks around the rapids down to Montreal. Need a crew to lock down. I ask everyone that I meet if they would like an adventurous free ride down the river to Montreal. No luck yet. At a little marina on the Canadian side of an unused canal. Thunderstorm approaching...gotta go. Wish me "lock".

Hugs, Curt.

The channel was narrow but deep enough, swampy, with a mud bottom and weedy shorelines. If I wasn't so worried about running aground and beating the storm I could have better soaked up the intimacies of the backwater channel. Finally, ahead on the left, I could see some masts through the trees and a connecting channel to the pond where the Iroquois marina was hiding. With nobody around and rain and wind and thunder and lightning just about upon us, I tied her up securely to an outer dock with lots of fenders between and hunkered down in the cabin for some supper (sardines) and the entertainment of the hellish wind, downpour, and thunder so loud you could feel it thumping against the hull.

Good timing. Lucky timing. Ten minutes later would have found me out in the river looking for an anchorage in the lee of an island or some sort of barrier for protection. I couldn't have run with the storm downriver very far because the first lock was only about a half mile downstream. With the power of the current and the winds of the thunderstorm, add to it the shorelines and shoaling hazards all unbeknownst to me, it would have been a soaking experience at best and a grounding experience at worst.

The rain and associated noisy storm that carried it; the sudden violence of it all, had moved on within the hour and the freshness of washed air and those magical streaks of sunlight through the gaps of darkened clouds, drew me out of the belly of Sweet Breeze and out onto the docks and over the grass I roamed. It didn't occur to me that this was Canadian soil, only that it was so utterly pleasant and fresh after the storm. There were frogs and herons and mosquitoes, and life was all around, like me, checking out the after-storm beauty or going about the business of securing food.

There was wi-fi available, so I wrote up one of my best and cleverest emails to the folks back home and as I was about to click on send, the power went out and my message got lost in cyberspace and once again this gadget world that I toyed with left me cold, and muttering some of those words my granddaughters should never hear.

Thursday, July 11th…up late — 6:30 a.m.… No hurry to do anything 'til the Marina office opens.

More of that after-storm, sensual bathing for me in the rich and heavy wafts of scented air flowing off the water and through the trees…everything wet and clean and tropical feeling. The backwater bay has that early morning ghosting of wispy fog, slowly swirling, unsure whether to rise or to hover over the water still longer. Even birdsongs can I hear. Friendly mosquitoes remind me that I am a food source as well as a sensual sponge.

Email Thursday, July 12th, 8 a.m.… Darn, forgot to call Canada Customs as soon as I entered Canadian waters yesterday. I guess I was too busy sailing and absorbing the scenery and trying to find my way toward some sheltered place before the thunderstorm hit at Iroquois, Ontario. Big winds and rain knocked the power out at the marina. Still trying to find a crewman to help me with the upcoming locks, but for now I must stay where I am 'till the customs officers clear me. Found my hearing aids and I can hear birds singing. Please send money if in jail or if I forget to promptly call customs again…hugs, Curt.

Attached to the front of the marina office is a large sign that reminds the visitor to check in with Canadian Customs immediately upon stepping ashore, if not before. Oops. Forgot. I did then call immediately. There were lots of questions on the other end of the phone and customs officers were dispatched to check me out.

When the agents arrived (darn it again, they were young and had that freshly out of training look) and I knew by their serious demeanor that I had done a bad thing by forgetting to call immediately and it became clear that I was in for a scolding and possibly more. They were very professional. My friendliest, grandfatherliest smiles softened them not a bit. As they questioned me repeatedly I couldn't help but notice what a gorgeous young woman she was (in a grandfatherly way of course). They jogged me back into the gravity of my offense with more questions. I was hoping that I wouldn't have to call my friend Hillary at the State Department to get me out of this fix that my poor memory and lack of nationalistic fervor and awareness had gotten me into. That's it! Not my fault, it's my memory!

It seemed that they were gradually arriving at a consensus of two that I was neither a terrorist nor a smuggler and that I had no weapons of mass or singular destruction except my pocketknife. I was to be put on a delinquent caller list but the $1000 fine would not be levied (because of my honest face and respectful demeanor, I thought)..."this time." I played the forgetful old man card too, because it was completely true. I promised that next time I touched Canadian soil I would call **immediately**...memory permitting.

Eventually then, I did get a really lovely smile that softened the sting of the mistrust of Canadian officialdom. The reprimand too was soon forgotten and I was back into the joy of this otherwise glorious morning in the backwaters of the St Lawrence, on water and soil upon which I could lay no rightful claim beyond that human, soulful, sensual absorption of nature that knows no borders. Back into the reveries of nature I slipped.

When the marina office opened, Mclissa, the attendant, had some more good news. Robert, the boss and owner of the marina, just might let her crew for me through the first lock.

Robert had some old attachments to the Alabama Crimson Tide; there was memorabilia everywhere, but the best part about Robert was his generous spirit. He agreed to let Melissa crew for me through the Iroquois Lock and would send another marina worker to pick her up. That was some really good news.

Melissa and I left immediately before Robert changed his mind and motored our way back out the narrow backwater channel to the shipping lane. I contacted the lockmaster by radio and we were locked through without any wait.

Just downstream, after exiting the lock, Melissa showed me where to let her off at another marina. I offered her some money in thanks, but she wouldn't take it. How to properly thank Robert and the crew at Iroquois Marine Services...just another of my many good fortunes with good people.

My next real challenge was not about sailing or finding my way but was another crew challenge. The next six locks, two U.S. and four Canadian, would also require more that just me aboard and as yet my best bet in finding crew lay with my young Canadian friend (and surrogate daughter) Lydia, who was in Kitchener, Ontario completing coursework and internship for her midwifery program. I had met her some years ago at a folk festival in a little town at the northernmost tip of Lake Superior called Red Rock. She was bold, forthright, and sweet (much like me) and we went for an afternoon sail on my boat. We happened to hook up and sail together because she walked down the dock, toward me and Sweet Breeze, and said something like, "Hi, I like to sail...why don't you take me out for a sail?" That's my Lydia. We have been friends ever since.

If I had any goal in mind, besides sailing to salt water, it was to find Lydia in Nova Scotia, where she had friends and was going to be staying later this summer. I didn't really need any goals, but having a stated goal made it easier to understand for all those well meaning and destination minded folks, along the way, who asked me where I was going or why I was going. Most times my answer to this often asked question would vary according to the snap judgment I would make about the questioner. If they looked and talked like conventional sorts I would just say I was sailing to Halifax to meet a long lost friend. If my snap judgment was correct, then they could grasp the answer immediately and knew I was a man with a plan, but If they had that alternative look of someone without a plan or a destination, someone relaxed and living the present moment, I would be slightly more forthright and tell them I was headed downstream to saltwater and beyond, wherever the wind may blow. "Cool," they might say, again if my snap judgment was right. But I really did want to find Lydia.

Lydia and I had kept in contact by phone and text messages throughout my sail. She knew some friends in Toronto who may want to crew for me just for the experience and adventure of it, but for now it was one lock at a time, one lucky break at a time, and one adventurous new acquaintance at a time.

The rest of this day was spent, as usual, putting on as many miles as was reasonable, chasing the variable winds and trying not to motor while allowing for an early stopover for the night. The miles both sailed by and motored by and the sights of the islands and the many braided channels of the river kept me peering towards the shores but also vigilant for buoys, keeping us in the main shipping channel. There were some farms and small towns to the right, on the New York side and lots of mid-channel islands on the left. If I had local knowledge of the river it would have been even more interesting to take some of the less used waterways off to the left around the islands, but I felt the need to play it safe and stay within the shipping lane.

Melissa, back at Iroquois, had made some telephone contacts for me to try to find a crewman for the Eisenhower and Snell Locks. My best chance to find an adventurous body seemed to be with the yacht club near Long Sault, Ontario called the Stormont.

The Stormont Yacht Club was my next goal. It was somewhere up ahead on the left shoreline back behind many islands, big and small, in the mysterious backwaters of the St. Lawrence. It would be my last chance of finding a crewman before the

American locks just ahead.

There appeared to be a family fishing outing on a houseboat, fishing and swimming off to my left, just offshore from one of the several islands with a dense forest canopy of hardwood trees. Houseboats looked like a roomy, stable way to enjoy being on the water. I could live on one of those but I would have to rig up a sail and a swing keel to make use of the wind. I couldn't motor all the time.

I was staying nearer to the New York side of the river because that's where the reassuring depths of the marked shipping lane was, but along the north shoreline was a string of smaller islands all connected by roads and bridges. This was another of those several areas of summertime water playgrounds that the St. Lawrence was revealing to me for mile after mile.

Now was the time to cut across the shipping lane and weave through the islands and shoals and bars toward the north shore. I could see the first lock in the distance straight ahead. The channels between islands looked deep enough, on my nav chart, if I carefully kept track of my position.

Long story short, rounding the end of the next island, deep back within a shallow bay I could see that friendly, beckoning forest of sailboat masts and some channel markers pointing the way.

Entering the marina proper, there was an easily accessible transient dock long enough for at least two boats, but a less considerate mariner had tied up right in the middle not leaving enough dock space forward or aft for another boat. I waved to a guy beyond the visitor dock and gave him the universal open armed, "Where can I pull in?" gesture. He gave me the "follow him" wave and Tom helped me squeeze Sweet Breeze into a tight open slip with my fenders keeping me off my immediate neighbor's boat.

It was one of those perfect summer days of short sleeves and shorts. Warm, sunny and bright. I followed Tom over to Harry's Cantina, which was a picnic table in the shade, next to the club's maintenance garage. Harry was the contact person that Melissa (through Ed, the phone contact at Stormont) said I should ask about a crewperson for the locks. Harry couldn't go with me tomorrow because of some tractor repair work that he had to get parts for but he said to, "Ask Rudi over there in the shade."

Rudi got me a cold beer from the fridge in the garage, looked me over, up and down, asked me where I was from and where I was headed and simply said, "Yup, I'll go with". It was almost too easy. I guess I wasn't just another pretty face...these were some "swell fellas" (as we'd say back in Minnesota).

After a brief acquaintance and a cold Canadian beer Rudi wanted to see my boat (to make sure it would go the distance perhaps). Then he volunteered to get some nav charts from his nearby home so we could look over the river ahead. We agreed to head out at 8 a.m. the next morning.

Email: July 11th, 6 p.m. Avoided a $1000 fine, "cause I look old and sunburned and pitiful."
Found a volunteer crew for the first lock ahead...Melissa was helpful, and pretty of course, and just

one more friendly Canadian who wanted to contribute her time to my adventure. At Long Sault now, found another volunteer, Rudi, at the yacht club. Great guy, not pretty, but will see me through the next two locks, the Eisenhower and Snell, dropping us about 60 feet...then four more locks to go. The river may have tidal swells at Montreal...need to learn about tide times and tidal currents but like normal, learn as I go. Gotta make a big salad now in celebration of new friends, hot weather, and good winds today, gusty though, almost lost dinghy off the cabin roof as a gust lifted it and tossed it over against the lifelines. The river is full of rocky reefs, must be vigilant. Otto gave out today so must steer by hand. Remember, better to lock down than to be locked up...hugs, Curt.

I spent the rest of the afternoon wandering around the grounds of the yacht club looking at the various boats. There was one on the hard, back in the weeds a ways that caught my eye for the classic lines and stiff looking hull design. It looked like a complete project boat that one ambitious yachtsmith could bring back to life with a good set of skills and a lot of free time. I loved to work on sailboats, but not now, Sweet Breeze and me were on a downstream agenda. I was just window-shopping. I do that at every marina.

We were getting close to salt water, but I wasn't sure how far tidal surges backed up into the St. Lawrence. It had to be somewhere below the locks at Montreal, one would think. How could the locks work with water flowing both ways?

I met an interesting lady at the clubhouse later that evening as I was about to shower up. She was using the wi-fi on a laptop. I told her, in a helpful and friendly way, just to strike up conversation, that it seemed to work better in the next room closer to the router (broadcaster). She asked what I was doing there and I replied that I was going to use the shower room. Then she looked me up and down and said, "No, you cannot, that is for guests and boaters." Maybe I looked like a hobo to her, a bit unkempt, unshaven, and I tried to laugh it off thinking she must be joking but she kept insisting that I leave. I was getting irritated with her attitude and she was getting more insistent. Couldn't she tell that I was the skipper of the good ship Sweet Breeze? That we had sailed a long, long way, and were reasonably harmless? Good that some other people came into the club room about then; more local club members and friendly. Our baffling discussion dissolved and I took my shower. The old adage came to mind, "What do you get when you argue with a fool? Two fools." I think I narrowly escaped being the second one.

I could never be sure what her problem was but I did learn that she was on the sailboat that had taken up the whole visitor dock by not pulling forward. Her strange behavior and the inconsiderate docking seemed like some sort of pattern of egocentrism or perhaps she was just nuts. I was okay with just nuts.

Friday, July 12th...waking to a chorus of bull frogs croaking...not as pretty as a robin's song, but interesting and new to me.

Straightening up the boat. Getting it ready for my guest, my crewman, my navigator, my line handling locksman...Rudi was my man. I hadn't had a guest on board since Sue jumped ship at Oswego and it only took but a few days for the cabin to "clutter up" considerably.

Rudi and I had a plan. We would lock down through the Eisenhower and Snell and head for the city of Cornwall, Ontario where Rudi's wife would pick him up for the drive home. There I would take on another crewman passenger...I hoped.

Rudi and I got along great. He was a kind of wannabe philosopher like me. We were relaxed together right away. He was a local sailor and he thought that we could take a shortcut through a shoal area between the islands to the shipping channel. I had avoided that possible route on the way into the marina as an unknown and risky area. I was pleased that I hadn't run aground since Lake Superior—they were some really anxious times—but Rudi seemed confident that we could slip through and I was all about short cuts.

There was plenty of water under the boat through the shoaling areas. Back onto the shipping lane and down the canal we motored and we were quick to gain access to the first lock and all was smooth. I think the Eisenhower dropped us about thirty feet. The currents above and below the locks were not as strong as they were upriver through the rocky channels and the pine crested islands. The river was broad here with more mud and sand and hardwood trees ashore.

Last evening, at the yacht club, between bites of a salad of wilted lettuce and other veggies a little past their prime, Lydia sent me a text message and asked me to contact her friend Mark in Toronto; he could possibly be a crew for me for the Canadian locks. Mark and I text messaged back and forth a few times. He wasn't working and wanted an opportunity to learn to sail. His tone of voice, when we finally had a phone conversation, gave me the impression that he didn't have a lot of extra cash and wasn't sure how to find transportation to Cornwall, Ontario where we could meet up. Very hesitantly, he told me that he could take a train to Cornwall but that it cost $120.

"Get on that train, Mark. Put it on a credit card. I'll reimburse you as soon as you get here."

"You sure you want to do that?" he asked.

"I'm very sure," I replied and I felt lucky to have made contact with him.

Mark thought that he could make it to Cornwall sometime tomorrow afternoon. It seemed like a done deal and Mark sounded like the "real deal" on the phone. Just another average day of good fortune for this old sailor far from home.

After the second lock, I asked Rudi about another shortcut to Cornwall. It was called Polly's Gut and cut across to the north channel at the upstream end of Cornwall Island. We were in the south channel and Polly's would save a few miles down around the far end of Cornwall Island, then left and back upstream to Cornwall.

Rudi nixed that shortcut. He said the current was too strong against us, especially if the dam upstream was partly open. A semi-smart skipper doesn't argue with a local sailor who is also, at the time, his pilot and navigator and local historian, etc.

Cornwall Island is about four miles long and one mile wide and was set aside as a reserve for the Akwesasne Mohawk Tribe of Canada. We sailed under a bridge that is an international border crossing between New York state and Cornwall, Ontario. Rudi told me that the bridge has been a controversial crossing because of smuggling and armed crossing guards and protests by the local Mohawks who don't want armed guards on their island. I'm not going to choose sides but history has an unusually long record of either a sly or blatant disregard for native rights or treaty rights by encroaching Euro-governments. Enough said.

We made slow but eventual progress against the river's current up the north channel to Marina 200 at Cornwall. We refueled at this upscale marina and carefully docked at our assigned slip between boats that cost many, many times what Sweet Breeze might be worth. One extravagance that I never wanted to use was a liability boat insurance policy that I bought for Sweet Breeze and me before leaving Duluth.

I had to find something on board to give Rudi...just a token of thanks for the help and the friendship. Thinking of a useful token, I had brought along a few hardwood handholds that I had made for boats or anywhere else that one might need a sturdy grip. Rudi thought he could use it on his sailboat.

My Newest Crew

Email: July 12th, Friday, 3 p.m. To Rudi and Ed and Harry and Ralph and Tom...the guys at the Stormont Yacht Club...the friendliest yacht club in 1500 miles of sailing. Special thanks to retired Commodore Rudi who crewed for me through the American locks and then caught a ride back home from Cornwall, Ontario. We told each other some sailing lies and learned a bit about each other on this short leg of locks, dams, and bridges downriver. At Cornwall now, once a millinery and textile producer with unused locks and canals through the city. Mark is on a train from Toronto...will meet him for the first time soon. He will sail with me to Montreal or beyond. Soon will be leaving English speaking Ontario on the left bank and New York on the right. Language will become a challenge with Quebec on both shores. Maybe Mark speaks French? Where is that Marna when I need her? (She is good with French, well, written French anyhow). Till we wi-fi again...Curt.

After writing an email and a short nap below, I heard a voice from above. It was Mark, tall, thin, smiling, and looking debonair in his new sun hat.

We got acquainted quickly. His big light-hearted smile got even bigger when I gave him a couple of hundred dollar bills from my stash. We stowed his gear and got his bed ready in the port V-berth where his long legs could stretch out. I had to tease him lightly, just to test him out, find out how seriously he took this life we were given. I liked his response...big easy smiles.

My mother used to say us boys had a hollow leg when we were young and she tried to fill us with her good cooking. We ate like we had voids to fill and now I had a young, "crewman in the making" who had little knowledge of sailing but I suspected knew well how to eat. Mark had passed a grocery store nearby...we agreed we would venture forth and reprovision our ship. A well-fed crew is a happy crew.

Already I was taking advantage of my new crewman's long arms as I piled on the grocery bags for the short hike back to the boat. As we shopped, Mark told me to watch for a green or red dot on some of the product packaging because it had a bargain price and that's how he was used to shopping back in Toronto on a budget. I think I said something like, "Get whatever you like Mark, red, green, or no dots, It's on me and you're worth it." We got some of his favorite foods and some of mine as well. Mark was not a picky eater so we made peace on that account right off too.

The old saying about beggars should not be choosy didn't take into account my good luck. Any warm body who could fog a mirror or cast a shadow would have got me through the locks okay, but I had lucked into a genuine article of a good guy.

Saturday, July 13th. Looking forward to getting to know Mark. Sailing classes with Curt.

I was up early catching up on my journal and getting that first comforting chai fix. Mark was soon after showing some signs of life and we would be underway with the sunrise; just a normal start for me, early on the water and hopefully an early mooring for the night. Mark said that he slept well and didn't need any coffee, tea would be fine, another good sign.

We motored straight into the wind leaving Cornwall, peering ahead onto the bright dancing reflections, searching out the channel markers. It felt like it would be a hot day when the sun climbed high.

"Red, right, return to port. That means the green, flat topped cans will be on our right all the way to the sea," my first instructions to Mark. Next, I tried to describe how to line up the green cans (right side channel markers) so that we could tell where the shipping channel was. On the paper chart I showed him where we were and where we were headed. With our binoculars I asked him to search out more buoys ahead to have an overall idea of our course on the right side of the shipping lane. Then I asked Mark to find our position on the chart plotter and steer us down river.

Mark had lots of questions and lots of smiles and once or twice I asked him to confirm our position and get us back on course. "Ohhhh yeah, I seeee." I was training him to coordinate our position within the parameters of the paper chart, the electronic GPS chart plotter, the depth meter, and most importantly our visual assessment of where we were with regard to shorelines and channel markers. We couldn't have our helmsman staring at the chart plotter and running into another boat or running aground outside the line of marker buoys or…!

Mark caught on quickly but I still watched over his shoulder for an hour or so and kept asking questions about our position until I felt assured that he had a complete grasp of our fundamental, "Navigation principles according to Curt." We were motoring with wind on the nose and the sails wrapped up tight; a good time, I thought, for Mark to get the hang of the helm while keeping track of position, heading, and course.

It was a long haul across the length of Lake St. Francis, against the wind for twenty-five miles. This was the first of the wide and slow waters of the Le Fleuve Saint-Laurent (St. Lawrence River) that looked like really big lakes and were called lakes. Off on the horizon to the south were the Adirondack Mountains of Vermont and New York. Ahead to the northeast, the lake narrows with Coteau du Lac and the main channel of the river to the left and the Beauharnois Channel leading to the locks and dam on the right.

The river left must drop about sixty feet through a series of rapids or falls or both because as best I can remember, the upper and lower Beauharnois Locks would drop us about thirty feet each.

Down the channel at the head of the upper lock were two powerboats with couples on board waiting for us to lock down together. I paid our locking fee ($30, I think, for each lock, at a credit card machine). We entered the lock on signal from the lockmaster following the powerboats along the left wall. Mark had tied the fenders (those inflatable vinyl "bumpers" that act as cushions to protect the sides of the boat) onto our port side; the lock attendants tossed down ropes, tied off up above, that we used to hold the boat near the lock wall and keep us from drifting fore or aft with the currents. We signaled that we were all set. Mark was forward and I was aft with the locking rope to stabilize the boat in one hand and a boathook in the other to push against the wall to fend off if necessary.

The powerboats ahead of us 50-feet or so had rafted up for the lowering process with outboard fenders between the boats, so the inner boat was close to the lock wall and the outer boat was tied alongside that boat.

As we started to slowly and gently sink with the water level we heard some hollering and looked quickly forward to see some scrambling and some angst as the power boat next to the wall began to tip away from the concrete lock wall and bang against it. It was immediately apparent what was happening and to the lock attendant above as well. The attendant cut the forward drop line instantly and the boat settled back onto the water and lurched around and banged into the wall a few times. The fenders appeared to be tied too far forward and aft and the beam of the boat clashed with the wall all the way down. Ouch!

Mark and I found it easy to control Sweet Breeze as we watched the drama unfold on the powerboats. The forward crewman must have tied the drop rope off on deck or a portion of the rope fouled and caught on some secure deck hardware. Catastrophe was averted by the quick thinking attendant above with a sharp blade in hand. I suspect there was some boat damage to the inner boat and possibly the outer boat as well. Not serious structural damage, but the kind of deep scrapes and creases that rough old concrete can leave on polished fiberglass when the two clash together... hard. Bet there were some words between captain and crew on the inner boat.

It was a short motor down the connecting canal to the lower Beauharnois lock as we followed the powerboats into the same process but without any drama or struggles this time. When the huge iron lock gates opened we motored out onto the broad vista of Lake St. Louis, an even larger lake than Lake St. Lawrence, with the skyline of Montreal ahead on the horizon across the lake, on our chosen path.

How many powerboats and jet skis can race around on Lake St. Louis at any one time? Hundreds, perhaps one thousand, was my best guess at the time. We had boats passing and boats coming at us and powerboat wakes that made a heavy chop at times on otherwise nearly windless water. It was fifteen miles of roaring engines and bikini clad babes on the bow. This was a time when I wished that gasoline cost about $40 per gallon. What a raucous waste of energy...of petroleum, that stored ancient sunlight which will one day soon be invaluable, for all of the amazing products made from oil... just by chemists changing its molecules around. But here we are, burning it just as fast as we know how. Enough said. I think. For now.

It was a relief when we finally entered the shipping canal on the south shore. Here it was narrow, quiet and intimate. The canal paralleled the main river channel and would lead us 18 miles to the two remaining locks before Montreal. St. Catherine's and St. Lambert's locks were at the lower end. The right bank of the canal was a Native reserve. There were kids walking and fishing...nice to see.

The locks were easy, uneventful, as they should be. I was reprimanded by the lockmaster, however, for calling him on channel 16, which was reserved only for emergency use, not for anything else. I plead ignorance and it was true. Mostly, I had used 16 to call bridges and locks for first contact and then would switch to the appropriate channel that they used. That was not the case here in Quebec.

We were in the land of many saints now. Quebec. Quebec, Canada...at least for now. Being sort of un-saintly, sometimes in language and sometimes in behavior I wasn't sure how the fit would be. Religion was always fine with me...fine for others, but I had little interest in the lessons of faith. Real life in the here and now was my faith. Acceptance and tolerance my prayers. The golden rule my ritual.

It had been a long, hot day on the water. Downtown Montreal was off to our left somewhere. We had made good about 80 miles with some current and wind, but mostly motor. Just below St. Lambert's lock and to the left around the lower end of an island was the huge amusement park left over from the Expo 67 world's fair, aannnd...a marina! There was a strong river current exiting the marina at the narrow entry and shallows on both sides.

We were tired and tied up to the fuel dock to the right of the entry, but it wasn't quite that easy. Mark made a dive for a dock line that I tossed poorly and short as the current swung the boat out from the dock. His sacrifice, scrapes and scratches on his chest from the dock was much appreciated. With no one around we made ourselves at home and showered with the water hose on the dock. The biggest and fastest roller coaster I've ever seen was on the island within a stone's throw. It was a noisy place but a most welcome tie-up for the night and neither the noise nor the bright lights were to keep us awake.

Sunday, July 14th...Bastille Day!

After some tea and some cereal we paid our bill for the night and gassed up. We made a plan thinking it would have been a good day to explore this big city, Canada's second largest, but it was not to be.

Quebecers do celebrate the peasants overrunning the Bastille in Paris in 1789 but to what degree we would have no first hand knowledge. Sweet Breeze could not make progress against the current in the main channel leading to the Montreal Downtown. Full engine power kept us at a standstill in the river. We tried for an hour but progress toward downtown was painfully slow. I think it would have taken us all day to make a mile upstream. The island marina where we stayed the night was fenced off from the Expo Park so we couldn't even walk toward downtown. The mainland area on the Montreal side was all industrial harbor with no place to tie up amongst the shipping docks and container ships. The whole of the lower shoreline was a commercial district. We would have to explore Montreal another time. We gave up and let the current sweep us downstream.

The river below Montreal was a weekend racecourse for powerboats. It was rare that a big power cruiser would slow down to minimize its wake as a courtesy so we were kept busy adjusting our course over the wakes and avoiding boats roaring around in all directions. Ship traffic was another hazard. Didn't anyone know that we were here for a quiet, relaxing cruise?

The current was strong and we were making good time. Past Île Marie and Île Bouchard, Île aux Prunes and Île aux Boeufs we flew. Farmlands and small cities on both sides as Quebec looked green and welcoming.

The heat of the day was draining us...cooking us. One way to cool off was to go overboard and clean the propeller. After every mile or two of motoring it would get clogged with a kind of sea grass that floated on the surface in mats. The engine would slow down noticeably when the prop became clogged so we would shut it off and take turns sliding overboard while adrift. While hanging onto the side of the boat we could reach down to the prop with our feet and pull the grass off with our toes. We waited until there were no boats or ships nearby because we had little steerage while adrift. It became a welcome mid afternoon chore for me. The sun and the heat of the day were starting to take a toll, my face was red and my brain was overheating, but of course real sailors like us would have little use for a dodger.

Finally it dawned on me. We weren't using the mains'l so we must make a boom tent to get out of the sun. I had a small tarp on board for just that purpose. What a relief! I should have thought of it days ago!

We were off the paper charts now. Too far east. We were checking position with my highway maps of Quebec, the chart plotter, and a booklet of the lower St. Lawrence that the young woman at the fuel dock in Montreal gave us; and of course we had the channel markers for the shipping lane to keep us in deep water.

My note in my journal that hot day of boats and weeds told of a near miss with a big ferryboat. I cannot recall the incident, which seems strange, but was probably because of the sheer number of boats and ships that we dodged that day.

In late afternoon we sailed by the town of Sorel, Quebec, on the right shore and I wondered if the winter boots were made there. Sorel was also where the Richelieu River ran in from the south. It was my absolute last chance to take the easy way south to Lake Champlain and connecting waterways to New York. I could shave 2000 miles off the seafaring route ahead into the North Atlantic and around the Maritime Provinces. We passed it with barely a thought.

Mark was hoisting and dousing sails as the variable winds came and went. It was good practice and he was a quick learner. We laughed and joked a lot. We talked about what we wanted to be when we grew up. I think we became friends for life that day...I felt that way.

It was another long day on the river, maybe 60 miles of dodging boats and boat wakes and floating mats of grass. We dodged the sun too, under the boom tent or down in the cabin. By evening we were looking for an anchorage somewhere out of the shipping lane. The big island to the left, just before Lake St. Pierre, looked like our best chance at finding refuge with good depth offshore a hundred yards and yet, just off our course a few hundred yards. We anchored. We set both forward anchors just to assure a good sleep in the strong current. Mark swam to shore to explore the beach. We had supper and were driven into the cabin at dusk by the bugs.

Monday, July 15th, bonjour, up at 5 a.m. The morning promises more heat.

Freighters are steaming hard upbound against the current as we regain consciousness after a restful night. There were no big wakes from ships during the night...good thing. Mosquitoes must be sleeping late so we had breakfast out in the heavy, warm air.

We hoisted anchors and the bow swung with the current pointing to the vastness of Lake St. Pierre. We had a light wind and light current for a few hours, but in the middle of the lake we needed the always dependable little Atomic 4 or we would have been stalled. The sun was intense again so we motored under the protection of the boom tent.

The chart plotter was beginning to confuse me. It showed Lake St. Pierre with expanses of green colored areas (normally depicting land) on either side of the shipping lane. That was new to me and didn't make sense. There was water for miles on both sides of the channel. It looked deep enough to sail off course anywhere in the lake, and it was, barely, mostly eight to 10 foot depths.

Mark is working out really well. He likes to cook and makes a great salad. He's cheerful and eager to help out. I am feeling lucky about his companionship.

We had brought along a French phrase book and an English to French dictionary. I asked Mark if he would look up and write out a list of phrases in French that I could quickly reference like, "Is there a store nearby with groceries?" Or, "can I have a fill of gasoline?" Or, for a lovely French-Canadian woman, "Would you like to sail off into the sunrise with me?" If I wasn't understood, I was reasonably sure that I could bring a smile with my attempts to use the spoken language, smiles being one of the most universal forms of non-verbal communication. Smiles often elicit patience. Patience facilitates communication and around we go again. It's been a good life strategy so far.

The weekend power boaters are gone...back to work to earn more gas money for next weekend perhaps? Lake St. Pierre, at about eight miles wide and 20 miles long, is mostly ours alone now. Belly up on the surface is an occasional three-foot-long, dead, sea lamprey or eel of some sort. I wouldn't have wanted to swim among them—dead or alive, their big round suction mouth had rows of short teeth.

We were on a northeast heading. We could begin to see the broad lake's end narrowing to the outlet where the river's current would again carry us to the sea. The highway bridge above the city of Three Rivers, Quebec was visible now, down the river.

From the water, Three Rivers doesn't seem to draw me into a desire to stop and explore. The waterfront is mostly commercial/industrial with massive church buildings dominating the skyline up from the waterfront. Probably Catholic churches... there are lots of Saints here in Quebec, and me not a very saintly sort.

Onward and downstream we go. There was no wind but the steady current together with the engine at just a fast idle give us five to six knots of speed-over-ground. We probably wouldn't make Quebec City today but more miles-made-good always made me feel accomplished. Our next stop was to be a surprising social exchange.

On the right riverbank was a small marina near Deschaillons-sur-Saint-Laurent (a small town, I think). We could both use a break from the hot sun and a gasoline fill. A young gal came down to turn on the gas pump and she was soooo pretty, sweet, and shy. Our tired old sun-dimmed squinty eyes sprang themselves open a bit even before I tried to speak forth one of Mark's prepared French phrases (requesting) a gasoline fill, please. She spoke no English and so began our bout of smiles and questioning looks back and forth, some head nods, sign language, and ultimately a gas fill.

The clubhouse high above the water was connected by a hinged aluminum ramp down to the docks. An interesting arrangement, I thought, that must be for high water levels at spring runoff.

Mark and I were able to buy two ice-cold bottles of beer from our marina attendant/bartendress but were told we must drink within the building. I noticed a big guy at a table wearing a Minnesota Vikings cap and nodded and pointed to his cap. He waved me over and asked where I was from. When I said Minnesota he wanted to tell me what a die-hard fan he was of the professional football team from my home state.

Charles was a biker from Quebec City, spoke good English, and moved his chair over so that his massive tattooed arms and body allowed space enough for Mark and me to join him and his girlfriend Bridget, at the table. Charles wanted to talk about the Minnesota Vikings (which I knew little about and didn't really want to learn more) so I questioned him about Quebec City and the St. Lawrence. He had grown up nearby and had gone away to play college football in the states. He was loud and likeable and I pictured his very thin girlfriend behind him on his Harley, invisible from ahead and shielded from the wind by Charles' bulk.

When we left the marina at the Deschaillons-by-the-St. Lawrence the bartendress gave me a hug and a kiss on both cheeks. So did Bridget. Charles didn't, but I was okay with that.

Charles must not have boated down the river ahead or he would surely have told us about the upcoming currents. About five miles downstream the current began to pick up. At one point, 10 miles downstream Sweet Breeze was racing along at 11.4 knots. Probably a lifetime speed record for the old girl, and for me in a sailboat.

When we motored into the marina at Portneuf there was a friendly and very helpful local marina fellow who also spoke good English. He was probably the Commodore of the marina harbor, I thought that because he reminded me about some general courtesies that I had overlooked. I had more to learn in Quebec than just the language.

I cannot remember his first name—let's call him Jaques—however, he asked me about the rapids upstream and our boat speed coming down. He said that 11.4 knots was far from the record.

"Is it always that fast?" I asked.

"Depends!" he smiled then stated in his strong French accent, "the tide, she runs up and she runs down. Now she runs down."

Some things were starting to make some sense to a Midwesterner...like the large green colored areas that the chart plotter showed on Lake St. Pierre. The chart plotter was trying to tell me not to sail into the green areas because they were tidal flats! Aha!

We were already in major tidal currents and didn't know it. That's what the long, hinged ramps and floating docks were about too!

Jacques looked away and back, askance let's call it, as if wondering how these boys had made it this far, not knowing anything about tides and currents. A little caution and luck had gotten me nearly two thousand miles toward the sea however, and guess what...the water was, at times, salty here.

I bought a tidal time chart booklet and Mark and I tried to figure out what all those tables and figures meant. Within were predicted the tidal times, heights and flows for each day. The high water mark on the rocks here at the marina showed that Sweet Breeze would rise at least ten feet while we slept.

Email July 15th...my French is so bad but someone always comes thru to rescue me before I say something embarrassing. At Portneuf, Quebec. A marina with tides. I need to learn fast about such things. Fuel dock gals in Quebec are all pretty and friendly. Very fast currents in the St. Lawrence. Sweet Breeze went 11.4 knots down a rapid. Didn't stop at Trois Rivières. Looked pretty industrial. Was expecting trade canoes and natives. Bundles of beaver pelts and muskets along the shore. Guess we're about 200 years too late.

Bought a tide table booklet...but how to read it? Hot shower? No, cool one tonight, high of 40 degrees C today. Over 100 F.

Sitting with a bunch of locals at marina. Feel out of place with language handicap. Mark and I cooked today.

New challenges everyday. Mark is great. So are you with supportive emails.
au revoir, Curt.

Tuesday, July 16th...if we read the tide book correctly for this area we should leave very early to ride the tide current out.

It worked. We rode the tidal current downriver. We had to keep in mind now that this river flowed both ways at about a 12-hour cycle. This just didn't seem right... doesn't water always flow downhill? We were told there would be little point to try to make progress (downstream) against the tidal current but if we timed the tides right our speed over ground *with* the current would increase dramatically. A boater on this part of the St. Lawrence would do well to be patient.

Our ride on the ebb tide was over at the bridge. The motor was laboring with little progress. We anchored near the south shore to wait out the reversal of the river's flow. I know this whole tide thing seems like a simple process but something about the timing of tidal currents is tricky to me. The best way for my simple mind to figure this out, with my visual and spatial concepts of things, was to make a mental water level mark on an object on shore, then check it occasionally to see if the water level was rising or falling. My theory on this mystery was that when the water reached its highest mark it would reverse and flow out to the ocean again and we would go with it. It seemed likely to me that an hour or two after high tide the water should start to accelerate to the sea.

I think my basic tidal water flow theory is correct but I also think there are complications in a huge river like this with surface currents and underwater currents often opposing one another. Suffice it to say, tidal currents would remain a mystery to me throughout the journey ahead.

While we waited at anchor we could have cleaned up the boat or rowed ashore in the seldom used dinghy. We read our books and watched the summer scenery instead...boats and ships slipping upstream with ease. I was monitoring our position to make sure our anchor was holding in the rocky bottom.

After about four hours at anchor the high water mark on shore was no longer awash. The water level here was dropping. Sweet Breeze had swung on her mooring and was pointing upstream now. To the Quebec City Yacht Club we motored...with ease I might add as the mighty St. Lawrence reversed and flowed to the sea.

Quebec City Layover

Not knowing where the next available fuel might be I was in the habit of topping off the on-board tank wherever gas was available. That was our first stop at the yacht club. We registered at the club desk next, were assigned our dockage then moved our boat and got ready (In our, "go to town clothes.") to hike up the hill to the city and explore.

I had been told (by acquaintances) all along my journey, to stop at Quebec City. The city did not disappointment me. There were gardens and paths, forested hillsides, historic buildings and lots of people to watch.

I lay in the grass near the art museum under the shade of big trees. It felt good, this horizontal repose on a steady surface. There were buskers and street musicians...I'm a soft touch and donate money easily. There were lots of restaurants and outdoor markets, lots of women of all shapes and sizes and colors to appreciate. We spent the whole day wandering. Mark hadn't been to Q.C. since he was a teen. I especially liked to sit on a bench and people watch.

We walked back toward the marina on an endless boardwalk, the Promenade, running along the crest of the hill above the river far below. That steep sided hill, a cliff in some parts, had helped protect the old fortified city in centuries past. Darkness caught up with us. We weren't sure which path to take down to the water through the dark, forested hillsides. The yacht club was a mile or two somewhere down there.

It seemed like we had walked far enough to encounter the steep, busy street that we had earlier ascended up to the 'Plains of Abraham' (the local historic landmark). I thought I knew the way. I had made mental notes of landmarks. But in the dark it was soon obvious that we were lost.

We happened onto a street with a kiosk and a city map with a streetlight above. From the map and some nearby street signs we discovered our current position. Thereafter we navigated our way through the maze of forest paths and roads, in near darkness, back to the marina. We were pooped. Late night showers it was, with two soundly sleeping sailors very soon thereafter.

Wednesday, July 17th...up at 5 a.m. to the coffee shop at the clubhouse.

Mark washed our clothing this morning. We had no laundry soap but that was fine with both of us. The clothes came out clean and fresh without it. Soap usage is a lot about commercial propaganda; a billion dollar industry and a mostly unnecessary polluter of precious water. I hold the same opinion of toothpaste and deodorant... hmmm, I hope that's not why Mark...

Mark has decided to leave today. He feels some pressure to take a bus to Nova Scotia and complete a building project for a friend. I think he knows he could stay and sail with me as long as he wants. We could sail to Halifax in two weeks but he feels the need to move on. I will miss him, yet I look forward to aloneness; the simple sovereignty of single-handing, self-reliance, the unknown challenge, alone.

The waitress at the clubhouse restaurant helped Mark to decipher the bus schedule and to find the nearest bus stop. We had plenty of time before his bus appointment so we went shopping at the nearby boating and nav. store. I wanted to get some paper charts of the river downstream, the Gulf of St. Lawrence and beyond.

Danielle at the marine supply spoke very good English, (I was learning that French Canadians often liked practicing English). Danielle took us under his wing. He knew the waters ahead of me and said it would be the toughest part of the river to navigate yet. Shoals, currents, and tides would need constant vigilance on my part. "Don't cut the buoys," he told me over and over as we poured over charts and the river routes ahead. (He meant for me not to take any shortcuts and watch carefully the boundaries of marked channels.)

Danielle was a sailor too, though his voyage to Florida was up the Richelieu River and the connecting waterways to New York City. "Around Gaspé," he said, "stay offshore about three miles to avoid the strong winds and currents." Gaspé still had that mystery for me, that sound of the unknown. He wasn't the first to warn me of the winds off Gaspé. We parted with a handshake and a final, "Don't cut the buoys!"

Mark was off to find his bus stop. His clothing and necessaries he carried in his backpack and shoulder bag. I was eager to get back on the water trail but the tidal currents were flowing upstream. Mark had left me some beer, icy cold. It was another hot and humid day with that heavy, hazy air. I waited, watching the boats at anchor outside of the marina to show me the first signs of current reversal by swinging around and pointing their bows upstream. Then we would be off, Sweet Breeze and me, down with the current and the wind, down to where the river broadens into the gulf, and more mysterious, alluring unknowns.

Quebec City was indeed a worthwhile city to explore. Not too big, about 170,000 residents, parks and arboretums, flora everywhere, healthy looking folks biking and walking, a historic culture preserved and integrated amongst modern conveniences. I was feeling glad that I had stopped and glad to be on the river again. Glad just to be alive.

My left foot and ankle had been swollen for quite a few days. No pain or tenderness, but it just didn't seem to be getting good circulation. Was my heart getting weak and not pumping fluids well, I wondered? I'm all about pumps and hydraulics. I thought it would be wise to figure out what was going on. I'm almost never ill; ailments of any kind are rare.

That interesting old city on the hill was upstream now and fading into the haze behind. We were carrying 5 knots easily with the wind and current scooting us along approaching the big island, Île d'Orleans, where the river splits around it. To the right, off starboard, was the main shipping channel, once again the route for us. The heavy, still air of the morning had turned into a freshening breeze from behind. It felt good to be on the water, alone and making such good time. The deep channel was well marked; once again the words of Daniellle crossed my mind, "Don't cut the buoys."

Lunch, (dinner, as we called it in the Midwest) was to be the last of Mark's salad. Thoughts of whales ahead, somewhere downstream; of tidal currents and their mysterious ways; of the money and the high standard of living that Quebecers appeared to enjoy; of the storm clouds forming behind to the west. Wonderings about the power lines crossing the river ahead, power lines on the grandest of scales—must be heading for the cities on the eastern seaboard, delivering power from the dams on the once wild and free rivers of northern Quebec? Thoughts of Mark, his easy ways and ready smiles.

It was exhilarating to feel the speed of the wind and current whisking us along. We were pushing seven knots now on the two mile wide south channel. We were looking at an easy 50-mile day. Then, almost suddenly, things changed.

The 15-knot tailwind abruptly switched to a 20-knot headwind. It happened so quickly, it should have been a warning of what was ahead. I expected a thunderstorm, but nothing like the intensity of what developed.

The sky overhead became too dark; late afternoon changed to near nightfall within minutes.

One other sailboat was out that day. It was nearer the south shore and appeared through binoculars to be seeking refuge at a harbor serving a small town. If there was a way to get off the water and into that marina I thought it wise to follow that sailboat. They may be locals and should know the way through the shallows, but it was not to be.

It all became a scramble now; getting the sails furled, doused, flaked, and secured; getting the engine started and…? Adrenaline mode. Steep-sided waves built quickly, an upriver wind against the downflow. Could we make it to the weather shore, into the protection of the marina following that big new sailboat with the wind gusting to 40 mph now? Lots of questions with no time to think through the best choice. I threw my life jacket on and cinched it up tight.

We headed for the lee shore and the path of the other boat toward refuge, but not for long. It appeared that the sailboat had run aground; it was no longer making progress toward the harbor. Visibility was such now, with the pouring rain, that I could no longer see the boat or the shoreline. My choice was made for me. Stay in the shipping lane and last out the storm. Turn into the wind and waves and hope that trusty little inboard engine holds my trust and faith once again.

The wind increased sharply again...60 mph? Standing waves of five to six feet tossed us up and plunged the bow under the next one. We were enveloped in the chaos of storm. No shorelines nor directions were apparent. The rain was not rain. It was wind driven sheets of water and airborne wave tops. I couldn't look into the wind. Lightning crashing all around. Waves coming over the cabin top now. My eyes stung from the velocity of the water hitting my face. My only sense of position was gained from the chart plotter, but we had to keep moving for it to get a fix on our direction and our position relative to shorelines.

Then another problem. The alarm on the AIS screeched at me from below that a ship was coming upriver; I could no longer risk staying in the relative safety of the deep water channel but must try for the windward shore of Île d'Orleans somewhere off to port. When I could open my eyes, visibility was 50 yards at most.

The wind now may well have been 80 mph, a straight-line wind, a full throttle wind and a nearly full throttle engine it now took to maintain steerage through the waves. The propeller was out of the water half the time and I didn't want to risk damaging the engine by over revving it fanning air.

The chart plotter was my only hope to get away from that ship's upstream course. If I could get over near shore in 20 feet of water we would be out of the shipping lane. I could no longer rely upon my senses. Visibility was nil and sound was everywhere. The chart plotter and the depth meter were the only way that I could discern where we were and where we were headed.

I recall yelling into the wind like a pure nut case. I guess I had to yell to hear myself above the crack and snap of lightning, the crash and booming of thunder, the howl of the wind, and the crash of Sweet Breeze plunging through the waves in the full force of the gale now. Maybe it was just my goofy sense of drama but it was spontaneous. I shouted at the top of my lungs, "Blow, you son-of-a-bitch, blow!" I laughed at the storm. Maybe it was to bolster my courage. Maybe it was some strange ancient connection between men and the sea that brought out such a hollering that I surprised myself. I knew Sweet Breeze could handle the weather if I did my part and kept her off the rocks and sand shoals.

The dinghy was fast filling with sheets of rain and wave tops but it didn't seem important as long as it wasn't pulling the stern of Sweet Breeze down. It was probably 30 minutes of this tossing about as a cork, screaming wind, water flying by from above and below.

We made it into 20 feet of water and the shoreline became visible. I scrambled forward on the pitching foredeck and yanked the latch pin on an anchor and let it rattle to the bottom, chain and all. Keeping in mind the tides, I tried to guess at the adequate scope of rode to let out without letting the current or wind push us onto shoals near shore.

The anchor was holding. We had made it. Soaked and shivering but none the worse, I dove below and got naked and dry with towels. She was still blowing and pouring rain, but we felt safe, my little boat and me.

Thinking about what had gone on out there in the channel a few minutes before and what was now just beginning to diminish in intensity, I knew that we were indeed in a thunderstorm. The mother of all thunderstorms.

I wouldn't call myself a storm wimp. I loved to snuggle under the thick boughs of a spruce in a thundershower or dress up in winter woolies and hike out into a winter blizzard. But this experience was sinking deep into my soul. The strongest storm I had ever experienced perhaps, and I had always loved to feel their power—in a house, in a tent, in a car, but never in a boat. This was a first. I had made the right choices and I felt accomplished, safe, proud of this tough little boat. But no time to gloat—another anchor to be set off the bow for insurance, the only way I would get any sleep that night.

The notes that I wrote in my journal that evening, safe and warm in the cabin, mentioned strong feelings expressed with words that cannot exaggerate the intensity of what that storm threw at us. I noted the sensation of steering the boat while swallowing and coughing rain and waves out of my mouth and lungs...of trying to see with eyes sprayed and stung by the driven torrents of rain and seawater...of always being certain of a white knuckle grip on one of my homemade handholds in the lurching cockpit, and finally, what a kinship I had felt with this old boat.

Would the calm of tomorrow morning reveal that other sailboat, the one heading for the lee shore, wrecked on the rocks or high and dry on some mud shoals? I hoped it would be a calm morning at least, one of those sweet, earthy-scented, clean-air, after-the-storm mornings.

Mud flats of the vast St. Lawrence.

For now, the rain poured down, the wind howled and the rigging hummed; sounds best heard from the security of the cabin. The boat pitched in the waves but the anchors were holding. I wedged my feet under the galley stove at the foot of my bunk, lying at an angle not quite on my left side or flat on my back. I had discovered that strategy weeks before on that rough night anchored off Long Point on Lake Erie. It helped to wedge me in the bunk. Boat motion would not keep me awake for long... it had been a long, trying day.

The Mountains of Charlevoix

Thursday, July 18th...up at 4 a.m. to catch the tidal ebb current outflow.

There was no wrecked or grounded sailboat to the south that I could see in the first gray light of dawn. It may have been over there somewhere but I couldn't spot it. If the boat survived the storm near the lee shore, Zeus or Poseidon, or maybe one of the Quebec saints, St Lawrence perhaps, had surely been looking out for those aboard.

I felt relieved and a little bit proud. Triton, the Greek messenger of the sea and the namesake of this sturdy boat of mine, had reminded me of the old sailor's axiom, "When in doubt go out." Once again, we had been tested and passed.

I remembered to empty the water from the dinghy while still at anchor. It was nearly half full of rainwater and wind-blown water; it would have pulled hard, like towing a small barge.

The first rays of sun on the broad St. Lawrence poked through between the horizon and the dense cloud cover. They accented and made sparkle Île d'Orleans, a couple of miles behind us now. We were making good speed, six to eight knots, with sails and current pulling. It was that special kind of, "Morning after the storm," that makes one feel fortunate to be alive...to be living on this precious planet and sense the pulse of wind, water, and this old boat quietly sliding downriver quietly, disturbing none of the pure magic.

It was the kind of morning that let my imagination run freely. Here I was, on the river to the sea, where once sailing ships from Europe had plied the currents seeking passage to the Orient, or failing that, seeking whatever riches could be found nearby. I imagined native villages along the banks at the mouths of rivers; streams socked full of Atlantic salmon and all the other fishes that could live where fresh and saltwater mixed. What must it have been like at the big Iroquois villages at Stadacona (Quebec City) or Hochelaga (Montreal Island)? How that life was impacted when Jacques Cartier sailed up this great river and wintered with the natives in the 1530s. On the shore to my left I pictured legions of bark canoes and farther up from the water's edge, bark dwellings with smoky fires for cooking, and racks for drying fish. I think I could have fit into that life, but just imagining it was probably more in accord with my dreamer's personality. It was, no doubt, a harsh life along the river, more about sustenance than romance. I was aware and thankful for the freedom; the life of relative ease and plenty that I had, with only the occasional, voluntary struggles that this sailing adventure entailed. It was, on this splendid day, just me, sailing the great river, the majesty of the green mountains...imagine that.

The steep green slopes rose from the water's edge. Deep clefts between them must have been the timeless work of tireless rivers tumbling to the Gulf from beginnings far north, back and beyond. Verdant forests were cloaking these small mountains to their very rounded summits.

For me, some of the best scenery yet was along these rocky bluffs and soon I was dreaming again, captured by thoughts of how the rivers ran and along which one I might build my latest cabin? Which mountain would need my exploring some day; which pool along which river would I stop to fish?

Some of the mountains had the scars of road building and logging; some had small hamlets in their valleys with tall, thin church steeples. I was drawn to the ones with only the timeless signs of nature shaping their faces, those that looked still wild and unexplored. I dreamt of returning another day.

Wind and current carried us into the broader expanse of the Gulf of St. Lawrence, not suddenly, but the river had widened now to about five miles. The big "Island of Hazelnuts," Île aux Coudres, to the right had a small town and a traffic jam of sorts where cars had lined up to wait for the ferryboat to the mainland.

Ski slopes and chairlifts described one of the tallest mountain faces on the near shore, left. The binoculars were at the ready now with intriguing scenery drawing my curiosity. There were some intermittent streaks of white showing through the trees where waterfalls tumbled over rock faces to the sea. Tiny cabins just up from the rocky beach were clinging to hillsides, not quite hidden from view. More very small settlements were set into notches in the hills with cleared fields on the most level of navigable slopes. Ever present were the tall, pointed church spires reaching high above the trees, reaching toward the promised heavens of the faithful. A railroad line followed the coastline, twisting and turning at the water's edge into deep bays and then out around the next cape. I finally spotted a short train made up of a few passenger cars rolling silently down the coast.

Mare's tails, those high wispy clouds, were the ceiling that day way up in the heavens beyond the church spires and the mountaintops. They usually signaled some impending weather change but I could never remember what change that was. The breeze was cool off the water but I wasn't complaining. I put on a thick, dark, wool sweater, a real heavy-knit seaman's sweater, a gift from friends Sara and Duck in Ireland...then some black pants to soak up some sunshine onto my legs. Quite a change from the heat of yesterday and the days before that.

Our speed over ground had gradually slowed to less than four knots. Tidal currents were flowing upstream again. I was no longer in control of our speed...there was this tidal thing that from now on would dictate the speed and direction of our journey. We motored over near the north shore, out of the shipping lane, anchored and read more of the book of the Norwegian immigrant pioneering on the prairie, by Rolvaag...and had an afternoon nap.

The water does not look clean here. There are a few big dead fish floating by and some of those three-foot-long eels that were floating in Lake St. Pierre upstream. We are, "downstream" now from some of the largest cities of the east central U.S.

and Canada; lots of runoff from agriculture on both sides of the river too, I would suppose, especially with those recent heavy rain events. About six weeks ago we had left from the uppermost and westernmost part of this watershed—and even there, way "upstream" at Duluth, the water has become less than pure.

Marna had been reminding me to pay close attention to weather reports. Mostly, I had been taking the weather as it came and made daily adjustments. I was often frustrated with the broadcasts from Environment Canada, not because they were wrong or because they were in French, but because it was so hard for me to pinpoint what area the forecast covered. They usually mentioned areas around cities or between towns but now the mystery was the weather forecasted for Charlevoix. I could not find Charlevoix on any road map or chart, yet the forecast that I thought covered the area we were now in said to expect 60 kilometer winds and temps down to -18 C... and snow likely. Holy crap! That can't be right. It's July. Sure it's a cool summer day but that's winter weather. Sure, I'd been sailing northeast for a thousand miles or so since Lake Erie but what kind of weather can they have up here in July anyway? Was Charlevoix nearby or 1000 miles north of here? I listened to the forecast several times and was sure that I heard it right. I didn't know what to think except to start looking for a safe harbor.

The weather was still fine and the tidal current was running downstream with the river. We might make more headway yet today but that spooky forecast of blizzard-like conditions caused some concern. It couldn't be right, yet I started to glass the north shore, the near shore, for towns with a safe harbor. All of my paper charts and chart books only covered the areas behind me now. I had sailed beyond the charts. It was up to the road maps that Kay had left me, and the chart plotter to show me the way. I really needed to figure out this weather forecast stuff. Where the hell was Charlevoix? Where are we now?

The nearshore scenery was still fascinating, green and gorgeous, rivers and hills, and in retrospect it was a shame not to thoroughly let it soak into my visual memory. That damn forecast for some big winds and cold weather had me distracted.

A few miles east of La Malbaie, Quebec I spotted some sailboat masts while glassing the shoreline and veered left toward shore. Here was a small deep harbor, well-protected, called Cap-a-l'Aigle.

Ivan (pronounced Yvonne) showed me where to dock and get secure before the blizzard hit.

Up at the marina office, Ivan and I tried our best to communicate, he in the French language with signing, facial expressions and head nodding, and me in English with the same. We came to the necessary understandings eventually. Ivan was patient and helpful. There was gasoline in a can that he had brought from the nearby town that I could buy.

I wanted to ask Ivan about the weather report but I thought it too complicated a question to wade through with our language barrier. We did, however, muddle through an exchange about, "Where the heck is Charlevoix?" On the map on the wall of the marina office I pointed to all of the nearby towns and cities while shrugging my shoulders...no towns called Charlevoix anywhere. Aha, and Ivan had a twinkle in his eye as he opened his arms as to say, "It is all Charlevoix." Call me slow on the uptake but I was running on the single-minded track that as with most of the other forecasts naming towns, or areas between towns, Charlevoix must be a town somewhere nearby. One frustrating mystery solved. Now to prepare for the "blizzard".

Back on the docks was a 50-foot long Hunter sailboat that would only fit on the main quay leading to the finger docks. A friendly couple was aboard, an outgoing, generous couple from Georgian Bay on Lake Huron. Ontarian's were they, and English they spoke.

About the impending weather...they chuckled. The forecast had caught their attention also. They too had listened and listened again on their marine radio. It had to be from last January they thought, with some scheduling mix up for the broadcast. I had guessed that too but since I was becoming unsure of so many things lately, tides, currents, weather forecasts, and where the heck I was exactly, their reassurance was settling. Then they offered me their downstream paper charts of the Gulf of St. Lawrence, since they were heading upstream and no longer needed them. I graciously accepted their gift. I was getting a more settled feeling, knowing where I was on paper charts as well as the chart plotter and correlating between both for reassurance.

I asked them (Bill and Shawnee) if there was a grocery store nearby. I was out of real maple syrup and some other staples that I was accustomed to. I hope it doesn't sound like I was hinting for more gifts but out of their expansive galley comes Shawnee with a bottle of maple syrup that they wouldn't be needing. (Or so they said.)

Shawnee and Bill were journeying also. Theirs was a two-year sailing loop from their home on Georgian Bay to Chicago, then down the Ohio and the Mississippi rivers to the Gulf of Mexico, through the Bahamas around the tip of Florida then up the Atlantic coast to the Maritime Provinces of Canada. Into the Gulf of St. Lawrence they had sailed and into this sweet little marina where their boat barely fit. They were on their way to Quebec City to meet up with family, then continue on west through the Great Lakes toward home. True adventurers...I could relate.

They were gone early the next morning on the flood tide. I had found a book, in my jumble aboard Sweet Breeze, about the locks and locking procedures that they would be needing upstream. I wanted to repay them in some small way for their generous spirit and welcoming ways. I was disappointed in myself that I hadn't gotten up early enough to see them off. The morning sky was gray and something between a mist and a drizzle was cloaking not only the local weather but also my spirits.

After all of my attempts, I still was unsure of how to read the tide tables and how to interpolate my location into the actual tide stations that were listed. The nearest tide station in the tables might be twenty miles from Cap-a-l'Aigle. When would that tide reach me here? It was frustrating to not know. My sense of control over my journey was waning, running in and out with the tide. My determination to figure out tides was being depleted and it affected my attitude. I liked to figure stuff out. I could obsess about it. The best I could determine was that I would have an ebb tide carrying me to sea at around noon today. Thunderstorms were in the revised weather forecast, the 60k wind and snow forecast had been replaced with another recording, but thunderstorms were an everyday possibility this time of year. I was paying little heed to afternoon thunderstorm forecasts...I had been to the mountaintop, so to speak, upstream at Île d'Orleans. I felt I could deal with their ferocity as the conditions arose.

There was a strange kind of frustrating anger welling up in me. Nothing violent or scary. Nothing I could really understand. Nothing that a few well-placed cusswords wouldn't help to see me through to the other, the brighter side, but still, I felt out of sorts. Oftentimes I couldn't find the location of the tidal stations on a map, let alone guess what the timing of the currents were at my present position. Losing control of my destiny is not easy for me.

My boat is a fucking mess. I can't find anything and it feels cramped, I bump into things in the close quarters. Things are getting that sticky feeling with a salt spray coating. I don't like sitting at a dock in a drizzle and feeling dumb. Headway is what makes me feel accomplished, not sitting around on a rainy day wondering why I am so slow to comprehend the tide tables. My raincoat starts to get clammy and leaky after an hour. It's a cold rain, but not snow.

Back in the boat I had discovered a port left open that was above most of my clean clothing on the starboard side of the V-berth. Rain had dripped onto my clothes. Shit. I would be needing some sunshine soon, for drying my wet everything and brightening my grumpy attitude.

It was wet everywhere but now it was getting *cold* and wet. Burning the propane galley stove in the cabin took the chill off but the water vapor from the propane flame added to the wetness all around. Warm and wet was better than cold and wet, however, and a hot cup of chai tea sweetened with real maple syrup and fattened with cream did considerable improvement to my attitude.

A really big part of my frustration, with things in general that day, I think originated with my damaged hearing. Weather forecasts and helpful advice given with a strong French accent are sometimes (often) heard wrong or incompletely. I try to pick out key words when people speak fast and incomprehensibly to me. "S'il vous plaît, parlez plus lentement," became my most useful French phrase, (please speak slowly) but even then my poor hearing cut out lots of the key words that helped make sense of a statement. I had hearing aids that, "kind of worked," but I usually forgot to put them in when I may have needed them. Okay, bad ears, bad memory, rain, bad attitude, and some bad words. And you thought I was perfect?

Email, July 19th...crabby and frustrated...and fortunate.

At Cap-a-l'aigle, Quebec, small marina. Never know if I can enter marinas at low tide but when I see a forest of masts thru binoculars I feel welcome. Found this after hearing bad weather forecast with snow and big winds.

Forecast was wrong and false. Maybe that is why I feel frustrated for the lost progress. Could have made another 30 miles perhaps. Will take forecasts with mixed feelings.

*Cold and rainy morn, waiting for ebb tide at noon to head for Tadoussac, whales (baleen), and beyond I hope. Can't find stuff in my messy boat. #@%$ and *%&#+%!!.*

Weathered big thunderstorm two nights ago. Winds and rain such as I have never experienced before. Sweet Breeze kept me safe. 60 mph winds or greater. Couldn't see to navigate as rain hurt my eyes. Had to pry my hand off the tiller to set anchor, such was my grip.

Hope to get beyond big tide currents soon so I can get back to a more normal schedule. Salt water now with kelp and more new things. Ivan at the marina speaks no English, and me even less French. He is great and helpful as we laugh and congratulate each other's new words.

Gotta try to organize boat now. Been in this small space a month and 9 days.

À bientôt, Curt.

My best guess in order to catch the tidal current to Tadoussac, about 50 miles downriver, and my next destination for a port of call, was to leave here at about noon. Little did I know then that only a couple of docks over from our berth, was a small sailboat that would delay progress further but much improve my sour attitude.

Philippe was coming back to his boat when I first met him on the quay. We exchanged friendly smiles and introduced. He was from Montreal on a sailing vacation with his friend Manon (pronounced man-oh') in their troubled boat named, Surprise. Philippe told me they were partners in the boat, it was a recent acquisition for them and it was indeed a "surprise".

I asked about some of the troubling issues of the boat and offered some of my collection of extra sailboat hardware to replace a bent connection clevis on their boat. It was a chance for me to repay the generosity of Bill and Shawnee in a karma kind of way.

The other pressing problem with the boat was the engine. It had an inboard Atomic 4, same as did Sweet Breeze and lots of other old sailboats. It had quit yesterday and they had been towed into the marina, a somewhat embarrassing way to enter for a sailboat, but considering the river current and the tidal current and the wind direction it may have been nearly impossible to sail into this tiny harbor.

We looked into the engine troubles and it didn't look simple or easy. Water, cooling water, was entering the cylinders somehow, fouling the spark plugs, and diluting the oil in the crankcase. The most likely part of the engine that would allow water into the cylinders was a leaky cylinder head gasket. Luckily, this was an easy engine to pull the cylinder head from and replace the gasket. I offered to help.

It wasn't so easy but between us we had lots of tools and determination. And we had Manon. What a nice woman. What a daring woman. Before we tackled the engine problem Philippe and I hoisted Manon up, in my new Bos'un's chair, to the top of their mast to fix their wind indicator. Not only was she unafraid but she was light. She probably weighed 70 pounds less than we men.

The engine was not such a quick fix. Cleaning the old gasket material off the cylinder block was as difficult as it gets. I had changed lots of cylinder head gaskets in my time but this one was tough. The old gasket must have been glued on. Manon took a taxi to the nearest town and bought us some good wood handled steel scrapers. Pocketknives seemed like the best tools for scraping the tight places and around the bolt studs. Philippe had found a new head gasket at another town earlier. Good that it was a common old marine engine with parts still available.

We were patient and diligent and spent most of the afternoon scraping, cleaning out the cylinders, then securing the head down upon the new gasket. I was fully expecting the engine to start and run and to feel like the hero I wanted to be. It was not to be so.

When we cranked the motor over water was entering the fourth cylinder again before the engine would start and clear itself. We were disappointed. The problem must be something else, Philippe was disheartened...but I was feeling buoyed by their warm company. It was just what I had needed to climb out of the minor funk I had sunk into that morning. The dodger covering the well accessing the engine was also a blessing...though real sailors and boat mechanics wouldn't need one but would be fine spending an afternoon working on an engine in the cold rain.

After some discussion in French, of which I understood approximately none, Manon and Philippe agreed to not pursue my next ambitious opinion, my current amended diagnosis was that the water must be entering the engine from the exhaust. It had to be. They seemed to agree on a new engine to replace the old Atomic 4.

I was to be a guest for supper on their boat after some vigorous hand scrubbing to get a few layers of engine grease removed. Manon was busy in the galley with cooking chores while Philippe and I shared stories and wine. What a fine meal of fish and salad, hot green beans and hearty bread dipped in olive oil. It was the best meal I had since leaving Duluth...thanks to Manon. They both were special acquaintances that soon became friends and I envied Philippe for having such a partner as Manon to share with. Philippe told stories until 11:30 p.m., way after my normal bedtime.

The Whales of Saguenay

Saturday, July 20th...sunny morning; gray thoughts and gray mood long gone.

It was a perfect, bright morning, birds singing and so was I...humming at least. The ebb tide would begin around noon so I had the whole morning to do as I pleased until casting off for Tadoussac, down the coast and up the Saguenay River.

Manon and Philippe were not excited about my latest ideas of fixing their engine but I thought it worth a try. I had done some late night web research and I thought I had discovered their water problem with the Atomic 4. They seemed a bit discouraged. Mechanical problems can do that and they didn't want me to leave at noon for Tadoussac because of the forecasted thunderstorms and wind gusts to 60 kilometers.

I needed a walk...some physical exercise. Up the road to the village—the very steep road—were all sorts of flowers and plants, trees and shrubs in yards, lining the roadway and the sidewalks. The greenery was good for my spirit and helped to satisfy my long distance curiosity—yesterday's glassing of the shoreline from a mile out—about the climate and plant species on terra firma. The fireweed flowers were opened halfway up their stems signaling that summer was half over. Hardy perennial roses were blooming in mixed pastels and that deep warm red that draws my nose to smell them.

The village was as quiet as it could be. It almost seemed deserted but it looked like the homes were well kept, quite old, and the little white church had a kiosk that told of its history...it went back centuries. I saw only one other person while walking the main street. If I had to live in a town, this one would do.

Email, July 19th...le Quebecois delay...Manon and Philippe at the marina didn't want me to leave for Tadoussac because of winds gusting to 60k. I think I would have left. Losing my 40-mile avg. with tide delays was grating on me. They offered conversation and supper if I stayed. Stayed to help them with their boat, fixed some things and helped hoist Manon to the masthead to fix wind indicator. From Montreal are they. Really nice and speak Anglais with medium accent. Quebecois are very good to me. Brought me out of my rainy morning funk.

Did I tell you that a young gal pumping gas at a marina gave me kisses on the cheek? A bright spot considering my own drab company of late, talking with Sweet Breeze and baking in the heat.

Big white caps on the river now as it looks like strong winds are here. Hear ship's horns too. Fog and strong winds?? Tidied up boat. Yes Marna, tidy makes me feel better.

Hoping to make Tadoussac tomorrow. Then following winds across to south shore the next day...Rivière-Trois-Pistoles or Pointe-au-Père.

Remember, the book will give more high adventure as I keep a daily log (journal). Ha...but I do. Keep a light on for me.

Broad reaching up the northeast coast of the river toward Tadoussac, the River Saguenay and the whales that came up the river to feed. A brisk southwest wind pushes us along at an ideal speed of 6 to 7 knots.

It was a mixed departure from Cap-à-l'Aigle with sad goodbyes to Manon and Philippe yet an inner intrigue urging me back on the water heading toward more unknowns. Sweet Breeze wanted to run too; I could tell by her heel into a steady wake and good speed.

The river water was mixed with the waters of the North Atlantic now and was icy cold and clear. The Charlevoix shoreline looked so precious. I was near enough to see that the trees were cedar and pines and the hills reminded me of the Sawtooth Mountains of Lake Superior's north shore but the scale here was even grander. I was having thoughts again, thoughts inspired by the natural beauty all around me. Thoughts about how selfish we humans are, living as though the earth doesn't really matter; doing the greenspeak thing, then going about our lives of seeking comfort as usual. Over populating and over consuming. We seem to be a species of perpetual wanting. Never do we earth creatures have enough. We could have lived very simply and wisely and saved our precious planet forevermore. Instead we have billions of our species, tens of thousands of thermonuclear devices that could eradicate all life almost as suddenly as the thunderstorm that was creeping up behind us. Time to stop with the philosophy and get the boat prepared for weather. The oncoming weather was imminent, but then, so is our demise as a species...dark thoughts they were, with dark clouds boiling up behind.

A black head popped up out of the water alongside the boat but was gone just as suddenly...before I could tell what it was. I thought it must have been a large otter or a small seal.

Winds were getting gusty and swirling about. There were ocean-going freighters stacked high with shipping containers steaming upriver. I guess currents didn't matter much with the power of the big diesels pushing. There was commerce to do, cargo to deliver, no time to waste waiting out tides or storms.

Those ships piled high with goods, made in China and other faraway places, had markets to supply in the U.S. and Canada. We were a global economy after all. We export good paying jobs and import the products that were once made locally. We have had our middle class moment in the sun. Now it's their turn. As wages in the growth countries of Asia increase, and wages here decrease, maybe the NASCAR circuit will move to China as well. Car races seem like such a waste of precious energy.

Maybe it's time for such changes, market driven changes, energy driven changes, all based primarily upon that stored, finite ancient sunlight in fossil fuels...who has it and can use it up the fastest wins I guess.

I had the sails reefed and secured. We were ready for a blow if it were to whisk down off the hills. As always, I wanted to capture what energy I could out of the winds and make use of that opportunity to gain some headway quickly, so I left some headsail up. It was still ten miles to the mouth of the Saguenay and a few miles upriver to Tadoussac. I wanted to anchor with the whales tonight.

The darkest part of the storm was heading overland to the north. We were on the southern fringe and got some medium gusty winds and lots of rain. I got soaked and cold again but as soon as things looked on the wane I ducked below and changed into some semi-dry clothes while Otto steered. I was having some of those fleeting moments, those infrequent thoughts of ending this adventure, I was in mostly salt water after all, but those thoughts usually only lasted until the next good breeze brought Sweet Breeze about onto a brisk sail. In retrospect, thoughts of quitting may have been prompted by being wet and cold and wondering why I did this to myself. I guess I was a comfort seeker too.

The sun was poking through, still high in the western sky, brightening my outlook both literally and figuratively. Powerboats and a small cruise ship were converging on the mouth of the Saguenay just a couple of miles ahead now. As the wind veered from west to north behind the thunderstorm we would lose its aid in climbing the river against the current. Powerboats were making headway up the river but Sweet Breeze was standing still, engine full ahead, sails luffing, speed over ground...zero.

It was decision time for us. Obviously, we would only be able to climb the river to Tadoussac with the flood tide. We would never make it against the wind and the ebb tide. We could wait for six hours for the flood but then it would be dark, not the best time to find the channel up an unknown river. We could anchor in the bay across the river mouth for the night, tucked up near the north shore, out of the waves and wind, and try to climb the river tomorrow.

An anchorage for the night seemed like the best choice so we quit straining that little engine and set sail for the bay and shoreline to the northeast. Getting across the river's current and around behind it put us into a big eddy where the waves and turbulent water would not make for a restful night, even if the anchors held fast. Bad choice.

Onward, northeast up the coast to the Baie de Bergeronnes. There was supposed to be a small marina there. Paul, a sailor I had met at Cap-à-l'Aigle, told me about it and suggested its refuge if I couldn't make it to Tadoussac. There was still enough daylight if I hurried. The north wind would scoot us along on a close reach on a mostly northeast heading.

It was one of those special magic times, those early evening magic times after the storm. The sunlight streaked through gaps in the clouds and made the hill come alive. Whales were surfacing and blowing off to our right. It looked like blasts of steam, accented in the streaking sunlight. We veered a bit more to port to avoid them. Whale watching boats were heading toward them. Big rubber rafts with big engines and tourists aboard hoping for a near whale experience. Earlier, crossing the river current, we had come alongside a Beluga whale, all white and ghostlike sliding up the river with far less effort than Sweet Breeze's aborted attempt.

More of those sleek, black heads were popping up near the boat, like the quick glimpse I had seen earlier that day. They were seals and in no hurry to continue their fishing or clamming...just catching some air and rolling their head to check us out with their big round glossy black eyes.

Scanning with the binoculars, I found the marker buoys ahead that must be leading to Baie de Bergeronnes marina but it was through mud flats, broad, flat expansive mud flats at least half a mile out from shore. It didn't look like adequate depth for us to enter but I could see and feel the draw of sailboat masts far inland behind a sea wall.

"Baie de Bergeronnes Marina, Baie de Bergeronnes Marina, Baie de Bergeronnes Marina...sailing vessel Sweet Breeze requesting dockage for the night...can I make it to the dock with our four-foot draught?"

"Stay on the green side of the marked channel and you might make it. We have about four-feet depth at low tide," was the welcome reply.

Radio contact can be the ticket to a good night's sleep. It's especially good contact when the person on the other end speaks English and knows the intimate details of the entrance channels.

I was stuck briefly in the mud just before the dock but powered through. Lawrence, a whale-watching skipper greeted me and sailors from adjacent boats helped me tie up. What a great little hideaway this was. I had that feeling, that secure sense of being where we were safe and welcome.

We were the fourth and last sailboat to make fast at the Bergeronnes dock on this cool, autumn-feeling evening...said hi to Paul, the sailor who had told me about this secretive nook off the St. Lawrence. Paul and his friends from Montreal were on a vacation sail. He said he and his crew of three were sailing to Rimouski, Quebec, about 50 miles across the river and down the coast toward Gaspé tomorrow morning. That was my plan too. I was thinking that I would stick with Paul, his local sailing knowledge had brought me to this hideaway.

I think that bergeronnes in English may mean bank or bluff. Even though this was my first real view of vast tidal flats at low tide, there was a steep bank (with a hinged stairway) up to the main building where there were showers and a restaurant (closing for the day) and a museum. What a cool place. Dennis, behind the counter at the café offered me some free milk and croissants that he couldn't use tomorrow because they got fresh supplies delivered every morning.

The view down onto the tidal mud flats from high on the bank was fascinating in the evening light. Small wading birds were exploring the mud flats and probing the network of streams that were still draining floodwater out and off to the river. It looked to be close to half a mile out to the vast St. Lawrence now.

The flats reeked of mild sewer gas, my first time to sense that olfactory delight. Could that methane (?) be somehow captured and used for energy?

A good wi-fi connection at the café allowed some quick research into where I was at Les Bergeronnes, Quebec. Recorded history went back to the 1500s to the whaling and sealing of the Basques from Europe. Before that, archaeological evidence of Native peoples that hunted seals and lived along the banks for probably millennia before that, has been found. It still looked to be a rich area for sea life of all sorts.

Email, July 21st .Yesterday I couldn't get sweet breeze to climb against the current of the Saguenay river so I sailed onward in strong gusts to Bergeronnes Baie and a marina I barely squeezed into thru shallow tidal flats...stuck once in the mud but got off.

Gusty wind and thunderstorm yesterday rushed me N.E. up the St. Lawrence. The storm was only a little sister to the one at Île d Orleans. Beluga whale surfaced quietly and checked me out. Seals popped up curious as to this slow and quiet vessel. Saw big dark whales in distance blowing and thrashing. Steered around areas where I thought they were, so as not to disturb.

Met Martin this morn. Quebec Indian of Inui tribe. Gave me food and free tour of local museum. He is the museum guide. Martin said he will take me brook trout fishing if I come back another year. He was curious to hear about the Native American tribes of northern MN.

Waiting for tide to come in so I can leave for Matane with favorable strong winds. Matane, Quebec about 100 miles. Maybe??

Some local sailors have told me I have sailed the most hazardous section of the most hazardous river in the world. The rest is easy they say. Winds are strong and gusty on the river. Currents and big eddies still toss us around, and tides still confuse me.

Tide rising, looks like I can sail with N.W. wind.

Gotta go. Hugs, Curt.

Last night's sleep was typical in that I awoke with a start a few times wondering where I was—threw open the hatch and stuck my head out, came to my senses and crawled back into Kay's sleeping bag that she had left on the boat for me to use (and would therefore likely never want returned). It was an atypical night in that it was cold...down into the forty's, Fahrenheit. The sleeping bag was not providing enough warmth for those temps. We were approaching the cold waters of the North Atlantic that explained the cool weather.

Today's forecasted winds held promise for a fun and fast sail across the river and down the shore of the Gaspé...fun because Paul and crew were going to leave with me and fast because of steady 20 knot southwesterly winds.

Before the flood tide provided us with the assurance that we could float out to the river channel there was still time to check out the museum in the multi-use building with the cafe. Martin, the museum guide and counter/staff person, let me wander through the exhibits and was typical of the warm response, beyond normal welcomes, that people served up to me daily on my journey. Language barriers were easily overcome with patience and that, "we're all in this together," attitude that most trusting people have. The museum had some of the best animal dioramas and local archaeological artifact displays that I have seen. The animal exhibits were done in a natural setting, not for entertainment but for education.

Paul and crew followed me and Sweet Breeze out to sea, down the narrow but well marked channel. With the flood tide coming in, upriver, and the wind blowing toward the northeast or downriver, the best option for taking advantage of the wind seemed to be to sail southeast across the river, taking the wind abeam (across the side of the boat).

Matane, Quebec on the south shore was probably too ambitious of a goal with such a late morning start waiting for the tide. If I made it that far, 90 miles or so, it would probably present me with the challenge of finding my way into a harbor after dark, besides, I loved to have sailing company and Paul was headed for Rimouski.

There seems to be an unwritten but universal culture amongst sailors that has developed eons ago. When two similar sailboats leave the same port at the same time heading for the same destination...it almost always becomes a race. Today was no exception, though Paul and I had never touched on the subject. The closest thing to a hint of competition was our wave to each other as we left the Bergeronnes side by side. I think we both knew then that the race was on.

Paul had every advantage. He had a longer and faster boat, probably a 33-foot sloop, a crew to help manage sails, and I was towing the dink (dinghy). I would need every strategy and trick I could come up with to remain competitive. We had about 45 miles ahead of us to try our skills.

I wasn't sure why, but I was pulling slowly ahead with the wind abeam on the 15 mile crossing. Otto steered well that morning while I kept tweaking outhauls, downhauls, sheets, halyards, and the boom vang, getting the best sail shape that I knew how to. I glassed the other boat frequently. There was lots of crew activity and they were keeping up now but about a half mile back. It was the best that I could do on that tack, but they were starting to close the gap quickly.

About mid-river Paul and crew overtook us on starboard. Another wave to acknowledge their passing.

We were out-classed and I knew it going in but as the morning turned to afternoon and they had pulled a mile ahead, there was only one option I could think of....if the tidal current was starting to reverse and beginning to head out to sea, perhaps we could gain some tiny bit of advantage by jibing over to a wing and wing run and heading more directly toward Rimouski. They were still beam reaching toward the south shore and pulling further ahead but if the current had indeed reversed I could ride it and the wind. I thought I might gain some speed downriver or at least be on a shorter course.

With the big genoa poled out on one side and the main'l on the other we were occasionally hitting eight knots, speed over ground. Paul's boat was out of sight now on the far side of an island near the south shore. They had probably jibed to a broad reach now and were heading downstream too.

I always thought Sweet Breeze was pretty nimble on a run. She was bowling along now with the waves, the current, and the wind. We could run in an almost straight line to Rimouski now if conditions persisted.

A few miles ahead our courses crossed and we waved. There were only a few boat lengths between us now, not miles as before. We were still on a run directly down wind and they were on a broad reach with the wind over their port quarter and heading back out toward the middle of the river, expecting to jibe again and into port on the south shore, I supposed. My strategy was simple—take the shortest distance between two points and hope that the advantage of current flow will balance out against their faster boat.

This is becoming a darn long racing story and is probably losing something in the telling, but suffice it to say, after 45 miles we pulled into the harbor on that late afternoon, fueled and tied up at Marina Rimouski about 15 minutes after Paul and his crew. I felt a wee bit proud of the old girl, a 50-year-old boat, and pleased with our teamwork.

Paul made me feel even better. He was amazed at our speeds and the close race considering the handicaps of the shorter hull and the dinghy in tow, and no crew to help. With a strong French accent he said something like, "You must be related to Popeye." Anyhow, it was a real compliment coming from a real sailor.

The sardines and salty chips, lunch on the crossing, were leaving me wanting. Marina Rimouski had a nice restaurant and the town was renowned as the seafood capital of eastern Canada. I ordered a big salmon salad and who should walk in but Mike and Jane, a sailing couple from Toronto and one of the four boats that I had met yesterday at Grandes Bergeronnes; they joined me for supper.

Rimouski seem like an odd name for a town in Quebec. It sounds so Polish...it must be. I guess if I put the accent on the last syllable like the locals do, then it sounds a little French. Ah, but no, I should have guessed. Rimouski is a word adopted from the dictionary of the MicMac Indians and means, "Land of the moose." It's a fair sized city with a shipping harbor that has Île Saint-Barnabé four miles long and about two miles offshore, buffering the northwest wind and waves.

Twice, Quebecers have told me about the great blueberry picking in the bush, back in the hills. The berries are quite large; "Three berries make a pie," I have been told with a twinkle. It must be a local joke thing.

Monday, July 22nd…up at 4:30 and on the water by 5:00; nice quartering wind from the southwest.

The St. Lawrence is about 25 miles wide here. I don't think of it as a river anymore so I'll call it the Gulf of St. Lawrence. It takes us northeasterly along the south coast, an increasingly rugged coast with hills stretching back from the water's edge. Hills, trees, and water. Unlike former president Reagan who, as I recall, said that, "Once you've seen one tree, you've seen them all," I believe that trees and forests are a precious natural legacy that supports all life. Some trees may even be as smart as some people…no names needed.

The wind was brisk that morning, just strong enough for some good speed at about five knots on a broad reach. The waves were not so pleasant. They were off the wind about 30 degrees and made for a fishtail ride sliding down their front faces as they rolled under us. I experimented with less and with more speed to try to find the best way to ride the waves with good steerage. More speed felt better; about 5 knots gave the most stable feeling and the best steerage.

By noontime the sun was getting hot and we were still barreling along. Earlier that morning I was trying to position my body into the sun to get warmed. Now I was trying to find some shade. On the water, the daily weather felt fall-like. It kept me aware of the fact that I was still climbing into higher latitudes…we had been heading northeast the last 1000 miles.

Email, July 22nd. A nice steady 20-knot wind and waves coming from the side, steep and choppy and confused. We experimented all day trying to adjust speed for a comfy ride without the rolling and twisting. We made it to Matane early but whimped out and pulled in. I wanted more miles than 50, but big smiles from Bridgette the dock gal, who spoke no English and didn't need to, convinced me to stay.

Besides, I needed salad fixings and cremé for tea. A half mile walk to a grocery store but a well-stocked store with all necessaries.

Met Joe and Nadia on dock with their 60-ft cruiser from Florida. I think Joe is a retired mafia boss with a young wife (half his age plus seven years…that's the formula). Joe is great. He said I have a hand like steel and the heart of a lion, with his Jersey accent. He loves my adventure; filled his tanks on "Countess" with 800 gal. diesel.

Will try for big miles again tomorrow…winds permitting…toward Gaspé.
Love y'all, Curt.

Late afternoon found us with Matane, Quebec in sight. The charts had indicated a marina at Matane and beyond that, farther up the coast, I wasn't quite sure where the next safe harbor was, besides, we had put in a 55 mile day and that felt substantial.

I was always reasoning with myself about distance made good. Was it enough for the day? Could I have done better? Should I continue on and make use of this favorable wind? Would I find anchorage if I did or would I need to stay clear of the coast and sail all night?

I was hot, hungry, and needed some local advice about the Gaspé coast ahead. If that wasn't enough reason to pull into Matane, I was also getting low on some of my favorite food provisions. Matane it would be.

Bridgette, the marina staff person, helped me to tie up to a dock in the frisky winds. I could tell she was a hard worker, moving about as quickly as she could, helping boats tie and retie in the winds. She spoke no English but she had a great shy smile. My smile had no pretensions of shyness.

Perhaps these winds were a harbinger of the winds of Gaspé that I had been warned about. I remembered that Danielle, back in Quebec City, had told me the winds come gusting down off the hills and sailing five miles offshore is safer and easier because they begin to dissipate over the water. More sailing challenges ahead it sounds like.

The Gaspé Peninsula of Quebec and I have had a romance that goes way back. I have always loved to pour over maps and dream; the wonder of faraway places I guess. I remember my old atlas of the world showed few towns and sparse settlement on the Gaspé coast. Just the sort of place I dreamt of exploring when I was a kid. Now, here I was, decades later, exploring the wonders of Gaspé; just me, my old sailboat, and the wind.

Our nearest neighbor afloat, at the marina in Matane, was a huge power cruiser named "Countess" from St. Thomas, U.S. Virgin Islands. She looked to be about 60 feet long, spotless and polished. Joe, her skipper, and I had to exchange pleasantries and curiosities. He and his wife Nadia and first mate Tom had spent the summer plying the coast northward from Boca Raton, Florida. They were taking on fuel, diesel, about 800 gallons in two tanks. I did some quick math...800 times $5.00 per gallon. More than I had paid for Sweet Breeze when I bought her.

Joe was a gruff sort. I suspected that he was used to having his way with things.

Originally from New Jersey, he said he was retired from running his trucking company. Possibly. More likely, thought I, he was a retired mafia boss. He had that Godfatherly way, a lovely young wife who spoke many languages, and the no-nonsense straightforward ways that I imagined New "Joyzee" bosses had. My imagination was delighted with his lifestyle and the little personal history he revealed. I liked Joe right off.

When I told Joe where I was from, where I was headed, and my single-handing of Sweet Breeze, he seemed amazed. He asked if I had no fear. Plenty, I replied. He said I must have the "heart of a lion" regardless...so far alone, so many unknowns each day, each night. His kind words affected me. Maybe I was becoming a sailor after all.

There was a real grocery store just half a mile down the road and across the river bridge. The kind that has a large selection of fruits and vegetables, breads baked on site, real foods beyond the boxed and canned food-like substances in the center aisles. I brought my new, complimentary, Marina Rimouski shoulder bag...perfect for hauling groceries.

Back at the boat, Joe invited me aboard the "Countess" for a tour and a drink, shoes removed of course. What luxury. Beautiful boat. Beautiful woman. I guess money has some advantages though it doesn't leave me wanting, I have a great old boat, vivid dreams of beautiful women, and I can leave my shoes on.

While Joe and I were chatting, a small fishing boat pulled alongside the dock. Holy mackerel! The fisherman and his son had a whole pail full of the most beautiful iridescent blue and shiny fish. They looked like a 15-inch version of those brilliant little "neons" that the dentist had in the glass tank in his waiting room. He offered us some if we would like. They were mackerels, looked delicious, and if the offer had arrived before my grocery trip and the pecan pie, I'm sure I would have taken a couple.

Tuesday, July 23rd...up and away at 4 a.m.

Getting on the water before the sun, with wind in the sails and unknowns ahead, gives me a feeling of peaceful excitement. The coastline over starboard intrigues me with its mountains and the cuts between that must hold some river gorges. Small towns at the river mouths hold onto their precarious footing against the mountain rising behind and the sea grinding at their frontage.

My watery world of the Gulf of St. Lawrence is about 30 miles wide now. The wind off the southeast shore puts us on a beam reach at 5 to 6 knots increasing to 7 to 8 knots as the miles fly by. The tidal current must be carrying us out to sea.

The Countess passed by out to port at about 6 a.m. Joe would probably put on a 150 mile day and I wondered where that would put him for the next overnight. Maybe to Port-Menier out on Anticosti Island. I'll probably never see him again but I hoped I would. Perhaps at Nova Scotia or down the eastern seaboard. Once again there was that tug at some inner self over losing contact with new friends. Nadia was curious about my single-handing, alone for days and nights. She thought I must like my own company...I had agreed.

Cooked some of my new potatoes and sweet corn in the pressure cooker for breakfast. I love my old pressure cooker—no spills or scaldings and if the top is left undisturbed after cooking something up, the contents are "canned" and will keep in the cooker without refrigeration. Its design, with the sealed lid, keeps the heat in and less propane is consumed too.

I think my body was craving something less sweet than the pecan pie I had indulged (overindulged) in last night. Potatoes and sweet corn was not my usual breakfast fare but then I had no usual breakfast fare. Whatever was on hand or nothing at all was the norm. Oftentimes I forgot about eating altogether when busy with sailing or glassing the coast, taking those mind photos for hours.

Sometimes I would just peer ahead at the waves and water for long periods, trance-like, one hand on the tiller, lost in thought, hoping to glimpse a whale or seal perhaps. With winds about, I kept glancing up to view the sail shape and would try to maximize our speed with whatever wind we could capture.

The late morning brought with it a wind change. My hopes of a one hundred mile day dropped with the wind. I suppose I was hoping to put on a really good bit of seaway just to prove to myself that my progress was not dependent upon carrying 800 gallons of diesel fuel, or even our own 12 gallons of gasoline.

The wind died suddenly and then did a 180-degree shift to the northwest. It blew cold now off the gulf. It also put us on the lee shore so I was expecting the waves to build, rolling across the 50-mile fetch of the widening St. Lawrence. My first thought was to head out another mile or two offshore to gain more sea way. We still carried good speed until the wind dropped off again, as suddenly as it had reversed direction an hour before. There was little choice now but to burn some of that 12 gallons of gasoline that we carried, still it seemed but a tiny amount of fossil fuel compared with what many boats consumed.

Passing Les Méchins, another small town off the starboard beam, caused me to wonder about the origin of the name. Was it about machines? There were commercial docks and a protected harbor with an industrial looking waterfront. Must be about machines...shipping machines. The oblique wonders of language. What I don't know I can have fun guessing about...just some of the things a lone sailor thinks about for amusement.

I've never thought myself a moody person, but I must be. Whereas a few days ago I had been feeling cramped within the confines of the boat, today I find myself telling her what a dear little boat she is. So solid and safe. So cozy and intimate. Today I love her design, her security. She wraps around me like a blanket.

With a 60-degree heading I can now see Cap-Chat ahead. There's always something of interest within sight...the highway along shore with its steep cut into the sheer cliff faces. Cars, colored dots barely visible, traveling at speeds unimaginable after six weeks of sailing. The diving seabirds with the yellow heads, hit the water from the air like a missile. "What are they called?" I ask myself as I search my memory of past nature shows and bird books and come up blank. Similar birds in the Caribbean were called boobies, perhaps a relative (northern gannets I later learned); beluga whales cruising along with me off to port, surfacing and blowing jets of vapor; small rafts of floating vegetation to avoid and keep the prop unencumbered. I would not want to clear the prop with my toes in this icy water.

A Canadian Coast Guard vessel passing by showing no interest in me. Good. Another wind shift; back to the east now causing me to trim the sails flat and tight trying to gain some pull from forward winds. The blank stare of the depth meter showing no digits now because of the great water depths here. Depths that reach far beyond the meter's maximum soundings.

Peering northeast, I think I can see Anticosti now, the one hundred mile long island guarding, or welcoming the offshore sailor to the broad entrance of the St. Lawrence and the Great Lakes beyond.

The afternoon's progress needed the help of the motor, with the diminishing and unfavorable winds. The surface of the offshore water was settling into a glassy calmness.

Coastal mountains and fiords kept drawing me landward, but in my imagination only. The coastal waters looked hazardous. Jagged rocks on shore strongly suggested the same thing just underwater. Breaking waves revealed the presence of rock reefs reaching out from shore. The view from a mile or two offshore would have to do.

The mountainous coastal scenery, the glassy water and my daydreams gave me no clue as to what changes were about to happen. Some welcome surface ripples from an offshore breeze brought me back into the thoughts of sailing again. Within one minute that breeze brought gusts behind it that heeled Sweet Breeze way over and made the rigging shiver. The sudden wind seemed to come out of the fiord, the deep bay shoreward across the mouth of which I was now sailing at top speeds. It was a welcome change from the drone of the motor but it was such an abrupt change it almost caught me off guard. I had thoughts that, even though it was late afternoon, with this new wind and faster boat speed I might make it to Cape Madeleine where I had heard there was a sheltered harbor.

The swirling winds didn't let up but intensified. I couldn't keep catching those winds on the beam with full sail or something bad would happen, yet I didn't want to fall off the wind and head out to sea, far off my intended course. I was looking forward to a peaceful night at anchor somewhere, not an all-night sail in gusty winds heading easterly, offshore in the North Atlantic. I reefed the main once and furled the jib a bit and still the gusts felt way beyond a controlled sail. These must be the freakish winds of Gaspé that Danielle back at Quebec City had warned me of.

Once across the mouth of the fiord the towering headlands with their seaward cliffs blocked some of the direct intensity of the blow but there was no likely anchorage or escape along the rock faced nearshore waters. It didn't take me long to decide that Cape Madeleine was out. Too far and too much wind from too many directions. Evening was approaching and a restful night at anchor somewhere was my usual goal, but these winds were really crazy and getting worse. Still, my sailor's will to make headway when the wind blows pushed me onward; if I could just keep the boat under control in the gusts; we were making some real distance with bursts of speed of seven to eight knots.

The chart plotter showed a bay with a wide mouth, a couple of miles distant and around the next headland. If the winds would settle down into something manageable we would keep reaching for distance beyond it, but if they kept up with their crazy ways I was ready to call it a day and look for shelter along shore.

Winds did not let up. The gusts were of an intensity that caused me concern not only about control but preserving the rigging as well. When they hit I tried to do all of the things I had learned to minimize the direct impact on the reefed sails but I couldn't point her up any higher or ease the sheets for fear of flogging the sails to rags. It was better to let the sails fill, let the boat heel and the loose objects in the cabin fly about. We skittered along this way until it became too much for me. I could see the lion's paws (normally called cat's paws, those surface ripples showing an approaching wind) coming across the water at us but the wind hit us too hard; something was likely to give way in the marginal rigging on this old boat. I started the motor and down came both sails, purposefully, to try to regain some semblance of control. Otto steered as best he could while I captured the main, tied the sail with one arm and hugged the boom with my other arm while on the cabin-top. These were some scary winds. Nothing was predictable about them. Straight-line winds were one thing, but these weren't like the thunderstorm blow of a week ago back at Île d'Orléans. These winds snuck up on us time and again with knockdown power.

The next bay was broad at the opening, giving little protection from the open sea, but we motored up into it looking for anchorage. There was a substantial river entering at the head of the bay so I suspected there was some alluvial bottom strata somewhere at the outflow. As we neared the river's mouth I could see that the current was too strong and depths too shallow to gain access upriver. To the right of the current was more of a mild eddy with deep water but I guessed there was poor holding for the anchor...sheets of flat shale or slate were on shore, running out to the depths, or so it appeared.

Any port in a storm, however. This was no port, but if I could get an anchor to hold against these winds this was port enough. I carefully motored into the eddy watching depths, checking both sides for boulders, keeping her pointed into the wind howling down the steep river canyon. With 10 feet of water depth showing on the meter I put the shifter in reverse at low idle and dashed forward to pull the pin on the Bruce anchor and let it drop, cleated off the rode with fumbling hands, then did the dash-crawl back to try to set the anchor into the bottom before swinging too close to shore. Watching the rode as I backed away from shore, the anchor skipped along a couple of times then grabbed and held, caught in a rock crevice I suspected. Close enough for now. Time to catch my breath and retie the mains'l to the boom before the teeth of the gale tore it loose and flogged it. The furled headsail was never a worry as long as the furling line was cleated off securely and the sheets taught and cleated.

I guessed that the gusts were 40 to 60 mph. The anchor was holding fast and the rigging was humming. I set the man-overboard mark on the chart plotter to check occasionally to see if we were holding at anchor or dragging it across the rock face.

Between gusts, the wind dropped to a quiet, almost friendly breeze, but then the next gust came howling with a still greater vengeance. I sat in the cockpit for some time just watching the rigging, the sails, and our position. Eventually I was feeling secure enough to climb down into the cabin and grab a cold beer as my reward for a long day and the likelihood of a long night ahead. After another hour or so of sitting in the cockpit and watching the shoreline and the chart plotter for signs of a dragging anchor, I was having the beginnings of thoughts of going below for some supper.

My appetite for food had left however and the precariousness of my situation tightened my chest. I kept standing and peering out the big side windows of the cabin for those markers on land that I had made mental note of before retiring below, still cautious and unsure of holding fast at anchor. Listening to the sounds of wind violence from above, but feeling secure below, I pondered how the fiord and canyon must act to accelerate the wind coming off the land. Something was acting on those winds. With each lull I thought perhaps the winds were dying out. Not a chance. A few minutes later the blow came back with an unreasonable velocity. The boat vibrated and made whirring sounds and groans as the gusts accelerated. We swung on anchor enough to cause concern about swinging into some rocks to the side. I had little appetite for the food I fixed.

Climbing back up into the weather, I thought it prudent to check again the anchor rode for chafing, but then I could see that the mains'l was getting torn loose from my sloppy, one handed, panic tie job on the way into the bay. I couldn't risk any damage to that old mainsail. I had no spare. This time I retied it for a hurricane.
I dropped a heavy anchor over stern on a swing to starboard to try to limit the lateral swinging back and forth that concerned me... something like a pendulum on a tall clock we swung, not that fast but still very disconcerting with unknown side depths and a falling tide.

Lucky we were that the claw (Bruce) anchor had found purchase on the rock bottom. I lashed the tiller before going below to ponder the situation, or read if I could relax enough. As I lay below, my thoughts ranged from the comforting sounds of rain striking the coach roof to more troubling thoughts, wondering if I would get any sleep this night with the calming lulls soon followed by the intense racket of the wind again, the cycle repeating every few minutes and the constant gnawing concern about holding our anchorage. Now I knew why there were hundreds of those tall, broad, white wind generators located high on the hills and cliffs all along "La Gaspésie".

I tried to relax. Sleep came in brief respites followed by startled awakenings with the wind roaring topsides. Frequent checks with the chart plotter's man-over-board mark showed that we were holding fast at anchor. At times I wondered how such a peaceful, relaxed day of sailing could turn to such a fitful night at anchor. Such is the life of single-hand sailing. It's just you and the weather. Sleep. Stand watch. Do it all. Your boat is your best friend. She'll do her part. I must do mine. She depends on your vigilance.

This was another of those times when a choice must be made between anchoring and trying for some sleep or heading out to gain sea room and sailing all night. Sleep was always my first choice. I plainly remembered the night on eastern Lake Erie with two hours of hard won sleep while Sweet Breeze drifted back into the busy shipping lane while hove to...then awakening with a start...trying to get my bearings and figure out how to get out of the way of those ship's lights bearing down on us. No more night sails I told myself then. Always try for safe anchorage I had promised myself. It was the lesser risk, with ships and shoals and other unknowns in nearshore waters and the black night melding into the black water. That, I remembered, was the most eerie, (Lake Erie) helpless of feelings.

At 3:30 a.m. the boat was pitching about. I was awake again and went topside to assess our current conditions. The wind had shifted to an onshore northeasterly. We had swung at anchor, dragged the stern anchor and were dangerously close to a shore with unknown bottom hazards. It was still dark but it was past time to get out of this bay. We were on the lee shore now with waves building and damp, cold, North Atlantic fog rolling in through the darkness.

The anchor lifted quickly from its fast hold on the rock bottom as soon as the bow got over it with a straight up pull. That was a relief...and some good luck. This was no time for struggle, either hand-over-handing the rode down the hawse pipe or fumbling hands pinning the anchor into its chock. With no one at the helm and no engine power, with total darkness and a heaving boat, hoisting anchor on a lee shore can be a critical time...then the dash/crawl back to the cockpit after securing the anchor, grabbing the helm and the engine controls and powering off shore to the safety of the open water. Things have to work out right the first time...the onshore wind and waves could have pushed us onto the rocks before I could reach the cockpit and power us offshore. But they didn't.

The safety of the open water was a fleeting feeling. Wind and waves were mostly on the nose out there. Even in the darkness I could feel the heaviness of air thick with fog. After a half hour of slight progress there seemed little point in pushing forward. There was enough gray daylight now that I felt I could find my way, despite the fog, to a possible harbor I had passed yesterday while I was trying to harness those fierce wind gusts. I hated to backtrack but it seemed the better option. Wind, waves, and fog were not my friends this early morn. Progress seemed a poor consolation if I were to entirely miss the shoreward views of this rugged, enduring coast.

We jibed about under power and loosed the big genoa. The pull of the sail felt good but was tempered by the defeated feeling of losing "way made good" yesterday. I did remember though that it was only a few miles back to the bay of Mont-Louis where I hoped I could find a protected harbor to wait out the wind and fog.

Nearing the mouth of the bay the fog thinned. I could see houses and shoreline structures; then off to the right was a heavy concrete dock with some big steel fishing boats languishing in its lee. We managed to wiggle in and tie up at a gap between some boats, with lots of fenders I might add, to keep us off the concrete and steel, fore, aft, and to port. No one was around so we made ourselves at home amongst the big hulks of the fishing boats. The fishing dock at Anse de Mont-Louis was all I needed to wait out the weather.

Checking the chart plotter, then rechecking, revealed that it was only about 15 miles east down the coast to Port Madeleine, where a marina was indicated. The plotter also said I had spent that uneasy night of last at Anse Pleureuse, tucked up as close to shore as possible, shuddering, shaking, and vibrating until the wind shifted onshore allowing our swift and necessary departure in the darkness.

If there was a restaurant nearby I thought that the night of big winds had given me excuse for a hearty breakfast, a reward for little sleep and lots of angst. Only a quick-stop type gas station showed any activity on shore but a walk was always a welcome way to stretch and explore a bit; get the flavor of the local folk and perhaps some tips about the weather and the coast ahead.

There were no eating places to be found but after it opened for the day, the fish store at the end of the big dock was like a museum of sea life. Of course there was a gorgeous young French Canadian gal behind the counter who spoke only as much English as I spoke French. We resorted to the universal language of smiles, head nods and pointing to the various creatures alive in tanks and freshly filleted. I didn't buy anything. Her friendly smiles and sweet ways were my breakfast.

From the protection of the bay and the breakwater it was hard to tell the weather out to sea. The fog had mostly lifted landward so it wasn't long before I was thinking of another attempt toward Port Madeleine.

Bending course to the South...at last....

Once back out to sea I wondered why I was pushing myself. Still there was fog. Still there was wind against us...but there was daylight now and a brightness in the air that hinted of a sun up there somewhere and soon perhaps a lifting fog. Still, what was it that drove me? Warmer weather? Destination Halifax? Meeting up with Lydia? Or was it just about getting as far as I could and still get back to Minnesota for my daughter's arrival from Germany sometime in the fall?

There was the dream plan too. Of leaving Sweet Breeze at Halifax for the winter, then single-handing across the north Atlantic to Ireland...then on to Germany's Baltic seacoast where my daughter and her husband have a cabin.

The challenge of a solo ocean crossing had been a spark within me since I read the first of many books by those who had made it. Also, since I really didn't want to fly anymore, for various reasons, it was one option for a trip to Europe and visits with old friends at Dublin, Ireland and my family in Berlin. This was a real possibility for next year.

After looking at charts of prevailing winds, ocean currents and distances, I thought Halifax would be a good base from which to set out. Once offshore a couple hundred miles we would be carried east by the Gulf Stream current. With some favorable winds and the current I thought I could probably make Ireland in 20 to 30 days. Then a short hop to England, around the Lizard, northeast up the English

Channel, along the coasts of France, Belgium, Netherlands, and through the canal across the Danish countryside to the Baltic Sea. Sailing along the German coast to near the Polish border would bring me right up to the Bach's cabin, the retreat from Berlin for my daughter and her husband and my newest granddaughter.

I would leave Halifax early summer next, before hurricanes became likely... perhaps.

As the fog occasionally thinned, here along the coast of Gaspé, I could see the outlines of the towering cliffs of Gros-Morne. It seemed a shame to miss any of the visual drama of this rugged coast due to the fog, yet I was driven to make Port Madeleine that day. How splendid it would have been to sail this coast on a sunny, clear day, but it was not to be and I was not wanting to wait.

The struggle against the wind was getting easier as the wind veered more to the north than east. With the wind shift, the fog drifted in and out again but was never so thick that I felt an insignificant particle enveloped in an endless gray world, as I remembered my feelings one day a month ago sailing down Lake Huron. Keeping about two miles offshore gave us the sea room to forgive a mistake and when the fog thinned I would peer ahead for sightings of boats or ships or...?

At the entrance to Anse du Cap-a-l'Ours there was a sailboat at anchor. The sun was out brightly and the fog was gone. Welcoming weather and always the welcome sighting and less lonely feeling that came with seeing a sailboat. Within this bay was the little marina just past Cape Madeleine that I had heard about. There we people on the docks and marker buoys leading us shoreward. We were soon tied up fast with some of the gracious help that boaters often offer.

There was no gasoline available but there was a woman fishing from the end of the dock who smiled and spoke fluent English. She introduced me to Ben, a crab fisherman who had gas in cans in his crab boat that he would sell. We made a deal and I replenished a few gallons to our fuel larder, returned Ben's can to his boat and thanked him for his kindness.

The fisherwoman offered more, translating French to English and back again. Her name was Susanne, a power boater from Montreal with her friend Marie. They were on a summer boating vacation along the Gaspé coast. Once again, after they heard my story of sailing east from the heartland of North America, they offered me their charts for my inspection and tea on their boat. What can I say? They were so good to me. Their contact was what I needed, or at least wanted, after the night of big winds and little sleep. I hoped to meet up with them again somewhere along the way, but like so many others on this journey, we were more like ships passing in the night, with but a brief glimpse into one another's lives, but what a warm and lasting glimpse they had shared.

Susanne brought on this recurring fantasy of mine...of a woman, a maritime hitchhiker, who wanted a ride to Halifax or Boston or Dublin, wanted to learn to sail, and was much easier to get along with than I was. Susanne was a beauty in many ways, her generous spirit being foremost. As I write this, many months later, those briefest of friendships show the warmth of the human spirit and give a glimmer of hope which takes me way above and beyond the great myth of human progress that our egos embrace.

J.P. and me

Once, a few years ago, a woman, a rather foreword woman, who later became a friend, asked me what my "status" was...whatever did she mean, I wondered? Was I married, gay, straight, from planet Earth or elsewhere? Later that afternoon while sitting at a picnic table near the marina and doing some serious people watching (there was a small walk-up lunch counter where locals and tourists were ordering food) a fella approached me with that curious look that suggested he was wondering about my "status". He probably knew that I wasn't a local and I thought that he probably was. He introduced himself as J.P. and spoke English very well.

"Jean Paul?" I asked. "Yes", he admitted, "but please, just call me J.P. Unless Jean Paul is pronounced correctly, I prefer to be called J.P."

"Tell me how to say it, J.P., see if I can do it. If not, I will call you J.P., Okay?"

"Zsha Paool"

"Again please, J.P."

"Zzsha Paoool"

"Like this? Zsha Paaool?"

"Close enough. You, Curt, can call me Jean Paul."

Thus began an afternoon car ride into the backwoods of Gaspé, up the river Madeleine. All of my French Canadian friends on this journey, the Quebecers who gave me advice and pointed me downriver, invariably corrected my poor pronunciation of their language. Pride in one's language is one thing but Jean Paul took it to another level.

I asked Jean Paul if I could hire him and his car to take me to a hardware store where I might buy some gasoline cans and fill them so that I would have more reserve fuel on board. He said that he would...that he often gives lifts to transient sailors and boaters like me.

We soon left in his small car for Grande Vallee, a town down the coast about ten miles where he said they would have gas cans...and anything else I might need. He was right. The town had one of those modern general stores that should have used the motto: "If we don't have it, you don't need it." My favorite kind of store.

I bought two-gallon and five-gallon containers for gas, good quality heavy plastic ones. Now I could carry close to 20 gallons of gas for those windless days ahead or those times when entering harbors and nearing dockage, setting anchors, or those coastal stopover and anchorages that had no fuel nearby.

Jean Paul told me that he was a French language teacher here on Gaspé. No wonder he was particular about words, language, and correct pronunciation. English was his first language as he grew up in Ontario on the shore of Lake Huron.

He knew his way around the back roads and the logging roads. We stopped at a roadside spring where ice cold water bubbled up through the gravel; the best drink I had since leaving Minnesota.

Farther along, on a one-lane winding gravel road, we stopped at a small trout lake that reminded me of so many of the clear water trout lakes in northeastern Minnesota that I used to fish. If I didn't know where I was or was blindfolded on the drive, I could have opened up my eyes and thought that I was back home in the Northwoods.

J.P. gave me a history lesson about the paper mill that was once located ahead on the Madeleine River. In places, we were driving on the old railroad bed that serviced the mill and allowed its construction back in the mountains. We were dropping fast now, deep into the canyon of the Madeleine, on a switchback road that was steep enough that I wondered about how his car might scratch back up the hills later.

The river's gorge was gorgeous. The water's color that deep greenish blue that said pure and fresh things to me. From an overlook I could see down into the water some 20 feet. It reminded me of a long ago hike along the Kern River in the Sierra Nevada of California. The color of the water...it so draws me.

Atlantic salmon (salmo salar) came up the river to this point, where the paper mill had been, but could go no farther until a fish ladder was built around the falls that had supplied the power for the mill. We walked down the steep path to the fish ladder where an attendant was counting the fish in the final step of the ladder. He kept a record of their numbers, declining numbers, of naturally reproducing fish throughout the north Atlantic. Without going into all the depressing reasons for their decline, suffice it to say I felt very fortunate to witness these beautiful fish, up to 30 pounds, a few feet from my face.

July 25th, Thursday. Awake at midnight to check the wind; again at 3 a.m. Tea water on to heat, good wind from west feels quite strong.

She had that warmth, that easy smile that draws me. I was taken with Susanne's kind ways of yesterday. She told me of the marina at the city of Gaspé where perhaps we could meet again...they were heading there next. I didn't even get her email address...maybe at Gaspé. Susanne...Manon...now if a man were looking for a sailing partner Quebec had its alluring female possibilities, oui?

Once more I had gone and left an early morning's safe harbor, this time at Anse du Cap â l'Ours, Quebec. At the first hint of dawn's light, I had started the motor and quietly slipped off the dock and out the passage to sea. With some serious second thoughts, I had left the camaraderie and comfort and wonder of the company of Susanne. I thought about that warm smile of hers, how it welcomed me into port yesterday as I motored past the end of the dock where she was fishing. She was a teacher on summer leave and a boater from Montreal. She spoke better English than me and invited me aboard her boat yesterday. She asked if I would stop at the Port of Gaspé down the coast, where we could meet up again. I told her I didn't know...that it depended on the winds and the seas. Those were my thoughts as I left another safe harbor...thoughts of Susanne. Would I ever see her again...?

Some part of me feels like a slouch if I'm not one of the first to shove off from port in the early morn. Is it about some silly competitive urge, I wondered? Or is it about not wanting to have that lonesome feeling from my past...of being left behind... of not venturing forth toward unknown and highly anticipated adventures, while others were? Maybe it comes from my fishing experiences as a boy...the best fishing was usually early, early, morning. "The early bird gets the worm," sort of thing.

This day I was off at first light, 4 a.m. The trip log on the chart plotter said we had traveled 3600 kilometers since leaving Duluth on June 7th. I was getting pretty good at metric conversions by now. In miles, we had sailed 2232. Once offshore there was a freshening wind from the west-northwest...mostly a following wind for us, me and Sweet Breeze. We were on an easterly heading at first, 90 degrees on the compass, bending just a bit south as the day were to wear on, holding about two miles offshore around the gradual curve of the Gaspé headlands.

Already there was a good roll on the water. For ease of sailing and better control I decided that the headsail alone would be enough power as we worked our way off shore. The waves were building quickly and I was starting to feel unsure of my choice to leave the security of the marina, with winds forecasted to reach the 25 to 30 kilometers per hour range. That was not the first time that I had second-guessed my choices but once offshore there was no turning back against the wind and rolling seas. We were holding a good speed of 5 to 6 knots as I tried to find the best angle to ride down the following seas as well as for a comfortable ride with adequate speed for controlled steerage.

Offshore from Grande Vallee, Gaspé Quebec, about 10 miles from the morning's peaceful beginnings, as the first (and maybe the only) boat to leave Anse du Cap â l'Ours, the waves were starting to reach scary proportions for a newby ocean sailor like me, on a small but stable boat, and I was starting to feel tense.

There was that tightness inside that my sailing adventures on Lake Superior had given me so many times before as I had pushed myself to gain sailing experience years before. Was it fear that made me tense? I remember sailing across Lake Superior the first time, from south to north, the Apostle Islands to Taconite Harbor, with a northeaster bringing on waves from the Canadian shore across a 200 mile fetch of lake, and having no way to know how big the waves could grow on this passage or if I could enter a tiny, rocky harbor in pitching seas. I was always conscious that Lake Superior, when angry, could break up 800 foot steel ships in open water and send them to the bottom. This was similar. I was having those same thoughts...why was I out here when I could be safe and secure at the dock? I was zooming in on the chart plotter's screen to see if there were any harbors that I could duck into should the sea conditions and my better judgment require a reassessment of my ambitious plans for miles-made-good.

It wasn't the thoughts of an impending storm. It was a mostly clear day. The winds weren't gusty. They were steady and strong. It was the way the waves were behaving. They weren't steady at all.

It was a reassuring distraction to see another sailboat about a mile off our port beam. That must have been "Conviction," my neighbors tied up alongside yesterday at the little bay and safety of the marina at Cap â l'Ours. Michael and his wife were from the north shore of the Gulf of the St. Lawrence, Sept-Îles, Quebec. He had told me yesterday that they would probably head for Rivière-au-Renard, (Fox River) weather permitting, in their big, forty some foot, Hunter sailboat.

They had caught and passed me. I wondered how they were faring in these building waves. Sometimes their mast would disappear from view behind wave-tops, then reappear as we were lifted up onto the next crest. Should I be farther out offshore? Maybe the wind was more disperse out there...the waves farther apart. Yet the further out, the more remote the awesome shoreline views. No matter the weather, after coming this far I didn't want to miss the cliffs, the rugged scenery of Gaspé as seen from the water. Whenever would I sail this shore again?

We zoomed past the towns of Petite-Vallèe, then Cloridorme, with rocks, hills and cliffs between the bays where the towns were tucked in along the coast. Then, finally, a heading south of east. East and north of east had been my heading for the last thousand miles. At last I was heading south. Only 10 degrees below east but a southing it was and south was what I had been looking forward to. It meant that eventually the water and the weather would warm. It meant that this following wind and sea may become a quartering wind and sea...and it may mean that we were sailing down a windward coast yet later today as we rounded the broad peninsula at a good clip. But for now, my hands were full, my mind was busy with the task at hand... keeping Sweet Breeze upright.

Not being a good estimator of wave height, my best guess was an average of 10-foot waves. Looking behind me, watching them approach, some seemed to crest at halfway the mast height. Those must have been the 15 footers. They were breaking into a boiling froth at their tops and it gave me pause. This was the time for extreme vigilance. Protect this old boat...and me.

I was tiring from the steering and the intensity of watching for those rogue waves that were much bigger than the average. Again and again I glanced at the chart plotter and zoomed out the screen to see if there were any caps (points) that I could safely hide behind until the seas became a bit more amicable. Too risky. Rocks and cliffs and unknown shoals, reefs, and depths. Better to ride it out with sea room offshore a couple of miles.

I put a boat cushion on the ledge at the companionway opening and sat, facing backwards, watching the waves approaching aft, steering with the tiller and attempting to catch the chasing waves at the best possible angle...an angle that would lift us and slide that energy under us without broaching or knocking us down. When the boat was getting slammed about I would kneel on the cockpit sole and grip the tiller. I kept low after taking a header into a stanchion base when I lost balance...no damage to my pretty face, just a minor bruise.

I kept trying to figure out the best sail combination for the safest speed. Our speed had to be fast enough to maintain steerage yet not so fast that we would surf down the face of the wave and get pooped (breaking wave filling the cockpit) in the trough. That was my strategy. It worked...mostly.

I felt, with meager confidence, that I could handle these waves, even waves twice this big, 30 footers, if only they were 100 yards apart and I had the best sail pull for the ideal boat speed to have the best steerage possible. In other words, if Sweet Breeze and I had every advantage.

These weren't those big swells of energy widely spaced that the wind transfers to the water and that the ocean was supposed to have. These were Lake Superior type waves. Very steep sided and close together. Cold, clear water. Very little time between waves to assess boat position relative to the next oncoming wall of water. Time and again. Hour after hour. Wave after wave. The morning passed toward noon.

This sail around the point of the Gaspé Peninsula was as trying as any rugged sailing day of my brief maritime career. The waves were scary big and I like to think that I don't scare so easily. The scrambles to keep Sweet Breeze upright bruised my old body in ways and places that I had no time to notice. The near knockdown by a breaking wave really got my attention. The big waves were lashing us from behind. I felt we needed more speed, more sail, to gain the steerage needed to steer around the breaking tops of the biggest waves. But how to hold steerage now, just for a few seconds, while I lengthen the sail in this maelstrom of wind and confused seas.

I managed to time it while in the trough between waves, lashing the tiller for an instant while I tried to uncleat the furling line for the headsail and thereby let out a bit more canvas. It worked for now. Steerage was better now but a wind gust could more likely push us over or force the bow down into a wall of water as we surfed down a cresting wave.

I lashed the tiller again and dashed below to grab the sturdy companionway hatch that I had specially reinforced, dashed topside with it and slid the hatch into place blocking the opening. If we were to get knocked down flat I had to keep the seas from filling the cabin. A cabin full of icy North Atlantic sea water would likely end this adventure, and all future adventures, for me and my old sailboat.

Here I was, a few miles offshore in some of the most challenging wind and seas anywhere on the globe...off the Canadian coast of Quebec's Gaspé Peninsula... known through sailing history for the fierce and sudden winds swooping down the mountains and rock cliffs.

That brilliant morning of fast sailing had quickly turned into survival sailing. I had a few days of survival sailing in the last 2 months on the Great Lakes and in the last few years of learning to sail on Lake Superior. Lake Superior teaches one quickly, surely, it yields no quarter and gives no second chances. Older salts had told me that if I could sail Superior I could sail anywhere there was water. That day off Gaspé I was hoping they were right.

I was doing okay. We were dry. Putting in lots of miles, veering a degree or two south every hour. Then two succeeding waves hit the port quarter. Before I had fully recovered steerage from the first one and was falling into the trough behind it, the second one hit us on the port quarter again and I felt her rolling as I heaved the helm very hard to port. Then the second wave broke over the port beam covering the deck with white water.

She came around. Barely, as I recall. I fell against the tiller and pushed it with my shoulder to port hoping the wind in the reefed jib wouldn't pull us down and the breaking wave wouldn't roll us flat or worse. And, luckily, I didn't break the tiller in my high adrenaline state toward regaining control. We came so close, but yet we hadn't broached, and by God, we weren't going to.

The cabin was a mess by now. We had been bobbed and pushed into so many steep angles, so violently of late, that most insecure items had accumulated on the cabin sole. So be it for now. There were more pressing things having to do with steerage and boat speed. How much foresail to maintain steerage...yet not too much, causing us to dive into any big lumps of churning water in the troughs.

Keeping my high-energy attention for the moment was the dinghy. I had set out more length to its painter (tow rope) with the hope that that forsaken little tub would then be able to ride over breaking waves and not get sunk or tumbled in the froth directly behind us as it likely would on a short halter. That extended line allowed the dinghy to surf down at high speed and pass us on the right and pass us on the left. Sometimes at its height of speed it would crash with a thud into the transom and with great force of impact causing me to startle if I didn't see it coming. These were times I had reminded myself again that I would cut her free in an instant if she filled with a wave or tumbled in the surf and sank. I thought she might sea anchor the stern of Sweet Breeze such that we would get pooped time and time again. I know, in retrospect, I would have cut her free with a quick farewell if I felt she endangered Sweet Breeze.

Alas, the waves were beginning to separate, to gain distance one from the next. It had been a few hours of high anxiety for me. Otto could not steer in big following seas like these. I was the helmsman, no lazy piloting today. I was obligated to steer with constant vigilance...obligated by my partnership with my sturdy old boat. I was learning the best speed and the best attitude that Sweet Breeze could hold to effectively shrug off the tall walls of water from behind. I would have been even more nervous if I had known that the tiller had been cracked and weakened in a steerage scramble that day. (On another trying day, a thousand miles and a month down the eastern seaboard I would finish off my wounded tiller in the Long Island Sound).

Gradually the waves ebbed after three to four more hours of diligent steering, always watching for those unusually big waves at unexpected angles from behind. Dinghy was still with us, a few inches of water in her bilge, just enough to tame her onrushes down the waves. I was relaxing enough now to view the village of Rivière Renard fly by in a bay on the shore two miles to starboard. Then finally, our magnetic heading shifted to 130 degrees and the waves and wind began to relax and so did I on our afternoon scurry around Gaspé.

The winds of Gaspé live on with me... no, not those caressing breezes we joyful sailors seek, but those infamous winds of Gaspé, blowing cold from the North Atlantic waters. Gaspé is fresh with me yet today. I can still sense the overwhelming power of tall water carried along by the indomitable, unrelenting force of the wind, carrying me in my little boat, that pitifully insignificant speck of ego called "self", on the adventure of a lifetime.

4 p.m. Wind abating, seas calming, fast sailing.

Two boats left Rivière Reynard. It always gives me a warm feeling seeing other boats on the water after a hard sail...a sense of relief or of feeling camaraderie with others or of feeling that I am not crazy for being out here alone at sea. Sometimes I think I must be a loner, but with reservations. Even from a mile distant, the other boats feel like friends I have yet to meet.

Their boats are longer and faster. They probably have a crew aboard to help out, to give reassurance and bolster confidence during trying times, to chuckle at the skipper's jests and jokes during easy times. The things a single-hander sometimes missed.

They sailed out and we sailed inward toward the coast. I guessed that they were making the shorter hop around Cape Gaspé and up into the broad bay of the same name, to the city of Gaspé, tucked back into a corner of the bay some fifteen miles shoreward. I could see that they were the long, fast, expensive newer models as they inched past to starboard. What might they think of this old sailor single-handing this old boat? Three years ago Sweet Breeze had a price tag of $3000 and needed lots of work. The boats off to starboard may have cost twenty times that...perhaps one hundred times what I had paid, yet here we were, plying the same waters, adventurers all. Sure they probably had an ice-making fridge on board but today we were the same, we float on the water and fly with the wind. Today Sweet Breeze, at age 51, was their equal...almost.

I didn't take many photos but as we rounded Cap-des-Rosiers, I had to hook up the autopilot and go below for the camera. My special friend in Duluth, Michele-of-the-Roses, needed to see a photo of her namesake some day.

Winds and seas were manageable now, pleasant even. I poled out the genoa to starboard and swung the main to port and clipped my makeshift preventer (accidental jibe preventer) from the shroud to the boom. We were running downwind wing and wing trying to keep pace with the long and sleek boats from Riviére Reynard.

Cap-des-Rosiers has the tallest of Canadian lighthouses, no doubt a result of the ship unfriendly shoreline and the long history of wrecks along this coast. From there the land rose quickly and dramatically toward Cape Gaspé. The views landward, the speed of a downwind run, the sun, the wind, and best of all we were now heading south...the angst of the morning's trials at sea had evaporated completely. A big, black fish slipped quietly by to port...perhaps a shark, maybe a seal, I only had a glimpse.

Cape Gaspé, as seen from the water, could inspire me to paint again...cliffs sheer and mighty with sea birds nesting and soaring, and the lighthouse crowning the headland.

It was a memorable sailing day. A day of drama. Some white knuckle sailing through the morning had brought on the rewards of that steady afternoon brisk sail with the visuals flying by of a stark and dangerous North American coast.

Late afternoon was bringing on that daily desire to find a safe harbor for the night. I had sailed off my paper charts long ago. Still I had my eyes, my binoculars, a road map of Quebec from Kay, and my trusty chart plotter.

The city of Gaspé and the marina there was the logical choice. It would be 15 or 20 miles out of my way, westerly, which completely goes against my inner compass which always pulls me toward the shortest distance between two points...the straight line between them that sailors call the rhumb line. From where I was, that would mean a heading due south, a nighttime passage of 150 miles or so to the northwest tip of Prince Edward Island. Was I up for that? I didn't think so.

Ahead a few miles, across the gulf of Gaspé Bay was an island offshore only about a mile. The road map said it was a Canadian national park and bird sanctuary. Bonaventure Island. Surely it had a dock or protected anse (bay). I began to glass the island from a couple of miles distant...was sure I could see a dock.

I tied up at dusk at Île Bonaventure. Tomorrow's winds were forecast to be from the northeast and the evening's northwesterly breeze was almost still now. We were all alone again and it looked like a restful night in the offing. The water was crystal clear and the depth seemed adequate for settling with an ebb tide. Still, I tied up near the end of the long dock with plenty of slack line for settling. Clunking one's ship on the bottom in the middle of the night was something to be avoided. A good night's sleep is so important, especially to a single hand sailor needing all his faculties to deal with tomorrow's unknowns.

The dock was long and sturdy. The creosote on its wood beams was awful smelling. There must be a better way to preserve wood than with some god-awful-smelly carcinogenic tars, I thought.

Seals were lounging in the seaweed just offshore. There were several small old cabins and beyond them I spotted trails leading inland. Fireweed was in the full bloom of late summer.

I probably should have hiked inland, testing the trails through the spruce and fir. When would I ever return to this island off Gaspés Canadian shore? I had the whole island to myself but was content on the boat, watching the birds and seals watching me having sardines for supper. Sleep came early but not before lying still, staring into the last light of evening, with some lingering regrets for passing the marina at Gaspé and the chance to meet with Susanne again.

The teeth of a nor'easter....

July 26, Friday...64 years ago a child was born...me.

We shoved off at first light from the most remote feeling and peaceful dockage, sans creosote.

I suspected there was probably some regulation that I was breaking by tying up for the night there, at that lovely, lonely island. "No harm, no foul," was my motto. Sue had called me a scofflaw a few weeks ago while sailing across Lake Ontario. Something I was doing did not set well with her more law-abiding nature. I had to look up the word. I guess the definition fit me sometimes.

I Set Otto for 180 degrees, due south...destination: Skinner's Pond on Prince Edward Island.

Scanning my meager supply of maps produced a likely sounding destination. Skinner's Pond. The name sounded like a safe harbor. The east winds forecast for today would be pushing across the side of Sweet Breeze, putting us on a beam reach heading straight south. It all sounded good to me...it was my birthday and after all, nothing bad would happen on this day.

Trying to find the right marine forecast for this area of the coast on Environment Canada's VHF weather broadcasts was always a challenge. Then trying to interpret the French language version and soon thereafter trying to decipher the often scratchy English version, also garbled by my poor hearing. This was an every morning frustration for me.

With this information I would try to plan a route that would take best advantage of the wind, seas, potential for miles-made-good, and finally bring me to a safe harbor at the end of the day. Any day my life may depend on getting those marine weather forecasts right.

I was feeling a bit timid after the trials of yesterday. Thinking back on the waves that were so confused yesterday morning...they were the biggest yet and steep and coming from different directions. It must have been caused by reflection waves bouncing off the cliffs of the Gaspé Peninsula...or maybe swells left from the winds of an outlying storm in another part of the North Atlantic. Today, thought I, perhaps if I just got offshore a few miles the waves would be more predictable. Those were my thoughts of an early morn. Darkness was all around but for the first gray hint of daylight spreading across the black waters of the Atlantic to the east. The nearly calm seas rippled only by the constant pull of this sailor's desire for more miles-made-good.

Environment Canada predicted strong winds from the east today. They called it a "strong wind warning" for small craft. I wish they would just tell me the velocity of the wind and let me decide if we could handle it. That "strong wind warning" always sounds so ominous.

My black and blue toe was not broken...tender but still flexible. It must have been damaged in a scramble yesterday when sailing hard in those big walls of water.

The swelling in my left foot was also getting back to normal size. I think it was caused by the way I curled it around and sat on it while at the helm for hours and hours, day after day. I kept a close eye on any physical/medical problems that might slow me down.

Warmer water and warmer weather were becoming a real draw for me now. It seemed like the last two weeks were a lot about wetness and chills. Heading south was good for my damp spirits. South meant eventual warmth to me.

My flannel lined pants were nowhere to be found on the boat. How does one lose things on such a small boat? Damn, I wanted those canvas pants with the soft feel of flannel inside. Long johns and a big wool sweater were substituted as the beginning layers to add some degree of comfort on this dark and gray early birthday morn.

Rain was predicted along with the east wind. So far little wind was felt as we left Bonaventure Isle. Grayness was all around now with a very light chill wind. It would take us 24 hours to cross the mouth of Chaleur Bay and reach the safety in the lee of Prince Edward Island. Sailing all night was nothing I looked forward to, especially with the potential for tall seas. But this was a good opportunity to put on some real miles...about 125 miles on a fast beam reach. That would be the best day's mileage yet, but could we handle 30-kilometer winds on the beam...in the dark? Just how big would the waves get? Only a few hours later those best laid plans and questions were to be answered.

After an hour the forecasted wind from the east picked up enough to set sails and enjoy the quiet ride. Shutting the motor down was always a welcome change of sounds. I had been below with my hot tea while the motor pushed and Otto steered. Hot tea and getting out of the chill air was my usual early morning comfort after getting under way, wind and waves permitting.

We were soon clipping along at five to six knots and putting on those miles anticipated. As expected, the waves picked up too and I could hear that Otto was starting to strain trying to hold our course in the lumpy seas so I put on more clothing, climbed topside and took over the helm.

We had about 40 miles to cross the open mouth of Chaleur Bay. That could take about five hours of fast sailing. If the weather slipped into a certain unpleasantness, there was still a plan-B available. Once across the mouth of the bay I could strike west and duck behind the islands that make up the southern lip of the opening to the vast bay. They were the first islands of northern New Brunswick and around the backside of Miscou and Lameque Islands we could hide from the wrath of the open ocean.

It wasn't long before the ride got really uncomfortable. I always got that queasy, seasick, icky feeling whenever the boat started a heavy roll. I have never been really full blown seasick but the warning signs were already there...the flu-like symptoms that made challenging sailing so doubly hard. Usually I could strike a balance between the mentally distracting stresses of sailing alone in rough seas helping to offset the rolling motion of the boat that would get me steadily sicker. The stress would help to ward off the sickness. The wind and spray in my face also helped to keep the sickness at bay and the anxiety felt of this developing bad choice was beginning to shift my thoughts toward survival...again.

As the waves built higher my outlook sunk lower. The wind was veering to the northeast...cold, right from the Greenland ice cap, or so it felt. Steady rain and salt spray was being carried by the wind. It looked like an old fashioned Lake Superior nor'easter was in the offing, only here we were offshore 20 miles in the North Atlantic.

My fanciful, Velcro laden rain jacket was beginning to feel cold and clammy as the rain seeped through, as it always did after about an hour's soaking.

I started to think about the forecast again. What if the winds reached 40k instead of 30k? I thought we could handle 30k winds. 40k winds I didn't want to think about. Plan-B was looking more appealing...wet, cold, half sick, and I was now beginning to think of survival over miles-made-good. I couldn't yet see Miscou Island but the chart plotter and compass said that a hard right turn would get me there.

Getting the mains'l down in the wind and seas would be the next challenge. My guess was that both sails would be way too much for me to try to control and probably way too much power and speed on a 20 mile southwest run toward the islands...and damn, now it had become two days in a row of hard, white-knuckle sailing.

I was feeling a bit of a chicken inside for heading for the islands. Could I have made the hundred-mile passage to PEI? Certainly I could. Did I want to test and torture myself that way? Certainly I didn't. It would have meant all night at the tiller in building seas and blowing rain and dodging 20 foot waves in the dark would have been tricky...maybe too tricky. I thought I was a smart chicken that day.

The weather worsened on the run to Miscou. Miscou was no miscue for me. It was the smart choice and when the low island began to show occasionally on the leaping horizon ahead of me, I let Sweet Breeze run her fastest on our sprint to safety. Spray and wave-tops were soaking us and once again I concentrated on keeping the reefed genoa full and watching aft for those occasional really big waves.

When the island came into view through the wind and rain, there was more than a mild sense of relief within me. We still had to stand off the island a few hundred yards to keep plenty of water between us and the sand shoals that the chart plotter showed extending out from the lee shore. The wind, rain and following seas were not abating yet but I was sure that I could find a respite somewhere in the lee of Miscou.

Finally, heading south again down the island's west shore the waves became more manageable. Only eight more miles to the bay between Miscou and Lameque islands, trying to keep 20 feet of water below us as the chart plotter indicated shallows all around the island.

We did it. It felt so good to drop the sails and slip up into the protected cut between the islands. Still steady rain and whistling wind, but only gentle swells there as we tucked up in the cut. The Bruce anchor wedged deeply into the sand bottom and gave us a secure anchorage in 9 feet of water. Looking shoreward, the high water lines indicated almost a low tide here. I was soon at peace again with the sea and the wind and this whole darned adventure.

Rain pounding on the coach roof, a change into warm dry clothes, hot food (leftover sweet corn and potatoes from way back at Quebec City), the snug cocoon of the cabin below. Even the howling wind in the rigging topside enhanced that secure feeling that warmed me. The angst of the last few hours was soon forgotten. Survival once again accomplished. Security once again relished.

But there was a lot to think about. First of all, I had to get rid of that fancy, so-called raincoat and get some real, old-fashioned rain gear like the local fishermen wore. No more miracle fabrics, thanks. Some good old "oilies" were in order...ones that would really keep a sailor dry.

Next, farther down the coast of Chaleur Bay, I would pull into the harbor at Shippagan, New Brunswick and look for some good paper charts. Something to back up the chart plotter and show more detail perhaps than my old road map of Quebec.

My father didn't raise any wimps, but parts of this sailing adventure had not been fun lately. I was warm and dry with a nor'easter howling above...but why, why was I here? I was having those thoughts again. What was I accomplishing? Was I having a good time? Was it still a fun time?

Wet clothes were hanging everywhere in the cabin...some dripping wet. The wind and water was very cold the last few days. The water was icy cold. Lately, this was not the sort of sailing I enjoyed. Lately, I had been daydreaming of hiking on solid ground.

Sure, I was surviving. There were times lately when that too was in question as me and my old boat were getting knocked about in serious seas. I was thinking that an Atlantic crossing would have been an easier sail than what I had gone through the last 50 days. There are so many unknowns along the coast. The weather, tides, bottom hazards, unknown harbors...some entries into safe harbors can be made only at high tide. Yup, barring a hurricane or an iceberg, we could sail to Ireland in 20 to 30 days riding the gulf stream and prevailing winds. Easier? Most likely, thought I.

I had been trying to figure out the marine weather forecasts and make wise choices based upon what I hoped was a forecast for my locale. Sometimes I would just tune in to the strongest marine weather channel on the VHF radio and hope that forecast was local because it gave the best reception. I intensely didn't like departing a safe harbor on hope. I wanted to know that I was hearing the right forecast for my current location.

For now, I was warm and snug. I hoped that the wind didn't shift and cause me to have to try to find another windward shore somewhere.

The wind was picking up speed but staying easterly. I could tell by the humming of the rigging and the motion of the boat. We were at anchor about a quarter mile offshore from Miscou in wide sand flats and we were warm and dry.

Yesterday had been a 90-mile day, though 50 of those miles were the highly anxious miles of big confused following seas. Today we had covered maybe 50 miles, and we were staying put...if the anchor held fast. I was feeling so glad that I had chickened out and changed course to the safe route behind the islands. We would have had winds at 40k or greater on a beam reach, triple reefed main and a patch of a foresail, five to six knots of speed and 24 hours at the tiller and who knows how big the waves would have gotten.

I felt that I should go topside in the gale and check that the anchor rode was not chafing as we swung in the cold, steady wind. There were many creaking sounds from my little ship, but before I checked anything I had drifted off to sleep again.

July 27, Saturday...a new day in New Brunswick.

It was a mostly restful night. When I poked my head out at 5 a.m. (We were now in a new time zone, Atlantic time.) the first gray light of dawn was enough to outline the islands. We were swinging south at anchor. The flashlight beam on the masthead fly showed the wind shifting to the north. Time to leave before seas kicked up on these broad sand flats of Chaleur Bay.

South it would be toward Shippagan, New Brunswick. I wanted a real raincoat. I loved the Quebecers but I was looking forward to speaking English. If my hearing was really sharp I know I could have done better with French but I was what I was, a slow listener, hard of hearing, and a lover of language, but with handicaps.

Shippagan had one big question mark for me though. To get back to the open ocean there was a cut (or a gut or a gulley) that wound its way through a lowland area east of the city, but the main highway to the islands crossed the gut on a lift bridge. I could not determine exactly how high the bridge would lift from my highway map and chart plotter. Sweet Breeze needed about 40 ft. of clearance for her mast and if she would not clear we would have to retrace our course all the way back north about 20 miles to the mouth of Chaleur Bay to get back to the coast. That would be hard for me, going north again and retracing water already covered.

I was in too much of a rush to get underway. The dinghy was half full of rainwater and was dragging hard...I had made way before checking the obvious. I had to drop anchor again, climb down into the dink and bail. In the process the painter sunk and got wound around the prop. This was not a good start.

Why had I not used floating (polypropylene) line for a painter? Why was I in such a hurry this morning? The water was way too cold for a dive down to the prop. I cut the line and slowly reversed the prop with power and luckily the painter unwound while I pulled on one end. Underway again.

Next, I carefully plotted a course south. Shallows extended far out from Île Lameque and I was not to run aground this morning too.

I called ahead to the Shippagan Marina and asked for help docking in the brisk north wind. Mostly a French response, but I think we understood one another and someone would be there to help with docking.

The fuel dock was an easy approach. I filled my tank and paid my dockage fee to some young Acadians in attendance. They told me about an Ace Hardware store nearby and a grocery store in our exchange of broken French-English.

It was a real hardware store and clothier where the local fishermen bought gear. I bought a real rain suit, rubberized and waterproof...also, some paper nav charts of the New Brunswick coast and the waters off Nova Scotia. Things were looking up. Even the sun was poking through occasionally.

The next challenge was to try to figure out if Sweet Breeze would fit under the lift bridge on the shortcut to the sea. The new marina attendant said, "Non, non, never to fit." The other two sailboats at the marina could not make it, he said, and my boat was equally as tall. "Non, non, not to try."

That was not what I wanted to hear. The rig on the other two sailboats looked taller than mine. I called the bridge operator on the VHF and asked what clearance would be possible at low tide. A little over 14 meters, he offered, again in a strong French accent that I needed him to repeat a few times.

Fourteen meters times 39.37 inches divided by 12 equals about 46 feet according to my 20-year-old solar powered hand-held calculator. Forty-six feet. How tall was Sweet breeze to the top of the mast? How best to measure her height alone and without climbing the mast? How to find her exact height?

Standing back and looking up and looking down and all around the boat, the pulley block that I had installed at the masthead and the extra halyard lined through it seemed like my best bet for measurement. I tied a small line to the end of the halyard and ran it to the top. Then I held the line taught and made a mark on it at the base of the mast. I pulled it back down and very carefully measured it with my 20-foot tape. Then measured it again, and again.

Long story shortened, I came up with an overall height from the water surface of about 44 feet to the tip of the mast.

Low tide was determined from the tide tables to be at 3:06 a.m. the following morning so I called the bridge operator again on the radio and asked if he could raise it for me at that time...that I would be there ready to pass under. I set my alarm for 2:30 a.m. and put it on my pillow before falling asleep that evening.

We, Sweet Breeze and me, were at the bridge in the dark at the appointed time. The darkness was good. I couldn't see the clearance, if any, and it always looks much closer from below when passing under a bridge.

We made it. Even the wind fly at the masthead was intact. There was some measure of relief. A fairly large measure. We did it...and saved some 40-miles of retracing our course, altogether, to the point just ahead, where we would reenter the Atlantic.

We had been told, by helpful Acadians, that if we cleared the bridge (which they thought unlikely) we should anchor and wait for high tide in order to navigate the four miles through the Shippagan gulley to the sea. We anchored. We waited. We quietly celebrated.

East of the Eastern Time Zone

This was the third time zone of my easterly sailing adventure. Central Time to Eastern Time to Atlantic Time...and a few hundred miles of easting yet to get around Nova Scotia.

I was tossing around the idea of motoring through the gully in the dark as the tide had begun to rise. There was no sleep to be had...there was that inner urge to put on miles, to embrace the day and whatever it presented. If we got stuck in the mud then we would just wait for the rising tide to float us off.

Leaving Shippagan, out the gully to the sea, I was having some mixed feelings. Thankful for small comforts...like the electric power at the Shippagan marina which allowed for my little electric heater to help dry out the cabin of Sweet Breeze and the wet clothing hanging everywhere within.

I was thankful for the marker buoys strategically placed to keep me out of the mud flats in the gully. They were cold steel painted red and green, but to this sailor they had a sense of warmth and of caring. Thankful for the snug cabin down below and the dependable little Atomic 4 inboard engine pushing us along and just barely sipping gasoline. Thankful to be underway again.

The other mixed feelings were about the people back home that I missed and my sweet dog Chickie. Slightly sad to know I would likely never meet again those folks I had met along the way who had helped in some small way or just smiled in return when part of me was seeking some human contact.

There was the draw of adventurous feelings...of new places and developing weather, of sailing ahead toward the bold coast of Nova Scotia...and all of the other unknowns that unfolded each day.

There was the rehashing of the events of the last few days. The wind and wave events that may have prompted fear within me. Whatever it was I had felt...fear, doubt, it never hampered my judgment or abilities to think and do what was needed for the survival of me and my old boat. For that I was doubly thankful.

There were lots of commercial fishing boats tied up along the south edge of the gully. Boats of all shapes and sizes and colors. Some were up on the hard ground looking old and abandoned, rusty and forlorn, but causing me to wonder of their history and the men of the sea who risked these waters in those hulks to make a living.

The morning had begun in shades of gray again. Thin fog. Low clouds. A light breeze from the northeast still. We reached the sea and motor sailed out a few miles to gain depth beyond the sand flats stretching far out from shore...peering into the grayness, watching and listening for waves breaking on the shallows. Not the kind of grand entrance into the Atlantic that a sailor would like...a fellow like me, with maritime ambitions off the maritime coast of Canada.

Not sure what day it is. Not sure of much in this fog.

The morning's heading was 190 degrees. That was a little west of south and was the first westing since the lower end of Lake Huron when I headed west across the lower tip of the lake for the slide down the St. Claire River to Lake Erie.

We were headed now for the Escuminac Point on the southeast lip of Miramichi Bay. It was to be a 20-mile passage across the mouth of the bay and I remember that I was feeling tentative. I distinctly remembered the trials of the last few days...the nausea of my rolling stomach in the rolling seas. The soakings in the spray and the rain. The struggles with single-handing the sails in gale force winds. But the forecast was for light winds today, still northeast but light. No strong wind warnings on any weather channel except for the northeast end of the Northumberland Strait and that was a long distance away yet.

The winds were light and so were my thoughts as the grayness all around gave me occasional glimpses of the low, distant shoreline of New Brunswick. But the grayness couldn't penetrate an inner joy that the open water sail was giving me.

We were sailing by chart plotter alone...that amazing gadget that showed me exactly where the boat was relative to land and sea. There were no visual reckonings beyond a quarter mile, just grayness.

Half way across the bay I was beginning to relax. Northeast winds were picking up but easily manageable on a swift broad reach, both sails full and pulling.

I often wondered why I so seldom saw another sailboat...none on the water the last few days. None since Gaspé Point. Was there some weather event in the offing that I didn't catch? Was it just too cold and nasty to be out? Were they all Sunday afternoon sailors hereabouts? Was I the only one going from here to there? I don't think I had seen 10 sailboats on the water in the last 2000 miles. I was not liking being a hermit on the water. Seeing another sailboat always gave me a sense of camaraderie.

Alas! Two big power yachts steaming by on port. I called them on the radio, just to chat but with no response. I wondered if they could hear the radio above the roar of the diesels. Probably not. Boaters were always ready for a friendly chat.

Occasionally the fog would lift or thin so that I could see a few miles. I would peer toward port then, hoping for my first glimpse of Prince Edward Island, somehow a landmark in my sailor's mind on this venture east. All I could see were big lumps of water. The waves were building but were big friendly rollers. Predictable and not confused.

When not paying attention to sailing that day my mind would wander to land-friendly thoughts...to thoughts of green forests and steady ground underfoot. To small trout lakes in northern Minnesota and campsites on their shores. To cold clear springs discovered on hot day hikes in the steamy, buggy woods, and the delight of their icy clear water after a belly full.

I think I was beginning to have had enough sailing for now...those thoughts of forest and foot travel seemed beckoning to me. What then, sailor?

Entering the western mouth of the Northumberland Strait, the fog thinned and I could make out Point Escuminac over starboard. The coast had not the drama of the Gaspé coast...lower and more accommodating looking from the sea. Fishing villages tucked into small bays.

I had set my sights on Pointe-Sapin now, about 20 miles due south. The chart plotter showed a small harbor there that looked like it would offer protection for the night, if we could squeeze in.

Northumberland Strait is the water body separating Prince Edward Island from the mainland and somehow I felt more secure as we entered. Though the strait averages about 20 miles wide, there was the imagined security of protection from northeasters off the open sea to the east. The reality was more likely that the strait could work itself into a hellish snarl of water if the wind was right.

The welcoming sighting of sailboat masts was not to be as we closed in on Pointe-Sapin, and that always gave me pause. Sailboats usually needed more water (depth) than the commercial fishing boats so I wondered if we would have enough water to enter, once within, would low tide leave us stranded in mud?

But the channel into the harbor was well marked with buoys and the depth meter showed that adequate water was under us. Just inside the break wall I tied up to look over the snug harbor but the creosoted timbers with old rusty spikes and odd hardware looked most unfriendly to the starboard rail. I hung out all the biggest fenders that I had but still didn't like the accommodations. I think Sweet Breeze was nervous too.

Fishing boats were tied up and lining the quays. Trucks were arriving piled high with lobster traps and crews of men and boys were unloading the trucks and piling the traps onto the back decks of the boats.

I so wanted to get out and walk around but our precarious dockage and the swells heaving the boat kept me on deck fending Sweet Breeze away from iron and old tires until I could figure out a better location.

I got to talking with a "young fella" fisherman, casting from the dock. He was trying for striped bass. Like most folks I met, he was interested in where I came from and where I was headed. My standard answers were "Minnesota," and "Halifax." My story often brought quizzical looks in return. Here at Pointe-Sapin a sailboat was seldom seen and one from Minnesota a rarity indeed.

"Where's Minnesota?" "How far west?" "Near Chicago?" "Winnipeg?" This fellow spoke English well. He had worked in the states for a long while but was back into New Brunswick's small town life...Boston was too big, too busy, not friendly.

His girlfriend arrived with some fast food. They ate and talked and they seemed a happy couple. I always like to see folks getting along...and watch their interactions.

I thought I had better move off this dock before my old boat became scarred for life. We moved into the center of the small harbor and I plunked down my Bruce anchor, checking the tide tables for draught at low tide. I didn't seem to get any dirty looks from the locals, the fishermen busy loading their boats, so I decided this would be the night's anchorage. With tides and raspy docks, I was learning that anchoring was my preferred alternative.

When I rowed the dinghy to shore the shore-caster brought me a bass, all filleted and pan-ready. What a nice welcome to this bustling little seaside hamlet of commerce and activity. The lobster season was to open in two days, I learned. I wonder if the guy who gave me the fish knew how touched I was by his conversation and his random act of kindness...those small things that happen in small towns, to a wayward sailor far from home?

I wandered a ways off the dock, away from the fishy smells and the methane odor of low tide...and smelled food. Smelled like brats and burgers on a grill. Following my nose, I rounded the corner to the community center building where a party of some sort was getting into full swing. Someone invited me in for a beer and a brat. It was a 50th wedding anniversary party... I felt a bit guilty about crashing it, but it had been a long time since a grilled sausage and some conversation in English presented themselves.

The simple humanity of small towns. Sometimes I contrast that with my visits to big cities. Cities where hurry and hustle leave little time for conversation. Where eye contact is to be avoided. Where folks exist in a contrived world, often visit their therapist, and may not know of such a life as at Pointe-Sapin, New Brunswick, Canada. Thank goodness for the draw of the big cities...that must be what is keeping the small towns small.

Down the Northumberland

Loud music was coming from a pickup truck as night fell along with a light rain. The old song, *Rock Me Momma*, rocking me to sleep, well not exactly.

Awoke during the night a few times...rain on the cabin roof one time. Awoke with a start another time as that recurring dream of sailing onto rocks or into another boat caused me to spring into action again in the middle of the night. Throwing the hatch open, peering into the night, taking a few seconds to get my bearings with a sleep-fogged brain, falling back into bed relieved that we were safe in a harbor somewhere. How many nights must I have that dream? How deeply was this sailing adventure seated in my psyche?

The first gray light of predawn brought me back to semi-consciousness. I could hear the activity of the lobstermen loading and readying their boats. Light rain and light fog felt not so welcoming nor heartening as an orange-warm sunrise, but I had places to go...south.

My new raincoat from Shippagan shed rain like it should. No Velcro on it anywhere, just big snaps to hold it closed. Simple. Very effective.

I taped a plastic bag over the top of my broadest sun hats to make a mini-roof with eaves to shed water from above. Very unfashionable I was sure, but I was to be reasonably dry from here on out. The hat reminded me of earlier times and the church ladies who taped plastic bags on their shoes and held them over their heads, lest their feet or hair get wetted on the dash from the car to the church. I guess that the rain and my appearance was not so important to me as a kid...even less important now, but I was getting tired of being soaked and chilled, day after day.

Before weighing anchor, the dinghy needed to be emptied of rainwater again. It was becoming a daily chore, not one of my favorites...take off my shoes, climb down into the little tub and bail...though I thought the cold fresh water was good for my pink, wrinkled feet.

We left the little hamlet of Pointe-Sapin when the daylight was adequate to show the marker buoys leading us back to sea. Light rain and fog and little wind. *Rock Me Momma* was still playing in my brain, as I often awake with a song going over and over in my brain. But Lord, please, not that one.

Thinking back over the last months of sailing out the Seaway, either I must talk funny or look odd. People I meet along the way often ask, "You're not from around here, are you?" It always makes me smile to think how alike we all are, yet a small difference is noticed immediately, and we become distinct. Well, I hope I am...distinct that is. It is simply not my nature to be like everyone else.

What would I do without that chart plotter? I would probably have sailed into the rocks long ago. Fog, again. Not only does the chart plotter screen show me where in the world I am, it also shows the water depths, the bottom contours, shoals and tidal flats, buoys and lights, towers and churches, tide stations and graphs, ports and marinas. What an amazing fucking gadget! In the fog, with no chart plotter and no visual references I would be constantly plotting my location on a paper chart by parallels of latitude and meridians of longitude obtained from a GPS receiver on another gadget. We would probably have been on the rocks miles ago.

Darn that song...still it was playing over and over in my head.

Last evening I had a great supper of fresh striped bass, sweet potatoes and onions. The sweet potatoes were still good from a month ago, purchased way back at Little Current, Ontario, on the top of Lake Huron. They had been stored in the "bilge fridge," where temps are usually cool and consistent.

Heading south again today...always a good feeling. South means warmer, right? A 190 degree heading. Motor sailing with the gas from the auxiliary tank. Staying below to keep warm and dry with Otto steering and the heat from the engine taking the chill off the cabin. Poking my head up every five minutes to check for boats and adjust Otto.

Sure am glad that I am a day ahead of the opening of lobster season. There would be lots of boats and lobster trap floats to dodge.

Only grayness all around, and lumpy dark water below. Had the last of my fresh Shippagan cherries for breakfast. I wondered if I could live on sweet, dark cherries alone? With afternoon, the fog thinned. Rainwater had collected in the dinghy again and ran to the back of it causing it to be a hard tow, slowing us down. The chart plotter showed an inland waterway along the coast protected by islands and long sand spits. There, I thought, I could safely climb down into the dinghy and bail her out again.

I had only used the dinghy once or twice in 2000 odd miles of sailing. Should I haul her up onto the foredeck, turn her upside down and lash her to the deck? But then the jib sheets wouldn't slide over so easily on a tack and would likely catch on something. The dinghy on the foredeck would prevent me from opening the forward hatch too. Once again, I wondered why I was dragging that troublesome little boat. It really didn't ask for much, however, and it certainly didn't ask to be towed all this way.

Alas, the sun broke through as we entered the protection of the natural near shore waterway, anchored and bailed out dinghy again and had some more "fresh" potatoes steamed in the pressure cooker. I felt like I was in a tropical setting, the sunshine, warmth...with all the present circumstances being relative to the cold and dreariness of the early morning. Sailing along these protected backwaters was a delight. Miles-long sand bars to the port offered protection from the open sea and anchorages could be found all around. It was not the rocky, foreboding shoreline of Gaspé. I felt I could be near shore here and not in deadly danger. Heading now for Cape Richibucto or Shediac, New Brunswick.

A strong wind warning crackled to life on the marine radio bands. It was for the seas of the South Magdaline...not sure where that was but here life was good, for now at least, so enjoy it.

Back out to sea for to make some miles. Made good down the Northumberland Strait. More rain again, fog, and the wind picking up out of the east-southeast. It was a perfect wind for a close-haul, 170-degree heading, but we were beginning to get tossed about.

Strong wind warning again on the radio for South Magdalene. That must be somewhere on the north shore of Prince Edward Island...?

Wondering and wandering? Can we make it around Cape Richibucto without tacking? Can I keep my lunch down in these seas? Where in the heck is South Magdalene? How can I be a better seaman? Sometimes I feel so inadequate...so many unknowns.

Though it was wet and dreary outside I was dry under my new raincoat and under my skin I was warm and feeling pretty good about my nearly two-month sailing adventure. Thinking ahead, and always trying to sail safely in the "right now," the awareness and constant vigilance, kept me from missing Marna or Chickie.

Peering ahead through light rain and fog for other boats...concentrating, fighting off the seasick feeling from the boat motion...but still we were making good headway, still close-hauled with flat sails and beginning to bend our course eastward past the Cape of Richibucto.

Apprehension low right now. Today this old boat and I are one. Sweet Breeze is so steady. When I need it, the motor runs perfect. Someone will be getting a darn good boat when we part ways.

Do I smell a skunk or is it me? Two miles offshore we were...hmmm.

When we were nearing Cape Richibucto the magnetic compass swung slowly off course about 20 degrees. Our GPS heading remained the same and our position relative to the unseen, fogged in nearshore, remained constant on the chart plotter. We must have been sailing through some magnetic disturbance area. Once again, the chart plotter kept us on course in the fog, with no compass backup that was accurate. Once again, I was thankful for that gadget.

These were times when memories of small waters crept in...trout lakes with clear, cold depths and a shoreline with a warming campfire only a few paddle strokes away. I had been on Sweet Breeze almost two months now and landward thoughts were creeping in more frequently. Days of cold fog will do that.

Wind and seas were steadily building and I could only go below for the briefest of moments without getting overwhelmed by nausea. Hauled the main down and reefed it cringle and clew.

To the port...a sailboat! Grabbed the mic on the VHF and call them on 68. Then tried channel 16 and made contact. Out of the fog it appeared...just the distraction I was needing. They were Canadians heading back up the St. Lawrence to Kingston, Ontario after two weeks of sailing around PEI. Much welcomed conversation for this single-hander.

The choppy seas were getting to me and I had begun to veer nearer shoreward to starboard, thinking perhaps I could slip into Bouctouche Bay and regain some appetite for food in calmer waters. We, Sweet Breeze and I, were making some good headway and so decided to keep going, but nearer to the shore to seek out some refuge if needed.

There were some marker buoys shown on the chart plotter that led into a bay ahead on the near shore. Close to shore the fog thinned and we sailed up alongside the outer red marker with the magic assist of the chart plotter screen. It seemed too early in the day to layover but the wind was veering from east to southeast and soon would be on our nose. Progress was slowing and the discomfort of the chop was causing me to seek reprieve. Food was the last thing I wanted but like other days I knew I would recover quickly once the heavy rolling motion eased up.

Watching the depth meter closely, the well-marked channel led us around a sand spit and off to the left appeared a field of masts. Here was a small hidden marina, unexpected and definitely well located from my standpoint...quiet water and just a mile or so off the open water of the strait. The desire for miles-made-good kept me constantly searching out stopovers not far out of the way or too far inland.

This was neither, and the welcoming committee consisted of Jules. He waved me over and helped me tie up at the only open space left, right in front of the office and services building. This was Cap-Cocagne, New Brunswick and as Jules explained it was not named for drugs but meant "land of plenty."

Jules talked a lot...fast too and in English or French, sometimes a mixture of both. But what a kind man was Jules. After some sardines and potatoes Jules offered to drive me to a gas station and get my portable gas cans filled and to a store for some groceries. We stopped at a fish store and I bought some fresh haddock for me and some for him to take home for supper.

Later that evening Jules returned to the marina and brought me a map of the Environment Canada weather forecast zones. The best map yet. Now I knew where the South Magdalene zone was and the rest of the named and labeled weather zones all around Prince Edward Island, Nova Scotia, and beyond. That little map was to sort out my confusion of forecasted winds and melt away my building frustration with the maddening uncertainty of not knowing what weather was predicted for where. That was Jules. He brought this sailor some peace of mind. What a thoughtful and kind man.

In the services building was a woman that had a hearing disability and we shouted at each other and asked for repetition often. We had the hearing problem in common and the sailing problem as well. She and her husband had a boat down the quay.

I met John and offered my assistance installing a new impeller into the water pump that cooled the engine on his old sailboat. Al and Krista came over and I learned of their Bristol 28, a sailboat designed much like Sweet Breeze, newly acquired from Maine for the unpaid docking fees of the previous owner.

Life was good again. The evening breeze was offshore and warm. The hot shower and shave made me feel almost sociable. My hair was long and out of control. Friendly folks were all around. Life was good again.

Tuesday, July 30. Up at 5:30, on the water at 6:15. Light winds as predicted.

Motored out to open water following the path of the buoys. A squall warning came to life on the VHF for the waters of South Malloy. I had no idea where that was and couldn't find it on the weather map that Jules had thoughtfully brought to me. Darn, same situation again...winds and weather forecasted somewhere in the coastal waters nearby, but I couldn't discern where. No matter. The frustration passed. We were sailing again and the wind was warm, light, and offshore.

If the wind is not brisk enough to carry us at a speed of at least 3 knots that is my signal to motor sail. With the sails full and the motor purring at a fast idle we can hold five to five and a half knots. A good speed for progress but the engine noise gets really old after a few hours. Everything is a compromise in this life.

I could see the bridge on the horizon to the east-southeast. The bridge to Prince Edward Island from mainland New Brunswick...the longest bridge in the world? Miles and miles long at any rate.

The length of bridges is fine to know but the height from the water to the bottom of the bridge is what concerns me. This bridge had clearance aplenty for our rig, never a concern because I knew the Northumberland Strait was a shipping route for the big freighters and they were several times the height of Sweet Breeze.

I had put Otto to work steering and went below to see if some certain persistent odors would follow me or if they emanated from the cabin.

Darn again, my ciabatta had molded and was not edible. My trusty 12-volt fridge was damp and smelly inside. I emptied it and wiped it as dry as I could and replaced my butter and treasured cold leftovers.

Keeping an eye on my new paper charts from Shippagan kept me busy. There were shoals about to be aware of. The depth markings on charts were a pet peeve of mine (another one). Some were in fathoms and feet, some charts showed depths in meters and feet or tenths of meters instead of feet. It was critically important to me in unknown waters to read the chart depths correctly and not get the units wrong. There should be a standard...but then, what other parts of life have universal standards?

A light fog began creeping offshore both port and starboard. The bridge was still visible straight ahead and it was not a lift bridge so no worries. Ferry boats, or were they big fishing boats, were making passage to PEI and back to mainland New Brunswick.

I got a phone call on my cell phone. Bill Long, a friend from back in Duluth, was driving to Nova Scotia and perhaps, he thought, we could meet up somewhere. Also Rudi, my lockmate from back by Cornwall, Ontario was heading for Nova Scotia.

And Lydia too, my long lost friend from Thunder Bay, Ontario was spending time in Nova Scotia at a farm with friends. Maybe too, I would see Mark again...that terrific young man we picked up at Cornwall and who helped me through the locks and challenges on the brilliant hot days from there to Quebec City (a warm day would be welcome now). Mark was the mate on Sweet Breeze for about 250 miles down the St. Lawrence River and a better sailing partner would be hard to find.

Ian and Robin, from Duluth, are somewhere off the coast of Quebec on the north side of the Gulf of St. Lawrence. Randy and Val, sailing Rover out from Duluth two weeks behind me are likely in the Thousand Islands of the St. Lawrence. And Shane and Mary, who I met up with in Detroit and also were sailing out from Duluth heading for Australia, were probably somewhere on the Erie Canal. Here I was, heading into the waters off Nova Scotia, another milestone and longtime goal within reach, alone with my thoughts...deep thoughts on being alone.

Marna called as we neared the bridge. She was driving on her way to work. Maybe I was feeling a bit melancholy but I wished that day she had made the call only a very special call to me. A call that wasn't a convenient distraction from a tedious drive to work. A call that would have been an important part of her morning, that she had planned for and anticipated and set aside just for me. Ah well, any call was most welcome that morning, and besides, when I had plans for an early departure and stuff to get ready, did I call anyone then? I think I was feeling a bit selfish, lonely, sad.

My thoughts may have been tainted by the book that I just finished...*Giants in the Earth*, by Rolvaag, the story of Norwegian immigrants in America settling on the prairie of South Dakota and scratching out a living from the soil. Their hardships were the story of perseverance with odds against them. But the part that is most sad to me is how their strong religious beliefs brought great anxiety into their lives. Not peace. Terrible anxiety, guilt, worry, and sadness, all inflicted upon themselves from their religious training and conviction, from their belief system. Their undying faith based upon stories and superstition handed to them as children and ingrained into them as absolute fact somehow replaced their joy with worry. So sad.

Such was their story...of hardworking folks whose good sense and good nature were overshadowed by the darkness of their religious beliefs. It seemed their joys were few and fleeting and recalling their story caused me deep thoughts and concern that day...concern as to whether the world and humankind would survive, despite religion and its fervent believers and the superstitions passed along and accepted as historical fact.

Whatever the outcome of this world I was determined to enjoy this life, this gift, this present sense of self and the beauty and wonder around me...the shiny black heads of seals popping up alongside in the fog, the sunlight streaking through, and the immense freedom of sailing.

It is called the Confederation Bridge, that eight-mile structure spanning the Northumberland Strait allowing free movement and transport from mainland North America to Prince Edward Island.

On approaching the bridge, high above I could see the long line of cars and trucks creeping along near the middle of the span. Were they waiting to pay a fee or was this some security check to see if they were terrorists, smugglers, or the like? Nobody was charging me a fee or checking me for contraband…I was free, the wind was free, the water over which we sailed was free.

After the bridge, the shortest route to the big bay and the strait between Cape Breton Island and Nova Scotia was a straight line, east-southeast along the coast of Prince Edward Island. Hopefully this course would bring us to an overnight safe haven without having to go northwest up into the bay toward Charlottetown. Southeast was a good direction. Anything south was good.

More seals popping up to look me over. I wondered if, in the evolutionary scheme of things, they were land animals that were readapted to the sea or if they were sea animals slowly gaining feet from flippers. This timeless Earth. The wonders of its creatures…the insignificance of hours, days, or years. How insignificant am I?

There were no afternoon breezes strong enough to hold that three-knot speed, my personal minimum speed for sailing without the assist of the motor. Motor-sailing it was, for most of the morning and for the afternoon too, unless something got the air moving.

How tedious the steady drone of the engine could become. I saw only one other boat today, it looked like a coast guard motor launch heading northwest off the port beam…a good direction for them, away from me. So far no stoppages, no boardings, no problems.

Sailed only about one hour today without the help of the engine.

It was the little engine that could, but there was oil on the surface of the bilge water lately. Not much, but it caused me some thought about where on the engine the oil would likely be oozing. Maybe the wind would pick up and the engine could take a long rest soon. If the wind did pick up maybe I could sail all night, maybe in the moonlight down the strait past Pictou Island and on to Cape George. But then I would miss the landward views of the coasts to port and starboard. But then I would be out in the dark in a shipping lane, like on Lake Erie, and I had told myself never to do that again. Miles-made-good would likely be sacrificed once more for a night's sleep somewhere along the southeast coast of Prince Edward Island.

As the afternoon wore on and I wore down, thoughts of finding anchorage for the night became primary. The light southeast wind and waves pretty much dictated a "tuck in" behind Prim Point. The north coast of the point should provide quiet shelter, its lee...if we could get there before dark and get hooked to terra firma whilst still able to see coastal hazards. There were no comfortable options of "feeling" our way along the darkened coastlines...they were rocky now, unlike the forgiveness of the sandy shoals along New Brunswick's coast.

As we passed across the mouth of Hillsborough Bay, on PEI's southeast coast, I knew that I was missing some of Canada's earliest settlements of the European seamen. I had heard that Charlottetown was a great and historic place to visit but once again, miles-made-good were the bigger draw for me.

Across the bay I dropped the hook in the dimmest of twilight in the lee of Prim Point. It felt like there was some sand on the bottom as I backed the Bruce anchor in to set it. The faint light seemed to outline a long dock to shoreward but the anchor was holding fast in the swells and the unknowns about the chances of dockage there kept us where we were. There were warm yellow lights from the windows of a home on the bluff near the dock. It had been a long day...70 miles from Cape Cocagne. I was ready for some supper, some quiet time without the engine, some sleep soon after.

Wednesday, July 31st...up a few times at night to check man-overboard mark for position... still good.

Getting up in the middle of the night a few times, climbing topside cold and half naked for a look around did not make for a restful night. Mostly any sound or unusual boat motion would awaken me. Always a light sleeper, a tentative anchorage in an unknown bottom made for only a slumber of sorts with most of my senses working as though conscious. Then there were the dreams...of drifting onto rocks or of ships bearing down on us and the startled, near-panic start and stumble topside to assess how to avoid disaster and awakening into a semi-conscious feeling of relief.

Such were my usual nights at anchorage...some worse than others, yet still, thankfully, there were some few nights that were pleasant and restful with few interruptions. I think it had to do with my thoughts of whether or not there were relevant safety concerns as I drifted off to sleep. Maybe it had become a kind of self-programmed sleep of caution and concern, or, if I was lucky, a program of a safe and secure feeling as I crawled into the sleeping bag, within the cabin...my layers of warmth and security. However it worked, it had kept us off the rocks, out of harm's way, not always well rested, but whole.

This morning was no different. The boat motion felt different and awakened me. Hillsborough Bay was starting to roll with the wind shifting to the west-northwest during the night. 3 a.m. and I was topside again, taking in the circumstances and considering my options.

The anchor was holding but with seas coming down the strait now we would drift onto the rocks of Prim Point if it lost its grip on the bottom. By 3:15 a.m. we were underway in the hazy light of the slice of the half moon.

Motoring around the point and standing off it a good safe margin, then with an east-southeasterly heading, I managed to get the sails set with the light of my LED flashlight attached to my cap. I set the gennie first this time for a run down the strait, then soon hoisted the main for more speed and a broad reach. The westerlies felt warm and welcome. Glancing up with the light on the sails and the masthead fly got us rolling down the Northumberland Strait in the dark toward Cape George.

Sweet Breeze sailing herself in the Northumberland Strait.

Keeping the wind over the port quarter kept me sharp and aware but soon the roll and pitch of the boat in the dark brought on that queasy, icky-sicky feeling that I dreaded. What kind of a sailor would I ever amount to? I lashed the tiller and dove below to search out the motion sickness pills that I also dreaded. They made me so drowsy (with lack of sleep contributing) that I could easily fall asleep at the helm (and frequently did) but they were the lesser of the issues of this early, early run in the dark. I loved the early morning starts, but not the rolling seas.

The last I had heard from my daughter in Germany was that she and her new daughter and husband were planning a trip to Minnesota in mid-September. I had to be there then. Was that my incentive to put on miles? Maybe that's why I pushed myself so hard...such long days sailing...or was it just my nature to take best advantage of winds when they blew and the opportunity to put on those weather dependent kilometers and miles?

At present rates of sea travel I hoped to reach Halifax, Nova Scotia in four to five days. Maybe there I would store the boat, or sell the boat, or continue down the coast to New England. I had no real plans beyond today...each day an adventure in itself, all waters and coastlines and weather events became new to me with each morning's first light. I guess that's why we sail.

I welcomed the warmth of the westerly, following winds. Three-foot waves sliding under her hull from the port quarter kept Sweet Breeze more active than I liked, though she didn't care. Some days it seemed I was a most unlikely sailor, barely tolerating the initial symptoms of seasickness, keeping my head up in the wind and my eyes on the horizon. The motion sickness pills were helping but soon after that came the overwhelming urge to sleep. The autopilot was working okay today, but working hard to hold course with the following seas. Still, I couldn't resist taking catnaps below. I had to or I would fall asleep at the helm. Five or ten minute naps followed by a quick climb up two companionway steps with my head above the cabin top, gaining a view in all directions...a look around with sleepy eyes for boats or ships and a check that the sails were still full and pulling. Then a quick check on the chart plotter for our position with regard to bottom hazards and if all was well, two steps down and another catnap.

Yesterday's 70-mile progress from Cape Cocagne was mostly the result of fossil fuel. We had burned three-quarters of the main tank's gasoline capacity. Today was as it should be...a little fuel consumed in the dark of early morning to get out in the safety of deep water and out into the wind. If the wind held, we would make Cape George and beyond with the pleasant sounds of only the wind, and not that monotonous, sleep inducing drone of the motor.

Thinking about Manon back at Cap â l'Aigle. Thinking about some of my other women friends. Bet you didn't know there was once another "Manon", another lovely French-Canadian, who played goalie in the National Hockey League! Thinking of Michele, back in Duluth. How important to me they were...wondering about their lives and what they were doing this day. Thinking about Marna and her grown kids gathering from Africa and Ireland at the lodge on the Brule River in northern Wisconsin. Women...wishing perhaps there was one aboard to share this adventure this fine sailing day...perhaps.

The trip log on the chart plotter registered 4140 kilometers from homeport in Duluth. A sailing day such as this was only missing a pod of porpoises leading us onward, riding the bow wave. I wondered if I would have such luck.

Local weather reports were windy. Sometimes wind speeds were forecasted in knots, sometimes in kilometers per hour and sometimes in miles per hour. Was that nautical-miles-per-hour I wondered? Whatever units of wind speed they were talking about, if it was less than 30, it was usually a "go" for me.

We crossed the path of a big ferryboat from the mainland heading out to P.E.I. at about 9 a.m. The following wind shifted more westerly putting us on a dead run. This old boat loved to run. We were holding five to six knot speeds as we passed the big island of Pictou. Life was good. No fog. Warm wind. Steady wind. Running down the Northumberland Strait on a summer day. This was my reward for the recent days of cold and damp fog. This was sailing and my spirits soared as well, with or without the porpoises.

By 11:30 a.m. I could see Cape George clearly on the horizon. If the wind holds like this we could make the lead into Canso Strait yet by nightfall.

The big genoa was pulling hard, poled out and tamed down by the heavy spruce pole I had made for just such wind occasions. The heavy pole kept the sail's clew from dancing high toward a luff or a backwind condition, if and when the helmsman's attention was not well focused on steerage (which was often enough after 50-days on the water). Otto couldn't steer anymore in the rolling, following, seas...I had to do it, for lots of hours this day.

Place names on the charts were entertaining me. Pugwash, Malignant Cove, Tidnish. The thoughts, dreams, longings, of many days alone on the water seeking entertainment and lightness wherever the single-handed sailor might find them.

Thinking of the big fishing boats passing nearby. The silent tolerance of the fishermen to us yachties. A wave of the arm usually, only in reply to mine. Their harbors a welcome late day relief to the lone sailor dreading an all night sail in unknown waters. I wondered if they, like my dad, would scratch their head and ask themselves, "Why would anyone go out in a boat if not to fish?"

Thinking of the label on my jar of potential lunch. Newman's Own Spaghetti. "All profits to charity." How un-American is that? A corporation set up to sell good, wholesome food and not reinvest the profit in order to make more profit in order to... but give it away? What kind of Capitalists are running that company anyway? What would the decision makers at Exxon-Mobil think of that kind of economic, corporate foolishness? Paul, I liked you in *Butch Cassidy and the Sundance Kid* but seriously, wherever is your good sense...and good old-fashioned greed?

I hoped Otto could steer through lunchtime, I didn't want cold spaghetti sauce but I had to go below to heat it on the stove. I was not about to heave-to, stall the boat just for cooking and waste this perfect wind.

With the leftover potatoes heating up within the sauce of the Newman's Own, I popped my head up above the hatch to check on the sails and the helm... then as I turned my head to look under the sails I think my words were, "Oh my gosh!" as I was met with an unbelievable sight. Forward, just ahead a hundred yards a huge and shiny black whale became airborne just for me. He must have been forty feet long. He must have soared clear of the water by ten feet. My spirits soared with the sight. How lucky to see this. A second in time would have missed it. Maybe this was Newman's Own charity just for me.

I steered to the right. The whale was going to the left. There could be more whales with this one. I thought I would not want to be within a pod of jumping, frolicking whales, and steered to get behind them. If one were to land on Sweet Breeze this sailing adventure would be over...but this was just a spontaneous precaution...not a fearful loss of any of the delight that I felt.

The effects of the sight stayed with me long after lunch. The power and speed needed to launch those several tons of flesh into the air astonished me...held me spellbound for many minutes afterward. That was my pod of porpoises. The gods of the seas were doubly blessing me that day with their oft withheld generosity of late.

Potatoes and spaghetti sauce seemed very plain now, after the whale's very personal display...just for me! Anything would have seemed mundane. Some butter added, improved the palatability. Some cheese improved it more. I was well aware of the lift to my mood that the whale and the wind and the warmth of the sun blessed me with this fine day. I felt at home on the sea this day.

Cape George was slow to arrive. It was so high and rugged I must have seen it from 30 miles distant. Even with the good wind and the consistent boat speed it was approaching ever so slowly...thinking ahead that once we rounded the cape's giant headland we could likely find a safe haven for the night somewhere in its lee. I took another motion sickness pill to keep me functioning (though drowsily) as we pitched and rolled and sometimes surfed down the bigger wave fronts.

Off to the left, to the northeast I imagined I could see all the way to the southern tip of Greenland...the mighty cliffs of ice and snow calving huge icebergs. When my mind was playing with imagined sights I knew I was in a good place. The fog and cold of previous times were behind me now.

If we made the beginning of the Canso Strait yet today it would be a 75-mile day all under sail. Not bad...still not the 100-mile day I thought I could make in good conditions but pleasing progress nonetheless.

The Canso Strait is the watercourse that separates the mainland of Nova Scotia from Cape Breton Island. Once through the strait and around the northeast tip of Nova Scotia I could head south again...better yet, southwest even. But for now, fascinated with the headland of Cape George to the right, the rugged greenery reaching down to the water's edge, homes perched high on cliffs reminded me of all the times I had sailed the north shore of Lake Superior...Palisade Head, Carlton Peak, Sawtooth Mountains...very similar as seen from the water of the big lake...the lake that taught me what I know of sailing, the hazards and the joys.

Glassing Cape George, I envied slightly the couple picnicking at a table below the lighthouse....the solid ground beneath their feet, their unheard conversation. Did they wonder where that yonder sailboat was from? Could they guess my adventures? Was I not the center of their attention at the moment? Was I as insignificant to them as I felt in this immense land and seascape?

I blew a blast from my conch shell horn. Then another, long and loud. Could they hear me? Would they wave? I must have been wanting to share my story of the jumping whale or perhaps just some human interaction, recognition, distant contact.

Then I wondered about that animal that once lived deep inside that shell that was now my boat horn. Were we related? What an elaborate and beautiful home he had built for himself. How many years must it have taken? Could I grind a hole through the calcified colors and extract him and eat him? I guess I could but I wouldn't want to. He put so much effort into homebuilding it seemed insensitive to pull him out. I would have to be very hungry, I decided.

Toward late afternoon, approaching the narrowing eastern end of St. Georges Bay, I could see an opening shoreward into a bay and a possible overnight anchorage. Ever so cautiously we entered the shallow bay with doused sails and motor power. It looked perfect. Total protection no matter the weather and a sand bottom ten feet down. I did all the usual semi-guesswork about tidal conditions. Was it a flood tide or an ebb tide? What was the high water mark landward? How much water did I need under the boat to stay afloat all night?

I had plenty of anchor line to drop and hold in deeper water but I never liked to. Near shore was a little riskier but far more interesting. I could see shore birds, fish were surfacing, and 15 feet of water would be plenty, was my conclusion.

The bay was called Havre Boucher and was indeed a haven for me. Tired and feeling secure, all the queasiness of riding the seas forgotten, I looked forward to a restful night within the protected waters of Boucher Haven. I felt greatly at ease and lucky to find this place.

My entertainment while eating supper was map reading...a typical evening event to see where I had come from and where I was going...tomorrow...weather permitting.

Once again, the place-names on the map triggered my imagination. Were I feeling unsure of myself I think I would head for Ecum Secum. Were I feeling downcast I would head for Blissfield or perhaps Sunny Corner. If I needed food or a naked and not so innocent woman, or anything at all I would head for the town of, Garden of Eden. New Brunswick and Nova Scotia seemed to have it all.

My last ballpoint pen was running out of ink, my journal getting dog-eared, and me getting dog tired.

Thursday, August 1st. A gorgeous calm sunny morn, a shoreline of spruce and rocks, Nova Scotia to the south and Cape Breton Island to the north and only one upstart to the deck during the night to come to my senses, ever slowly figuring out where I was and why I was there.

I felt pretty important seeing all the car and truck traffic backed up as the lift bridge to Cape Breton Island was lifted just for me. I had called the lock and bridge operator on channel 11 and got instructions for locking down the modest drop of a foot or two, the last lock on my sail to the sea.

To the right just beyond the bridge a huge mining operation was starting up for the day. The hillside was gouged deeply in an open pit that must have been dug for access to some mineral or metal ore, I surmised. I later learned that it was a huge gravel pit mainly for use on Cape Breton Island where gravel was scarce.

My thoughts ranged toward some of the scars we have made on our Earth-mother...this one small compared to the open pit iron mines of northern Minnesota, the mountain-top removal in the Appalachians for coal and one that bothered me more than most as I was driving my little truck into the mountains of Alberta with the Canadian Rockies blurred by the white dust of a mine at the entrance to Banff National Park. It seemed so out of place there, obscuring the view and long held anticipation of entering the heights of those most spectacular of mountains...views obscured with the dust of "progress".

One other scar on our Earth Mother bothered me more than most. It was my first trip to the Caribbean...the U.S. Virgin Islands and the huge dusty mine on St. Thomas, later to have learned that it was the opposite of a mine...it was the huge landfill dump for the islands where little was recycled and refuse deposited by the kiloton for another generation to deal with.

But for now, I needed some gas. I was not perfect. But I didn't burn much gas and almost none at all yesterday in 75 miles of travel. Part of the draw of sailing was the potential for travel adventure and sightseeing with minimal environmental impact. I was not perfect...but I was aware of what we were doing to our precious planet.

The Canso Yacht Club at Port Hawkesbury was just ahead a couple of miles on the left bank and it was decided to be our next opportunity to step back on steady land. It was an easy approach, good depth, and a fuel dock with room to swing into.

Wayne the attendant fueled us up. Then I moved us over to a finger dock. I bummed a ride up the hill to a grocery store with Wade, a resident boater and reprovisioned the boat's larder with all that I thought I could carry back down the hill. Beer, paper towels, chocolate bars, granola bars, and some fruit for good health. Probably some sardines too, my usual light-to-carry protein source.

Upon beginning to write an email to the folks back home and some I had met along the way, I discovered that the keyboard on my laptop was malfunctioning. Some letters wouldn't work...the 'a' and the 's' and the 'd'. I gave up and went for a walk on the docks. There I met a couple with a C&C 30 sailboat with engine troubles. They were Nova Scotians heading for the Bras d'Or Lakes of Cape Breton Island. The electric starter wouldn't engage with the flywheel ring gear on their Yanmar diesel. I could have been a smart ass and asked why they thought they needed a starter...it was a sailboat...but I remembered all the times the little Atomic 4 in Sweet Breeze had saved my smart ass.

He had taken the starter out and it was typical looking and fixable, I thought, from their telling of its symptoms, but the wind was starting up from the west again and I was soon afloat and heading east again. Later, I thought I probably could have fixed the solenoid by turning over the copper contacts to a new surface and saved them a bundle of cash for a new starter. But generous and helpful though I truly wanted to be, the selfish inspiration of the favorable winds drew me and my little sailboat out into Canso Strait and east toward the open sea. It was late morning already but if we hurried we might make the old fishing village of Canso on the northeast tip of Nova Scotia before dark.

Those big steel nuns and cans are becoming old friends on this sail. I'm speaking here about the red and green marker buoys that show the seaman the safe route through shoal waters. Some do even more than visually show the way...some sound off as they rise and fall with the swells. How clever. The whistle buoys make a low groaning sound that when first heard by this mid-westerner-turned-sailor, gave me visions of big sea creatures. I thought they must have a flexible diaphragm that is activated somehow by the motion of the buoy in the waves, directing a blast of air through the big, deep sounding whistle. Then there are the bell and gong buoys, simpler in design with a bell or gong that is struck by a hammer that swings with the motion of the buoy in seas. The sound buoys could become useful in dense fog...yes they certainly could.

There was no need for sound warnings on this day. The air was clear, the sun was bright, and the wind warm and offshore as we sailed away from Port Hawkesbury heading southeast down the Canso Strait. The relatively narrow strait, mostly only a mile across, felt intimate and one could take in the sights of forest and development on either shore...my favorite kind of sailing, taking in all the visual wonders of a shoreline that was new to me.

Just a few miles down the strait the waters opened into the breadth of Chedabucto Bay. To the left were forested islands with more intimate passages leading, I thought, up to the well known sailing haven of the Bras d'Or Lakes region of Cape Breton. To the right, the open waters of the bay were cut some 15 miles landward into the Nova Scotia shore. This afternoon's goal was for a reach or a run across the bay to Canso, and another safe haven for the night.

It became a reach. A close reach. First, with only the genoa pulling. Then the genoa and double reefed main as I cautiously tested the quartering wind. Eventually I shook out the full mains'l and full genoa as I gained confidence that the wind was steady and not coming in big gusts. We heeled to 25 then 30 degrees occasionally, and flew across the bay. Sweet Breeze was showing her stuff. At one point I could hear the propeller whirring as the water flew past and shifted the transmission into gear to stop it, hopefully when it was parallel to the keel. The turning propeller was drag that was slowing our progress to some minor degree but crossing the bay as fast as possible in strong winds was my pressing goal. We would make Canso early at this rate.

It was to be an exhilarating sail, fast and a bit wet with spray. I had gained confidence in myself and my old boat in all the various weather and wind events of the past 2000 miles or so. I gave Sweet Breeze full reign. She had a bone in her teeth. I think she liked the freedom of the steady wind and the prospect of the open Atlantic just ahead.

Fast sail to Canso with northeast tip of Nova Scotia on horizon.

Always, one of the hardest things for me to do alone is dousing sails in stiff winds and rolling seas. It also is one of the most critical and dangerous things. As we approached the shoals and rocky islands, the waves breaking over house-sized boulders at the tip of Nova Scotia, dousing sails was a special challenge.

Furling up the headsail was usually not a big deal. I could stay in the cockpit and brace my feet against the sidewall with the furling line in my right hand and the working clew in the left. I would try to point the boat upwind but not enough to luff the big gennie...with some wind holding the sail's shape I could better furl it up tight and neat, easing out the clew in one hand while hauling mightily on the furling line with the other hand. Sometimes I would have to sit on the starboard locker to maintain position without getting tossed onto hard fiberglass surfaces.

Hauling down the mains'l was another thing. It could not be powered at all or the slider clips would bind in the track and she would not go up or down. This meant a full luff with the bow to the wind. Holding the boat into the wind while getting the sail down was never easy in seas and blows. Someone had to mind the helm. Someone had to douse the sail. Someone had to capture the flogging sail and get it flaked or at least manhandled, bunched and tied to the boom...and the full crew (me) doing all these things in quick time must stay on the pitching craft first and foremost.

That's how it was that day...the scramble of getting control of the sails, safely offshore in seas, getting the boat ready to enter a tricky, rock strewn, unknown harbor under motor power, a one man crew, never an easy maneuver for me. But it worked once again...the most dangerous moment when on the cabin-top trying to tie the main to the boom with one hand while desperately grasping onto the boom with my whole other arm wrapped around it...getting hit with a wave, loosing the sail to lock both arms around the boom and start over, trying to finish the sail capture before the next wave hits and dive into the security of the cockpit. This became my normal procedure in stiff wind and seas...it almost never went smoothly but yet I am here to tell about it.

Entering the Canso harbor was tricky for me...lots of rocky hazards and unsure of the several buoy placements and the route they marked. The area was much like a Boundary Waters Wilderness lake, bald rock islands and craggy shores, but my canoe this day needed five feet of draught. Motoring through the islands we avoided a shortcut called False Passage, the name giving me a likely clue. Between the chart plotter, visual sightings, and bottom watching we wiggled our way into the arms of mother earth at the little marina.

Soon after tying up and settling down another sailboat arrived from the south. It was a small sailboat with a large crew. Kelvin was skipper with a crew of young guys getting a taste of sailing. They came up the shore from Halifax and were heading into Chedabucto Bay to Kelvin's cabin tomorrow. After he learned of my journey, Kelvin offered me his paper charts of the coast from Canso to Halifax, which I gladly accepted and promised to leave them with his hometown friend when I reached Halifax.

Paper charts were great for a backup to the chart plotter, especially along such a complicated coastline. The difficult thing for me, as a single-hander, was tracking progress on the paper chart while steering and sail handling. Getting my bearings straight took some pretty intense study of a chart that showed all the local ragged complexities. It seemed I never had the time while tending the helm and sails. The chart plotter worked better to track my position while navigating unknown waters alone...but Kelvin was generous and I was grateful.

Canso was the end of the road for travelers driving north. Two travelers tenting nearby, Ken and Gwenn from Pennsylvania made acquaintance and we talked of adventures near and far. They were campers, explorers and kayakers. The islands and coves just offshore looked ideal for their sport and we talked into the wee hours (9 p.m.) aboard Sweet Breeze.

Canso was a milestone for me. It was here that I would turn hard right and begin heading south. South into warmer waters. It meant meeting up with Lydia, my long lost Canadian friend, somewhere landward in Nova Scotia. It meant an end to the sailing adventure (probably) somewhere down the coast. I was feeling accomplished, satisfied with my performance, looking forward to solid ground. I had sailed to salt water...that having been my only destination. I could keep going, forever if I wanted to, but my thoughts were turning to homebody things that I was beginning to miss... my friends, my dog, my cabin in the woods on the river, my projects to finish and new ones to begin.

The plans and thoughts of sailing across the big pond to Ireland, then up into the Baltic to visit my daughter in Germany, were losing their romance, their draw for me. Without meaning to sound arrogant or overconfident, I was feeling pretty certain that I could fairly easily accomplish that adventure if I wanted to, barring an iceberg or some hellish hurricane. Sweet Breeze could do it if I did my part. Mostly it was about not wanting to surrender to that sick feeling from motion sickness, that subtle torment that had taken from me the pleasure of sailing so many days past. Maybe I would get over that icky queasy feeling after a few days out in the ocean but why take the chance? Maybe I was a landlubber after all?

Friday, August 2nd. Up at 5 a.m. Cool and foggy, looking forward to the rugged and varied coast of N.S. On the water by 5:30.

Nearshore islands, bays, coves and fiords. My charts showed a most interesting shoreline with passages in and around and between the islands. This was to be a nature lovers vista cruise, this Atlantic coast of new Scotland.

There was only the lightest of breezes...nothing worth testing with the sails.

Rounding Cape Canso and entering Andrews passage, patchy fog whisked most of the much anticipated vistas away. Charity, Sherewink, and Spinney Gulley Island were somewhere off to the right. To the left I could occasionally catch glimpses of Andrews Island, but this was obviously rock and shoal waters and my concentration was on the chart plotter screen plus trying to sight marker buoys when the fog thinned...(I read sometime later that Andrews Passage should only be attempted during days of good visibility...maybe someday I would learn to read about where I was going instead of where I had been.)

I hated to miss all the visuals, the rugged shores and hills beyond of rocks and spruce, but how long must one wait for the fog to lift...hours, days, weeks? This coast was known for fog. Onward.

This shoreline would be entirely unforgiving for boats and sailors out amongst the rocks and the swells. Best to pay close attention to the chart plotter and a sailor's sixth sense that had kept us off the bottom since mid-June in Lake Superior.

Motoring with little wind well offshore for safety. Strong wind warning crackling to life on the VHF from Environment Canada. Where exactly the wind was predicted for I could not discern. Somewhere on the Nova Scotia offshore waters in an area that I could not find on maps or chart plotter. So be it. The hell with it. It always pissed me off to know there was considerable weather somewhere nearby and not know where. Little wind here. Lots of fog and rocks.

We made good time motoring all day, watching, watching, peering into the fog for...mostly boats. I knew I was missing the views of this most grand and intricate shoreline. So be it. The hell with it. Lots of fog and rocks, swells, and little wind.

Plotting a course on the chart plotter was an everyday requisite in these unknown waters. Checking and double checking and scrolling the screen forward and back and zooming in and out, all were part of my normal process of maneuvering through the islands and shoals in fog...or even on a clear day...and all the while trying to be as certain as I could that I hadn't plotted a course toward wreckage. Without the chart plotter I would have been burning the midnight oil drawing lines on paper charts in preparation for the next leg of the coast. It would be difficult to steer, navigate, and sail, while constantly checking and double-checking position by GPS coordinates. Luck would have to see me through if I had no chart plotter. Without it, I think I would have headed out offshore five miles or more and stood off that distance until something changed...the fog lifted or I couldn't stay awake any longer.

Liscomb Island was somewhere ahead and it had a northeast coast that may provide a quiet night at anchor in its lee, away from the prevailing and building southwest wind and swells. That would give me about a 60-mile day. Good enough with conditions such as they were.

Saturday, August 3. Up with the gray dawn to nose Sweet Breeze out into the open ocean. Wind on the nose with fog...fuck it, not again today.

After motoring and motor sailing against the wind most of yesterday my thoughts were blowing landward...to wait out the southwest wind and hope for a change...any wind but southwest.

Liscomb Island had given me a decent night's sleep in its lee. It was a pretty big island, about two miles by one mile wide, still it always amazed me how the swells and waves could bend around into the lee of such good protection and make for a lot of boat motion at anchor. The physics of bending waves...water waves in general were a mysterious phenomenon to me. Energy from the wind converted to waves on the water. Yet the water didn't really travel with the wave but the water was only the medium for the kinetic motion of that energy...something like that.

Suffice it to say I didn't want either the waves or the wind on the nose again for a while. Back into the lee of Liscomb Island and to the left was the Liscomb River and its estuary where it met the sea. A few miles upriver the chart plotter showed some sort of marina. Upriver we went.

It proved out to be one of my best choices. There was a tiny marina there with about six berths just downstream from the first rapids. We snuggled up into one where Peter, the attendant, thought we might settle onto bottom at low tide. I thought not and decided to give it a try. Chester would know.

Liscomb Lodge and Marina, I soon learned, was famous among boaters for its gracious host, Chester. When he arrived to work that morning he thought we could give it a try at the shallow berth.

I met some of my favorite people on the docks at Liscomb Lodge...sailors like me who had taken respite from the fog and southwest winds...Joe and Yvonne from the Ontario side of Lake Huron...Henry and Marie from around the west side of Nova Scotia near Wolfville. Wind and fog-bound we were...short term castaways tossed into the friendly wake of others of similar ilk.

Chester offered his car to Henry and Marie for a jaunt to Sherbrooke, a few miles north and east, a historic sort of period town with the sights and sounds of a preserved settlement of Europeans who immigrated to Nova Scotia. They graciously asked if I would like to go along and it was just the sort of thing that I wanted to do... be land-bound and with a bit of local history to learn.

The water-powered sawmill at Sherbrooke was the main draw for me. It was a reciprocating vertical stroke type mill, something I had read about and one of the earliest types of water-powered sawmills. Sawmills always fascinated me. They were magical...they could reveal the beauty and utility of lumber from a gnarly old log. Pure magic. Spending the afternoon with Henry and Marie was very easy.

More southwest wind in the forecast so we all stayed another night on the river. I ate too much good food at the lodge...typical landward behavior for me.

Sunday morning's forecast still told of fog and a southwest wind. The urge to move on waned with my foreknowledge of the motion sickness that the day would bring if I chose to beat into the wind and waves. Fog on this rocky coast leaves no margin for error. It was an easy choice to stay another day and enjoy the fine company, sights, and food.

My big plan for the day was to hike up the Liscomb River to a fish ladder built around a rocky gorge and falls to allow Atlantic salmon to reach the upper parts of the river and reproduce. It felt good to hike, to get my legs working again beyond the confines of a boat. It felt good to smell and taste the scents of the forest...to imagine the salmon on their upstream struggle.

Sadly, the Atlantic salmon is an endangered species now. Dams and habitat destruction, acid rain, over-fishing, and pollution have decimated this once prolific aquatic missile of the northeastern streams of North America. As the oceans acidify by absorbing excess CO_2 from our burning of fossil fuels, the likelihood of any recovery by the Atlantic salmon is slim. I try not to think about the species that are presently going the way of the passenger pigeon. There are many.

I am not, however, going the way of the passenger pigeon, nor is my species. We eat too well. We adapt too well. We reproduce too well. We care too little.

Supper at the lodge with my sailing friends and live music...this land life could draw me back from the sea some day. Stayed up until the wee hours again...probably 'till 10 p.m., but I needed to get going tomorrow...either sail it was, or give up and rent a room at the lodge.

Monday, August 5th. Left the dock at 6:30 a.m. Patchy fog, light wind on the nose.

It was nothing similar to the sunny, fair winded race across Chedabucto Bay from Hawkesbury, Cape Breton to Canso, Nova Scotia just a few days ago. This was all about being cautious...tentative even... not my normal M.O. for sailing. This was fog, shoals, rocks, ledges, islands big and small, all along a shoreline unknown to me. Being attentive, nervous, and keenly aware of our position staved off the motion sickness for now. We were making good progress on generally a southwest heading, weaving our way along the coast of Nova Scotia, peering ahead and to the side through the fog looking for marker buoys or other solid objects while staying course on the chart plotter's rhumb line...but as the morning wore on, the wind and the waves on our nose picked up and it all started to wear me down, taking its toll on my spirits but not my determination to keep my old boat off the rocks. I took a motion sickness pill as our speed dropped from five knots to barely four knots. Even the stress of feeling our way was not enough to keep the flu-like symptoms at bay.

I do remember the intensity of plotting a safe course on the chart plotter... rechecking several times that the course avoided all shoals...then trying to find and plot the route to a likely secure anchorage and a safe overnight at the end of the day's rhumb line. Once again, without the chart plotter and its ability to show me my location in the fog (Within 10 feet, its manufacturer claimed.) I would be land bound until the fog lifted or worst case, land bound as wreckage.

I don't remember all of the islands along the coast that I tried to tuck behind and sneak between to both straighten my course and to seek respite from the wind and waves. It was either that or head out into the waves of the open sea, though the near shore open ocean was probably fogged in too. Risking the trickier passage through the islands was my preferred route. I knew for certain that the offshore route would be rough and sickly for me. In the lee of some of the larger islands I sought a reprieve from the rough seas. It was a short lived reprieve but worth it to relieve that awful and debilitating ill feeling that fogged my brain and tried to distract me from my most conscious need of navigating with vigilance at all times.

Such was that day's sail. There were times when I sought out anchorage in the lee of islands to rest and have lunch...only to find a rocky bottom and a doubtful attachment for the hook. I remember passing near a long island to port, watching the depths and the shoreline for some indication of a sand bottom only to find a bedrock floor with no purchase for the anchor. I remember seeking out a headland that might have a sandy lee shore offering some time to anchor, relax, and regain some confidence.

All the while the seas were getting rougher. I hoisted the main and sheeted it tight to help dampen the boat motion...it helped. It became difficult to move around on the boat with the heaving and sharp seas but it looked like we were past some of the tightest slips between the rocks and shoals. The islands were getting bigger too and with the afternoon we fought for headway.

Thank goodness for that dependable little Atomic 4, the little inboard engine that could. I could have tacked and gained little more than frustration under sail power alone. Motor sailing was keeping me on the rhumb line and mostly sane.

We went seaward out around Taylor's Head, then swung back a bit landward following the twisty turns of the rhumb line on the chart plotter. The main bent to the wind as we headed toward the Pope's Shoals, Drunken Dick, and Tucker's Ledge. Then a bend left, outbound again through the run between Baltee and Tangier islands, toward the lee of a big island that may have some sand. Straight ahead, Borgles Island had some deep cuts on its lee shore that promised sand bottoms. That would mean an early stopover for the day but I felt I had earned it, unless of course the wind abated or switched directions and the patchy fog lifted...then perhaps I could sail onward (but I really didn't want to).

Borgles Island it would be. It just felt too good. I had motored into the deepest bay in the lee of the island and backed the Bruce anchor into sand. No large rocks were evident within the swing of the boat at anchor. It felt secure. There was 15 feet of clear water under us...plenty to keep us afloat in the tides. The boat rolled only gently in the swells. I could read. I could eat well. I could plot a course for the next leg through the next maze of hazards to Halifax and I wasn't leaving.

I had sailed and motored through some of the trickiest, most dangerous waters of my recent sailing career (and probably anywhere on the planet) through patchy fog and rough seas. My old boat and I had gained half the distance to Halifax that day. My stomach soon settled down. Life was good again.

Tuesday, August 6th. Up early with the first gray light. Fair night's sleep—only one midnight rush topside to waken and decide where the hell I was.

We had to head southeast a couple of miles to get around the shoals extending out from Borgles Island. Still the wind was southwesterly, on the nose again. A stronger wind than yesterday's but with lighter fog...take your pick.

More wind means more boat motion. It wasn't long before I was thinking of a pill to stave off the dreaded pitch and roll sickness plaguing me lately. We motor sailed through the morning with the main flattened with vang and sheet as tight as the old sail would stretch.

It was one more day of navigating between islands and around rocks with seas growing a bit from yesterday. We were barely holding four knots of speed over ground and it wasn't even noon before I was looking for some place to hide. It would have worn me down and made me weary but there was no time for weary. Followed the shore of an island to port but nothing but bald rocks leading down to the water's edge. No anchorage off that one.

Passed just outside of another big headland with a broad bay opening up on the right, but no respite from the seas anywhere near that I could tell. Soon after crossing the mouth of the big bay the motor sputtered and died. "Okay, Sweet Breeze is a sailboat after all, not a problem," I told myself. We would lose a little speed and miles-made-good but Sweet Breeze could climb the wind pretty well, if I could hold up my end.

That was the first time in 5000 miles or so that the engine failed me. I really would talk to myself...it seemed to bolster my confidence when things ran afoul. We would need to watch closely for shallows as we tacked sharply off the relative safety of the rhumb line.

The increased intensity of sailing now may help get me over the motion sickness and ensuing drug induced drowsiness...there was always an upside. There was no option of checking out the motor now...not until a safe anchorage was attained somewhere. Otto couldn't steer in these seas. There was no heaving-to or letting her go adrift with shoals all around. This was a time to sail.

After about an hour of beating upwind, the wet cold fog, the heavy boat motion, the lack of much progress and the dead engine all combined to create an anxiety within...a cause to find the first protected anchorage and reassess what the heck I was doing out here. It would take me a week to get to Halifax at this rate and I wasn't having fun.

We made a hard right turn and sailed into the nearest broad bay looking for an island or point to get behind for a rest and some engine analysis. We were just getting past some of the more formidable rocks and shoals along the coast and sailed up behind one of the few remaining islands and dropped the hook and doused the sails.

It was an easy engine fix. All gasoline engines quit if they lose either ignition or fuel. This time it was fuel. I had never changed the fuel filter since I bought the boat so that seemed the likely problem and it was. I had a spare filter and installed it and I had engine power again.

Off we went motor sailing, into the wind again but making good progress and back on the rhumb line. Beating across the mouths of some broad bays we made it to Wedge Island, about 12 miles from Halifax. We tucked up close to shore and into a small bay somewhat protected by a rocky point. There was no valor to be had beating into that wind so the plan was to have lunch and wait it out. Maybe by evening it would subside.

While fixing some lunch and feeling at peace again with my watery world, I was thinking of the folks I had met along the way and the several times I had heard them tell of the tricky or dangerous waters of their locale...from Lake Superior to the St. Lawrence River to the coast around Gaspé. Nothing, so far, was any more hazardous than sailing on the fog shrouded rocky Atlantic coast of Nova Scotia. I'll bet there are lots of wrecks along this coast and fishermen who never returned. Such were my thoughts with lunch at anchor.

The afternoon passed as I finished reading the book about the Buffalo Soldiers. That's what the Indians had called the Negro cavalry that the U.S. Army had sent to fight the tribes that wouldn't relinquish their lands peaceably or starve quietly.

The afternoon winds were still strong at 4:30 that day. From below I could hear the rigging humming as I was drowsy and reading. Maybe with the evening the blow would subside and I could make the remaining 12 miles or so to Halifax.

Such were my thoughts through the afternoon, but as I boiled some cauliflower for supper and listened to the songs of winds in the rigging still, my thoughts shifted a bit...I thought then it might be wise to sleep with my clothes on that night at anchor behind Wedge Island, just in case. I recalled that tenuous night a few weeks ago back on the Gaspé Peninsula, where the wind came roaring down off the hills but the anchor held fast over a ledge of slate. This was not at all the same wind, just a gentle reminder...best sometimes to sleep with your clothes on.

Wednesday, August 7th. Up at 5 a.m. Strong smell of methane gas. Must be low tide. Cold in cabin...can see my breath. Drank hot tea until there was enough light to make way. Calm seas. Calm wind...good to get some miles before that southwest wind started up again. Halifax will be an easy run from here.

From the open sea it was about 10 miles up the passage to Halifax. Freighters, container ships, and a few small boats were giving me some water traffic to watch. It was a calm morning, weather wise, and we motored on up to the dock at the Maritime Museum like we knew right where we were going.

It felt welcoming, the sun's warmth, people all around, low cost dockage right in the heart of the busy harborfront. The first person I met was Robert tied up just ahead of Sweet Breeze in his small sailboat. He told me where to pay my dockage fee and told me how to avoid paying it. Robert was from down by the southern tip of Nova Scotia, Cape Sable, and had sailed his boat to Halifax to work for the summer at one of many restaurants catering to tourists on the waterfront.

Robert was a talker. I soon learned of his three-week marriage that failed and of his troubles with the law, along with tales of sailing adventure. He was a true character of sailing lore and may have had the makings for a modern day Howard Blackburn. (A famous and infamous Nova Scotia fisherman who wound up in Gloucester, Mass. after his years of plying the treacherous waters of the Maritime Provinces.)

Minutes after Robert headed off to work I was greeted by Canada Customs agents. It was nothing like the last time back in Iroquois, Ontario. I felt welcomed by them, not like I was a terrorist or smuggler until I had proven otherwise. They were a couple of older guys, not looking for their first arrest of a foreign national. I think they had rekindled some small faith within me that government officials indeed still operated by courtesy and common sense.

I spent a couple of days on the Halifax waterfront. Tourist watching was interesting at first but soon I had seen enough overfed and underdressed people slurping smoothies and stuffing fast food and placating small kids.

The Maritime Museum and some other interesting working boats kept me wandering the docks. A couple of wharfs down was a large restaurant. Tied alongside was the largest single-masted sailboat that I had ever seen, rigged as a cutter. Black, shiny, and sleek, perhaps 100 feet from sprit to stern, impeccable shine everywhere, one of the huge polished sheet winches probably cost many times what my whole boat cost. There looked to be a crew of two or more that kept busy polishing the brightwork and keeping her gleaming in the sun...the whole scene shouting a definition of sailing much different than mine. I once tried some polish on Sweet Breeze but upon standing back to admire my efforts I really couldn't tell the difference...she shone more at heel with a bone in her teeth.

I walked into the city to a computer store and bought a plug-in keyboard so that I could once again send emails to the folks back home without using the dollar sign key for an S and some other creative substitutions.

Call me hard to please, but the hubbub of the Halifax harborfront soon lost its draw and fascination. Halifax was a goal reached but there was nothing to keep me there. I guess it was a fine city, as cities go. The pull of new sights along the coast and the aloneness of the single-hand adventure were drawing me seaward again after only two days of the wharf-side semi-social life.

"Where was I headed?" I had been asked so many times along the way. Up 'till now I had mostly replied, "Halifax." It seemed like a reasonable goal to most and it seemed to satisfy most destination oriented folks and kept me from trying to explain that I really had no destination beyond a continuing sailing adventure.

Halifax was an interesting old seaport, but I had seen enough. Cities were only cities to me, all much the same. People were entertaining to watch and chat with... for awhile.

I met up with Rod, Kelvin's friend and returned the loaned paper charts. Rod was the sort I would want to become friends with but within the hour I was sailing southeast out the long bay to the sea. There was no fog that morning.

On my way out of the Halifax harbor a huge cruise ship was steaming in. I had chosen a good time to leave. The waterfront of Halifax would be teaming with thousands of tourists.

Sailing was fun again that day with the wind in my face, no fog, the sails pulling, and my sights set on Lunenburg, somewhere down the coast.

We were delighted with the wind and sun off and on through the afternoon. Two other sailboats were heading down the coast to our landward so naturally I tried to keep up with them by plying the wind to our best advantage. We kept up with them the whole of the afternoon but they stripped off up to Mahone Bay or Chester as we neared Pearl Island. I imagined we were all part of a flotilla, sailing together day after day and meeting at a common destination at day's end. That would be my ideal sail...others to meet again and greet again and tell lies to as we explored the coast and tested our sailing skills throughout the summer. The fair winds and sunshine had brought out the sailor-dreamer in me again...that which the fog had too frequently obscured in recent days.

I sailed into Lunenburg Bay, around the jetty, past the defunct looking fish plant and doused sails in order to motor around and find likely dockage. It was a most interesting waterfront.

As it turned out I found a private dock down from a marine store and tied up and paid up for the night. I snuggled Sweet Breeze up close to another small sailboat of unique design and left room at the end of the dock for one more boat.

Bill was the skipper of the unusual boat just ahead. I loved Bill right off. The whiskers, the sense of humor, his 6 foot 4 inch frame crammed into the tiny cabin of his boat, the hot coffee and conversation in the morning. He had sailed over from Chester, Nova Scotia to sample the music at the Lunenburg Folk Fest which was on for the weekend. Bill was a high school teacher and I guessed his classes were not dull.

Dockmate Bill at Lunenburg, Nova Scotia.

Across the slip and tied to a big commercial dock was the Farley Mowat, a rusting hulk being cut up for scrap. She was once a proud ship, named after my all time favorite author of sensitive, fun reading books of his life experiences. I had read Farley's books since I was a boy and he felt like an old friend...a like-minded naturalist sort with a dry sense of humor and an unquenchable sense of adventure.

I was sad to learn that the ship had been seized by the Canadian government for interfering with whaling or seal slaughter activities, set afire at some point and was now being scrapped out. All for trying to preserve endangered sea life. Makes good sense doesn't it...government nonsense. It reminds me of locking up people who protest nuclear weapons and the insane stockpiling of warheads. Mutually Assured Destruction (MAD) of sea life or of humanity itself. What sort of fools are we? Aren't we supposed to be intelligent?

That night a strong southwest wind screeched across Lunenburg Bay. Roller coaster waves tossed us through the night and I was up twice to check fender placement and dock lines trying to make sure there was no contact with the dock or with Bill's boat. A big catamaran had taken up the space at the end of the dock and was absorbing some of the energy of the waves fetching across the bay. It was not a restful night's sleep.

Lunenburg was a most interesting waterfront and town. Fishing, shipping and pleasure boating were the history on the shoreline. Farther up the hill, the early German settlers did some gardening and attempted farming the thin soil. Their brightly colored homes gave the town a European flair. It could have been a Baltic Sea town had I sailed across the Atlantic to visit my daughter in Germany like I once planned. I walked the town from end to end and bought some gifts for the folks back home...a bag sewn from a sail for Lydia, should I meet up with her soon.

Saturday, August 10th. Up early, coffee with Bill. Thinking of a landlubber's breakfast in one of the many restaurants.

It was folk fest weekend in Lunenburg. Tourists were everywhere. I walked the streets through the morning getting some exercise and looking for someplace to use wi-fi and send out an email update.

Mark, the young guy that sailed with me through the locks above Montreal and on down the St. Lawrence River to Quebec City was in the neighborhood. I got a call on my cell phone from Catherine, his girlfriend, telling me that they were on their way to Lunenburg in Mark's old van to meet me and haul me across Nova Scotia to near Wolfville where Lydia was staying with friends at a farm.

This was good news. A car ride across the countryside...something I looked forward to. Seeing Lydia again, finally, and Mark again, my young Canadian friends who both had those big warm smiles that penetrated my old wind-and-age toughened skin, and my squinty eyes from the bright sun of late. I liked sharing their warm, young, strong energy. This was to be a welcome change from the two months of my social sailing, meeting nice folks along the way and then losing them forever as I sailed away the next day.

Back on the Farm

Driving across Nova Scotia with Mark and Catherine was a simple pleasure... one often taken for granted that I had not done for a while. The speed of traversing the countryside by car seemed surreal to this coastal sailor who often had the same view of a distant shoreline, and the bleak sameness of the horizon on the other side, for several hours at a stretch.

The rural life of the small farms and country homes sped by before I could digest it with my eyes or with my thoughts. I was more accustomed to the mysterious wonder of the distant shoreline...to ponder what was at the head of a deep bay or around the next point and I usually had hours to contemplate the view and imagine the details of a shoreline a few miles to starboard. I found myself turning my head as we passed something of interest, trying to absorb more details of the view at such a lightning speed of 50-mph. This was life in the fast lane.

Mark's old van had seen better days so he thought it pertinent that we open the hood and check for leaks and loose things before we lost them, but it got us to the Gaspereau Valley without breakdown...to a little old farmhouse and barn that could have passed for a homestead in Minnesota or Wisconsin.

The farmers were Alex and Selene and it was a day of celebration with their array of friends arriving from near and far. Tents were set in the yard and foods were cooking indoors and out. Mothers and babies were fondling and feeding. Men gathered in small groups to reacquaint. I was absorbed in the sights and sounds, met a few new folks, but as usual I was content with sitting off to the side and watching and listening...this was a lot of hubbub for a lone sailor.

I kept expecting to see Lydia amongst a group or coming out of the house... would I recognize her? Others must have wondered who I was, this old guy crashing their mid-summer bash. I learned that Lydia was somewhere tubing down the river and introduced myself as her long lost friend. There were lots of welcoming smiles. She would return later and I had time to wander down the road looking, looking at the trees and greenery, looking into an abandoned metal building that had housed a sawmill, looking for a clue as to what the finished wood product was like from the derelict machines left behind. History and sleuthing, favorites amongst my pastimes.

Back at the farm, their son Rolly was the happiest, most joyful 2-year-old I ever had the pleasure to meet. Alex and Selene and their friends all had a warmth about them. The interaction with them was heartwarming for me, so much more so than the casual, antiseptic brushings with the tourists of Lunenburg and Halifax.

The big hugs from Lydia were what I was waiting for. No disappointment there. And her smile, that shy brightness that I remembered and could see in my mind at times as I sailed. We sat together on a bench in the yard, talking, listening, smiling. It was hard to find the quiet place, like where we had first met, on the dock at the very top of Lake Superior, Red Rock Ontario, and shared a supper in the cabin of Sweet Breeze. She still had that infectious energy. We walked to the yurt she had set up and to her new-old car that she wanted to show me. Her face glowed with shyness and appreciation when I gave her the gift of the tote bag made from the old sail. Land life was good, here on a small farm on a small corner of Nova Scotia, soaking up the largess of these very real people.

Lydia and me at the farm in Nova Scotia.

Lydia had graciously set up and offered her yurt for overnight accommodations. Someone else loaned me a sleeping bag. The solid sense of lying on mother earth with only fabric between was a subtle sensation that I at once noticed, both for its hardness and for its connection between human body and earth body.

Sunday was loosely organized into a work detail to disassemble and pack away a very large yurt. Alex was a builder of yurts and his business was their sale and rental. Down the valley to the north his palace yurt had been erected. Rented to provide the shelter for a wedding and big celebration, it was now due to return to storage at the farm until the next event.

For four of us, the disassembly was almost an all day project. Alex had boundless energy, could climb around the structure like a monkey, and directed the sequence of the take down. I did my best but was not as agile as the young guys nor as at ease in the heights of the structure as we removed the poles from top to bottom. It was an amazing structure, round, roofed, and about 40-feet in diameter. All made from hand cut sapling poles and cotton canvas.

We feasted on more good food when we got back to the farm. We had put in a hard day taking down the big yurt and packing it into Alex's trailer. Catherine and Mark and I left for Lunenburg late that afternoon. What a memorable and unusual experience that whole weekend was for me...thanks to Mark and Lydia and Catherine and all the others. How lucky I felt to have been included, and still I was looking forward to the quiet solitude, swallowed up by the belly of my old boat, and new adventures on the water soon, weather permitting.

Monday, sometime in August...up late like a landlubber. Coffee with Bill. Gave some money to Bill to pay my dockage when the store opened...Bill I would miss.

As soon as we motor sailed out around the next point to the south the patchy fog was back, of course, and so was the southwest wind. The chart plotter was to be my eyes again. It showed reefs to port and starboard and at times I could see waves breaking where no land should be.

The navigation hazards all had names...Little Hope Island, Hellreef, Point Enrage. This was another time on the coast of Nova Scotia to pay strict attention to my exact position and heading.

I would catch myself cursing into the wind, like a sailor I suppose...maybe just to add some color to a conversation with myself and Sweet Breeze. I think she knew that when I was cursing loudly I would do my part.

We made it to a semi-calm cove called Dog's Hole and dropped the hook. We weren't making good headway anyhow and I was on edge, cursing the fog and the wind. Someday this wind would change direction and I was in the mood to wait.

I was feeling unsettled. Maybe I was lonely anchored here in the fog, but I almost never felt lonely. I wasn't sure what was bothering me. Maybe I had become spoiled by the warm and gracious company of the folks at the farm. That was only yesterday though. But here I was, at a place called Dog's Hole, thinking of a warm fire and friends.

Enough of that. Wanting what cannot be. What *is*, that's all I had. I had a safe anchorage for now, a snug old boat for company, and some sailing business to attend to. It was about time to check the rigging again...looking for signs of wear or anything loose. The starboard aft-shroud needed tightening, but other than that the standing rigging was holding up well...as it should with all the recent days of motor sailing to a close reach. The last time that any real strain was applied to any wires was on the fast beam reach across Chedabucto Bay toward Canso. Maybe that was what stretched that shroud.

Checking the tide charts showed a five-foot variation in depth hereabouts. There was seven-feet of water under us now and we were at low tide so all should be well for the night if the wind stayed steady and we didn't swing too far toward shore on anchor. I pulled the boat manually forward by the anchor rode and could plainly see the Bruce on the bottom, securely backed into the sand and gravel with the weight of 20 feet of 5/16 chain leaving it undisturbed by my strong-arm inspection method.

I often checked the anchor this way in these clear waters of the north Atlantic... it was one of the double checks that made for a semi-restful night's sleep in the lee of an island or a point. Even so, there was, almost every night, the startled awakening and the flash charge topside to see if we were in trouble...whether awakened by such a dream or by a sound. Sleep like last night's rest in the yurt would be most welcome.

Before darkness, in the cold creeping fog, two sailboats came into view heading into Medway bay. I wished they would come alongside and anchor or raft up for the night...but of course they had another plan and I was feeling wistful, alone in the damp cold.

I did some productive chart plotting for tomorrow's route through the reefs and islands. Maybe we had made good 30 miles today. Poor headway, but safe. It took a quarter tank of gas to gain that dismal distance.

From my bunk below I could hear the mournful wail of a whistle buoy. It reminded me of the mooing of a cow.

Tuesday, August 13th. Up at 4 a.m., back on a sailor's sleep schedule. Too dark to make way. Hot tea. Light fog. Light wind.

There was light enough to get under way at 6 a.m. Starting the engine and hearing it come to life always gave me a sense of companionship and control. These were unfriendly waters to boats of all kinds and that surefire little engine made staying off the rocks while hoisting anchor possible without panic.

I often went through the steps in my head before I would weigh anchor to get offshore quickly with the engine, or without the engine...how I would sail into an anchorage too. I have done both while single-handing sailboats both out of necessity and for the experience. Who knew? Any day that 50 year old engine could develop a serious illness and I wanted to be ready both mentally and method-wise to sail into and out of a safe night's anchorage. Hopefully I would never have to hoist anchor and try to sail quickly off a lee shore without the engine's help. A few weeks ago both boat and I would certainly have been cast ashore on Lake Erie's Long Point without the push of that sweet sounding little engine.

Were it not for the bird life there would be little scenery as the day passed with scant headway in fog ranging from light to dense. I spent some hours blowing the conch shell horn every few minutes as warning. Could it be heard above a fishing boat's diesel I wondered? I dreaded motoring or motor-sailing in the fog. With the steady drone of the engine I could not hear waves breaking on reefs or shores. I would not hear the engine of another boat either.

Against the wind, what were my options? Anchor and wait was the only safe option and that had its risks too...of storms blowing up and a wind change that could put us on a lee shore.

Everything was gray that day. There was no horizon...air and water were as one. A dead gannet floated by. I stared ahead trying to spot that fishing boat or log before it spotted me. There was not much progress at this speed but I could not sanely motor at five or six knots and only see ahead a few yards...sometimes a hundred feet, occasionally a hundred yards.

There weren't many highlights on this day but one that stuck with me...a few small birds flying out of the fog and fluttering near Sweet Breeze. They were Mother Carey's chickens. I recognized them right off. Sailing to salt water was one goal, whales another...seeing the little storm petrels with the interesting nickname was high on my list of things I had hoped to see. I'm not sure why they were important to me... maybe there was a romantic sailing connection with them as they are said to have led fog bound sailors to harbor. They are also said to warn a sailor of an impending storm. They were gone as quickly as they appeared and my joy faded into the fog gray of everywhere.

Once again, it was the chart plotter that allowed me to get by with even a 30-mile day in these fog bound shoal waters. I thought that there must be lots of wrecks along this coast, especially from the days before electronic navigation tools. I was more than determined not to join them. It was a day of staring at the chart plotter and then straining to see straight ahead...checking and rechecking my course plotted through the offshore hazards. No mistakes. Nothing could be missed. Nothing.

Somewhere up ahead were the washed rocks, Big Dick, Little Dick, and The Bastard lying in wait for the unwary or tired navigator. The chart plotter showed me where these washed rocks were and how I could sneak between them in the fog. But I was tiring. The concentration was wearing me down. Somewhere ahead was also a small island with a small bay aback from the rising wind and seas. That was my goal for a rest and some lunch. Only 30 miles-made-good again.

Why was I doing this? One mistake would likely be fatal in these frigid building seas and submerged rock piles. Was it the challenge of man against the sea? I don't think so. The sea would win in the end. After the warm camaraderie landward at the farm just a couple of days ago, perhaps one would maybe come to his senses. Then again, just a couple of nice days, some sun and some favorable wind and sailing would be fun again. But not today. Definitely not today. Maybe the weather would change.

Ram Island had the shape of a water bird on the chart plotter. In the lee of the bird's neck, between the topknot and the shoulder was a tiny bay opening to the northeast. That was the only island far enough offshore that I could possibly safely approach for a rest, but there were shoals all around the entrance to that little bay and the seas were rolling. It was either there or keep feeling our way through the rocks and fog.

A cautious and indirect approach got us into the small bay. The gravel and boulder shoreline rose steeply from the water's edge and the nearshore depths were good. I could see a sand bottom out about 100 feet from shore and in 20 feet of water and dropped anchor, trying to get the boat centered in the bay so that the swing would not bring us onto the rocks on either side at low tide. It was a relief to get off the rolling gray seas and into the dark rolling swells of the bay.

It was a stark and strange little island. Birds were everywhere. Gulls, cormorants, gannets, small shorebirds, between the boulders on shore and sea ducks riding the swells. (I learned later that puffins also resided somewhere up the craggy, steep cliffs.)

I put on my raincoat and sat topside watching and waiting to see how close we would swing toward shore and submerged car-sized boulders. Not yet feeling safe I stayed there in the cold, the wind-blown rain, watching our position change. When it appeared we could not swing onto rocks I went forward and heaved in on the anchor rode until I had pulled the boat shoreward a ways, then dropped the big plow anchor too. Between the wind and the big swells I couldn't predict where we would swing but felt secure enough, for now, to climb down into the plunging and banging dinghy and bail the rainwater, then even get below and try to dry out and warm up.

I was determined not to move from this tiny bay until the fog cleared, that's what I told myself anyway. More clothing, some hot food and a good book were the comforts I found below...listening to the rain pelting the cabin-top, the racket of the gulls, the steady roar of waves crashing onto the lee shore just across the neck of the island and the wind in the rigging. It was me and the birds. This was home.

As I read McMurtry's, *Anything For Billy*, a saga about Billy the Kid, I was frequently interrupting myself with thought. What was I doing here tucked into this treeless rocky island where birds sat motionless facing the wind, looking like stumps of former trees. What I had accomplished today was a fool's journey...seven hours and 30 miles of risky travel with nothing to see, no land in sight, one seal alongside, a dead gannet afloat, and Mother Carey's chickens, little storm petrels dancing on the water just for me. The only bright spot were the birds until Ram Island appeared so suddenly and dead ahead through the fog. Even though I knew there was a town and protected harbor just a few miles to the west, I was not moving until the fog cleared.

The rest of the day I kept busy and warm. Lazy busy...reading, napping, poking my head above deck every half hour or so to check that the anchors were holding. Wondering why I was here.

Would the fog ever lift on this coast? If only two clear days would present themselves I could make Cape Sable on the southern tip of Nova Scotia and begin the passage across the Gulf of Maine to the coast of the good old U.S. of A.

There was always that push-pull thing...feeling secure where I was yet feeling antsy to put on some sailing miles. More napping, reading, and questioning my sanity.

Finally, before dark, I climbed down into that lurching little tub that Sweet

Breeze had drug for a few thousand miles and bailed out the rainwater again. I let the painter out on the dinghy about 20 feet hoping it would drift away and stop ramming and banging into Sweet Breeze as swells and wind tossed it around. Maybe I would get some sleep that night with more blankets and less noise. It was a snug cocoon in the belly of my little boat. Life was good, tenuous, uncertain, but safe for now.

Wednesday morning, August...gray dawn and fog.

Listening to the weather forecast for Nova Scotia's southwest shore gave me some hope. Winds were to come in from the LaHave Bank offshore. That would put us on a close reach instead of a motor sail upwind. Promising...but not in this fog. Staying put today. Yesterday's damp chills had left my body overnight and with some occasional bracing against some nearby structure with my arms and hooking my feet under the stove I was able to stay in the bunk and even get a little sleep.

This seemed like a good anchorage for now. So far we were holding position and the plan was to stay put. There was no room in this bay for an anchor to drag...too many boulders down there. More tea. More reading. More writing in my log/journal.

The best outdoor scenery in this bay was below...large brown jellyfish swaying with the swells, a bed of plants and other animals that I knew nothing about and couldn't identify. Around noon I started to get antsy again. I knew I could find the town of Lockeport in the fog with the guidance of the chart plotter and I had enough gas to make the seven miles or so.

Antsy won out. But first, how to get out to sea if the chart plotter quit? Plan B. Once past Ram Island, 135 degrees by compass heading would see us to the open ocean around the reefs and rocks, then once a few miles offshore sail straight south, 180 degrees, there would be no reefs all the way to the Florida peninsula.

We were off. We had to be. I couldn't sit through another gray foggy day rolling at anchor in this tiny bay hoping the anchors would hold fast. What sanity I still harbored I held dear...the better risk seemed to try to find Lockeport in the fog.

We made it to Lockeport without bad events, but not without a big tense knot in my stomach and the best of my navigator's vigilance. There were rock hazards all along my route and the swells were as big as any I had yet encountered. The relief was great when a tall red nun or a fat green can, marker buoys, appeared out of the fog sometimes only 30 feet away, just as the chart plotter predicted.

The approach to the Lockeport harbor was well marked with more buoys and the tiny marina even held two sailboats. The fog-bound helpless feeling within was gone. Solid ground again and lots of big fishing boats docked and moored.

All the boats had radar equipment (their eyes in the fog) but me. I didn't even know how to read a radar screen. The sun would come out eventually and once again my eyes would be my radar, able to determine where to sail and where to stay clear. One day I would even be able to look back and see where I had been. The fog would lift someday along the Nova Scotia coast. Anyway, life was good again, safely here ashore, and the relief of "no worry" dockage overpowered the desire for miles-made-good...for now.

At the restaurant next to the marina, the second person I met was Bruce, a commercial fisherman. He asked how I had found Lockeport in the fog. By guess and by gosh and by chart plotter, I replied. He gave me that raised eyebrow look that suggested I was lucky. And where did I come from he wondered? From the little bay in the lee of Ram Island, I confessed...before that, Duluth, Minnesota. He knew it well and had hid there once himself, Ram Island that is, not Duluth.

Bruce then asked where I was headed? "Not sure," my usual reply, "but I'll know when I get there."

Back on the dock, Darrel, the skipper of one of the sailboats, offered to take my gas cans in his car and get them filled at a station in town. That kindness would save some heavy lugging. He and his wife and dog were provisioning for a sailing adventure starting tomorrow. They were locals heading northeast, up the coast of Nova Scotia. They had struck a better bargain with the wind than I had, with the prevailing summer blow coming from the southwest.

Kimmy, another acquaintance, wanted to come aboard and see my home on the water. She had a farm and horses somewhere nearby so I gave her the western pocketbook I had just finished. Her husband gave me a ride a mile down the shore to a beach house that had hot showers...only it didn't, but the walk back on a long sand beach was just what I needed, squishy, abrasive sand underfoot, but feeling solid and firm to me.

The wi-fi at the restaurant allowed me to catch up on emails and weather forecasts. It sounded like the fog would lift tomorrow...after three days socked in.

Rod and Gail, owners of the larger sailboat told me of the electrical system difficulties their boat was having and I offered to have a look, went and got my test meter and listened as they told me her symptoms. I discovered that their alternator had no output, unbolted it from their Yanmar diesel for them so they could get it repaired or replaced.

My troubleshooting efforts had earned me a hot shower on their boat...their kind offer of hot water I readily accepted along with the big fresh towel, then supper at the restaurant on them. They insisted. People weren't always bad...sailors almost never. That night I caught up on my sleep requirements with some restful slumber, unlike the last two nights.

Thursday, August__?...up late this morn. Environment Canada weather channel called for wind and no fog on the southeastern shore.

There was no hurry to get underway, even with the good forecast. I wanted to reprovision my little ship with some of my favorite foods and the Lockeport grocery store wouldn't open until 9 a.m. I had my usual few cups of tea while seeing my dock-mates Darrell and family off on their sailing adventure up the coast. Rod and Gail were to follow me down the coast later when they got their alternator repaired and installed.

Sardines, a few fresh vegetables, and some treats like fresh frozen blueberries made up the contents of the bags from the grocery store. I even found some good bread, whole grain (not that white stuff).

With the paper navigation chart that Rod gave me, (he had two of the same of coastal southeast N.S.) the fresh food and the promising weather forecast, we were soon off toward the Atlantic, sailing again, for Cape Sable, the southern tip of Nova Scotia, another milestone goal in my recent sailing career.

Rest assured, I really am a sailor man, but once again the wind was on our nose as we cautiously poked out into the broad reach of the Atlantic out beyond the Lockeport headland off the coast of Nova Scotia.

Really, you know by now that I didn't look forward to listening to the monotonous drone of the engine all day, but motor sailing it must be in this foul wind. I had not the patience to tack and tack and tack again trying to gain headway toward Cape Sable. It was sunny and clear and I could see where I was going but the rhumb line was my true path, it was the shortest route and darn it, I was determined to make the Cape before the dangerous sounding winds of the afternoon were forecasted to be upon us. I had learned to pay attention to a "strong wind warning" from Environment Canada a few weeks past, back on the waters off the Gaspé Peninsula.

The normal gray and rain and fog of this Nova Scotia coast took away most of the enjoyment of sailing for me. It often became a determined effort of survival, of staying off all the hidden rock hazards and some few miles-made-good.

Today was different. It was good to be at sea again. There was bright sun. There was wind, foul though it was. I could see the remarkable coastal shoreline of gray rock and green forest and the distant strip of a distant white sand beach. I could see waves breaking as they passed over rock piles far offshore.

Maybe I'm just a tourist after all, but I love the visual experience of seeing the coast. That's what coastal sailing should be like...and the secure feeling of actually seeing the offshore hazards helped too. It made yesterday's anxious tension in the fog, as we tried for Lockeport, one more harrowing memory.

We stopped for an early and peaceful lunch at anchor on the lee shore in the large bay at Cape Negro Island. Sailing was fun once again. The sun, the good food and the views all around made the difference. Sweet Breeze and I were one again, neither needing the security of a dockside mooring, equal partners again in our biggest sailing adventure together.

Beyond were the rock piles called The Salvages, others called The Halfmoons... they were more shelves of solid bedrock poking up just above the surface, far offshore and supporting a remarkably stark and forlorn lighthouse. Many of the lighthouses viewed on this journey were white and prominent and proud looking. Not this one. Grey and brown, it didn't look like a place I wanted to visit, only a place to give wide berth to and perhaps a wave of thanks for marking another danger to ships, small and large, mine being of the smaller variety.

Cape Sable was in view and the promised potent winds of afternoon greeted us soon after rounding the outside of Blanche Island. Sweet Breeze and I plowed ahead for a while as the wind and waves increased, just like forecasted and straight on the nose as usual.

Out around the next long point, its prominent lighthouse and some huge military looking buildings making it memorable to me, the waves were coming straight on and I was tiring of ducking the spray and the rough ride was wearing me down. The seas were building with the wind as we headed straight for the lee of Cape Sable Island.

We struggled for over an hour to gain Bullhead Wharf at Stoney Island Harbor on the southeast side of Cape Sable Island. Cecil, my latest acquaintance who happened to be walking on the dock, offered to tie us up at the tall fisherman's wharf as I tossed the lines up to him. There must be lots of tidewater change here with the height of the dock being so prominent I thought.

Cecil was just another bright spot on my long list of seaside acquaintances ready to help out as I had sailed into countless ports before. The dock surface was about six feet above the deck of Sweet Breeze so a climb up the pilings was required to square off with Cecil. He worked at the big fish plant at the head of the wharf and lately the plant was shut down for lack of fish so he had some time off.

I was just glad to get off the rolling seas at the southern tip of Nova Scotia and I was feeling accomplished for having safely sailed the whole Atlantic Coast of Nova Scotia, mostly in fog and into headwinds. Sweet Breeze was glad or lucky to have never touched a rock offshore or nearshore. We knew if she had we would likely not be afloat today. The beautiful and rugged coast of Nova Scotia, challenging in the sun, most dangerous in the fog, and mostly behind us now.

Cecil offered to take me to town to get gas in my portable cans. He had his small truck out on the wharf and time was slow now on the island until the fish started coming in and the fish plant reopened. He said he came from a long line of settlers on Cape Sable and believed he had about 700 cousins on the island. I didn't know how that would be possible but it was not for me to question his lineage.

As we drove the road to Barrington Passage, the town on the mainland, we drove the land-filled road that made the island no longer an island. With the passage filled in, the local fishing was spoiled as the tidal currents could no longer stream through the strait, flushing it and bringing in new nutrients and fish. Neither Cecil nor I were pleased with the "progress" that cars and roads had brought to the island, but that took nothing away from the generous nature of my latest friend and chauffeur and nothing was lost from his telling of more island lore as we drove back to the big dock jutting out from the fish plant.

Calvin and Me

Back on the wharf Cecil introduced me to the lone fisherman who worked the offshore waters that summer. His name was Calvin. Calvin Blades. He fished alone. He was a long-liner. A bottom fisherman for halibut, haddock, and cod. Those words didn't mean a lot to me then but he was readying his boat for a two day run out to some fishing banks about 40 miles out to try his luck, and I was fascinated with the stuff he was loading.

I asked Calvin if I could tie up for the night…"Stay as long as you like, no one would care. It's pretty dead around here right now." There were several big fishing boats tied up and rafted together out away from the dock. I tried to get him to talk some more without interfering with his work. I was fascinated with watching him load his boat with barrels of lines and barrels of ice. What kind of fishing did he do, how did it happen, what species did he catch? I was full of wonder about his work-life on the sea.

He would be leaving about 8 p.m. this evening and be gone until Saturday morning he thought. First he had to buy a few groceries and get some things from home. Never having been accused of being shy (not since girls and my 14 years of age had nervously collided), I boldly asked Calvin if he would like a partner for the fishing trip. Before he could answer I said I would try to be helpful and at the least stay out of the way. That I could drive the boat if needed and was generally pretty handy with boating things and that I had just sailed 3000 miles of coastal waters alone.

Calvin said he had been fishing alone for 30 years…and looking me over again said matter-of-factly, "Yup, you can come along. Be ready at eight. Tie your boat up to that big lobster boat over there so you will have no tide worries." I gave him a $50 bill and told him to get some of his favorite foods for the trip. He hesitated, didn't want the money, but I gave him my reasons for wanting to pay my way and he finally said, "Okay…be ready at eight," and he was off in his truck.

I was excited as I ran Sweet Breeze up alongside a big steel 60-ft trawler and decided where to put fenders and ties and raft lines so that the boats wouldn't clash with wind and major tidal surges while I was gone. I was having second thoughts too, a little concerned about leaving my boat, but when would I ever have this opportunity again? It was decided.

With asking Calvin I was really just thinking out loud, testing our new acquaintanceship, not expecting an affirmative to my query. It kinda felt like asking a woman to marry me (or better yet, sail off with me) on the first date. Holy shit. We were really going fishing.

All that I brought along were some warm clothes and a camera. I asked Calvin if I should call the harbormaster and tell him about my boat tied alongside the trawler. Calvin said, "No worries, nobody cares. That trawler won't be going out for a month."

Calvin had a warm smile and a twinkle in his eye. I got some shouted conversation started in the roar above the diesel. I recognized the roar. It was a GMC 2 stroke diesel, a "Screamin Jimmy," no wonder it was so damn loud. The sailor in me just had to ask, did we have plenty of fuel, spare parts like v-belts for the engine, spare fuel pump? He understood my concerns. He said nothing but he smiled and pointed to spare parts hanging on nails all about the pilothouse

As we got acquainted he became this warm guy with a great smile. He was a Micmac Indian of the First Acadian Nation band and had been fishing for 30 of his 48 years. He had a wife and she required that he call her on the VHF radio every two hours or so. What would she do if, like me, he got engrossed in some project and forgot to call? Maybe that's why I wasn't married. Calvin had a son too…an upcoming fisherman? I asked, carrying on the tradition? He would not come fishing, Calvin said. Computers were his only interest.

At the transom of his 43-foot wood and fiberglass boat were 20 plastic tubs with long lines coiled within, hooks tied to the mainline every three fathoms with a frozen piece of squid on each hook. I think the four long lines were nearly a half-mile long each and were contained neatly by the tubs with the tail of the first line tied to the leader of the coiled line in the next tub.

When we got out about 35 miles he studied his special chart plotter to find where he was allowed to fish according to regulations. Overboard went a weight and a float with the first long-line attached and off Calvin went to the throttle…6 knots of boat speed and the line peeled out of the first tub at amazing speed with a big stainless steel hook and a squid flying aft about every 2 seconds. Were one of those flying hooks to catch a man unawares …something I didn't want to imagine. I watched from a safe distance as one tub of line after another sailed up and back and into the blackness of the ocean beyond the lights at the rear of the boat.

Calvin had baited all those hooks by hand and arranged the lines in the tubs so they would feed out under power. He had done this on the days prior to our leaving for the fishing grounds. About three miles of line and thousands of hooks. Amazing… the preparation for baiting and coiling his lines so that he could loose and set them, alone, with speed and efficiency.

Alone. He was a single-hander too. We had that in common but I only tried to cover distance while single-handing my old sailboat. Calvin covered distance and eked his living from the sea at the same time.

My biggest challenge on the fishing trip was dealing with the cigarette smoke. It was almost smoke free out on the work deck but there was a cold wind off the water that drove me into the pilothouse. In the pilothouse, out of the wind, the cigarette smoke was thick. Calvin smoked incessantly, nearly without interruption. The smoke collected in the lower forward cabin where my bunk was, so that if I wanted any sleep I had to swim through and into it. My lungs were a precious part of my anatomy and I always tried to protect them but this time it was smoke and sleep below deck or no smoke and no sleep and shivering out on the working deck. I chose smoke and sleep.

The pilothouse on the boat had the modern electronic nav gear. The chart plotter would graph where we had been so when it became time to find the first float marking the initial end of the long line it was easy to find.

When I woke up, dawn was brightening the eastern sky. Calvin was running out the last of his baited long-lines. He was fast and efficient handling the lines and buoys and the boat. I mostly tried to stay out of the way as I took a few photos and made some scribbles in my journal.

The seas were kind to us on my first offshore fishing trip. As always, I felt queasy, out of sorts with the boat motion, lack of sleep and the ever-present cigarette and diesel smoke but I never got sick.

We went adrift after the last buoy on the last line was tossed overboard. Calvin shut down the diesel. The silence was deafening. Breakfast was bacon and eggs fried in a brand new fry pan on a camp stove. I thought I may have contributed the fry pan to the boat with my grocery money contribution. Perhaps Calvin thought his crusty old fry pan was no longer adequate with a guest on board. Washing dishes and frying pans was probably not a high priority on this fishing vessel.

Now it was Calvin's turn to crawl into a bunk and catch up on sleep. He'd been awake all night running out the lines. His was not an easy life...he was his own boss though and I recognized the need for that part...another thing we had in common. Calvin didn't smoke cigarettes while he slept.

Hauling in the catch...

The fish had big eyes. They were bottom feeders from the depths and the darkness. Cod and haddock and cusk were the primary species covering the bottom of the first tub. Calvin steered the boat with one hand and gaffed off fish from the long-line as he winched it in. The fish fell into tubs of ice while the line was coiled into a plastic barrel. He did all these motions with only two hands. I was useless...would have gotten in the way if I tried to help.

Cusk was a species I had not heard of. It looked like a relative of the cod but plain, without the shiny colors. We had a similar freshwater fish back in some Midwestern lakes that we called a burbot or a lawyer. They were a slippery, eel like fish, much like a cusk. No wonder someone had named them lawyers.

Occasionally a skate or a small shark (dogfish) would be winched up from the depths. These were tossed back and became feed for some other species I suppose. Maybe lobsters dined on them when they reached the bottom. I didn't know a lot about life on the ocean floor but I thought it must be a fascinating ecosystem way down there.

Speaking of ecosystems, the boat's ecosystem consisted of all the bare necessities for the job at hand, and a few extras; the rustiest old 12 gauge shotgun that I had ever seen; a harpoon like spear with a barbed business end attached to a light line. Tools of the trade? What was this, a whaling ship?

Occasionally only a fish's head would be attached to a hook as the long-line came in. "Seals," said Calvin with a disgusted look and shake of his head. That gave me a clue as to the old, rusty shotgun.

After another nap on my bunk in the forecastle, Calvin was smiling when I stumbled up into the pilothouse. It was the "money fish" that had came in on the last line hauled up...a halibut of about 60 pounds, that caused the smile. He said that fish would bring him $5 per pound and pay for the fuel for the trip.

Calvin and the Money Fish.

All the fish were cleaned with fast hands and a flashing knife as we were heading back to his homeport. The offal tossed overboard brought gulls, shearwaters, and other birds in for the feast. The dark outline of a 6-foot shark caused the birds to scatter from the surface alongside just as quickly as they had appeared...I supposed that not many fish parts made it all the way down to the lobsters on the bottom.

Calvin told me that we could have a TV dinner for supper, heated in the microwave oven on board or we could feast on fresh fillets of haddock. Haddock, big fillets fried in a whole stick of butter within the galley's new fry pan was my menu choice. It was an all you can eat fish fry, so fresh they curled up in the pan. We had plenty. Why not? We had about 400 pounds of fresh fish aboard packed in ice. Not a good haul for Calvin but with the halibut there would be some profit.

With darkness approaching and 30 miles to go back to the Bull's Head I could see the tiredness in his face and the fatigue in his motions. I suggested to Calvin that he go below and catch up on some sleep...that I could drive the boat back and that I would wake him when we approached the shoal water so he could take the boat into the wharf in the dark. He thought about it for a few seconds before giving me a quick nod to the affirmative and then heading below. He was entrusting me with his boat, his income, his lifestyle his future, and possibly his life, so I felt more than a little pride with his confidence in me.

I woke him about four hours later when we were half a mile out and Calvin groggily steered us in to his spot on the wharf at the Bull's Head. He didn't say much about our adventure together but as we parted ways I felt a close connection that went beyond words...our mutual respect for one another and a sort of brotherhood that men of the sea seem to have. We shook hands and hugged and promised to keep in touch. He handed me $30..."change," he smiled, "from the grocery money."

Calvin and I had not agreed on everything. At one point, while motoring out to the fishing grounds I had asked him where his trash bag was...he smiled and nodded his head to the side of the boat. Over the side he meant. "Everything...even plastics?" I exclaimed.

"Yeah," he shouted above the engine, "You one of those environmentalists?"

"Well, yeah," I shouted back. "Aren't you? Your livelihood depends on a clean ocean doesn't it?"

It wasn't for me to push the topic farther, I was a guest after all. I started a trash bag from one of our grocery bags. Much later, when I moved my stuff and the trash bag off to Sweet Breeze as Calvin and I went our separate ways, I noticed some items in the trash that I hadn't put there.

I can still picture Calvin two years later as I write...his rugged features and his black smiling eyes with the tiny web-like lines in his weathered brown skin...the cigarette perpetually hanging from the corner of his mouth, his strong hands always busy.

I climbed down onto Sweet Breeze for a quiet and smoke free sleep. The morning was to begin another milestone for me on this sailing adventure. If the weather forecast was fair or at least favorable we were going to begin the crossing to the coast of Maine with the break of day, a 200-mile passage. I was feeling the draw of a new adventure as one had just drawn to a close.

Gulf of Maine / Bay of Fundy

Up at 6 a.m. and tuned in the weather channels on the VHF...even before I put the tea water on to heat. I was feeling the urge to get out around Grand Sable Island and test the winds and seas. The forecast was for light winds in the areas of Forchu and Grand Manan. The Grand Manan weather region covered much of the route from Cape Sable, Nova Scotia to somewhere on the northeast coast of Maine. Forchu was behind us up the coast of Nova Scotia.

Patchy fog was part of the forecast but then patchy fog was always part of the forecast on this Atlantic coast. It sounded like a go for me. Start the crossing to the coast of Maine and hope for no sudden storms or extreme weather events in the next two or three days.

Sweet Breeze and I were ready for this leg of our journey. I wasn't sure what to expect. The tides in the Bay of Fundy were the largest in the world...as high as 28 feet I had read. Those kinds of tides must mean tremendous tidal currents with so much water moving to and fro every 12 hours. We were about to sail across those currents, or maybe with those currents, depending on what wind power we would encounter and attempt to harness.

With decent winds I thought we could make the passage in two days and one night. We needed wind. I didn't carry enough gas to motor 200 or more miles and I sure as hell didn't want to motor 200 or more miles even if we could.

So far we were sailing a beam reach in light air on a southeast heading to round the southern tip of Nova Scotia at Cape Sable. The stretches of beach that almost looked tropical off to starboard, these, my last views of Cape Sable Island.

I was not sure which route I would take to cross over to Maine or if I would take any route this day. It all depended on the winds and the ocean currents and how things felt to me. I had heard from other sailors that most folks crossed over from Yarmouth, Nova Scotia, up the coast to the northwest, cutting off about 50 miles from the open water passage.

This morning I was all about feeling the wind and the ocean currents and trying to decide whether the direct course between Seal Island and Mud Island would work or whether heading more north up the coast toward Yarmouth was the faster choice.

So far we had burned a quarter tank of gas just climbing up the wind and current to a few miles east of Seal Island. I wondered when, or if, the current would reverse and start to carry me northwest out into the Gulf of Maine as the ocean waters rushed up into the Bay of Fundy. That's what I thought would happen but I didn't know when or how that might feel.

Two more hours of a snail's pace against the current and I noticed us picking up speed on the chart plotter's speed-over-ground knot meter. That's when I decided to go for the crossing. The speed increase was the first encouraging sign and then a pod of porpoises off the port bow was the clincher for me. Those were my first porpoise sightings and I took it as a sign of a safe passage.

We picked up speed as we sailed close-hauled and most carefully (in a broad fog bank) between Seal Island somewhere on the left and Mud Island to starboard. I couldn't see either of the islands and watched the depth meter and the chart plotter intently. There were broad shelves of sand somewhere below that stretched out between the islands and depths were holding at only around 20-feet.

Shortly beyond the islands the fog thinned, the depth dropped way off and the atmosphere brightened. We were sailing in the open ocean for the coast of Maine now. The wind was on the nose again but there were no more bottom hazards so we could make deep tacks for hours, close hauled, and sometimes feeling the assist of the strong current. If I could set up my sheet-to-tiller steering rig perhaps I could catch up on some sleep on a long tack.

The Bay of Fundy must be filling with that massive volume of tidewater for those 20-plus foot tides because our tack to the north was much faster than the one to the west. I was developing a plan...sail with the current into the bay and when it reversed, sail with it out the bay to the west. It sounded simple enough and it worked to maximize our speed and conserve fuel in the light, but foul air.

With the fog mostly gone I could still see land far to the right...the mainland of Nova Scotia with the islands out in front. Over there somewhere was Yarmouth, if I still wanted to find it and wait for better winds for the passage. But no, my doubts had sailed away and we were moving briskly now with the current...big whirls were showing on the surface and in some areas small standing waves were riding on the currents of this vast river in the sea.

We made a long tack in the afternoon toward the north-northwest at seven knots speed for about 10 miles, the speed mostly due to the current. As the speed began to drop off below three knots we did our 90-degree tack and headed back toward the rhumb line, very slowly in the light afternoon wind, but still, this was sailing and I felt at ease out there in the Gulf of Maine. Whenever we made the coast of Maine would be just that...whenever. As usual I had no agenda, no schedule, no itinerary, and lately, no worries.

Zooming out on the chart plotter and sliding the cursor ahead showed that we had about 120 miles to Bar Harbor, Maine, but we could meet the coast anywhere... wherever the wind and currents carried us. It made no difference to me.

The gentle sail made for some gentle thoughts and the quiet out there made for some quiet observations. Shearwaters would sail in on silent wings, alight nearby and check me out for a few moments before moving on. Some species of small tern would dance among mats of floating vegetation and pluck out some sort of delicacies. The birds seemed to be going my way. Storm petrels (Mother Carey's chickens), did their water dance for me and gulls sailed low overhead checking to see if I might be a fishing boat with some lunch potential.

Evening was very quiet and almost still. We were moving only a knot or two toward the west every hour with the sun bouncing off the wave tops and brilliantly lighting our gently rolling watery path. It was feeling right just to be out there, about 70 miles from either coast now, almost adrift...almost in a dream.

Light and variable winds were forecasted for the night, so where the morning would find us I could not know. I set the sails for a heave-to and lashed the tiller and went below into that snug bachelor's den...that nest on the starboard bunk where books and snacks were easily within reach. That womb on the sea where gravity, it appeared, would be all I needed to stay in the bunk tonight. Life was good and sailing was fun again.

Sunday morning, August___? Cool with very little breeze. More birds winging west.

While the tea water heated on the stove I went up to the cockpit and checked the M.O.B. (man-overboard) mark on the chart plotter that I had set last night before going below. The good news was we had drifted eight miles overnight to the southwest (with the outgoing tidal current from the Bay of Fundy I supposed). Southwest was a good direction for us, mostly parallel with the coast of Maine but on a parallel south. South was good because eventually the water and wind would warm. Maybe one morning soon I would go topside to check out the day and not see my breath in the chill air.

I had on my big wool sweater from my friends in Dublin this morn. It was a gorgeous morning on the sea and looking east toward Dublin the sun was flashing its brilliance off the wave tops. Though I didn't pay much attention to clocks it seemed the days were getting shorter. I supposed I would be moving back into the eastern time zone from the Atlantic zone soon...maybe today, but what did it matter? Somehow it just felt good to be sailing west, or trying to if the wind would pick up.

If the wind did start up it would likely be from the "sow-est." That's how the "Bluenoses" pronounced the prevailing wind direction off their coast. Bluenosers were what the Nova Scotians were affectionately called as a nickname. I wondered if their noses were perpetually blue from the cold Atlantic winds. Calvin, my fishing buddy of a few days ago had used some vowel sounds that took a little getting used to. His favorite affirmative expression was, "right own," which of course was simply..."right on."

Last night I had slept well at sea but got up a few times as usual to check our position and make sure their were no ships bearing down on us. I had left a light on all night in the v-berth so that it would shine through the windows and also switched on the masthead light. Hopefully the pilot of a ship would be using his vision occasionally as well as his electronics. The wake of a ship tossed us once during the night...it woke me and I flew topside to see its lights in the distance heading back toward the east.

The marine forecast was for light winds the next few days off the East Coast. At this part of my journey light winds were fine, much better than storms and it didn't matter when I made the coast. I would get there eventually.

Whenever a mild breeze would come our way I would steer to try to catch it and fill the sails and feel the boat accelerate slightly for a while. When there were no ripples on the water I would start the motor and head west or a little north of west looking into the horizon hoping for a hazy glimpse of the coastal mountains of Maine.

Conserving gas and catching each little breeze kept me occupied most of the morning. I had poured the last 5 gallons of gas into the main tank from the portable cans, which I thought would give us about 40 miles worth of fuel when I needed it.

The only chart for my passage to the coast of Maine was my state highway map of the main roadways, but the map covered a large portion of the gulf too. I extended the crude latitude and longitude grid offshore with pencil and straight edge and tried to approximate my position using the GPS coordinates off the chart plotter.

It wasn't that I didn't trust the chart plotter showing my relative position but I had been out of sight of land for over 24 hours now and had a lot of time on my hands. It was good to have a backup to the chart plotter, crude as it was, and it gave me something to occupy some time with. Otto was steering.

Sea birds were my favorite pass time. Maybe it was the large mats of floating vegetation that brought the birds far offshore. Maybe I had made a wrong turn and had slipped way south into the Sargasso Sea (known for its huge mats of floating greenery). Seriously, birds are a wonder though, one we take for granted sometimes, until we consider their amazing flights over water.

Land ho! I could see the hazy tops of mountains 35 miles to the northwest. It really was a thrill for me. I felt a little like I had just sailed across the ocean. I guess I had, a little 200-mile stretch of it. There was a satisfied feeling within, mixed with apprehension, and tempered with the confidence I had gained in my old boat and myself.

At the time I thought the tallest mountain in view was Cadillac Mountain of Acadia National Park on Mt. Desert Island, Maine. It had to be, as I rechecked our position and heading. We could be there in seven hours at our current five-knot sailing speed. It was 2 p.m. now. We might make it before dark if the wind of late held.

I had some salty junk food and something sweet to wash it down to celebrate... potato chips and orange juice. The next exciting thing I saw was a whale blowing 100 yards ahead and coming straight at us. I grabbed the winch handle and vigorously tapped the side of the hull thinking the sound may warn him of our presence. Something did...he veered off a bit to port and surfaced about 100 feet away as we passed.

As the afternoon passed into early evening we made good time but the waves grew with the southwest wind making sailing a chore requiring my full attention. No more reading for me as the coastal detail grew sharper ahead.

The next visual wonder for me was the really huge, really fast white boat bearing out from shore and off to port a mile. It would stop dead in the water, then its engines that I could hear from a distance, would fire up and off it would fly again for a mile or so at an amazing speed for such a huge craft. Some days later I concluded that it was a whale watching boat full of tourists out of Bar Harbor, Maine.

The next challenge was small marker buoys with lines attached. They were everywhere and some were more densely gathered and some more spread out. It became a minefield of lines and buoys. Damn, as though I didn't have enough to do handling sails and keeping my Sweet Breeze upright with darkness closing in and with the building seas. They must be marking lobster traps down on the bottom, I surmised. They were everywhere.

We were sailing fast now, dodging floats and lines. I wanted to reach some likely anchorage bay or cove before total darkness set in. Then we entered a fog bank. Ick... more tiring challenges requiring anxious attention after a long, long day on the water.

I marked a cove on the chart plotter that would have protection from the west and southwest. I think it was Seal Cove, behind Bunker Neck of Little Cranberry Island, 10 miles distant.

This was not the welcome back to the states that I had imagined. There were no fireworks and music in the park like my welcome, a month or so ago, when I sailed through the darkness into Port Stanley, Ontario (the celebration was actually Canada Day but I was playfully imagining it was for me). This was a heck of a way to welcome me back to the good old U.S. of A. Big waves and fog and a minefield of lines, floats, ships and lobster boats.

We passed in front of a cruise ship leaving Bar Harbor. I quickly changed the range of the AIS on my VHF down to one mile. I couldn't be concerned now with anything but immediate danger. AIS (Automatic Identification System) sounds an alarm when a ship's signal is detected nearby...my only eyes in the fog.

It had become a normal part of sailing for me, I guess, when a lazy afternoon of relaxed sailing, with time for reading and napping quite suddenly changes to the high anxiety of fast sailing in fog with unseen hazards all around and darkness approaching. Sailors will know what I mean.

We made it though. At 9:30 p.m. we were anchored in 27 feet of water in the cove protected by Bunker Neck. The fog lifted for a few minutes to reveal a spectacular sunset of color and quiet, oranges and pink and blues swirling above the dark rolling mountaintops of Mt. Desert Island.

With darkness came on some warm yellow glowing lights at a home just ashore on Little Cranberry Island and I wondered if they wondered where that little sailboat came from, anchored out front in their bay? I wanted to tell them I had just arrived after sailing single-handed for 3200 miles amongst so many coastal and offshore challenges. "Not bad for a blueberry farmer," I would prod them. That evening had become a welcome far exceeding my expectations.

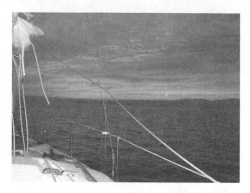

Monday, August 19th...awoke with the gray dawn and a sense of accomplishment.

There was 13 feet of water under us now so the tide hereabouts must be at least 14 feet. I guess I was finally learning something about tides, their ebb and flow and slack times.

We weighed anchor and motored carefully through a myriad of lobster floats across the channel to Seal Harbor. There I asked a lobsterman where I might get gas. "Nothing but tourists at Bar Harbor," said the fisherman. "Try Northeast Harbor. Nothing but money over there...maybe gas at the Clifton Dock." I thanked him and motored on out of Seal Harbor with some lobster boats going out to check their traps.

I was the second boat to tie up and wait for an attendant to open the little marine store and fuel dock. The first boat was a center cockpit ketch with a delightful older couple as skipper and first mate spending their summer exploring and re-exploring the complex coastal waters of Maine. I guessed that they had been skipper and first mate for a lot of years together. They invited me aboard and gave me coffee and told me of the local sights and their favorite places to visit nearby. "Don't miss the gardens on the hillside above Northeast Harbor," they almost implored. It was obvious that they were green plant folks like me.

A half hour later I was tying up at a very busy commercial dock out in front of the harbormaster's offices. There was a big piece of earthmoving equipment ever so slowly driving from the dock onto a skow, yachts of all sizes (mostly twice the length of Sweet Breeze), loading with provisions. I walked up to the office to inquire about anchorage or mooring possibilities at the front desk. Then I asked to speak to the harbor master about putting a For Sale sign on Sweet Breeze.

There was no anchorage area, only mooring rentals for $25 a day. That was no surprise. Twenty-five bucks was not so bad. A small For Sale sign would be okay too. Then out to weave through a hundred boats to find mooring ball #258, my home for the next few days.

This time I remembered to call U.S. customs to inform them that I was back in the U.S. of A., after a month in Canadian waters and on Canadian soil. Damn it though. I was in violation again. I should have called when I stopped at the Clifton

Dock for gas an hour ago, but never gave it a thought. I thought it would probably be a fine and jail time for this transgression as I waited for the customs officer to water-taxi out. Double damn...I'm just no good with rules.

I got lucky again. He was an older guy just like the pleasant Canadian ones back at Halifax last week. Only a minor scolding did I receive and he was gone after a couple of questions about fruit on board. No $10,000 fine threats like the youngsters back at Iroquois, Ontario had given me (with their sidearm weapons at the ready and bullet-proof vests bulging their chests even a little more), for forgetting to call them right away. Somehow the youngsters in uniform did not make me feel safe from smugglers and terrorists, but made me feel like I must be one or the other until I could convince them I was neither. It reminded me of my travels to Mexico City where young men in uniform with guns seemed to have an almost visible shroud of testosterone mist around them.

There was never a dull moment for me at Northeast Harbor, Maine. I loved just sitting in the sun on Sweet Breeze and watching boats coming and going. When that got old, there were shore-side places to explore and the town center only a couple of blocks up the hill, catering not just to tourists with the usual fare of tee-shirt shops and jewelry, but including a real grocery store and an old fashioned, well stocked hardware store. No MALL*WARTS allowed.

Dinghy, the plastic tub we had dragged for 3000 miles was finding good service now. It was a long row to shore, good exercise, but sometimes I felt lazy and called the water taxi service for a lift. I would tie dinghy behind the taxi boat (she was used to being drug around) in case my return time was after taxi hours. That was a convenient service included with the mooring fee.

Sure it was a tourist's environment. The docks, the boaters and their boats, the late summer winding down, and family vacations coming to a close soon, but still, the harbor and town had a quaintness that kept me there...and I wanted to sell Sweet Breeze. If I was to make it back to Minnesota before my daughter and family arrived from Berlin I had to get moving. Sell the boat, buy a car and reorganize my life for land travel. Northeast Harbor seemed like a great place to hang out while I tried to get those things to fall into place.

Pearson Tritons like Sweet Breeze had a reputation for their durability and their sail-ability in all the conditions one might encounter. Sure, she was 50 years old but I thought she was in fine shape for her age and wannabe sailors would surely line up to take her off my hands after a few strategically worded ads were placed.

That's not exactly how things played out. She was worth $10,000 in my estimation with a solid old hull and deck and all kinds of new gear plus a bullet proof, rebuilt Atomic 4 inboard that never failed. I had good Internet wi-fi at the marina clubhouse so I got some ads uploaded with handsome photos of her best side. She looked good. I would have bought her. But I was soon to learn that not everyone loved her as I had.

Sweet Breeze at Northeast Harbor, Maine.

I asked everyone that I met that had boat connections if they knew anyone looking for a great old sailboat. Next, I had some thoughts about how to locate a good used car or small pickup truck. I shopped on the Internet but found little that suited me. This was such a lovely corner of the planet to be in that I could easily get distracted from buying or selling much of anything. Each sunny day was just a joy to be alive.

Mount Desert Island was large by my island standards. There were lakes up in the hills (called ponds), roads, highways and trails to get around on, but it was not badly spoiled. Actually, for the most part, quite well preserved.

L.L. Bean, the big retail store had provided busses on the island to help keep down the car traffic. What a great idea, free bus rides all over the island. Park your car, park your boat, take a bus all around Acadia National Park which was a large part of the island. I seldom find the opportunity to praise a corporation for public service but I must give Bean's its due. Even with the busses, cars were everywhere on the island and traffic jams were common. I was glad that I didn't have a car.

I enjoyed the bus ride to Bar Harbor and sat up next to the driver who talked a mile a minute, telling me tales of the local lore. The fisherman back at Seal Harbor was right, Bar Harbor was all about tourists. I didn't want to be a tourist, I was a sailor after all, perhaps a rung or two above tourists on the social ladder of my invention. Besides, I could have sailed over to Bar Harbor just as easily as riding on a bus full of noisy tourists...I could have. And I could have talked to my old boat instead of the bus driver as I had been doing for the last 10 weeks. I could have....

Seriously, I did take a bus to the entrance to the park and paid for my park permit. Then I felt free to hike the trails and carriage roads throughout the hills, up to the ponds and the high overlooks. In between hikes, I must admit, I loved to watch tourists, meet them perhaps, exchange smiles. I know now that I am a thorough introvert but some one-on-one social exchanges were a good check to see if I still behaved in socially acceptable ways or if I had been talking to my boat for too long.

I hiked woodland paths up to Jordan Pond and Bubble Pond. I hiked some of the carriage roads, that only allowed horse carriages, bike or foot traffic, to the intricate old stone bridges that spanned creeks babbling down the mountainsides. The quiet greenery of the forest drew me within and refreshed me. The crowd of tourists at Jordan Pond, the pavilion, car traffic and the noisy restaurant, gave me reason to hike onward.

High in the hills the first tinges of fall colors were showing on the hillsides. Bubble Pond was more remote with some rugged talus slopes coming down from Cadillac Mountain threatening to fill the lake someday. The clear water with no car access suggested native trout to me.

My favorite jaunts were in the hills just a short row away from my mooring. Just as the sweet couple at the fuel dock had said, the gardens on the hillsides were serenely spectacular. A wooded, sun-dappled path would lead me into an arboretum of native and exotic plants tastefully arranged in gardens with mini-paths radiating into secluded displays of the greenest nature. Small ponds from springs broke up the greenery and carefully placed rocks kept the hillside trails from eroding. Memorable, quiet, early-morning jaunts that were a delightful start to the day.

Back at the clubhouse one morning Joe and I started to chat. He was the captain on a huge motor yacht that he had skippered up from Florida with the boat's owner and his family. We had more in common than boats (actually there was nothing in common between Sweet Breeze and Joe's charge beside the fact that they both floated on water).

Joe was an outdoorsy guy from upstate New York and we both loved the rural life. Under those trendy dark glasses, I think Joe was a hick like me but he had a role to play...skipper of an enormous motor launch. Unlike Joe, I could be my regular bumpkin self. We became friends with some common threads through the proximity of our uncommon boats. Joe gave me a tour of his boat. The engine room and the dining room furniture were most interesting. On the tour, Joe tapped into his stash of venison in a freezer and I left with a package of organic red meat to go with my mostly vegetable and fish diet. Joe Yaghy was my kind of yachty.

One of my water taxi drivers had an interesting story. Bruce was from Grand Rapids, Minnesota. Not far from my cabin back at Camp Cotton. For most of his professional career, he taught religion at a university in Chicago but he decided to retire to Mt. Desert Island and be a part-time water taxi driver. There were lots of interesting folks around with interesting stories and I sought out the one-on-one conversations wherever likely prospects presented themselves.

I could only be a "tourist-like" sailor for so long. Used cars were not presenting themselves nor were used sailboat buyers. My big bag of long overdue, well worn, aromatic clothing had been washed, dried, and neatly folded at the Chinese laundry by a lovely young Mexican gal with a smile and accent that I immediately knew was deserving of a healthy tip of more than a few pesos.

My galley was well provisioned from the grocery store...so much food that I paid to have it delivered to the seaside dock near Dinghy. I caught not one mackerel to add some fresh fish to my larder though I tried many casts from Sweet Breeze.

I struck out on my offer to accompany a lobsterman, one morning, who happened to be a lobsterwoman, which would have made for more fishing stories to tell. Another potential tale was in the offing but she would not take my bait...eternal fame from when my book was published and on a bestseller list.

My spirit was refreshed from all the woods walking of late and it was time to sail on while I still had some money in my stash on the boat. Southwest, down the coast of Maine it would be, on the morning's ebb tide.

Sunday morning, August__? Guess I'll Never be a Gentleman….

There is this dumb old sailor's adage that goes something like, "Gentlemen do not sail to weather," and it means that beating into the wind is to be avoided...at least if you wanted to preserve your dry and elegant attire and your sense of what is proper. It must have been a saying that carried over from bygone times when sailing was for the well off and the well dressed.

Well, there was little hope for me becoming a gentleman on this Atlantic coast. Winds were almost always from the same direction that I wanted to go...southwest. That meant sailing against the wind trying to make headway down-coast and being battered by the waves and thoroughly wetted by spray and, on a little boat like Sweet Breeze, sometimes the waves also swept across the foredeck to spread out in your lap.

Being a fresh water sailor from the Great Lakes, this continually being wetted with saltwater spray for countless miles left me feeling sticky and clammy. I generally liked the 64-year-old pores of my epidermis feeling clean and relatively unclogged.

The trendy joys that the sun block cream ads touted left me feeling like I needed a hot and sudsy shower, besides, the chemicals in that stuff was being found in the waters of Antarctic seas and just maybe it wasn't being tested with regard to long term use on humans. Cottons and linen shirts were my sun blocker of choice. They had been tested for centuries to no ill effects or side effects. Long pants covered my legs.

But back to the salt spray. It left my clothing stiff, but even that was better than the thought of being covered with a salty and greasy (sun block cream) coating like a cold bratwurst from the fridge or one of those thick cut potato chips that were the newest way to satisfy one's salt-fat cravings.

Sailing close-hauled into the wind was normal for me now, at least for the last two weeks, since Canso, on the northern tip of Nova Scotia...but today was different. A northwest wind it was. Offshore and brisk and it put the wind abeam at times and even aft of center. Yup, sailing was fun again. The vast waters, the intricate arms and islands of Penobscot Bay went by all too quickly. We were sailing dry and warm with the thrill of the heel and the joy of near top speed.

I even had to slow down a bit passing Stonington and Moose Isle for to sail safely amongst all of the boating traffic. The Fox Island Thoroughfare kept my head turning like an owl's trying not to miss the lay of rocks and forest, boats of all kinds, and uniquely styled homes perched up beyond the tide lines.

There were sloops like Sweet Breeze. There were cutters and ketches, yawls and schooners...and a motor yacht so huge it took up most of the marked boating channel while it swung at anchor off North Haven. Those folks on that yacht obviously knew all about conspicuous consumption. Deciding which jacket to wear for dinner was not my idea of adventure on the water. Sure I was making judgments but I would rather have adventure over comfort any day. I thought Sweet Breeze and me were likely having lots more fun than they were. Rich folks...sometimes I felt sorry for the adventure, the real life that passed them by while they sipped Vermouth and chatted not so demurely. Sure I would like to have a million dollars, it would be fun deciding how to give it away.

We had put on lots more miles-made-good yet that afternoon before we anchored up early, in a shoreward cove, in the lee of Ash Island for the night.

There were lots of reefs and bottom hazards on the route from Northeast Harbor that day and the vigilance to always know position tired me out in those complex coastal waters...that and sail handling and steering. I expected a peaceful night at anchor with protection on three sides. Once more a cold drizzle had started. The yellow lights of homes on shore beckoned, perhaps it was their comfort that I was wanting to share?

A quiet evening at anchor usually brought back thoughts of the day's experiences and sightings. With a smile I thought of Sweet Breeze at Northeast Harbor...feeling like a Model T at a new car show...the gleaming Morris Yachts fresh from the shop where they were built and all of the polishing and scrubbing that my neighbor boaters passed their days with...why was I so different?

I spent my days at Northeast Harbor hiking and exploring and Sweet Breeze didn't shine, she swung on her mooring...waiting. My neighbors...for all of their visual perfection, their brightness and polish, I wondered if their docile, gleaming lifespan would include half of the adventure that my old Triton had provided.

When I bought a car they didn't shine much after the first week either but brought me on many an exploration near and far. There seemed to be a pattern developing here.

Monday, late August...up at 4 a.m. and gone at five.

Out and around Ash Island the force of the wind and waves gave me my first clue to what the day's sail would be like. Wind and waves on the nose again...big swells and slop over the coamings and spray in my face. Oh yeah, fog of course, and then rain as well. I'd had my vacation in the sun at Northeast Harbor.

Being the lazy sailor that I am and not out to prove how much misery I could take before I got sick or discouraged, I very soon started looking for some protected harbor or anchorage. My choice was Tenant's Harbor up ahead about 10 miles. That was a miserly amount of progress for a day but I felt that I should wait for some sort of pleasantness in weather and sea conditions. I had no schedule or destination after all.

Tenant's Harbor was a deep cut inland with good isolation from the turmoil happening out on the sea. I grabbed a mooring ball that looked seldom used, and looped through the heavy old bridle that I was accustomed to using. Then I went below and cooked some venison and onions for a late breakfast.

The Maine coast was such a delight of rocky shores with spruce and an occasional home or cabin above the tide lines, small towns and hamlets tucked into bays, that I didn't want to miss it sailing by in the fog. Most of the 300 mile shore of Nova Scotia was hidden from me by fog.

I recalled the swift sail yesterday. The sun's warmth and the clear calendar-photo views. The pod of porpoises in Penobscot Bay. I would wait for the fog to lift.

I felt I should row Dinghy over to the dock and see if I could find a library or restaurant with wi-fi. Had my ads placed a few days ago to sell Sweet Breeze attracted any responses I wondered?

The wind was Southwest and gusty. It would be a strenuous row to shore now against it but I was feeling well fed (lazy) and good about my world. The sun somewhere above would even give the fog a bright warm glow at times. I checked my old boat's attachment to the mooring line and rechecked it again as we swung about in the wind. I listened to the wind in the rigging and was glad I was not out at sea somewhere fighting it again.

My journal needed some attention so I did some catching up with the writing. Good that I did that everyday or you, the reader, would likely be reading something far less fascinating right now—or—perhaps something much more interesting conjured up from my imagination.

I worked up the ambition to row to shore when I was finally satisfied that Sweet Breeze would still be there when I got back. Unknown moorings left me wondering how secure they really were...the lines and heavy stuff underwater that I couldn't see may be chafed or rusting away...I had no way to know. I dropped an anchor and snubbed it off just for insurance.

The worst feeling a sailor can have is to see his boat drifting off to sea after rowing to shore. I know. It happened to me in the Apostle Islands of Lake Superior a few years back. That time I rowed the dinghy so furiously to catch my boat that I coughed blood for two days...but I caught the boat before it was wrecked on the rocks.

Tenant's Harbor had a restaurant just up the hill from dockside and I became engrossed in watching the live lobsters in the shallow tank. They are a strange animal to me. Big vicious looking pincers and shiny eyes and all sorts of appendages poking about. There were some fish parts in the tank that they were tugging at, sorting out their pecking order it looked like.

The rest of the town looked like what I imagined a New England town should look like. Neat older homes lined the main thoroughfare, where porches facing the street and the harbor would have been a great place for morning tea. No Mall*Warts along main street here at Tenant's Harbor, only a little general store with hardware and groceries...just the way it should be.

The library was closed but by sitting on the grass alongside I was able to pick up the signal and catch up on my emails. No real, serious sounding emails of interest in buying Sweet Breeze so far and nobody with a good small car that wanted to bring it to me so I could see it.

Tuesday, August__?...up at 4 a.m. to a calm harbor. Lobster boats heading out in the dark. Waiting for daylight to find my way.

Left downcoast for Boothbay Harbor with the first gray light of dawn. The most challenging part of plying these coastal waters, especially in early light is the lobster traps with their floats and lines. Thousands, no, tens of thousands. Getting a line tangled in the prop or hung up on the rudder would be a small disaster for me. This was not the warm Caribbean water that would make for a delightful dive and swim to untangle. This water was really cold. This was not water from the Gulf Stream, this was water from the "Greenland stream", or so it seemed.

Out around South Island the swells were rolling but not a lot of wind, just enough to set sails and shut down the motor. The winds were light and more offshore than yesterday...more west than southwest.

Somewhere ahead through the complex of long points and coastal islands was Boothbay Harbor where my friend Dean, back in Duluth, said he had friends who I should visit and use as a local connection to sell the boat and buy a car. He gave me a phone number and an email address to reach them so I left a message that I was sailing in today and could I look them up?

The sail and motor sail that morning was most pleasant and the views shoreward were captivating for me. It was more of my favorite mix of trees and rocks and coastal waters interrupted occasionally by a seaside home or a village tucked up in a bay with fishing boats out front. More calendar views highlighted and brought to clarity by the morning sun.

Boothbay Harbor was still sleepy when we pulled in about 10:30 a.m. I pulled into the city dock and tied up to ask some questions and find a more permanent dockage. The waterfront was a mix of old and new. I tied up at the Tugboat Inn and paid for a night's dockage.

The streets were getting packed with cars and once again I was glad to be afoot. This was indeed a tourist haven with shops for fudge and gifts and seafood but not entirely spoiled...yet. The harbor was a haven for pleasure boats and work boats and boats for tourists to see the waterfront from the water. I liked the old homes and the walking bridge across the harbor connecting both sides with a shortcut.

In one of the old homes was a vast used bookstore packed with room after room of books where I bought about six that would keep me reading for a while. I used the wi-fi at the dock to contact my friend's friends via email, but neither phone nor email raised any responses. I even bought some fudge.

Catherine, the piano player, entertainer, fine singer at the lounge and hotel where I was docked, was most interesting to talk with. Everyone has a story. Part of her's was about days long past when she was a part of a really big name folk music group. She wasn't Mama Cass but she was good enough to be. I can't remember the folk group she sang with but it was a big-time group. I too loved to sing and stumble around on the strings of a guitar.

Catherine made it look too easy and sound too good. I came back in the evening to hear her sing again and sip a beer. I turned in late, snuggling up with a fantasy that Catherine would soon be tapping on the coach roof and asking to share my bower below decks, where we would softly sing old songs together, share our stories, as Boothbay Harbor, Maine fell quiet in the warmth of a late summer night.

She didn't show and I decided to cast off early in the morn for Portland. Damn fool romantic old sailor.

Foggy Passage to Portland

Wednesday, August___?...up early as usual. Light fog on nearshore waters. Sailed around the west half of the harbor before leaving.

The west half of Boothbay Harbor was residential, with moorings out front and homes on the hills. I think I may have been looking for a likely out-of-the-way small, family owned marina that was just hoping for the opportunity to store and sell Sweet Breeze for me. A place that would say, "Wow, isn't that a Triton?" as I sailed up to the dock, doused the main and stepped to the dock all in one motion. On second thought, it looked a bit upscale for me and my old boat, there in the western bay but it was an early morning excursion worth the views.

The coast of Maine should be a whole summer's sailing adventure or even that of a lifetime. A week would barely allow time to explore one of the miles long bays reaching far inland or the many smaller arms of water attached to that which beckon the explorer. But I was sailing the coast of Maine in a week. Still I was not in a hurry because everyday was a new adventure and all the sights and sounds were new to me...I had no place to be but wherever I happened to be.

Out from Boothbay and around the point I happened to be in fog. Hardly noteworthy. Worth writing about? Only because it caused me to miss so much of the shoreward views and it caused me much consternation, concentration, and some anxiety...and it caused me to cuss out loud. Now I had lobster boats, floats and lines, bottom hazards of reefs and shoals and ledges...and fog. This had become a normal day of coastal sailing for me but it was taxing even *my* patience.

My nature is to take what nature gives and make the best of it. Nature wasn't giving me that much lately.

Sometimes there was enough wind to shut the motor down. That was a major relief because then I could hear the thump and growl of the diesels in the lobster boats. It was up to me to avoid a collision. They were busy checking and moving from one trap to the next.

They were out making a living. I was out making an adventure. I would probably show up on their radar screen but I didn't expect they had much time to look for boats as they were searching for the next float marking a trap.

One narrow miss, probably a 100 foot miss as we saw and veered from each other at the same time. That made me even more cautious and vigilant peering into the fog ahead. I could hear their engines on all sides but the suddenness of their appearance in the fog always gave me a jolt. I tried to follow the sound from their engine to try to guess their heading to avoid any unplanned meetings.

My best estimate of distance to Portland from Boothbay was about 40 miles. It was mostly a nerve wracking 40 miles all because of the fog, plus, I was missing the coastline and all of the complexities of islands and coves and bays...that exquisite combination of rocks and trees and water that nature had been slowly working to perfection for a long time...and I was missing it all.

The last few miles were the worst. More boat traffic was heading back to Portland after a morning's fishing and the fog was thicker than ever. I was blowing my conch shell horn until my lips got sore. That was my foghorn and there were a chorus of other horns all around.

Suddenly there was the deep, rumbling blast from a ship's horn directly behind me and I think the low rumble of the blast made my hair stand on end. How to get out of its way when I can't see it. Was it 100 feet behind us or a quarter mile? I held my course. There were too many boats around to make any maneuvers that could cut across their paths. My course was to stay as far to the right as I could, right next to the red nuns when they showed themselves in the fog...the freighters and ferrys should be out in the middle of the marked shipping channel...my strategy for avoidance and survival.

As sudden as the ship's blast, the fog dispersed, just for a moment, but long enough that I could see the Spring Point lighthouse. It briefly showed through at the end of a rock cobble jetty. I ducked across the channel and behind the jetty as quickly as I could. I really felt deep relief knowing that I was out of the way of boats and ships and ferrys.

With the drizzle turning to rain I grabbed the nearest mooring ball, tied on and went below to take a deep breath and fix a salad. We were socked in with fog again so

I really couldn't tell what was around us but I was certain we were out of the shipping lane and that was enough for now.

I wasn't below for long. Something was pounding on the hull and it was a heavier thud than the customary banging of the dinghy. Topside in the rain I discovered we had pulled the mooring loose and were up against some kind of temporary sea wall made of canvas and floats.

There was no damage anywhere so with the engine engaged we dragged the mooring back to about where I found it and turned it loose, went a bit closer to the jetty and dropped anchor. I went below again to get out of the rain and the blare of foghorns and this time I stayed, snug, snacking and reading, my below decks M.O.

The rain on the coach roof was a most pleasant sound...safe, warm, dry. I told myself I was never to sail in the fog again...well, unless tomorrow...? I guess I recovered from sailing anxiety quickly, too quickly for my own good sometimes.

Thursday morn, August__? Got up late.

It was a bit of a shock...the view as I poked my head above the companionway hatch. The fogged-in acre or so of my entire visual world, when I ducked below last evening, had become amazingly vast this morning. There was a marina nearby packed with pleasure boats. A ship at dock was loading not far away. Big green islands were across the channel with old homes and new homes. An intriguing old fortress of some sort was sitting derelict and alone on a broad, rocky island farther up into the bay.

What I must have missed yesterday...blinded by fog, surrounded by a constant shroud of grayness and that spooky symphony of foghorns. Today there were colors, nothing bright and shining in the sun yet, but colors and the sharp visual definition of objects all around. There were distant views too and a horizon above the city of Portland.

This bay would take a week to explore by sailboat but I knew I wasn't staying. The forecast was for off shore winds this afternoon and that meant smooth sailing and some speed too...some real miles-made-good, to somewhere downcoast. Sunshine forecasted later too, no fog. A perfect forecast for a coastline tourist like me.

The broad opening to the Atlantic hereabouts is called Casco Bay but the interest for me now would lie to the north, up long finger bays reaching miles inland. Portland was on such a finger. Farther up this one was a city called Falmouth and beyond that was Yarmouth. Did the river Fal enter the bay at Falmouth and the river Yar a few miles beyond? And up at the head of the bay, how did Freeport get its name? Words and wonder...such are the entertaining thoughts of a lone sailor in such foreign lands on coastal Maine.

Up the bay at Falmouth, I was told, there would be a big marina that mostly catered to sailboats and perhaps, thought I, they would be excited to be the chosen purveyors of Sweet Breeze's future. After some fuel at the magic marina that appeared when the fog lifted, it was off to Falmouth we were, past the old fort on the island and the other winsome views toward all the shores that captured my imagination with more and more wonderings of the local history...the canoes of local Indians plying these bays for seafood and sustenance and the ships of the first Europeans seeking profit in trade or passenger fares.

We motor-sailed upwind and through a maze of moored boats to Handy's Boatyard. I really just wanted an experienced salesperson to give me an idea of the local market for a sweet old boat like mine. Would she sell? If so what might be her worth in the money trade...I knew her worth many times over on the sea, in a blow, and as a personal friend.

I waited for an hour or so while the "sailsman" was busy with other duties and then I became encumbered, distracted more likely, with delightful thoughts, the anticipation of sailing downwind. I watched the wind pick up on the water out front and shift more to the north. That may mean following winds down the bay and downcoast.

Handy's would have to hope for another old Triton to come along. How the wind beckoned me when it came up from behind. We were sailing off toward the sea. Not long past Portland we sampled the seas again as we nosed around Cape Elizabeth. We struggled a bit around the cape as the waves there were confused and tossing us all around.

Another small sailboat like Sweet Breeze, it looked like a Cape Dory, was also struggling around the Cape but turned back toward Portland. Did they forget something at home or did they know something that I should have known. They had a crew on board too.

Surely this confusion on the surface would settle down with the slack-tide or with a bit more distance seaward. And it did. After an hour or so of getting slapped around by waves hitting us from all quarters, the wind veered to the east of north and gained some velocity in the easting.

Even after such a late start, with these following winds and waves we could put on a few miles before nightfall. And where would nightfall find us? That was my next question. I decided we could make Kennebunkport if the wind held, and if it didn't, there were other bays and necks that should provide some protection from the open Atlantic.

Curtis Cove sounded interesting. Stage Island Harbor looked like it was well protected if it was deep enough. And just maybe the Bushes at Kennebunkport would welcome me if I hailed them from just offshore. I knew they had a seaside cottage somewhere nearby and I should be arriving around suppertime.

Waves of three to four feet would sometimes ride on top of a swell making it an eight to 10 foot wave. Sweet Breeze would surf on these briefly if I caught them just right. I have said before that swells were almost never swell for us to ride. Today they were swell. They were meeting us on the port quarter. There was enough wind to steady the boat and keep up enough speed to, in effect, slow the passing of the swell and gentle the ride as it passed. Ha! It was blowing a northeaster and we were going southwest. How about that!

Toward evening as we rounded Cape Arundel heading inland I was looking over the huge seaside homes, palaces really, that I guess were unabashed statements of how much wealth one had gathered.

One had a huge flag flying...big as at a Perkins Restaurant. That must be the Bushes, true patriots that they were, but no, it turned out they were just some other hugely patriotic folks with a huge seaside home.

Another one had a series of marker buoys offshore a half mile or so. I sailed up to one to see if I could read the attached warning sign. It said something like, "Stay back. Do not sail closer to shore than these markers." This must be their cabin ashore I thought, but this is no way for the Bushes to welcome a lonely sailor, and a shirttail relative at that, thought I.

Sure, I hadn't announced that I was coming, but still, so unwelcoming was that sign on the buoy. So ungracious, I thought. I waved but no one saw me or waved back. Maybe they were having supper and I was late.

To hell with them then. I wasn't going to stop and visit...well maybe if they pleaded with me, but even a sailor can tell the difference between a welcome mat and a, "Stay the fuck away," sign. Barbara, you looked a lot like my grandmother on the Bush side, but now...you would never know.

Breakwaters extended out on both sides of where the waters of the Kennebunk River met the sea. As always, I cautiously entered, glancing at the depth meter every few feet forward as I inched Sweet Breeze up the river. There was a man fishing off the right seawall, I waved thinking maybe it was one of the Bush boys, a distant cousin who, like me, enjoyed trying for the family supper. He didn't wave back... perhaps it was!

Inching upstream, not knowing if I would get stuck in mud or what, I finally saw the welcome that I was hoping for...sailboat masts. They were a signal to me that there was depth in the river and maybe a place to tie up as well.

I asked at the marina for info on dockage for the night. There were two choices... tie up at a finger dock for $135.00 for the night orrrr...take a city mooring ball out in the river for free. Hmmm. Hard choice.

The mooring ball was close enough to somewhere that I had wi-fi service. Some big boat nearby may have had a powerful router that the receiver in my little Netbook picked up. I wouldn't use much broadband service, honest, just a few emails.

It was a most peaceful night at Kennebunkport and I was almost over my hurt that the Bushes had snubbed me. Back home, at my palace on the Whiteface River at Camp Cotton, it wasn't like that...we welcomed everyone.

Speaking of welcomes, the phone call from Jay and Sara, Marna's sister and her husband downcoast a ways at Gloucester, MA was a welcoming distraction as the quiet evening waned on the River Kennebunk.

They had been following my progress throughout my "big sail" and were wondering when I might reach their area. They offered me use of their mooring at the marina on the northeast side of the Gloucester harbor and other common amenities that this sailor found to be generous and welcoming. I was looking forward to seeing them again and their little city with its rich history of fishing, sailing, and seamanship.

I sent Jay an email that said, weather permitting, I would be there soon, and drifted off into a most restful sleep, secure on a mooring in a small river, after finishing the terrific book, *The Land Remembers*, by Ben Logan.

Friday, August__?...up with first hint of light in the east. Down to the sea in my ship, the downeast sea, at 6 a.m.

Sunshine makes all the difference. Of course the wind was on the nose that morning, but with the sunrise over the water off the port quarter, it was only a tolerable inconvenience.

We close hauled with flattened sails and the motor pushing and tacked as we tried to stay close to the rhumb line and hold about five knots. It was an easy course to plot today...mostly just a straight line from the Kennebunk to the northern end of the canal and river across Cape Ann.

The landscape was changing quickly ahead. There were more sand beaches and fewer rock promontories. Most of the islands of Maine were behind us now and the water ahead had few bottom hazards...and there was sun this day and so far no fog. Sailing was fun again.

Starboard tacks had brought us about five miles offshore but even that far out the buildings up on Bald Head Cliff were massive. What could they be?

The starkness of the tall lighthouse and the lighthouse tender's home on the barren rocks of Boon Island made me wonder and hope that the tender once had a very complete library in his home. That would be a lonely life, even for me. I might like a wife or a companion were I the tender...then again, a good dog might do.

Seas and winds were of the reasonable kind that one would hope for on a late summer day. The autopilot (Otto) was steering well again after I had discovered and tightened an intermittent electrical connection.

I was thinking lunch, but my favorite foods were beginning to get picked over aboard Sweet Breeze. From the fridge I found some green beans, some left over canned stew and some wild rice from a few days back. I heated them all together and added a can of spicy tomato basil soup for a base. It was a rather pleasant concoction due to the tomato basil and I had difficulty throwing away food that was still mostly edible. A good spicy soup base makes anything mostly edible.

Ten more miles down the coast we were approaching a most interesting group of rocky islands. Appledore, Smuttynose, and Star Island all in a tight group about eight miles offshore. They drew me in close. Their stark, rocky appearance caused me to wonder why people chose to settle there. They had built homes but was there soil enough to grow crops? Was there grass enough to graze sheep or cattle?

I sailed up as close to the islands as I dared with the ledges and shoal waters reaching offshore. My curiosity was piqued. I wanted the best views possible. There was even a town-like group of buildings on Star Island and the islands were connected with big blocks of rock, placed by men and machines.

My guess was that the first economic draw of the islands was not the potential for animal husbandry but of eking a living from the sea. White Island just to the south had another of those very tall lighthouses. I decided that I must do some research someday about this island group and the history of settlement there.

With early afternoon and that interesting island group left in our wake, the wind picked up a bit and with it our speed. I noticed that on the starboard tack I would start to feel queasy as in the beginning nausea of seasickness, but on the port tack I would recover and feel good again. There must have been some particular boat motion that the starboard tack generated that my system didn't like. I took one of those motion sickness pills that alleviated the sick feeling but gave me the yawns and once again, I would nearly fall asleep at the tiller.

As I glassed the shore I was amazed and saddened by the excess that we human beans so proudly display. They probably call them their beach cottages. Massive homes lined the shore of what I thought must be the New Hampshire coast now. Whatever happened to the wisdom of the adage, "Live simply in order that others may simply live"? It must have not been spoken hereabouts or perhaps it was something that the homeowners thought other people should follow.

We were speeding along at five to six knots now and that was good, if we were to make Gloucester today. The shoreline beaches now stretched for miles and were not developed at all along Plum Island. My faith was renewed that there were some planners who thought ahead, who set aside and protected lands from development by us needy humans.

The sun was warm now and the curving white sand beaches could have been in the Caribbean. This was indeed a pleasant day of sailing...and through the waters of three states in one day. The miles-made-good and the warmth of Ipswich Bay helped erase the lingering snub that I had been dealt back at Kennebunkport.

Schooner Weekend....

The passage across Cape Ann through the canal and river was intimate and warm and crowded. Was it Labor Day weekend or did these folks always party and play on the water? Perhaps they had heard about my big sail and were celebrating my arrival.

The current carried us both inland and south, winding amongst real Massachusetts marshland on the right, tiny floating cabins and boaters everywhere else. But I loved the activity, the smiles and waves. Almost every boat had a full crew of partygoers raising their glass or bottle to my journey.

There was light wind and I felt I could have sailed silently amongst all the activity, and if I had a crew I may have, but alone, the motor gave me the control that I needed through the tight spots. There were many tight spots and one needed to pay close attention to the marker buoys or run aground.

Where the current reversed just beyond a big marina, it took all of the motor's thirty horsepower to gain Gloucester's western harbor past the narrows at the drawbridge. The powerboat behind us nearly had to give us a push.

But I had arrived. Gloucester was another milestone for me and Sweet Breeze and we had put in about a 50-mile day. We poked all around the inner harbor before calling Jay and Sara and I could sense the history of men and boats in the wharfs and dry docks. It was indeed an interesting seaport with no golden arches anywhere in sight.

Brown's Yacht Yard was full up with boats for this was the annual Schooner Festival Weekend at Gloucester, but the attendant, Greg, told me that I could anchor out amongst the moorings and use the facilities at his marina.

The harbor was full of boats at anchor and all the public moorings were taken but I found an opening where my neighbor, in a long and shiny sailboat, helped me to determine how much scope would allow us to swing about without clashing. My first impressions were that this was my kind of town...even on the busiest weekend of the year.

I was always a bit puzzled by how a fleet of boats could all swing at anchor and never clash. Here was a perfect example with a maze of boats on all sides of Sweet Breeze. After a period of sitting and relaxing and watching boats and boaters, when I was satisfied that we could not swing into our neighbor on either side I pulled the dinghy up close and stepped in.

We rowed over to the west side of the inner harbor, tied off on a dinghy dock and immediately spotted Jay and Sara at the Heritage Center. There was some sort of celebration going on and Jay and Sara were taking part. After a brief meeting and welcome, I had to part ways for now and continue my mission.

Some quite a few years ago, one of the first books that I had read about sailing was about the history of a Nova Scotian born fisherman named Howard Blackburn. His tenacity for life and for adventure at sea are stories told and retold, again, with likely nothing lost in the telling.

Howard was never lacking in courage or determination. Most of his adult life he fished out of Gloucester and when he and his partner were fishing away from the mother ship their dory was caught in a storm. Howard's partner froze up till he died but Howard rowed the dory long after, his hands were frozen to the oars. For five days he rowed until he came ashore on the Newfoundland coast. Howard survived but lost a few body parts, their being frozen beyond recovery.

It had been a few years since the reading of Howard's tale had started me thinking about sailing as I operated and managed my blueberry farm in northern Minnesota. My current mission was to have a beer at the bar that he opened in Gloucester. A kind of rite of passage for me. Blackburn's Bar was somewhere up the hill and I meant to have that beer.

No, I had no pretension that I was another Howard Blackburn but I felt I had certainly tested myself this, the summer I spent at sea.

I remembered the thunderstorm off Île d'Orléans in the St. Lawrence River below Quebec City with the blackest skies, the torrents of rain and the strongest winds I could ever imagine. Horizontal rain flying at such speed that I could not look forward above the protection of the coach roof, the chart plotter was my only eyes. How under bare poles and full engine I made it to an unlikely anchorage.

I remembered distinctly the wind and waves off the tip of the Gaspé Peninsula, our near knockdown in seas and the hours spent kneeling on the cockpit sole steering while watching aft for those big breaking waves that wanted to pick us up and roll us over.

The hundreds of miles of fog along the coasts of Nova Scotia and Maine were fresh in my mind. That we made it through hundreds of miles of shoals and rocks, ledges and fishing boats in dense fog with no radar gave me an acute sense of the here and the now.

No Blackburn was I, but I wanted that beer. A thanks to his spirit for the jolt he had given me some years back...to tackle a new challenge...single-handed sailing. But it was not to be.

I walked the streets of Gloucester and I found no Blackburn's. Finally I gave up and asked someone who looked like a local. I learned that Blackburn's Bar had closed for remodeling and was now called Giuseppe's. It had no draw for me.

My shoulders slumped a bit as I walked the streets further along and then circled back down again by the waterfront. There I found a small restaurant that was to be my Blackburn's. A poor substitute for the romance of the real thing in my own mind, but they served beer and seafood, there was an attractive woman at the bar, I would tell her my name was Howard, and it would have to do.

Saturday, August__? Or is it September? Up early and motored to Eastern Point Yacht Club in the rain.

Gloucester was gray and cold in the early morning hours, unlike the warm welcome of the afternoon and evening of yesterday. A cold light rain was becoming a cold heavy rain and the wind was on the rise. There was another sailboat heading my way but they continued on out to sea in fog and rain.

I was glad it wasn't me this time sailing out into the fog. There was a forlorn feeling deep within me that I didn't understand as I watched the boat toss in the waves past the breakwater and gradually disappear in the fog. Part of me hoped that there were two people aboard...the warmth of two seemed comforting to me just then.

Swells were bending around the corner past the jetty making it tricky staying on the forward deck as I tried to grab a mooring before the wind blew us back away from it.

The attendant came out in the motor launch and took me to the clubhouse where Sara was waiting. I was soaked and cold and not in the best humor but Sweet Breeze was secure on Jay and Sara's mooring and Sara had the best of ideas...take a hot shower while my clothing was dried and warmed in a clothes dryer. A thorough warming and the dry clothing did wonders for my attitude.

Jay and Sara were great and their generous offer of their mooring most appreciated, however as Sara brought me back to town to meet Jay and buy some groceries, I realized that I was too far from town out here off Northeast Point. I wanted to be where the action was...back in the Gloucester harbor where the schooner fest was happening. Later that afternoon as the weather cleared I sailed back to the inner harbor and the mooring field and there I was to stay for several more days.

Checking emails back at Brown's dock was not encouraging. There were no solid sounding responses to buy Sweet Breeze and no used cars or trucks for sale locally that appealed to me. So be it. No hurry. No worry. This town felt friendly to me and when the timing was right she would sell and I would buy a car with the proceeds and head for Minnesota.

Saturday evening the parade of boats around the harbor kept me chuckling. It was part of the planned festivities and my first ever boat parade. The creative lighting and festive decor on boats large and small demonstrated the creativity and good humor of boaters. I suspected they may have loosened the cork on a rum bottle or two.

Once again, well fed and in high spirits, I whimsically trifled with the idea that the boat parade was part of the welcome that the community had planned for *me*. Then the fireworks began and glittered the sky and I was certain. Gloucester knew how to make a sailor feel special all right.

It was long after dark before the harbor began to lay quiet and settle down, as I lay in the starboard bunk and rehashed the day. How the gray and cold of the morning had been melted away by the warmth of afternoon sunshine...and by the camaraderie of boaters, of their high spirits, humor, and welcoming smiles.

Sunday morning...picked up Sara at Brown's dock.

Today was to be the parade of schooners and Sara and I were heading out to sail amongst them, but for Sara, it was love at first sail. Sara had impeccable taste in sailboats for she recognized Sweet Breeze for what she was...a no frills boat that will sail well, easily, and take you anywhere. I thought I had my new boat owner aboard as we put the old girl through her paces, but later Jay explained to Sara that one old sailboat in the family was sometimes one too many. Jay had been rebuilding one for a few years. It was back to the emails for me, and the responses to my Internet ads.

Monday began gray and foggy. I put some honest effort into cleaning up the cabin on Sweet Breeze and tidying up the deck and cockpit. I'm afraid I wasn't the neatest sailor but then I had been living aboard the boat for almost three months now. My attitude was more about keeping things handy, if you know what I mean.

I did get the 12-volt fridge cleaned and figured out though. I discovered it would automatically shut down to conserve battery power if the onboard voltage dropped below a predetermined level. After I lowered the setting for that "shut down voltage" it worked fine all the time.

Dinghy and I rowed around the harbor looking for someone who could fill the propane tank for the galley stove...and eventually got it filled.

Received an email from the City of Kennebunk. The mooring that I used in the river a few nights ago was not free after all and I owed the town twenty bucks. That was still a bargain and I mailed them off a check.

Tuesday, Wednesday, Thursday, Friday....

Jay had given me a contact with a fellow who traded in used cars who might want to trade a car for Sweet Breeze. That could be a quick, tidy, and perfect deal for us both. I took Eric for a test sail but for reasons of his own there would be no deal. I think he was looking for a bigger boat for family outings. We Americans mostly like bigger...except me.

Sara talked Jay into taking Sweet Breeze out in the bay for a test sail too and Jay could appreciate her stiffness and ease of sail handling, but it boiled down to too many boats...not enough time. Jay helped appease my broken salesmanship spirit by borrowing a bicycle from a neighbor for me to get around town with. Now I had wheels and the independence they offer.

I explored the town and some of the outlying regions, stopped and talked to the locals and gained an appreciation for the friendly and real people that lived and worked in Gloucester. They were blue-collar worker bees. The folks who worked at Brown's Yacht Yard treated me like a guest...the gal behind the counter, Val, had a bit of a hard shell, but under that was a warm person who gave me a big hug on Friday when I had decided to leave and sail on down the coast.

Gloucester was a bike friendly town of curved streets. I suspected the roads originally followed cow paths and foot trails as they wound around the hillsides. There was no grid work of streets where they were aligned with the compass points and it was easy for me to get turned around on a gray day with no sun for reference. I would just head downhill then toward the bay and recover my bearings.

I made a loop along a coastal road out toward Rockport on Cape Ann one afternoon. The scenery there was about the rugged coast on one side and the big homes of those who could afford the view on the other side of the road. The speed and the intricate detail of the fast moving scenery still fascinated me after so many miles of coastal sailing and the hazily slurred slow motion scenes held fixed for hours from far offshore.

Marna's brother David also lived in the area and we got together to drive to nearby Beverly to visit their mom who was in her 90s. That was another of my reasons for sailing into Gloucester...Blackburn's, and getting to know the rest of my best friend Marna's family, especially their mom who likely wouldn't be around too much longer.

I liked David. We had a good, "getting to know you" chat on the drive to Beverly and back. Were we to stay longer at Gloucester I would have liked to get to know David better and his work with photography, but, as it happened, the wind shifted from southwest to west on Friday and I felt the urge to sail away.

Sailors can be flighty that way. Gloucester had captured my attention for almost a week and a town must be a special place to keep my attention for that long. I begged off the kind invite to dinner with David and his wife, returned the bike, paid my bill at Brown's and got that big hug from Val. The late morning wind was offshore. Me and my old boat were offshore soon thereafter.

The sail down the coastal waters and across the breadth of the deep bay leading into Boston harbor was pleasant and uneventful. I had thoughts of sailing into Boston to check out the market for parting ways with my boat but the skyline of tall buildings far up into the bay did not draw me in. Tall trees draw me in—tall buildings, not so much.

I sailed a straight course for Plymouth. The Mayflower II and Plymouth Rock had some attraction for me. The late afternoon had me coursing Plymouth Bay and the Plymouth harbor channel following a big sailboat on a winding course through shallows and mud flats. It was a tricky course for a newby like me and I tried to keep up with the other sailboat as it showed the way around the long bar and finally up into the harbor.

It cost $100 just to tie up to the fuel dock for the night but it was close to the action at the center of the harbor and I thought that was where I should be. My cash stash was running low but plastic was working for paying my dockage, fuel, and provisions of late. The Mayflower II was tied up nearby and Plymouth Rock, with the date 1620 chiseled into it, was resting quietly just a short walk away.

On close inspection, the Mayflower looked like a mighty clumsy vessel to me. Blunt on bow and stern, top-heavy in appearance and very smelly, it was interesting... from the dock.

The "rock" was pretty ordinary. Nothing to hold my attention for long there either. It was a warm and gorgeous evening though and there was live music in the harbor park so I wandered amongst the tourists and sat in the grass listening to a well-done version of David Gray's *Babylon* by some local musicians. The song brought on a temporary wave of melancholy that evening...of lost loves, lonely times, even here in a crowded park. Yet I knew that any sadness was only temporary for me...offset by a lifetime of personal growth through adversity...somehow I always would come out smiling, that special gift I had been given and that deeply felt thankfulness for my own good fortune.

Most of my moods were short lived, down ones especially, as I was easily distracted by the next view, sound, or sensual stimulation and the entertaining thoughts they carried to me. An unrelenting curiosity—another part of my good fortune.

When I walked back to the boat, the gentle acoustic songs in the park were drowned out by the rock band at the marina's restaurant. There was to be no sleep on Sweet Breeze with that racket going but they quit pretending to play music at 11pm. What was one to expect for a hundred bucks?

Saturday morning...two cups of tea and off to sea.

I wasn't the first boat off the fuel dock that morning at Plymouth. Two sport fishermen were gassed up and heading out in their powerboat rippling the glassy water ahead of me winding through the channel and out to sea.

Today was to be another milestone of exploration on the "downeast" coast for me and my old boat. The sun was rising over the tip of Cape Cod some 25 miles off port. We had a stiff wind across the starboard beam and sailing was fast.

Rather than go way out around Cape Cod I had heard there was a channel that cut across a narrow part of the foot of the cape. I didn't know what to expect in the channel but it would cut off about 100 miles from the route far out around the cape so that channel was my choice.

It wasn't long before we were tacking up the channel with the mains'l and the motor pulling hard with the wind and a strong current against us.

What the afternoon wind would bring there was no telling but I knew that the current would reverse sometime or at least slack off...maybe when I reached the midpoint in the channel. We struggled to make way tacking as close to either shore as I dared, then back the other way trying to stay out of the way of the powerboats taking the straight-line route.

The interesting shoreline activity made up for the struggle. Folks were fishing and picnicking and biking. It reminded me of some of my river trips in canoes with the rounding of the next bend showing a new panorama.

The current eventually reversed but the wind didn't. It was still on the nose. No matter. The motor and the current were winning the struggle to Buzzard's Bay... slowly, painstakingly slowly. It took most of the day to gain the eight-mile shortcut across Cape Cod. It was sunny and warm though. No fog. Sailing was slow but life was good.

As Buzzard's Bay opened up ahead we were bucking waves now too. Progress was exceedingly slow yet, and now it was a very wet progress too from the spray and occasional wave over the bow. We gave up and ducked in behind the second point on the right where a sailboat was moored at a small bay.

The lee of Hog Neck gave us the respite we deserved after tacking most of the Cape Cod Canal and the first two miles of the bay.

At anchor there I watched as boats struggled to gain headway down the bay banging into the waves and clawing their way close-hauled. No thanks. I added a quart of motor oil to the "little engine that could" and lubed the distributor shaft. That engine didn't ask for much after helping me through over 3000 miles of sailing since early June.

I got a text message from my daughter in Germany while having lunch. She said on the message that she and her husband and my newest granddaughter would not arrive in Minnesota until late November. This was great news for me and took off all of the pressure to hurry back to Minnesota for their earlier planned arrival in late September.

There was no rush for anything now. Maybe I could sail down to Charleston or even further south now? Maybe I should just sit here at anchor for however long and wait for a wind shift so we could get down Buzzard's Bay without the struggle?

No hurry now...no worries either. This was a great place to enjoy a sunny afternoon watching...watching boats banging their way into the frothy mouth of Buzzard's Bay where the waves have fetched up some fury from somewhere downcoast. It was easy to imagine their struggle knowing that I didn't have to join them.

The afternoon passed into evening as I caught up on my journal, began reading another book, and listened to public radio. Having no schedule again suited me just fine, though I should get back home to Camp Cotton sometime soon to relieve my house guest/caretaker Terry, in case she wanted to get back into her normal routine in the city.

We stayed the night anchored just outside of the marked channel (on the near landward side) heading up into Onset Bay. Into the late evening motorboats streamed past following the channel, back up into the bay somewhere beyond my view. Sometime around 2 a.m. the nearby blasting of a horn brought me topside in a groggy hurry.

A power boater was the rude one, apparently honking at a sailboat that had anchored in or too near the channel up the bay. The sailboat must have came in seeking shelter after dark when the buoys were hard to find, but all the noise was not the most sensitive way to let them know that they could be in the channel. It reminded me of the incidents of road rage that I had heard about. This must have been an example of water rage as he continued to blast a really loud horn and I went back to bed.

Southwest winds were in the forecast again and we weren't the first sailboat to leave Onset Bay to head back into the teeth of the wind at daybreak the next morning, hoping to make some headway before the winds and waves grew with the day. Somehow the distant company of other sailboats always made hard sailing a little easier. Maybe it is a misery loves company thing.

The motor was needed to get far enough out into the bay to have room to tack. Progress was slow and unsteady, wet, cold, and frustrating. At the rate of headway we were making we would not even make it out of Buzzard's Bay today. I could tell that the struggle against the southwest winds was taking a toll on me. My attitude was slipping easily into dark places once again. Beating into the wind for many days of the past weeks was wearing me down.

On the right shore at Mattapoisett Bay we sailed in just far enough to get out of the waves for a respite from the beating we were taking. Sweet Breeze could handle it but I needed a break.

I was in the habit of craning my neck upward watching wind direction intently for the last three months. During and after a late lunch at anchor I watched the masthead fly gradually start to show a wind shift to the west of southwest. A half hour later the wind had moved all the way to the northwest. We immediately set sail back down Buzzard's Bay hoping for a beam reach with an offshore wind.

We got the wind on the beam...more wind, as it turned out, than was comfortable after testing it for a few miles. We were holding five-six knots now easily but heeling a lot and stressing the rigging. I got the mains'l down one reef and the headsail furled a bit. The speed felt good but the sails didn't seem to balance well and I would push the tiller hard to port to keep our heading when the gusts of wind hit us.

Crrrack! The wood laminations of the tiller separated and it folded over near the attachment to the rudderpost. This required some quick action or my old sails would soon get beaten ragged luffing in this new blow.

I dashed below for duct tape and some scrap wood pieces I had stashed under the port settee. A wood splint of old oak molding on either side of the break wrapped with the duct tape and we had regained steerage in a minute or two. Just like the junkyard at Camp Cotton (where the nearest hardware store was 35 miles away) my mini junkyard aboard Sweet Breeze had saved the day...and maybe more.

That was enough struggles for the day though. In toward the coast we sailed looking for some calmer seas and some sand to set an anchor into. There was a makeshift spare wooden tiller stowed aboard also and I thought I might need it properly installed before long.

Call me hard to please but the wind was strong and the anchorage I found was peaceful so we spent the afternoon fixing the tiller better with glue and C-clamps and reading books somewhere just offshore in the waters between Massachusetts and Rhode Island. I truly hated to waste that strong offshore wind but there was a long bay ahead with a five-mile reach inland and the waves coming out of that bay to windward would be hard on me.

Instead, I called friends back home on my cell phone. Michelle checked my Gmail inbox for responses to my ads to sell Sweet Breeze. Nothing. Maybe she would sell at Newport or Bristol. She was born at Bristol, Rhode Island in 1962. Surely someone there would recognize her worth, pay me a few bucks, and feel their life was now complete.

We spent the night anchored...up near a windward shore, not sure exactly where, but Newport, Rhode Island would be our destination for the early morning sail...weather permitting.

There must have been a special event in progress at Newport, or...had they heard that I was coming...?

Sailboats were everywhere in and around Newport. All of the docks and moorings were full of boats. I wasn't even sure that I going to pull into the mouth of Narragansett Bay on this fine sailing morning and stop at Newport or Bristol. When the weather was right for sailing I really wanted to sail, but I had to see what was going on at Newport, Rhode Island...sailboat haven.

The only fuel dock open for business, the Goat Island Marina, was lined with boats and the attendants moved some 100 footers to make an opening for Sweet Breeze. Just weaving through the fields of sailboats to get to the dock was a challenge. Squeezing between the two million dollar sailboats to get fuel called for some precise boat handling. There was no room for errors here. Any error would be very, very costly. Two strong young attendants helped Sweet Breeze to ease into the tight space and I topped off all my gas containers and the main tank.

I stopped to visit with some folks on an attractive old wooden sailboat on a mooring in a vast field of moored boats. They were having morning coffee on deck and the conversations turned quickly to where from and where going.

They were from New Rochelle, New York, down the coast a ways. I had heard that city's name spoken before, back on Lake Superior a few months ago when I met another sailor heading for Duluth, Minnesota. They knew Doug! What a coincidence...of all the boats here at Newport, I had stopped to visit with the one whose crew was acquainted with my new friend Doug who was by now in Montana with his Cape Dory.

Pat and Joe and their skipper Jon were going shoreside for breakfast but were heading downcoast as soon as they were ready. We agreed to sail together, just for the fun...they in their cutter rigged 50 foot Rhodes and me and my old sloop Sweet Breeze.

While they had breakfast I motored over to old Fort Adams protecting Narragansett Bay. The massive garrison was used from 1800 through WWII and was now a state park. I have always been drawn to those indomitable old stone bastions of democracy...maybe it went back to my boyhood and my penchant for building forts. It was so impressive from the water. I didn't have the time to tie up and take the tour so I filled my eyes and my memory with the outer stonework and the greatness of the forever quality of its architecture. I reminded me of the stone buildings in Zurich that were 600 years old and still in fine shape.

It was challenging, trying to keep up with the Rhodes, close hauled on a port tack, a southwest heading with a south wind. I should have stopped at Block Island but I loved to sail in tandem with another boat. I should have stopped at a hundred places that I sailed past in the last three months. When would I ever get this way again?

The old wooden Rhodes was a mile ahead. I had sailed a 40 foot Rhodes on Lake Superior and felt that it was the most responsive sailboat that I had ever had the pleasure to encounter. Pat and Joe's boat, now way up ahead, had sailed around the world several times...it was their home and their transportation and their retirement dream. Jon, their skipper, owned a marina at New Rochelle and had told me to be sure to stop by on my way down the Long Island Sound...that I could stay for free as long as I liked. They were just a few more good people to add to a very long list of good folks I had met on this journey.

Somewhere in the darkness off Fishers Island they had waited for me to catch up. I motored after them in the dark for what seemed like miles. They were headed for a dock somewhere inland. All I could see was their boat lights and an occasional marker buoy in my four-cell flashlight's beam. I hoped they knew where they were going. We stayed as close to their stern as possible without running into them through a night fog and the complete blackness of a twisty-turny channel.

Some days later I learned that we had tied up for the night at the Dog Watch Cafe, Stonington, Connecticut, where we had a beer out back around a campfire... then a late supper and a nightcap aboard the Rhodes before I thanked them for letting me tag along. I really didn't know where I was except with some new friends.

First daylight on the following morning brought back my visual bearings, less darkness, and fog. A few days later I traced our route on a Google map with my laptop. Sometimes it was more fun to see where you had been than where you were going. Darkness and unknown waters makes boating really interesting. Boaters know what I mean.

Would it be Charleston or Savannah…?

I backed away from the Rhodes at dawn's gray light. The progress downcoast was pretty good lately and I felt that I needed to keep it up. Yesterday was a fun buddy sail and fairly fast at times covering about 40 miles from Newport with a late start.

I really was really thinking about Charleston or even Savannah, Georgia now as I motored away from shore…well Annapolis at least. Trading Sweet Breeze for a car or a small truck was still a hope at one of those sailing meccas.

The gray day ahead, as it always seemed to do, dampened my thirst for sailing adventure. Yesterday's sun, wind and exhilarating sail was lost in this day's dark sky and building seas as we scratched our way past Fishers Island and into the Long Island sound.

We sailed with another small sailboat with two aboard for a few miles as they tacked back and forth but we mostly held course close-hauled again. When they peeled off toward Long Island I felt damp, alone, and mildly seasick.

By early afternoon I had enough of the sickness, enough of ducking under wave tops splashing across the cabin top. I was wet, cold and getting generally pissed off about everything. I may have uttered a curse word or even put together a whole string of them and I started to look for a haven on the Connecticut shore.

I was not having fun and the seas were getting bigger, steeper and nearing the danger point for me, alone. As usual…chart plotter to the rescue. It showed me the way across the bar at the mouth of the Connecticut River and once within the breakwater channel I felt the purest relief.

Could I have kept going, dodging and ducking waves beating into the wind at a snail's pace…? Of course I could have and would just as likely be here today to tell my story. But why? I was beginning to detest this fucking southwest wind and this sticky wetness of salt spray in my clothes, in my hair, on everything I touched there was brine.

Okay, it wasn't the brine so much as the whole discomfort of this damned situation. I had already tested myself and my boat in big wind and seas many times. Off Gaspé in the Gulf of St. Lawrence and in Lake Superior with that damn northeaster coming across from the Canadian shore and trying its best to throw us up on the rocks near Grand Marais, Michigan. I just felt that I had nothing more to prove! Nothing more.

Fear wasn't ruling my choices. I had faced that a number of times already and stared it down and survived. Why was I doing this when it wasn't fun?

The marina up the river a mile was welcoming but way upscale for me and my old boat. My 28-foot boat would cost $100 to tie up for the night and electric hookup was some dollars extra.

That was all okay. I was just glad to step onto a dock and get my inner ears settled back inside my head and the gyro that they normally gave me, gyrating again.

This would probably not be a likely place for a good buy on a used car or truck... the parking lot had a Lamborghini and a Maserati and other cars with long, foreign names. I was thinking Ford or Chevy.

I washed my briny, smelly laundry at the nearby inn and must not have looked like a thoroughly normal guest. More like a homeless person I guess, just judging from the curious looks of other guests. That's okay, my briny clothes and whiskers were earned. If they only knew.

I smiled and told them I was the laundry boy...did they have any briny clothing? I could put it in with my load...on my quarter? They weren't sure if I was kidding.

Some of the inn's other guests came over by Sweet Breeze and I had fun with them as well. "She can be all yours...she's for sale," I said. Actually one guy seemed quite interested but reached into his pocket and came up a few grand short. We laughed.

With my cash stash running low and my fridge foods needing to be eaten, I had a quiet evening on the boat and some conversation with a sailing couple that pulled in along the other side of my dock in their C&C 44. Really a nice guy, sailing the coast with his wife in retirement. They too had sought out shelter from the turbulent Long Island Sound.

My last day of sailing....?

As we nosed around the breakwater, the seas looked doable. Of course, I was the first boat out the Connecticut River that morning with just the gray dawn's light. And, of course the wind was southwesterly and on the nose. But hey, I thought, one day in seven with a fair wind and sunshine should be enough for any self debasing, self flagellating sailor... right? And of course the sky was gray with a light rain falling.

Suck it up and get tacking, I told myself. What's a little more salt spray, cold rain and misery? Real sailors don't need a dodger. Stop thinking about your warm cabin on the river back home, I told myself. One more wave in the face can't hurt.

After a few hours I couldn't see much. I tried to wear my glasses to block the spray but they became brine coated and pretty opaque. I double reefed both sails to get the boat back under control but made little headway...with barely enough speed for steerage. I took a motion sickness pill to help stave off the blah and sick feelings that were capturing my body and spirit. And I was conjuring up a string of oaths that my granddaughters should never hear.

Around noon I started to scroll around on the screen of the chart plotter looking for a calming respite toward Long Island or the mainland. The Long Island coast was farther away and didn't seem to have any deep inland cuts or long points to get protection from the sound.

A place called Harry's Marine well inland at Westbrook, CT looked like a place to call home for a while. I liked the name. It sounded like a family run operation, not some vast marina chain corporation. We flew in on a beam reach past the breakwaters and into the calm river mouth heading up to Harry's. I started the motor and doused the sails on my old boat...for the very last time as it turned out.

Parting ways with Sweet Breeze

I tied up on the fuel dock, as far forward as I dared, to leave room for more boats behind me and walked up to the office through the boat yard. There were older boats propped up awaiting a caring owner to return...none as old as Sweet Breeze but still we both seemed to fit in better than at Saybrook.

When I entered the office/workshop Harry Jr., some local boaters (and some dogs under the table), were having a morning coffee break. Marguerite and a friend were chatting. Harry was working on an old wood stove making it serviceable again... something I would have done. I liked the ambiance. Informal. Friendly. Dogs. Harry's was a family run operation. I decided to stay awhile.

Harry didn't sell boats for owners but there was a boat broker nearby that he suggested I contact. I called Ted the broker and made arrangements to meet later, or tomorrow...whenever he had the time.

Just down the road from the marina were a couple of restaurants. The first one was called Ed's Lunch and the second one was Bill's Seafood. Harry's, Ed's, and Bill's. This sure sounded like a small town on a first name basis. Things were looking up. I decided to stay awhile longer.

The lunch counter at Bill's was nearly full and I (just happened) to sit next to a very pretty gal named Raylene and her friend Lee. Raylene reminded me of an old girlfriend and her salad looked good too so I ordered the same. The waitress was busy but not too busy to smile...big, free ones.

Raylene and Lee were interested in my sailing adventure so we had a leisurely lunch together with conversation between bites. They were retired and lived nearby. If I needed a ride to look for a car or to get some groceries they offered their services. Things were falling into place here everywhere that I turned.

Westbrook, Connecticut must have been that destination that I hadn't known about until I reached it. Raylene gave me her phone number just in case I wanted to take them up on their kind offer for transportation.

Back at the boat I spent the afternoon reorganizing some of the disorganization that had happened in the last few months of sailing and living aboard. I took some photos of the inside of the cabin, trying not to show the clutter of my lifestyle.

The photos were for the Craigslist ads that I was placing up and down the east coast towns from Maine to Georgia trying to sell the old boat. I spent the afternoon trying to put together and place some strategic and attractive ads with my Netbook and some wi-fi Internet service.

Surely buyers would soon begin to compete for ownership of Sweet Breeze.

Maybe it would be like just a few years before when I sold my blueberry farm... prospective buyers there were bidding the price up with offers way above my asking price. Or when I sold my previous sailboat the next day after taping a For Sale sign on it in a marina in Duluth. Maybe not.

The next morning I awoke on Sweet Breeze at Harry's and unlike most mornings in the past three months I had no desire to sail onward. None.

I felt that I could almost live somewhere around Westbrook...on the outskirts of course, I needed to have some woods nearby, but it was a welcoming sort of town for a blue collar sailor like me.

Ted came by to look Sweet Breeze and me over. He didn't show a lot of enthusiasm about the prospects of selling her, especially in her live-aboard, cluttered condition. I promised I would do better at cleaning her up but I had nowhere to stow all of my stuff. Ted, somewhat reluctantly I sensed, agreed to help with the sale. Another plus for my choice to stay here and get my land-life begun again.

Raylene and Lee agreed to pick me up at Harry's and take me used car shopping. I didn't find anything I really liked at Tony's or Bernie's used car lots but we had a fun drive around the town as Lee gave me some lessons on the local history and we found some more car lots on the far side of town.

They dropped me off at a West Marine boating store where I found just the right replacement tiller for the broken and barely repaired one on Sweet Breeze. I bought them lunch at their favorite restaurant and ice cream cones for dessert and we had a delightful afternoon...but no car.

Harry Jr. loaned me his bicycle so I had wheels and began to explore the countryside around Westbrook. The shaded, wooded lanes with clapboard homes along the Menunketesuck River was what I thought a New England town should look like. I found an old cemetery with headstones dating back to revolutionary war times. A passenger train whizzed by on the outskirts of town...some real mass-transit that we all should be using...or bikes.

Four years ago, when I first spotted Sweet Breeze in the big boat shed in Superior, Wisconsin it was love at first sight. Was I so different? Where were the real sailors on the east coast that wanted a real sailboat? An affordable one that could take them around the world if they had dreams of sailing afar. They were not lining up making me offers. No matter. She would sell eventually. Maybe if I kept lowering the price... well perhaps?

I found a good car, thanks to Lee's daughter but getting the money from my account in Minnesota to pay for it was not easy. Security and passwords put up roadblocks. Eventually I had to borrow the money from my former wife back in Minnesota who had it transferred to a local bank.

Long lines at the State of Connecticut License Bureau gave me second thoughts about living here. I was just not cut out to stand in long lines for anything. Small town Minnesota was all about short lines and few people.

Before the car arrived, Angello, my dock mate with a powerboat and an SUV brought me grocery shopping. Angie was my man. We hit it off. He and his brother

Tony reminded me of *Click and Clack, the Tappet Brothers* on public radio.

Angie was so loud in the grocery store cracking jokes that I was laughing too hard to be embarrassed. The next day Angie brought me to Waterbury to a big Sears store where I bought a car-top rack and a big car-top storage bag. We had a pretty constant verbal banter going between us whenever we were together. If I lived around Westbrook I was pretty sure we would be good buddies.

A couple of mornings later, with the car packed to the hilt and the bloated travel bag topside threatening to collapse the roof, we were on the road at 4:00 a.m. heading west. Daylight arrived as we crossed upstate New York on the thruway along the Erie Canal. Evening found us near Tobermory, Ontario at a little campground sitting around a campfire having a late supper. I was in the woods again. I always felt at home and safe in the woods.

Pencil drawing Terry Millikan drew of Curt's spirit tree, a white pine above the Whiteface river near Camp Cotton.

Afterword....

Perhaps another book at another time could tell the whole tale of my final parting with Sweet Breeze. I think the old boat just didn't want to leave me. She knew when she was loved unconditionally. If she were able to love me back we might still be together.

Before leaving Westbrook for Minnesota, I did have a real, honest bite from a potential buyer from Boston. Horacio drove down to Westbrook from Boston, eventually, after getting the wrong town name from me on an email. I had told him that we were at Westport, CT and that's where he and his family called me from. Damn, I felt bad about their detour because of my confusion of town names.

Anyhow, Horacio forgave me when he and his family arrived at Harry's and out sailing we went. They were about the sweetest family ever...Horacio, his wife and two kids. Mexican-Americans, educators at universities near Boston, we had fun and I smile still when I recall the visual picture of Horatio beaming at the helm of Sweet Breeze...just before he steered us into the mud off to the side of the channel. He had much to learn about marker buoys.

The rest of Sweet Breeze's suitors I only met on emails or phone conversations from my cabin in the woods in northern Minnesota. A few came and looked her over with Ted supervising the introductions. Harry's had lifted Sweet Breeze onto the hard now, and prepped her for winter, if she didn't sell before that.

There was one interested buyer who remained in contact with me all during the following winter as I was home writing this book by the fire. Her name was Jane and she lived on Cape Cod. She had the fondest of memories of the Pearson Triton that her dad had when she was a girl learning to sail with the whole family aboard.

Twice she visited Sweet Breeze down the coast at Westbrook but was not sure about so many of the details of the equipment on board and the leaks on the deck that may have worked their way down to the bilge.

I sensed her apprehension...her hesitance about all the unknown problems that an old boat can present or that can show up with the passage of time and weather exposure. I also sensed that Jane needed a diversion from personal pressures and problems. And too, I got a little tired of answering emails and calls from others about the boat...most were nice folks but a couple of them were downright snotty about their approach and further contact with them didn't improve their boat side manner.

One day in July, I called Jane and told her she could have Sweet Breeze. No strings. No money. Just pay Harry and Ted any fees that I might owe and sail her up to Cape Cod. I would send her a bill of sale and it would be a done deal. She sounded disbelieving but kinda giddy about the prospect.

Sweet Breeze is at home on Cape Cod now. Jane is still a little disbelieving and a little giddy. I am in a warm log cabin on a river in northern Minnesota with no briny waves to duck and have just finished my first book...and dreaming of a new adventure, though I know not where. This afternoon though, I'll go for a hike along the frozen Whiteface River, just below my cabin, hoping to see a gray wolf.

Hugs,

Curt.

Acknowledgments

Perhaps a better title for this page would be Encouragements. Friends and family were usually supportive of my adventures on the water and always supportive of my adventures on the written page.

Most of many thank-you's should go to my parents. They have endowed me with the genetic makeup that has resulted in good health and an adventuresome spirit. They raised us kids with the attitude that we could do anything that we set our minds to.

Dear friend Marna Banks always supported and encouraged my adventuresome spirit. She was there when I set sail in my first boat 'Sea Mouse' on Pike Lake and after the 3500 mile sail to the sea on Sweet Breeze.

Friends Jim Banks, Sue Wilmes, Dave Poulin, Rudy, Matt, Lydia, Mark, Randy Sorenson, Mike Savage, Thom Burns, my sisters and brother and my grown up kids Randy and Amanda all had a part in the sailing adventures, backgrounds, and the stories that followed.

Thanks also to Cotton, Minnesota's 'Old School Lives' for their generous sharing of wifi Internet connections.

About the Author

Curtis is the youngest of a large blue-collar family raised in northern Minnesota.

He has had many jobs throughout his work life, the most important being a father and grandfather.

Writing is only one of many challenges that occupies his free time, and most all of his time is free time. Living in the woods and learning from nature is important to his sense of well-being.

He divides his time between his cabin on a river in northern Minnesota and his cabin on a ridge in the Ozarks of Arkansas.

To order additional copies of

FROM BLUEBERRIES TO BLUE SEAS

Contact Savage Press by
visiting our webpage at
www.savpress.com
or see our
Savage Press Facebook page.

Call
218-391-3070
to place secure credit card orders.

Our email address is:
mail@savpress.com